INFORMIX
Basics

ISBN 0-13-080799-0

9 780130 807991

90000

PRENTICE HALL PTR INFORMIX SERIES

To See A Complete List Of Informix Press Titles, Point To
http://www.phptr.com/~informix

INFORMIX
Basics

Glenn Miller

Prentice Hall PTR
Upper Saddle River, New Jersey 07458
http://www.phptr.com

Library of Congress Cataloging-in-Publication Data

Miller, Glenn, 1959-
    Informix basics / Glenn Miller.
        p.   cm.
    Includes index.
    ISBN 0-13-080799-0
    1. Application software.   2. Informix software.   I. Title.
    QA76.76.A65M55   1998
    005.75'65--dc21   98-36692
                                                       CIP

Editorial/Production Supervision: Maria Molinari
Acquisitions Editor: John Anderson
Development Editor: Jim Markham
Technical Editor: Kimberly Kirk Ringer
Editorial Assistant: Linda Ramagnano
Buyer: Alexis Heydt
Cover Design Direction: Jerry Votta
Art Director: Gail Cocker-Bogusz
Series Design: Claudia Durrell Design

 © 1999 Prentice Hall PTR
Prentice-Hall, Inc.
A Simon & Schuster Company
Upper Saddle River, NJ 07458

The publisher offers discounts on this book when ordered in bulk quantities.
For more information, contact: Corporate Sales Department, Phone: 800-382-3419;
Fax: 201-236-7141; E-mail: corpsales@prenhall.com; or write: Prentice Hall PTR,
Corp. Sales Dept., One Lake Street, Upper Saddle River, NJ 07458.

10 9 8 7 6 5 4 3 2 1

ISBN 0-13-080799-0

Prentice-Hall International (UK) Limited, London
Prentice-Hall of Australia Pty. Limited, Sydney
Prentice-Hall Canada Inc., Toronto
Prentice-Hall Hispanoamericana, S.A., Mexico
Prentice-Hall of India Private Limited, New Delhi
Prentice-Hall of Japan, Inc., Tokyo
Simon & Schuster Asia Pte. Ltd., Singapore
Editora Prentice-Hall do Brasil, Ltda., Rio de Janeiro

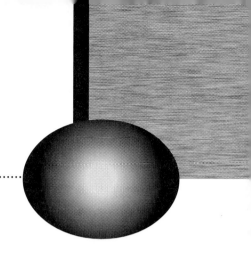

Contents

PART 2 • SQL FUNDAMENTALS

PART 3 • SQL ADVANCED TOOLS

PART 4 • INFORMIX PROGRAMMING

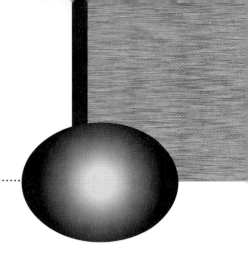

About the Author

Glenn Miller is President and co-founder of Tsunami Consulting Group, a Denver-based information services provider. Tsunami, an Informix Solutions Alliance Partner, excels in developing industry-leading e-commerce and data warehouse applications.

One of the first Informix Certified Professionals, Glenn has been a hands-on developer and administrator of Informix products since 1984. He currently works on an Informix-based Data Warehouse for MCI. Glenn is also a co-author for *Informix Unleashed*, and can be reached at glenn@tsunami.com.

He plays a mean game of chess.

Acknowledgments

Extraordinary thanks go to my contributing authors: Bob Davis, Kevin Kempter, Beth Popovich, and James Risinger. They did more than fill in where my expertise was lacking. Their breadth of experience, good humor, and professionalism made this a much stronger book. I'm proud to have my words bound together with those of my friends.

At Prentice Hall, Development Editor Jim Markham molded the misshapen early pastiche into a coherent lesson plan. Under his vigilant aegis, there was never a doubt that this project would succeed. Technical Editor Kirky Ringer rooted out numerous insidious errors, and kept me from overwhelming the reader with inscrutable arcana. Where I've strayed from their admonitions, the resultant mistakes are mine entirely. Thanks also to Acquisitions Editor John Anderson, who signed me to author this book, and Maria Molinari for putting the final pieces together.

Finally, special thanks to my Tsunami partners-in-crime: Pete Abell, Matt O'Kelley, and Rob Peterson. For months, they were strong enough to carry the load for me in directing our ongoing food fight of a company. Thanks, guys. I can take my turn at bat now.

Oh, and "Thanks, Dad."

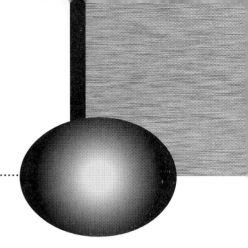

Introduction

This book is an introduction to the Informix product line—my world, where for over 14 years I've developed, designed, administered, and managed Informix applications. Along the way I've had the opportunity to teach Informix concepts to dozens of co-developers who have been with me in the trenches. Many times I wished I had a guidebook to make the job easier. This is that guidebook.

Who This Book Is For

This book is for you if you need a tour guide through the admittedly complex suite of Informix products, or if you need a jump start to developing applications. If you are a novice programmer new to the Informix environment, you will find value here. If you are a savvy power user with plenty of ambition, this book will help launch you into the development arena. If you are experienced with other database development tools, you will find here enough universal principles to allow what you already know to be used as a springboard to your becoming a strong Informix developer.

This book is a tutorial, offering hands-on examples that will provide you a solid foundation for applications development. It does not attempt to cover every facet of the Informix product suite, but rather it distills the key concepts into manageable lessons that are directly applicable to most development efforts. Someone who knows everything between these pages is someone I'd like to have developing an application with me. When that person is you, send me e-mail to glenn@tsunami.com. We'll want to talk.

What You'll Need

This is a book describing the basic Informix product line, so you will need to have the following basic products installed to complete the examples: an Informix database engine, Informix DB-Access, and Informix-4GL. Chapter 1, "The Informix Product Suite," describes these and other Informix components. You'll also need an experienced database administrator to install these products and instruct you how to access them. Finally, for some chapters, the following software is also required: Informix-ISQL; Informix ESQL/C; UNIX Korn shell.

A few background skills could make some of the material herein more familiar. A basic knowledge of structured programming concepts and operating system fundamentals would provide a good foundation. C language programming skills could also be a small plus. But if you read this book serially, letting its tutorial, stepwise examples unfold, you'll find that you have all the tools you need.

How This Book Is Organized

After this Introduction, the book is organized into five parts, comprising seventeen chapters, and is followed by two appendixes. Part 1, "Getting

Started," introduces the Informix product line, the relational data model, and the primary tool you will use to manipulate your databases—DB-Access. You should scan these topics even if you already have a passing knowledge of the fundamentals, if only to ensure that you build the sample `music` database used throughout the rest of the book.

You'll become intimately familiar with the sample database in Part 2, "SQL Fundamentals." You'll learn how to create databases and their principal components, tables. You'll see how to examine not only a database's structure, but its contents as well. You'll see how to add your own data, change it, and delete it. You'll also learn how creating simple forms and reports can simplify even these fundamental procedures.

In Part 3, "SQL Advanced Tools," you'll explore more of SQL, the industry-standard language used to interact with relational databases—the kind this book describes. You'll discover advanced ways to extract relationships from your data, and how to build queries of surprising depth. Additionally, you'll explore Stored Procedure Language, a programming tool that allows you to embed your SQL statements within procedural language rules of any complexity. This part ends as a springboard to the following one.

Part 4, "Informix Programming," shows, at length, how you can write custom Informix applications. You'll progress from building the simplest "Hello, World!" example to writing programs of surpassing complexity. You'll discover that by keeping individual parts of your programs direct and purposeful (using functions), by segregating discrete operations into isolated functions (modularity), and by incrementally building ever-larger working programs from smaller functioning components (stepwise refinement), you'll discover no practical limit to the applications you can create.

The remaining sections are bonuses. Not strictly addressing SQL or programming proper, Part 5, "Advanced Topics," and the appendixes provide complementary material that can help you become a more complete Informix developer. These topics include data migration and database administration tools, as well as how to create the sample database. While not strictly mandatory, the lessons of Part 5 can differentiate an educated programmer from an effective one. Appendix A, "The Sample Database," contains the instructions for building the database upon which the book's examples are based. Following those instructions will save you time and make the exercises clearer. Finally, Appendix B, "Administrative Tools," describes some of the ways you can look behind the scenes at your Informix databases and processes. It's a useful aside.

Conventions Used in This Book

This book uses different typefaces to help you differentiate between Informix commands and regular English, and to highlight important concepts. Actual Informix code and keywords are in a special `monospace` font. In examples where the input and output of a command or program are presented, the user input is typeset in **`bold monospace`**. Placeholders—terms for which you substitute values—are typeset in an *`italic monospace`* font. New or important terms are typeset in *italic*.

The book contains some special features to help you navigate the Informix product line. Syntax diagrams show you how to use a specific Informix command. Here is an example, from Chapter 5, "Basic SQL," describing the syntax of the `update` command:

```
update table-name
    set column-name = value
       [, column-name = value ...]
   [where condition-list]
```

where *`table-name`* is the name of the table whose rows you are updating, *`column-name`* is the column whose contents you are replacing with *`value`*, and *`condition-list`* is an optional set of conditions that describe and restrict the rows updated. The new *`value`* can be a constant or an expression. The syntax of *`condition-list`* is identical to that for the `select` statement.

Within the syntax diagram, square brackets (`[ ]`) surround optional elements. Ellipses (...) signify that an element can be repeated. A pipe (`|`), not shown in this example, separates alternative choices. Otherwise, the typeface parallels the rest of the book's conventions.

note *Don't fret over the syntax shown for the `update` statement. By Chapter 5, when you see it again, you'll have learned all you need for it to make sense.*

This book also contains an occasional sidebar, such as the following, which calls attention to and expands on an adjunct topic.

Some Hygiene *Dos* and *Do Nots*

DO

Brush your teeth after every meal.

DO NOT

Forget to floss.

You'll also see Tip, Note, and Caution boxes. Tips provide useful shortcuts and techniques for working with Informix. Notes offer extra details about a concept being described. Cautions help you avoid common problems.

 Don't ignore the Caution boxes. They can help you avoid problems that occur frequently.

Each chapter ends with an Extra Credit section containing answers to common questions relating to the chapter's material. Exercises and Exercise Answers follow each Q&A section. The exercises give you an opportunity to apply the material in a hands-on fashion. You should work through the exercises before proceeding to the next chapter, because some of the examples in subsequent chapters build on exercises you are expected to have completed.

About the Web Site

For your convenience, the sample database in this book is available on the Internet. When you are ready to install the database, point your browser to the following URL:

```
ftp://ftp.prenhall.com/pub/ptr/informix_sco.w-052/miller
```

Appendix A contains the detailed instructions for extracting the files you need, but the instructions are also available at the site listed above.

Part

1

Getting Started

Welcome aboard your Informix cruise ship, the flagship of the *Prentice Hall Informix* line. I'm Glenn. I'll be your tour guide. This is Isaac: he takes drink requests. Notice the enchanting music in the background. That's "Sounds of the Okefenokee Swamp," one of the twenty-two albums in my collection. You'll hear choice cuts from each of them as our tour progresses. Settle in; this ride starts off slow, but gets pretty wild as the chapters unfold.

In this part you'll be introduced to Informix: the company, its products, its database manipulation tools. This is no whistle-stop tour. You'll have plenty of chances to step off the bus (ship, bus, train—whatever) and mix with the locals. They don't bite.

In Chapter 1, "The Informix Product Suite," my technical conscience and pocket billiards nemesis Robert Davis gives you the Informix once-over-heavily. His introduction serves first as a high level fly-over, but contains enough details that you ought to revisit his words again after you've finished the book. You'll find that you've learned a thing or three.

Chapter 2 is where I step to the chalkboard and deliver the "Data Modeling 101" sermon. (One thing you'll learn, if you haven't already, is that I mix metaphors shamelessly.) In this chapter, I'll pontificate on what you need to know before you start creating databases and tables. That's Chapter 4. In Chapter 2, you'll learn the fundamentals of relational databases, and how to design your own.

In Chapter 3, "DB-Access," you learn how to use DB-Access, Informix's primary user interface tool. By the end you'll have a good facility with DB-Access, which is necessary, because you'll need to use it throughout all the remaining chapters. Also by then, you'll need some cool tropical refreshment. Isaac: If you don't mind, get some of those little umbrellas ready!

The Informix Product Suite

Before you dig in to the "meat and potatoes" of database development with Informix, you will benefit by becoming acquainted with the extensive suite of products available from this leading database vendor. This chapter begins with discussions on relational databases, client/server computing, and the scope of Informix applications. Following these discussions will be a brief, yet encompassing, history of the company.

The remainder of the chapter, as the title suggests, will be dedicated to a high-level look at most of the products offered by Informix today.

You may want to read this chapter twice. First, read it as an introduction to the Informix product suite, the company, and the relational model. It will provide you an important skeleton that the rest of the book will flesh out. (Don't try to memorize the details of the various products and utilities.) Then read this chapter again when you have completed the book. You'll be surprised how clear some of these admittedly arcane details become once you've used the products hands-on.

caution

Quicksand Chapter. The material in this chapter can trap the unwary. Bring along a rope, and if you feel yourself being drawn too deeply into the details, gingerly pull yourself out. Scan these important topics to gain a broad overview of the Informix product suite, but don't feel compelled to plumb the murky depths on your first reading.

What Is a Relational Database?

An Informix database is a *relational* database.

In basic terms, this means that the data is stored in *tables* made up of *columns* and *rows*. In other types of databases, the data may be organized in flat files or arrays. Relational database theory, however, provides a set of rules by which all types of data can be represented using only tables, columns, and rows.

A relational database, in its simplest terms, is a collection of data that is grouped into one or more tables. When you create a database you are actually creating a set of tables that have specific relationships among one another. A table can be thought of as an array of like items organized into columns and rows. Each table represents one *entity*, or one type of thing described by the database.

Each column in a table represents a specific characteristic or *attribute* of the entity the table describes. For example, in the `music` database used throughout this book, the `performers` table is made up of five columns: `last_name`, `first_name`, `sex`, `birth_date`, and `death_date`, each of which describes one attribute particular to a performer.

A row is one instance of a table entity, one example of the real-world thing this table describes. Each row is composed of the attributes that define the table, and stores values in each column appropriate to its instance of the table.

In Chapter 2, "Data Modeling 101," you'll apply these principles toward the building of your own `music` database.

Relational databases store and manage data. With them, you build databases and manipulate the data within the database's tables. That manipulation is limited to the following four types of operations: inserting, selecting, updating, and deleting. Chapter 5, "Basic SQL," is where you will begin to learn the hands-on means of implementing these relational operations.

What Is Client/Server Computing?

Client/server, in its simplest terms, refers to the ability of a *client*, or requester, to submit a request for services to a *server*. The server interprets the request, accesses the appropriate information from the database, and sends its response to the client. In the simplest scenario, the client and server run on the same hardware platform. Although this is not generally the industry perceived client/server environment, it nevertheless subscribes to the client/server definition.

The industry perception of client/server computing states that the client and server reside on separate computers. This enables the application code to reside in the client environment and to consume separate resources from that of the server on another machine. This type of environment also allows the client to use a number of different tools to manipulate information, as well as permits greater freedom to request data from more than one server.

A client/server architecture (see Figure 1-1) consists of three primary components: *front-end* software, *middleware*, and *back-end* software. Front-end software is the client software, which sends requests for services. Middleware refers to the software that supplies an *application programming interface (API)* for distributed applications. This level also includes communications software that manages the service requests the front- and back-end software generate. The back-end software is generally the server, which receives and processes client requests. In true distributed environments, it is not always clear which component is the front-end and which the back-end. In this kind of environment, the front end for a transaction may be the back end for another transaction. In most scenarios, however, it is easy to distinguish between the client, the API, and the server.

The client is generally a desktop computer, such as a PC or an inexpensive UNIX workstation. The server hardware is more com-

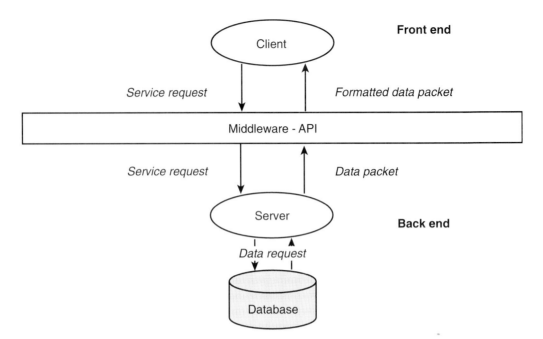

Figure 1–1 *Client/server architecture.*

monly a larger *symmetrical multiprocessor (SMP)* machine. In a client/server environment, there is a good deal of flexibility in the configuration of the processing. Processing can take place primarily on the server, leaving the client behaving as a *dumb terminal*, typically with some type of *graphical user interface (GUI)* front-end. Processing can also take place primarily on the client side, leaving the server with nothing to do but fetch data. This latter method, using a smart client, is generally a cheaper solution, since the processing is performed on less expensive hardware. That cost is often offset by added complexity, as new problems are introduced in maintaining the code on each client.

The Scope of Informix Applications

Informix supplies a comprehensive set of enterprise information management products ranging from database servers to GUI and data access tools. The types of database environments Informix supports range from small workgroups to large data warehouses. The products Informix offers can be classified into the following categories:

- Database engines
- Data access tools
- Development tools
- Administrative tools

Each of the variety of database engines, or *servers*, that Informix offers manages the structure of, and access to, all types of data. These data types range from conventional alphanumeric types, such as character and integer, to more content-rich types, such as video and HTML.

The data access and development tools allow you to operate on these data types to solve business problems. The focus of this book is to show you when and how to use the most important of these tools.

In the client/server model the Informix engines provide the back-end processing, whereas the development and data access tools are the front-end. Informix has chosen to include the middleware software with each of its front-end tools.

Database Engines

The database *engine* is the backbone of the database environment. The engine, also known as a server or an *instance*, is essentially a mechanism to control access to data in a database. Although the database engines explored in this section have different features, capabilities, and even architectures, they all perform the same rudimentary function. Each manages incoming requests for data from the client, retrieves the requested data from the database, and passes this information back to the client.

INFORMIX-SE

INFORMIX-SE (Standard Engine) for UNIX is an SQL-based database engine designed for small- to medium-range applications. This engine is a good choice for environments that need the power of *Structured Query Language (SQL)* but not the complexity that can accompany database administration. Since there really are no configuration requirements, the engine is ready for use immediately following installation.

 note   *SQL is a text-based database language that has been adopted by most database vendors as the standard language used to build and query relational databases. Since SQL provides the basic building blocks of relational database management, you will see this term frequently throughout the rest of this book. You will also have the opportunity to become quite handy in implementing SQL, from performing basic data manipulation to writing complex queries.*

Unlike the other Informix database engines, INFORMIX-SE does not require the use of *character-special* or *raw* devices to store data, but rather makes use of the native UNIX operating system and file manager. Database tables and indexes are stored as UNIX files beneath the Informix installation directory. Because the data is stored in these UNIX files, backing up the database is as simple as backing up any other set of UNIX files.

INFORMIX-OnLine

The Informix-OnLine servers provide more power than INFOR-MIX-SE and are ideal for larger multi-user *online transaction-processing (OLTP)* systems and *decision support systems (DSSs)*. The architecture of the OnLine engine differs from INFORMIX-SE primarily in that it manages its own *shared-memory* resources and disk I/O. When shared memory is implemented, instead of each server process referencing its own data space in memory, common segments of memory are used by all processes. Shared-memory architecture greatly improves performance by reducing memory requirements and disk I/O, and by providing a high-speed mechanism for communication between processes. More detail on shared memory and disk management will be provided in Chapter 17, "Database Administration Fundamentals."

Current versions of INFORMIX-OnLine (versions 6 and higher) use Informix's *Dynamic Scalable Architecture* (DSA).

DSA employs threads, or *lightweight processes*, to perform database management activities. By managing several threads simultaneously, DSA's *multithreaded* architecture allows parallel query processing within an SMP environment, as well as the capability to dynamically allocate processes. In very general terms, this multithreaded design means that fewer processes are needed, and that one process can do the work for more than one application. We will take a closer look at the multithreaded architecture and the impact it has on your development environment in Chapter 17.

INFORMIX-OnLine XPS

INFORMIX-OnLine XPS (Extended Parallel Server) was the next logical step up from INFORMIX-OnLine Dynamic Server. XPS, like the Dynamic Server, incorporates the multithreaded DSA architecture, but, unlike the Dynamic Server, XPS is designed to take advantage of *loosely coupled* or *shared-nothing* computing architectures, including SMP clusters and *massively parallel processor* (*MPP*) systems.

A loosely coupled or shared-nothing hardware environment like the SMP cluster or MPP is made up of a set of servers or *nodes* connected by a high-speed network or *interconnect*. Each node has its own set of processors, memory, and disks, and runs one instance of the database server called a *co-server*. XPS is able to distribute database tasks across multiple CPUs within a single co-server as well as across multiple co-servers. Through data, control, and execution partitioning, these co-servers can run in parallel while operating independent of each other.

XPS is optimized to support *very large database* (*VLDB*) applications, including data warehouses and large-scale OLTP environments. As you might imagine, the task of managing one of these VLDB environments could be extremely cumbersome. To ease the pain, XPS provides an administrative environment called INFORMIX-Enterprise Command Center that is designed specifically for managing VLDB distributed databases. The Enterprise Command Center permits the configuration, monitoring, and control of all co-servers from a central location.

The ability to increase the number of co-servers in a share-nothing environment makes XPS even more scalable than the Online Dynamic Server. Whereas the OnLine Dynamic Server is scalable to a point within the confines of an SMP environment, a number of benchmarks have shown that XPS scales linearly as additional co-servers are implemented.

INFORMIX-OnLine Universal Server

With the advent of the World Wide Web and multimedia computing, organizations began to realize that their *relational database
management systems (RDBMSs)* needed to be able to handle more
than the traditional alphanumeric data types. The need for the
capability to handle content-rich data types such as image,
HTML, spatial, sound, and video had become apparent.

Informix and Illustra combined forces to create the INFORMIX-
Universal Server, an *object-relational database management system
(ORDBMS)*, designed to integrate these nontraditional information
types with the alphanumeric data types. The Universal Server is
built on the Informix Dynamic Scalable Architecture, which provides it with high performance and scalability. In addition, Universal Server accepts third-party, reusable software "snap-ins"
called *DataBlade* modules. Each DataBlade module extends the
capabilities of the core database server. As an example, if an
organization wanted to include photo images of each employee
with his or her file in the human resources database, a DataBlade
module that provided this imaging capability could be added to
the native database server. A single SQL query could then be written to pull up an employee's file, including his or her picture.
What's more, DataBlades can be built that actually consider the
content of the complex data types, and allow custom functions to
be integrated directly with the database engine. With Informix
DataBlade technology, organizations can now tailor their servers
to fit their unique information requirements.

INFORMIX-OnLine Workgroup Server

INFORMIX-OnLine Workgroup Server is designed for developing
and deploying small—2 to 32 users—client/server and Web/intra-
net applications across an organization. The Workgroup Server is
based on the Informix DSA architecture and runs on Microsoft
Windows NT. Because it is targeted for distributed workgroup
users with little or no database administration experience, the
package comes with a set of GUI-based tools that reduce the complexity of typical database operations. Installation, setup, configuration, and administration activities are all simplified to point-
and-click processes.

OnLine Workgroup Server has integrated Netscape's FastTrack Server and Navigator to provide Web application connectivity as a standard feature. It also includes INFORMIX-Universal Web Connect and Web-DB Publisher to assist in Web development.

Data Access Tools

Now that you know the types of database engines that will manage the databases you create on them, the next question is, "How do I create my database and then access the data within it?" The next section covers three Informix data access tools: DB-Access, Informix-SQL, and INFORMIX-NewEra Viewpoint Pro.

DB-Access

DB-Access, unlike the other two data access tools in this section, is not a separate product. This tool comes bundled with the Informix database engine and is ready to be used immediately after engine installation. Because DB-Access will be looked at in great detail starting in Chapter 3, only a brief overview of the product is needed here.

DB-Access is not only a data access tool, but also an effective database management tool. In a nutshell, DB-Access provides a means to access, modify, and retrieve information in a relational database. A query language menu is provided for users to write, execute, and save SQL statements.

A schema editor permits users with appropriate permissions to easily create, modify, and drop databases. Within databases, they can view and maintain tables, indexes, constraints, and table partitions without using SQL. DB-Access also provides a means to obtain information about database and table architectures, all from within a friendly ring-menu-based interface.

Informix-SQL

Informix-SQL (ISQL) is not only useful as a data access tool for the novice to SQL, but may also be used by a developer to prototype database applications. Unlike DB-Access, Informix-SQL is a separate product and must be installed separately from the OnLine engine.

Five built-in tools come with ISQL. Two of them, the interactive SQL editor and the interactive schema editor, are very similar to their counterparts in DB-Access. The other three, a forms package, a report writer, and a menu builder, are exclusive to ISQL. All of the tools share the common Informix ring-menu interface and are integrated.

With the forms package, called Perform, beginners can create complex data entry screens with very little experience. These screens can be used to query, modify, add, and delete data from multiple tables. Perform can also be used by developers to build prototype multiscreen forms that may contain multiple field data displays and perform complex table joins. Perform's internal data validation ensures the integrity of information, making it nearly impossible to corrupt data.

The Ace report writer allows the user to control and format information returned from an SQL query. Custom reports that query data from multiple tables can be developed with very little programming. Formatting features such as automatic page headers and trailers, as well as adjustable page layouts, ease the building of report files.

The menu builder allows you to create custom vertical menus without any programming. This tool can integrate the pieces of an application by tying together forms, reports, SQL statements, and other menus.

ISQL has the same command line capabilities as DB-Access. We will cover ISQL in more detail in Chapter 6, "ISQL Forms and Reports."

INFORMIX-NewEra Viewpoint Pro

INFORMIX-NewEra Viewpoint Pro is actually a suite of GUI development and database administration tools designed to create small to mid-sized applications in a codeless environment. New-Era Viewpoint Pro may also be used as a data access tool for developers and end users. The suite of tools includes:

- A GUI form painter: permits end users to create GUI forms that may be used to run queries, browse the database, or perform data entry and data manipulation activities.

- A report writer: allows a user to automatically create and print graphical reports using only the mouse.

- An application screen builder: a GUI front-end used to create screens necessary to allow end users to move among the forms and reports available in a completed application.

- A database schema builder: allows the Database Administrator to perform essentially the same functions that DB-Access permits, all within a GUI environment. In addition, this tool may be used to create SuperViews (see below).

- An SQL editor: a GUI-based SQL editor similar to the interactive SQL editor available in DB-Access and ISQL. In addition, the SQL editor includes a history pop-up menu that allows a user to reexecute or modify any of the previous 20 SQL statements.

- A SuperView builder

A SuperView is a named set of relationships that models database data in a specific way. A SuperView is similar to a *view*, which you will learn about in Chapter 8, "Advanced SQL Queries." A typical view is like a table, except that it is created from a subset of one or more actual tables in the database. An example where a view might be used is when an application requires users to be able to look at certain characteristics of other employees, like office extensions and pager numbers, but not confidential information, like salaries and personal phone numbers. In this case, a view could be created so that when it is queried, the user would see only the nonconfidential information.

Development Tools

The following section covers a number of different development tools and packages offered by Informix. These products assist you in designing end-user applications and provide you with more flexibility and error checking capabilities than the data access tools we looked at previously. Specifically, we will discuss the Informix-4GL product suite, INFORMIX-ESQL, Stored Procedures, and INFORMIX-NewEra.

Informix-4GL

4GL stands for *fourth-generation language*. A 4GL is an English-like programming language that allows faster development time, and is easier to learn and maintain than a *third-generation language* (*3GL*) such as C, COBOL, or Pascal. In fact, a 4GL is normally pre-compiled into a 3GL before final compilation into machine code.

The Informix-4GL product family consists of Informix-4GL Rapid Development System (4GL-RDS), Informix-4GL Interactive Debugger (4GL-ID) and Informix-4GL Compiler (4GL). Like all Informix application development tools, the 4GL family is built on industry standard SQL. Chapter 10, "Your First 4GL Program," shows these tools in practice.

Informix-4GL Compiler can be used as a development tool itself, although it is not as powerful or fast as developing with RDS and ID. The 4GL and 4GL-RDS development environments look basically the same, with the primary exception of the debugging options within RDS. Both implement the standard Informix ring-menu development format. No matter which tool you use, 4GL gives you the capability to build menus, forms, screens, and reports as supplements to your code, as well as the capability to invoke ISQL without having to exit the 4GL development environment.

Informix-4GL Rapid Development System   This interpreted version of Informix-4GL decreases compilation time, and subsequently increases developer productivity. Code written with RDS is compiled into *pseudo-code (p-code)* and executed by a p-code runner after being read into memory. This p-code does not run as fast as the more streamlined executable compiled by Informix-4GL Compiler, but for developing and debugging purposes quick compile times are much more critical than quick runtimes.

Informix-4GL Interactive Debugger   The Interactive Debugger enables a developer to enter a running program and perform debugging operations. Among other things, a programmer can:

- Control the execution of a running program
- Interactively view and change the contents of variables
- Watch a program execute step by step

4GL-ID is also a powerful maintenance tool, because a new programmer can become familiar with existing code more easily and spot existing bugs more readily than without such a tool.

INFORMIX-ESQL

ESQL is an SQL API that permits the embedding of both static and dynamic SQL statements directly into a 3GL program. In a static SQL statement, all the components are known when the program is compiled. A dynamic SQL statement, conversely, does not have all its components available at compile time, but rather receives all or part of the statement at runtime. Chapter 15, "ESQL/C," explores this distinction between static and dynamic SQL in an instructive manner. Currently, Informix has ESQL product releases available for C (INFORMIX-ESQL/C) and COBOL (INFORMIX-ESQL/COBOL).

ESQL supports both *Data Definition Language* (*DDL*) SQL statements as well as *Data Manipulation Language* (*DML*) SQL statements. DDL refers to SQL statements that create, modify, or drop database objects such as tables and indexes. DML, as the name suggests, refers to SQL statements that manipulate data. The `insert`, `update`, and `delete` operators are all examples of DML.

A developer can therefore embed SQL that creates databases and other database objects such as tables, views, and indexes in the 3GL code. Additionally, `select`, `insert`, `update`, and `delete` operations, as well as SQL that connects to database servers, may also be embedded in the 3GL code.

Once an application is developed, INFORMIX-ESQL automatically links the Informix communication libraries into the application. These libraries make the application network-ready and capable of working in client/server environments without additional middleware products or tools.

Stored Procedures

A *stored procedure* is a user-defined function that is stored in a database rather than in a code module. It is typically used to improve performance when executing frequently repeated tasks. Performance is improved because the procedure is stored in the database in an executable format, allowing you to bypass the repeated parsing, validity checking, and query optimization that accompanies executing external SQL statements.

Stored procedures can perform any function that can be performed using SQL alone, but are normally created to expand SQL capabilities. Some of the capabilities a stored procedure can implement that SQL by itself cannot are:

- Defining and assigning values to variables
- Defining control structures, such as `if` statements and `for` loops
- Designating return values
- Implementing error-trapping and recovery
- Generating debug output

A stored procedure is written using a combination of SQL and *Stored Procedure Language (SPL)*. SPL statements can only be used inside the boundaries of a `create procedure` statement and an `end procedure` statement. When a stored procedure is created, its execution plan is optimized at that time and stored in an internal database system catalog table. The first time the stored procedure is executed, its executable is loaded from the system table and stored for public use in a reserved portion of shared memory. Because of this shared function feature, stored procedures are often created to reduce application development times.

Stored procedures are often used in conjunction with *triggers* to enforce business rules within a database. A *trigger* is a contingency mechanism that sets off an event or chain of events within the database when a triggering event—an `insert`, `update`, or `delete`—occurs on a table. A trigger may execute a stored procedure when the triggering event occurs. Both stored procedures and triggers will be covered in depth in Chapter 9, "Stored Procedures and Triggers."

INFORMIX-NewEra

INFORMIX-NewEra is a graphical development environment designed to make graphical database application development both quicker and easier. NewEra includes:

- A Window Painter
- An Application Builder
- A database application programming language

The Window Painter is a graphical form painter and code generator used to create the graphical interface for an application and, in essence, prototype the application at the same time. This tool permits the creation of typical GUI window controls such as radio buttons, menus, edit boxes, and scrolling lists.

The Application Builder allows you to manage large applications spread out over many files. With it, application modules can be compiled into C code or p-code, similar to 4GL RDS. A debug option is also available. The programs managed by the Application Builder may be NewEra code generated by the Window Painter, C, C++, or NewEra code a developer has written.

The database application language supports an object-oriented (OO) architecture as well as the traditional programming approach. The object-oriented language provides standard OO constructs such as class creation, inheritance, and reusable application components. Many class libraries are already created for NewEra, but you can write your own to implement business-unique features.

In addition to being client/server- and Web-ready, NewEra's environment is optimized for developing INFORMIX-Universal Server-based applications and DataBlade modules.

Summary

In this chapter you were provided with a high-level overview of Informix and the types of products that Informix offers, as well as an introduction to relational databases and client/server computing. The primary goal of this chapter was to provide you with a framework for the rest of this book.

In our broad look at database engines, we stressed the multithreading capabilities and scalability of the Informix Dynamic Scalable Architecture. The engines investigated (INFORMIX-SE, INFORMIX-OnLine, INFORMIX-XPS, INFORMIX-Universal Server, and INFORMIX-Workgroup Server) support environments from the small workgroup setting to the massive decision support SMP cluster and MPP systems.

Informix provides a variety of data access and development tools, all of which base their functionality on SQL. The data access tools (DB-Access, INFORMIX-ISQL, and INFORMIX-Viewpoint Pro) provide a means to easily view and modify database data and structures. They may also be used to test and prototype applications and to create reports. The development packages (Informix-4GL Compiler/RDS/ID and INFORMIX-NewEra) allow the creation of flexible and secure end-user applications. INFORMIX-ESQL allows you to embed SQL within 3GL code, whereas stored procedures permit repetitive tasks and business rules to be embedded within the database server itself.

Extra Credit

Q&A

Question	Answer
Can I run SPL directly in DB-Access?	No. You must create a stored procedure first, and then you may execute the stored procedure from within DB-Access.
Can I implement a for-loop in an SQL statement that I write in the DB-Access Query Language screen?	No, SQL alone does not support control structures such as the for-loop. For tasks such as this, you need to use a procedural language tool such as SPL, ESQL/C, or Informix-4GL.
Can I write a C function that calls a 4GL function?	Yes, the Informix 4GL API allows this functionality.

Exercises

1. Join your local Informix Users Group.
2. Surf the Informix Web site (http://www.informix.com).
3. Explore the comp.databases.informix newsgroup.
4. Take a look at the documents in your $INFORMIXDIR/releases directory. There is important release-specific information in these files.

Data Modeling 101

Data modeling is the creative process of translating real-world items like customers, bank transactions, and music collections into the database parlance of entities and attributes, tables and columns. You model items so that you can know how you will store information about them in your database. Whether your database is large or small, its purpose is to let you track data that reflects something that actually exists. You need to model that existence before you can build your database.

Introduction

This type of modeling is analogous to an architect's crafting of architectural design drawings that show a building's perspective, how its elements relate, and the components of each room. An effective model is the blueprint for building a database—the Rosetta stone that translates subject matter expertise into formal relational parlance.

Data Modeling Terms

Let's start with a few definitions. There won't be a quiz, but there are a few terms with which you must gain early facility. The remainder of this chapter will expand by example on the definitions presented in Table 2-1. You don't have to memorize these just yet, but you may need to refer back here as you read the rest of the chapter.

Table 2-1 **Essential data modeling terms.**

Term	Definition
Attribute	A logical name for a characteristic of an entity. Attributes in a logical model map to columns in a physical model.
Column	An element that describes a row in a table, like the birth date of a performer or the title of an album.
Constraint	A restriction mandated by the designer and enforced by the database.
Database	A collection of related objects that describes the format and content of a discrete business model. Some elements of a database include tables, indexes, constraints, views, synonyms, stored procedures, and triggers.
DBA	Database administrator. An Oz-like megalomaniacal figure with a constant mien of exasperation. Has been known to design, maintain, and tune databases. Genderless.

(Continued)

Table 2-1   Essential data modeling terms.

Term	Definition
Domain	The set of all legal values for a column.
Entity	A logical container that describes a single kind of real-world thing. Entities are items in a logical data model that translate to physical database tables.
Foreign key	Column(s) in a table that identify a single row in a related table.
Logical modeling	The realm of database design concerned with what a database stores, why certain entities exist, and how they relate.
Null	An unknown or inapplicable value for a column.
Physical modeling	The realm of database design concerned with how and where the logical model is physically implemented on a database server.
Primary key	The set of columns that uniquely identifies a row.
Relational database	A database where all of the information is stored in relations, or tables.
Row	One element in a table. A set of data that describes a single instance of a real-world item. Pointy-headed geeks refer to rows as tuples (rhymes with "couples"). We don't.
Schema	The Data Description Language (DDL) recipe used to create a database and its contents.
Table	A database container comprising rows of like data, each described by columns that define it. Formal scholars and dweebs refer to very well behaved tables as relations.

This list may look imposing, but don't be daunted. The remainder of this chapter shows these modeling terms in practice and demystifies them by showing you how to model and design your own database.

Building a Model

The major components of your relational data model will be an *entity-relationship diagram (ERD)*, and the column domains and definitions that compose it.

Define the Project Scope

It should go without saying—although in practice it does not—that before you can model something, you must understand it and limit its scope. The data model reflects one *miniworld*, a very small tile in life's brilliant mosaic, and does so with a single diagram. In the interest of presenting as much data as succinctly as possible, the goal is to keep the model small and familiar.

By way of example, the small, familiar application used to teach the basics will be a music collection, specifically my eclectic assortment of tunes. I have recordings that represent assorted genres, recorded on various media, from diverse performers. For some albums I have multiple copies. Not only that, I'm also interested in some background data on the performers, as well as valuing my entire collection. In this chapter, and throughout the book, we'll develop and use this music collection to show both general relational principles and the broad Informix toolkit.

Fasten your seat belts. Here is a look ahead. Figure 2–1 shows the completed data model.

Take a look. It won't hurt you. The ERD in Figure 2–1 identifies *entities* (boxes) and the *relationships* (lines) between them; hence its name. The rest of this chapter explains the conventions used in this diagram and shows how the model is derived synthetically; that is, built gradually from the identification of its fundamental database components.

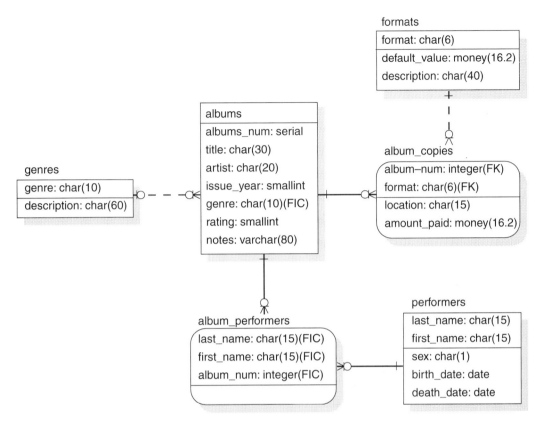

Figure 2–1   *The music data model.*

Define the Entities

Entities are the *things* in your database. They correspond to the real-world physical objects and events that your system describes. The entities are further described by the attributes they contain— the adjectives, if you will, of the nouns that are the entities. Thus, for example, albums are reasonable candidate entities for the music database, with traits like their title or their performers as potential attributes.

The first step in creating a model is to identify candidate entities. The traits listed in Table 2–2 help you identify and distinguish the entities in your model.

With these traits in mind, we might consider trying to segregate the information for this music collection into nascent logical groupings, candidate entities that might form the skeleton of the

Table 2-2   Traits of entities.

Trait	Definition
Distinguishable	Not decomposable to dissimilar objects. For example, a single entity does not store information on both performers and the albums on which they performed. These groupings are dissimilar: one describes people, the other events in which the people participated.
Relevant	Within the scope of your miniworld, and about which further descriptive information is to be stored.
Generic	Not an instance. An entity is not one occurrence, such as "Stevie Ray Vaughan," but instead is a template to store a collection of items with traits in common, like "performers."
Independent	Not a feature or trait of another entity. This is true only for kernel entities. Association and characteristics entities (see Table 2–3) specifically *do* describe other entities.

data model. You could consider groupings such as Albums, CDs, 8-tracks, Artists, Ratings, Performers, Titles, Costs, and so on. As yet, the traits are too abstract to allow significant progress. One set of rules that helps impose some structure on these early groupings is the classification of all entities into three types. Table 2-3 explains these classes.

Given these classifications, it's most productive to first identify the kernel entities of the target system. For the `music` database, those entities appear to be `genres`, `formats`, `performers`, and `albums`. Why not label as entities things that are more primitive than albums, such as ratings, for example? In this case, there is nothing further to describe about a rating, which is to say that a `ratings` entity would not be relevant to the miniworld. Why not have one entity for CDs and another for each other music format,

Table 2-3   Entity types.

Type	Definition
Kernel	An independent entity whose elements have existence regardless of any other entity. In the completed data model, the kernel entities are `albums`, `genres`, `formats`, and `performers`.
Association	An entity that describes a many-to-many relationship (see the section "Cardinality") between other entities. For example, the `album_performers` table describes such a relationship between the `albums` and `performers` tables. The related entities may be of any type.
Characteristic	An entity that describes some other entity. In our model, `album_copies` further characterizes `albums`. Characteristic entities are meaningless without the entities on which they depend.

like 8-tracks? The reason is that these items represent mostly the same thing: the music they each contain. The term "albums" as used in this model represents the music in the abstract, not any instance of that music, regardless of how it is recorded. The instances of the recordings are distinguishable from the ideal of the albums; thus, separate entities (`albums` and `album_copies`) are needed to reflect this distinction. Other questions remain, but the remainder of this chapter will continue to refine the criteria used to organize items in the data model to answer them.

Entities of whatever classification have properties that describe them. These properties are the attributes of the entities. A key question about entities is "how are they distinguished?" That is, which properties compose the primary key, the set of attributes that uniquely identifies an instance of an entity? Even more fundamentally, the question is "what are the attributes that describe each entity, from which a primary key can be chosen?"

Define the Attributes

An attribute is a characteristic of an entity. In an ERD, attributes are shown inside the entities they describe. Table 2-4 shows the traits that identify attributes in a relational model.

Table 2-4   Traits of attributes.

Trait	Definition
Atomic	Not decomposable. An attribute must contain a single value, never a list or other kind of repeating group. Furthermore, an attribute should not store disparate values that might be treated separately. For example, the `performers` entity will include separate attributes for `last_name` and `first_name`. Since the last name is to be treated separately from the first name (for example, as the basis for sorting) it would not be acceptable to combine the two columns into one `name` column.
Relevant	Within the scope of the model. There is no reason to track data that will never be used.
Similar	Of the same type. Each entry for an attribute shares a common domain, or pool of legal values. As such, no single attribute should be designed, for example, to store both names and dates.
Specific	Not a generic placeholder. Attributes with names such as `other_data` are malicious.
Autonomous	Not derived from other attributes. A relational database should not store the same data in multiple places. Thus, traits that can be calculated or derived, such as the number of rows in another table or the sum of other columns, should not be stored as attributes, but rather should be computed when needed.

A primary goal of data modeling is to reduce redundancy. Such reduction allows efficient data storage and permits easier updates. Try to adhere to the maxim of one fact in one place.

Consider again the `performers` entity. We are interested in some personal data about each performer, such as sex and age. Should these both be defined as attributes? Although sex contains all of the traits of an attribute, age does not. Instead of being autonomous, age is derived and should instead be calculated as needed (you'll do this in Chapter 9, "Stored Procedures and Triggers"). The more appropriate atomic attributes are `birth_date` and `death_date`.

Primary Keys

In each row, each instance of an entity, either one attribute must contain a unique value, or the values of a set of attributes must be unique as a unit. In the `performers` table, the combination of `last_name` and `first_name` makes each row unique. As such, these two attributes together are designated as the entity's primary key (PK). Likewise, for example, a given `genre` uniquely identifies an instance of the `genres` entity. As a consequence, other tables can now reference a row, and look up its properties by supplying the PK values.

Sometimes, more than one set of attributes can be considered the primary key. The choice of which of these *candidate keys* to select as the primary, and which to leave as *alternate keys*, is often subjective. For the `albums` table, `album_num` is chosen as the PK for easier reference by other entities, but the combination of `artist` and `title` will also always be unique and thus remains an alternate key. Although the ERD does not identify alternate keys, they are reflected in the constraints embedded within the database's schema (see "Constraints" later in this chapter).

Foreign Keys

One goal of modeling is to reduce redundancy. This means not storing the same data in several places; that is, not all in one table. An effect of this separation of data is that to find all of the information about a thing—for example, to list all of the information about your Beatles CDs—you need to relate the associated entities back together (you'll do this in Chapter 8, "Advanced SQL Queries"). You create the structure for this by designating as foreign keys (FKs) the attributes that identify other entities. To find data associated with another entity, you can refer to that entity as needed, using the values in the FK attributes. The following section describes these relationships, a core component of relational databases.

Define the Relationships

Relationships are what make a relational database, well, relational. Relationships are the associations between entities that can often be described with verb phrases such as "act on" or "has a" For example, it is reasonable to say an album has a genre, or that performers act on albums. The primary traits of the relationship that the model must capture are *reference*, *dependency*, and *cardinality*.

Reference

Any two entities that relate, or reference each other, do so specifically via referential integrity (RI) between the two entities. RI is a key concept that describes the FK-to-PK relationships between tables. FKs are those columns that identify a single row in a related table. RI states that any columns designated as FKs must either contain values that exist as a PK in the related table or be null. For example, in the `albums` table the `genre` column is an FK to the `genres` table. Therefore, no values may be stored in the `genre` column of the `albums` table that do not already exist in the `genre` column of the `genres` table. In this case, there is also a business rule that states that it may be appropriate for an album's `genre` to be unknown or inapplicable. Thus, having a null value does not break an RI constraint.

Dependency

Dependency indicates whether this entity is optional or mandatory in the relationship. For example, an album copy can exist only when the album it references exists—no copies of imaginary music are allowed. Conversely, for example, not all albums have performers. (Really. Check out "Sounds of the Okefenokee Swamp.") Only association and characteristic entities have dependent relationships. Knowing the dependency of a relationship will help you identify RI rules and not null constraints, described later in the "Refining the Model" section.

Cardinality

Cardinality defines the number of rows that the relationship represents. There are three choices: one-to-one (1:1), one-to-many (1:n), and many-to-many (n:n). These choices refer to how many rows of one table reference rows in the other. For example, a given performer might perform on many albums, or a given album might have many performers. Thus, the `albums` and `performers` entities have a logical n:n relationship One of the goals of physical database modeling is to try to translate all 1:1 and n:n logical relationships into 1:n physical relationships. This translation aids in data integrity and efficiency. The final music model consists of only 1:n relationships and, for the above n:n relationship, resolves it for implementation by creating an association table.

 tip   *Resolve n:n logical relationships by inventing an association entity at their intersection that describes the events at which the entities relate.*

Draw the Model

Let's revisit the ERD to look closely at the entities, attributes, and relationships therein, and the diagramming conventions used to portray them. Figure 2-2 is a subset of the music ERD, with an explanation in Table 2-5 of the diagramming conventions used.

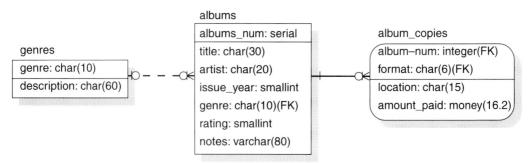

Figure 2–2 *Entity relationships explained.*

Table 2-5   ERD modeling conventions.

Object	Convention	Business Rule
Attribute	Columns above the line	Primary key. This set of attributes uniquely identifies a row, so there should be no duplicates of these values within a table. Also, no parts of a PK may be null.
Attribute	FK	Foreign key. Values in these columns must be present as a PK in the table they reference. A relationship line shows the referencing table, and every line represents a FK-PK relationship.
Attribute	Data type	The kind of data the field may contain. For example, an integer data type may not contain character data. The data type is the most obvious means of enforcing an attribute's domain.
Relationship	Crow's feet at end	The *many* side of the relationship. In Figure 2-2, there can be many albums for any given genre, and many copies of any given album.

(Continued)

Table 2-5   ERD modeling conventions.

Object	Convention	Business Rule
Relationship	Single crossbar at end	The *one* side of the relationship. In Figure 2-2, each album copy refers to a single album, and each album is classified with at most one genre.
Relationship	Circle	An optional relationship. That is, not every row on the other side of the relationship line requires a matching row on this optional side. In Figure 2-2, every `album_copies` row must have an associated `albums` row, but every other relationship is optional.
Relationship	Dashed line	An independent FK relationship. In Figure 2-2, the existence of a genre does not depend on any given album.
Relationship	Solid line	A dependency FK relationship. Represents the relationship between a characteristic or association entity and the entity on which it depends. In Figure 2-2, the existence of an album copy depends on the album it represents.
Entity	Square corners	A kernel entity. Signifies an independent table.
Entity	Rounded corners	A dependent entity. Identifies a characteristic or association entity.

It is not important that you memorize these rules. What is important is that you recognize that such conventions exist, and can be used to embed many business rules succinctly into a single diagram.

Refining the Model

In all real-world cases, creating a useful data model is an iterative process. Candidate entities are proposed and then sometimes rejected or refined. Attributes are assigned to entities, and then may be moved to other entities, split into components, or discarded. This refinement is a natural outgrowth of the attempt to map fuzzy real-world items and events into the rule-bound terrain of the relational model.

An aid to this refinement is to consider the modeling process from alternative perspectives. What follows are small expositions on two facets of strict relational modeling: formal data integrity and normalization. Each topic reveals finer points on the relational model. The previous rules and the following explanations are not exclusive, but rather complement each other in a slightly different context. By considering both these formal rules and the earlier guidelines, you can continue to refine and have confidence in your data model.

Data Integrity

Data integrity comprises the following three areas:

- Entity integrity
- Semantic integrity
- Referential integrity

Let's explore these rules with specific attention to the `music` data model.

Entity Integrity

Entity integrity ensures that each table has a primary key, which by corollary means that all rows must be unique. Table 2-6 summarizes the traits of every primary key.

Table 2-6   Traits of primary keys.

Trait	Definition
Unique	Not duplicated. The fundamental role of a PK is to distinguish rows from each other.
Invariant	Unchanging. This is not a strict rule enforced by all theorists, but it should be.
Not null	Must have a value. No part of a PK may be null.

Design your tables so that the primary keys need never be updated. The primary key's value should be so tightly integrated with the actual row it represents that updating it would be tantamount to creating a new row.

These PK traits have some consequence for the `music` data model. Consider the unique PK constraint as it applies to the `album_copies` entity. The restriction mandates that you cannot have two albums of the same format in your collection. Is it reasonable to prevent storing the data on, say, two CD copies of `Abbey Road`? At the very least, you would need some other characteristic to make the two copies distinguishable. You might even need to invent an artificial primary key, an otherwise meaningless number, with which you could tag your copies. Every data model contains some compromises. One of this model's compromises is to not allow multiple album copies, but such choices are ones you as a designer have to make based on your own understanding of the model's miniworld.

Consider now the restriction that no parts of a PK may be null. This is necessary to reflect that null values are not comparable; that is, they are neither the same as nor different from other null values. They are unknown or inapplicable. In the `music` data model, the PK of the `performers` entity, the place where details on each musician are stored, is the combination of `first_name` and `last_name`. Yet not all performers use two names professionally. What about Madonna, Jewel, Yanni, or Enya? One choice is again to invent an artificial numeric key as with `albums`, and professionally this is the option most often chosen, but too many such keys can make a database unfriendly for casual users. Another option is to use the last names (Ciccone, Kilcher, Hrisomallis, and Bhraonain) even when the performers do not. The compromise chosen here is instead to own music only by artists with two names. It is not a perfect choice, but the world does not map exactly to strict relational rules.

Semantic Integrity

Semantic integrity is the principal that data must be appropriate for the attribute, the column, in which it is stored. It must be meaningful semantically to appreciate the contents of a column based on what you call a column, and how you store data within it. For example, if a column is identified as an `integer` data type, this column must contain only whole numbers, not character data such as letters or symbols.

Domains   The set of all legal values for a column is known as its domain. For example, in the `performers` table the `birth_date` and `death_date` columns both draw from the set of dates. We could be more specific than merely specifying that these columns contain date values, as opposed, say, to text fields. For example, we could say that these dates must lie between 1/1/1900 and 12/31/2099, or any arbitrary range we choose. Domains encapsulate the customized, user-defined business rules that an application demands.

Most database tools, Informix included, have no direct physical tools that support the complete logical concept of domains. Instead, we specify domains using these three components:

- Data types
- Constraints
- Naming conventions

In general, when columns share domains they can be reasonably compared: tested for equality, related to other tables, aggregated, and so on.

Data Types   Every attribute, as it gets mapped into a column, must be assigned a data type. In Chapter 4, "Creating Databases and Tables," the entire range of datatypes is enumerated, with explanations of each. At this point, you merely need to recognize that such categories as character, integer, date, float, and money exist.

A domain is enforced first by specifying a data type appropriate for a column. This data type is the most effective means of enforcing a column's domain. With it, for example, you can ensure that only money-type data is assigned to the `amount_paid` column of the `album_copies` table. In addition to dictating a column's domain, data types restrict the type of operations that can be performed on a column. For example, a character-based description field cannot be summed; nor is it meaningful to find the length of a date field.

Constraints   Constraints are the database tools you use to enforce the business rules and domains of a data model. These are actual physical data restrictions that you specify, and that the database enforces on your behalf. Table 2-7 shows the five constraint types available within Informix.

Table 2-7   Constraints available within Informix.

Constraint Type	Enforces
not null	Existence of a value
unique	Uniqueness of a column or combination of columns
primary key	Same as unique constraint, but its nomenclature suggests that it has additional stature (see Table 2-6)
references	Referential integrity
check	Domain validation via an SQL-like clause

The ERD shows each of these except the check constraint. For that, you have to look at the database schema—its recipe for creating the database and the objects within it. The schema also specifies the other constraints, but you can also infer them from the ERD itself. Each of these constraint types is used in the `music` data model, specified completely in Appendix B, "The Sample Database."

Chapter 4 shows the formal syntax for specifying domains with the Informix toolkit, but at the initial modeling stage you need only consider the pools of values that will be appropriate for the attributes you define. You can decide, for example, that an album's rating must be between 0 and 10, or that the sex of a performer should be limited to male or female.

Naming Conventions   The more consistently tables and columns are named, the more meaning users and developers can ascribe to the names. Although Informix does not mandate strict naming conventions, you should consider adopting your own guidelines. For example, consider having all table names be plural. This reflects the fact that a table is a set of multiple rows of data.

The rules for naming columns can also be restricted to enhance meaning. For example, although two columns in the same table cannot have the same name, columns from different tables can, and should, share names when they share domains. Thus, you can recognize which columns can be related to which others based solely on the column names. It is especially important that columns participating in an FK-PK relationship be named the same.

Another naming convention arises from Informix's limitation that database identifiers such as column and table names be no longer than 18 characters. Should you be forced to abbreviate, do so consistently. Do not abbreviate "number" sometimes as "num," elsewhere as "no," and other times not at all. In the `music` data model, the only abbreviation used is "num" for "number," but it is used consistently.

Referential Integrity

The concept of referential integrity has already been introduced in the "Reference" section, but this section explores some consequences of having the database enforce RI via its referential constraints. The earlier discussion considered mostly the creation of data in the referenced table, and the idea of preventing the creation of a referencing row if the value in its FK does not exist as a referenced PK.

Consider instead what ought to happen if a primary key that is currently being referenced were to be deleted. If a performer were to be deleted that was referenced in the `album_performers` table, RI would be violated. This cannot be allowed. In Informix, a constraint could be applied to enforce that such a delete does not occur, but preventing the deletion is not always the appropriate action. In fact, there are three options available when considering deleting a referenced PK:

- Restrict—Do not allow deleting a referenced PK. This is the default.
- Nullify—Upon deletion of a PK, set all columns that reference it to null.
- Cascade—Upon deleting a PK, also delete all FK rows that reference it.

It is unfortunate that our ERD does not depict which of these business rules is applied to each relationship. For that data, you need to examine the schema directly, and look at how the referential constraint is defined. The default for all FK relationships is to restrict the delete of referenced PKs, and in the `music` data model this default is used throughout. However, you need to be aware that other options are available.

Notice that no mention has been made of what to do when a PK value is updated. There is a reason for this: we *never* update primary keys. Ever.

Normalization

Normalization is the process of adjusting a data model so that it consists of tables that conform to strict relational tenets, or *norms*. At its core, the process calls for removing redundancy from the database. Additionally, it ensures that the attributes of each entity are exactly dependent on the whole primary key.

You need to see these definitions not only because they will serve you well in your database career, but also because everyone expects you to know them. Here you'll get the précis on the topic with little stern textbook formality.

A fundamental concept that underlies all normal forms is that they are refinements of relations, the formal way of describing a well-behaved table. Specifically, a relation is a table that has a primary key, whose attributes are all non-null, whose rows and columns are in no particular order, and on which all attributes in the table depend.

First Normal Form

This rule (abbreviated 1NF) says that each column must contain an atomic value—no repeating groups are allowed. In our database, for example, it says that we cannot store the list of performers for an album anywhere in the `albums` entity. Such a list would be a repeating group, a list, an array. Instead, we must design another entity such as `album_performers` to store the associations between `albums` and `performers`. Tables with repeating groups are unnormalized.

Second Normal Form

The normal forms are cumulative. For example, for a table to conform to second normal form (2NF), it must be in 1NF and comply with the additional 2NF constraint that all of its attributes must be dependent on the whole primary key. That is, it can have no *partial dependencies*—those based on a subset of the PK. For example, it violates 2NF to store data about a specific album in the `album_copies` table. Although `album_num` is part of the table's PK, it is not the entire key. Rather, the entire PK is the conjunction of `album_num` and `format`. It follows that in order to have partial dependencies, a table must have a multipart key.

This rule exists so that data will not be stored redundantly. Consider the effect if an album's rating were stored in the `album_copies` table. Each copy of an album, each instance of the same music, would have to independently store the same rating. Each time you cared to update an album's rating you'd need to do so for every copy of the album you owned. The 2NF rule exists to obviate the kind of data anomaly that can occur when such multiple updates do not occur in sync.

Third Normal Form

A table is in third normal form (3NF) when it is in 2NF and contains no *transitive dependencies*. A transitive dependency occurs when a nonkey attribute is dependent on other nonkey attributes. Consider the effect if, in addition to the genre, the genre's description were also stored in the `albums` table. Insofar as each album number is atomic (1NF), and the PK has only one part (2NF), such a model violates none of the other normalization rules. But this transitive dependency—genre description depends on genre, which in turn (transitively) depends on the album number—creates redundant data. It forces a duplication of the genre description for every album that shares a genre.

When you notice a violation of 3NF, it is a signal to create a new table, one such as `genres` (in this case) where the erstwhile transitive dependency is extracted to its own table.

The Higher Forms

There are in fact more normal forms. There are 4th, 5th, and the unlikely sounding Boyce-Codd normal form. You will not need to know about these.

tip

When asked about your normalization methods, mention offhandedly how you always "consider the higher forms: 4th, 5th, Boyce-Codd, but then back off to 3rd for practical reasons." Others will nod knowingly. This bluff works at any level.

Summary

One doesn't build a house without blueprints, or a database without a data model. The question is not: *Must I have a data model?* Instead, the question is only: *Will it be explicit and useful, or implicit and disorderly?* Be a good database citizen and construct your model before building a database on flimsy scaffolding.

A data model consists of an ERD and the supporting detailed column and constraint definitions. In our case, those supporting details are captured in the database schema, the formal recipe for database creation. The ERD shows the entities, or areas of interest, of the database and how they interrelate. Many detailed business rules are depicted by the use of consistent diagramming conventions.

Modeling is a process of refinement, of assembling and reassembling the relational constructs in an attempt to mirror the imperfect real world. By applying the tenets of data integrity and normalization, you can refine your model until it is the best compromise between relational formality and objective reality.

Extra Credit

Q & A

Question

As an invariant primary key, performer name seems to be unacceptable. Some performers change their names over time. John Cougar Mellencamp née John Cougar becomes John Mellencamp. And what about The Artist (formerly known as Prince)?

Answer

You think I'm happy about this? The real world is a notoriously messy place. One makes compromises in a data model, such as excluding such protean noms de plume from being recognized as the same person. If it were available, you could use something about the performer that doesn't change, such as Social Security number, as your PK. In practice, an artificial system-generated identification number is usually invented to accommodate such artistic freedom of expression.

Why is `album_copies` treated as a characteristic entity and not an association entity? Its PK seems to depend on both the `albums` table and the `formats` table.

Sometimes the distinction between these entity types is hazy, and in practice the labels are not critical. The choice of PK for this entity is imperfect in any case. It mandates, for example, that you cannot store multiple copies of the same album format. One modeling answer is to invent an artificial sequence number, perhaps called `album_copy_num`, which resets for each album, and have that plus the `album_num` be a composite PK. Such a structure models a characteristic entity more accurately.

Exercises

1. Have a Piña Colada.

2. Some albums seem to fit in multiple genres. Who's to say that the Jackson 5 Christmas Album isn't also gospel, or even pop? Identify the changes required to the data model if a given album were allowed to belong to more than one genre at a time; that is, if the `albums` and `genres` entities had an n:n logical relationship.

Exercise Answers

1. Here's the recipe:
   3 ounces light rum
   3 tablespoons coconut milk
   3 tablespoons pineapple, crushed
   Blend all ingredients with 2 cups of crushed ice. Strain into a coconut shell and serve with a straw and a little umbrella.

2. The creation of an additional entity would be needed—one that associated `albums` to `genres`. The 1:n relationship that had been enforced by designating `genre` as a FK in the `albums` entity would be removed, and a new entity, `album_genres`, added. This entity would have a 1:n relationship to each of the entities it referenced. Figure 2-3 shows the subset of the data model that would change.

Figure 2–3 *Resolving a many-to-many relationship.*

DB-Access

DB-Access is your friend.

Introduction

As a developer, Informix *power user*, or database administrator, you will likely use DB-Access more often than any other Informix tool. This important interface is the chief way in which to perform the following:

- Enter ad hoc queries
- Execute SQL command files
- Examine the structure of your database
- Create databases and tables
- Connect to database servers
- Modify table structures
- Build and modify stored procedures

You can do some of these tasks with INFORMIX-SQL, but not all of them. You'll see in Chapter 6, "ISQL Forms and Reports," how ISQL is best suited for creating data-entry forms and simple reports. INFORMIX-NewEra Viewpoint Pro, another front-end tool, provides a graphical interface for examining the database structure and building queries, but is not shipped with every Informix installation, as DB-Access is. This chapter presents you with a guided tour through DB-Access, with a chance to explore its various components as well as the structure and contents of the `music` database.

Environment Basics

This section addresses the fundamentals of launching DB-Access in a UNIX environment. It contains some instructions that may be unnecessary if your system is already properly configured. To find out whether it is, try the following from your UNIX command line:

```
$ dbaccess
```

If your environment has been properly defined, you will see the DB-Access main menu, as in Figure 3-1. If you don't see the DB-Access main menu, you may to need to get assistance from your local DBA or system administrator. Generally, you'll need to have certain *environmental variables* set properly for your current Informix installation.

 UNIX is case-sensitive. In general, all commands are lowercase, whereas environmental variables by convention are designated in uppercase. Sloppy programmers occasionally violate these conventions. We won't.

Environmental Variables Defined

An *environmental variable* is a value defined for your login shell that customizes your current session. A strength and weakness of UNIX is that you can customize your own environment. You'll see

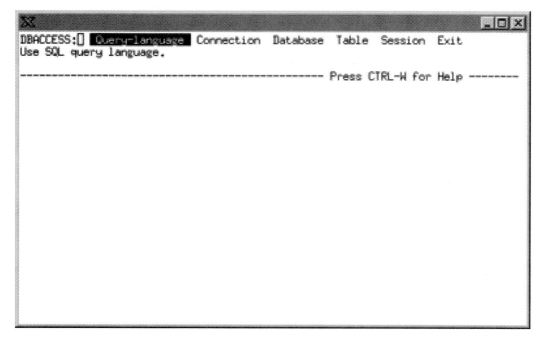

Figure 3–1   *DB-Access main menu.*

here enough fundamentals to get started doing just that. You set your environmental variables in a login script or dynamically during your shell. They allow the Informix products to recognize the values specific to your operating environment.

For DB-Access to run, you'll need to assign the proper values to a few environmental variables. These variables, and the values they must contain, are as follows:

- INFORMIXDIR, the directory in which your Informix products are installed
- INFORMIXSERVER, the logical name of your database server
- TERMCAP, the file that defines how terminals are defined
- PATH, the list of directories that contain commands available for you to execute
- TERM, the type of terminal you are currently using

Examining Environmental Variables

To see the value of all your variables currently set, type:

```
$ set
```

Look through the output for lines like the following:

```
INFORMIXDIR=/informix/7.2.UC3
INFORMIXSERVER=music_server
TERM=vt100
```

Of course, the values assigned to your variables will differ from those shown here. You use the `set` command to view all variables that have values.

You can determine the value of an individual variable with the `echo` command, as follows:

```
$ echo $INFORMIXDIR
/informix/7.2.UC3
```

The `echo` command displays the values that follow it on the UNIX command line. Notice the `$` symbol preceding the `INFOR-MIXDIR` variable. In UNIX, it signifies the *value of* operator. With it, you indicate that the value of `INFORMIXDIR` is what you want displayed. Compare the previous command to the following one:

```
$ echo INFORMIXDIR
INFORMIXDIR
```

If, by using `echo` and `set`, you determine that you need to assign values to or change the values of certain environmental variables, you will need to set the variables explicitly.

Setting Environmental Variables

You use standard UNIX commands to set environmental variables. The method varies with the type of shell you use. Table 3-1 shows how you set your `TERM` variable to `vt100` in each of the most common UNIX shells. It also shows the name of your *login file*. Your login file is read whenever you log in; you can embed environmental variable assignments there to have them set automatically upon login.

You can use this same method to set the other environmental variables previously listed.

Table 3-1   Setting environmental variables.

Shell	Assignment Operation	Login File
Korn (K) shell	`export TERM=vt100`	`.profile`
Bourne shell	`TERM=vt100`	`.profile`
	`export TERM`	
C shell	`setenv TERM vt100`	`.cshrc or .login`

Commands Map

By now you should have set any necessary environmental variables and launched DB-Access. Your screen should resemble Figure 3-1. DB-Access comprises several submenus, each of which is accessed by selecting an option from the main menu.

Press the space bar or the arrow keys repeatedly to examine the descriptions for each menu option. You select a menu option by typing the letter in its name that is capitalized (usually the first letter), or by pressing Return when the option is highlighted. You move from any menu to its parent menu with the `Exit` option. To save space, this option is not reproduced on each of the menu maps that follow. A map of the main menu is shown in Table 3-2.

Table 3-2   DB-Access main menu map.

Menu Command	Command Description
Query-language	Use SQL query language
New	Enter new SQL statements using SQL editor
Run	Run the current SQL statements

(Continued)

Table 3-2   DB-Access main menu map.

Menu Command	Command Description
Modify	Modify the current SQL statements using the SQL editor
Use-editor	Modify the current SQL statements using a user-specified editor
Output	Run and send query results to a printer, file, or pipe → Output submenu (see Table 3-4)
Choose	Choose a command file as the current SQL statements
Save	Save the current command in a command file
Info	Gives information on tables in the database → Table Info submenu (see Table 3-3)
Drop	Drop an SQL command file
Connection	Connect or disconnect from a database environment
Connect	Connect to a database environment
Disconnect	Disconnect from the current database environment
Database	Select, Create, Info, Drop, or Close a database
Select	Select a database to work with
Create	Create a new database → Create Database submenu (see Table 4-1)
Info	Retrieve information about a database → Database Info submenu
Drop	Drop a database
cLose	Close the current database
Table	Create, Alter, or Drop a database table

(Continued)

Table 3-2   DB-Access main menu map.

Menu Command	Command Description
Create	Create a new table → Create Table submenu (see Table 4-7)
Alter	Alter the structure of an existing table → Alter Table submenu
Info	Display information about the tables in the current database → Table Info submenu (see Table 3-3)
Drop	Drop a table
Session	Retrieve information about the current DB-Access session

There are over 140 menu options within DB-Access. In this chapter, you'll see a small fraction of them—the most useful ones. At your leisure, you should traverse the various menu paths, but for now we'll explore the Query-language menu, the Table Info submenu, shown in Table 3-3, and the Output submenu, depicted in Table 3-4- Notice while exploring that the name of your current menu is displayed on the left of your menu selections. This guidepost can help you track your location.

Table 3-3   DB-Access Table Info submenu map.

Menu Command	Command Description
Columns	Display column names and data types for a table
Indexes	Display information about indexes for the columns in a table
Privileges	Display user access privileges for a table
References	Display user reference privileges for a table

(Continued)

Table 3-3 **DB-Access** `Table Info` **submenu map.**

Menu Command	Command Description
`Status`	Display status information for a table
`cOnstraints`	Referential and check constraints
`Reference`	Display referential constraints → Reference submenu
`Primary`	Primary key constraints
`Check`	Display check constraints
`Unique`	Display unique constraints
`Defaults`	Display column defaults
`triGgers`	Display header and body information for a trigger
`Table`	Select a table from the current database
`Fragments`	Display fragment strategy for a table

With the `Query-language` option, you create and run SQL statements. The `Table Info` option allows you to examine the structure of your database tables. We'll start there, and use the `Table Info` submenu options to explore the sample `music` database.

The `Table Info` Submenu

There are two ways to get to the `Table Info` submenu from within DB-Access. The first way is by selecting the `Query-language` option, followed by selecting `Info` (see Table 3-2). Alternatively, you can select the `Table` option and choose `Info` after selecting a table. Each method allows you to choose a table (pick albums) and then points you to the same submenu, which should resemble Figure 3-2.

When DB-Access prompts you to choose from a highlighted list, you can either type in the name of your selection, or use the arrow keys to select the value you want. If you want none of the options, use Ctrl-C to interrupt the selection and return to your previous menu.

From this point on, Informix Basics *uses the sample* music *database. For details on how to create and populate this database, refer to Appendix A, "The Sample Database." You can still take the tour without the* music *database, but until you create a database— any database—you will be unable to explore all of the DB-Access features. If you like, instead of using the scripts in the Appendix to generate the database automatically, you can jump ahead to the next chapter to learn how to create the database and tables manually.*

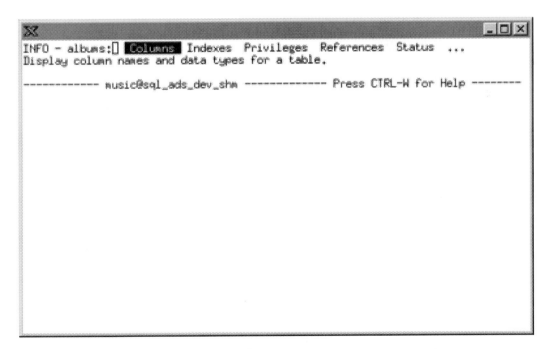

Figure 3–2   DB-Access `Table Info` submenu.

This menu lets you examine the structure of your tables, including their indexes and constraints. In this chapter you will examine the completed database that was designed in Chapter 2, "Data Modeling 101." In Chapter 4, "Creating Databases and Tables," you'll have the chance to build the database yourself. You'll need to have familiarity with these menu options so that you can verify the correctness of the tables you will be building.

note   *The ellipses (. . .) in the ring menu signify that more options are available, but cannot fit on the screen. Use the space bar or arrow keys to display the next screen of menu options. You can still use a menu option's first letter to select it even when it is not currently shown.*

The `Columns` Option

Examine the columns in the `albums` table by selecting the `Columns` option. You should see a screen like Figure 3-3.

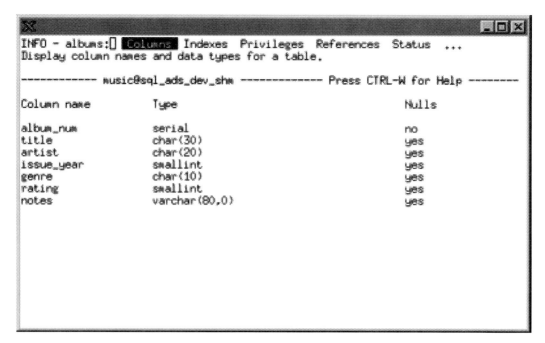

Figure 3–3   DB-Access `Table Info:Columns` option.

Compare the display to the design for the `albums` table, developed in Chapter 2. Notice that each column has a specific type, which represents how it is stored in the database. In Chapter 4 you'll learn about each of the Informix data types, and how to choose the appropriate one for each column you design. In brief, the `char` and `varchar` data types hold character values of differing lengths, the `smallint` type holds small integers, and the `serial` type holds an auto-incremented integer value.

The `Indexes` Option

Now, look at the indexes for the `albums` table, by selecting the `Indexes` menu option; see Figure 3-4.

```
INFO - albums:[]  Columns  Indexes  Privileges  References  Status  ...
Display information about indexes for the columns in a table.

--------------- music@sql_ads_dev_shm --------------- Press CTRL-W for Help ---------

Index name          Owner     Type     Cluster   Columns

  103_9             informix  unique   No        album_num

  103_10            informix  unique   No        title
                                                 artist

  103_11            informix  dupls    No        genre
```

Figure 3–4   *DB-Access* `Table Info:Indexes` *option.*

Informix has created these indexes to enforce the constraints that were included in the design of the `albums` table. Indexes are internal data maps that Informix uses to enhance performance and enforce constraints.

Although you need not try to understand each item shown in Figure 3-4, you should note the columns labeled `Type` and `Columns`. The unique index that exists on `album_num` ensures that no two `album` rows can have the same `album_num` value. This index thus enforces your primary key constraint. Likewise, the composite unique index on the combination of `title` and `artist` enforces your alternate key constraint. Informix uses the last index to enforce the referential constraint between the `albums` table and the `genres` table. This constraint ensures that each value you store in the `genre` column of the `albums` table must exist in the `genres` table.

There are more data on this screen than we'll describe, and some menu options that will remain unexplored for now. You'll have plenty to keep you busy just following the guided tour, and you can always come back later to explore any details you miss this time around. Please keep your arms inside the tour bus.

The `Status` Option

Let's resume our DB-Access tour. Choose the `Status` option. You'll see a screen like Figure 3-5.

This useful screen allows you to see at a glance the number of rows in your table of interest. The `Row Size` is the sum of the lengths of each column in the table. The remainder of the data on this screen are self-explanatory.

The `Constraints` Option

You'll remember from the previous chapter that several types of constraints can be defined. With the `Constraint` submenu, you can examine each of these.

tip

The `Constraints` submenu is the only place that allows you examine a constraint's components easily. When your application attempts to violate a constraint, say by trying to insert an illegal value, the error message returned by Informix contains only the name of the constraint. In this submenu you can identify the definition of each constraint by name.

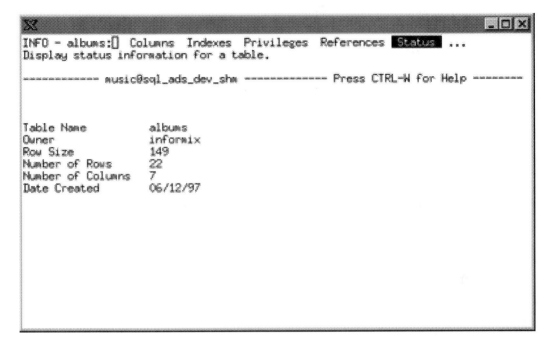

INFO - albums:[] Columns Indexes Privileges References [Status] ...
Display status information for a table.

─────── music@sql_ads_dev_shm ─────── Press CTRL-W for Help ───────

Table Name   albums
Owner   informix
Row Size   149
Number of Rows   22
Number of Columns 7
Date Created   06/12/97

Figure 3–5 *DB-Access* `Table Info:Status` *option.*

Since every constraint you have is shown here, this screen is a good way to find out which constraints you have entered and which are missing. This will be especially useful when you are creating the tables and constraints in Chapter 4. Take a moment to explore each of the constraints defined for the `albums` table. Three of special interest are described shortly.

The `Reference` option from the `Constraint` submenu (see Figure 3-6) shows any other tables that the current table references. In this case it shows that each value you store in the `genre` column of the `albums` table must exist in the `genres` table. Notice how the constraint name parallels its function.

Now choose the `referenceD` option (Figure 3-7) to examine the converse: those tables that reference the `albums` table.

This screen shows the details of how this referencing relationship is enforced. Consider the first row, the `ac_fk_albums` constraint. Its name conveys that the `album_copies` table (the `ac` abbreviation) contains a foreign key (the `fk` abbreviation) that references the `albums` table. The second column on this screen identifies the `albums` column that is referenced by the `album_copies` table. In a well-defined database, this will always

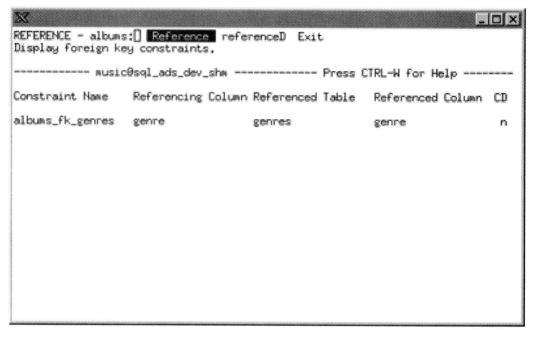

Figure 3–6 DB-Access `Constraints:Reference:Reference` *option.*

be the referenced table's primary key. The third and fourth columns confirm that it is the `album_num` column of the `album_copies` table, which references the `albums` table. That is, every `album_num` value in the `album_copies` table must exist in the `albums` table. Finally, the last column shows that no cascading delete is in place for this relationship. You'll remember from Chapter 2 that a cascading delete is a database-enforced mechanism that automatically deletes referenced rows when the row they reference is deleted. For simplicity, our database contains no such automatic deletion mechanisms.

Finally, choose the `Check` option from the `Constraints` submenu. You should see something like Figure 3-8.

Notice again how the constraint name (`ck_album_rating`) parallels its function. This is the product of good design.

You should get comfortable navigating the `Table Info` submenu; you'll be sure to revisit it often as you develop Informix applications. The only menu of more value within DB-Access is the `Query-language` menu. Let's explore that now.

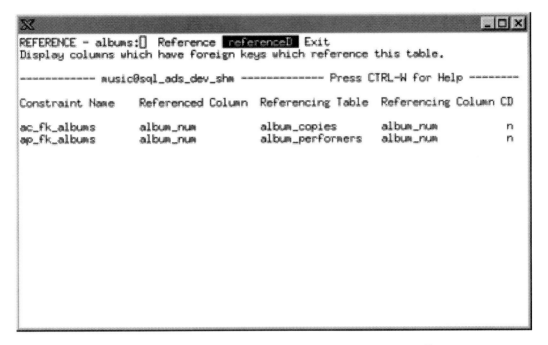

Figure 3–7 DB-Access `Constraints:Reference:referenceD` option.

The Query-language Menu

Within the `Query-language` menu you write and execute ad hoc SQL commands. You can also save your SQL statements in command files, then modify or execute them later. In Chapter 4, you'll see how to use this menu to help you build and run SQL commands to create tables and indexes. In Chapter 5, "Basic SQL," you'll use this same menu to insert data into your database and selectively retrieve it. In this chapter you'll learn the mechanics of the `Query-language` menu.

The New Option

From within DB-Access, choose the `Query-language` option from the main menu. Refer back to Table 3-2 for a map of these

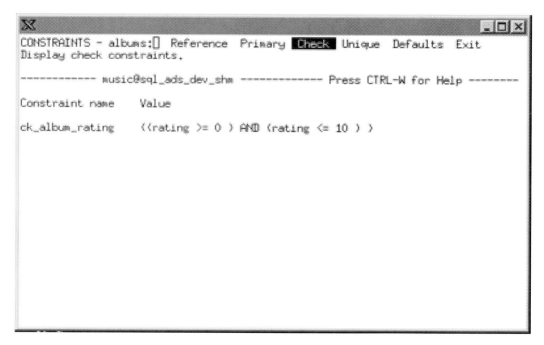

Figure 3–8   DB-Access `Constraints:Check` option.

important options. Choose the `New` option so that you can create an SQL statement, then type in the command shown in Figure 3-9.

caution   *All current statements are lost when you select the `New` option.*

tip   *From with the SQL editor, you can press Ctrl-W to see the otherwise hidden help screens. These screens summarize the syntax of many basic SQL statements.*

The **Run** Option

Press Esc to save your query. Then choose `Run` from the `Query-language` menu. Your screen should look like Figure 3-10.

You've just created and executed a `select` statement, the fundamental operation provided by SQL. In Chapter 5 you will learn many more details about the command you've executed, but for

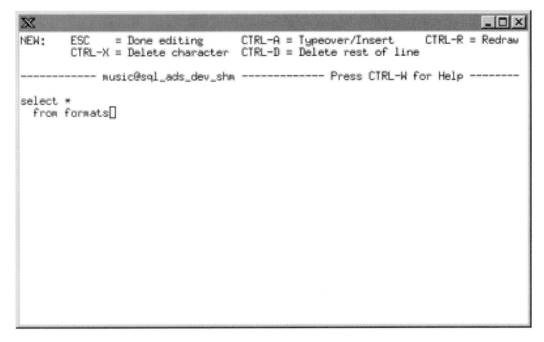

Figure 3–9 DB-Access `Query-language:New` *option.*

now you need only to see that it retrieved all of the rows from the `formats` table. For the remainder of this chapter, we'll use variations of this simple statement to show how DB-Access manages SQL *command scripts*.

A *command script*, or *command file*, or merely *script*, is a file that contains SQL statements. Its suffix is `.sql`. Command scripts can contain any number of SQL statements. A command script is not independently executable; you need an SQL driver to run it. DB-Access is an SQL driver that lets you create, manage, and run your SQL scripts.

The `Save` Option

Save this query by selecting the `Save` option. Enter `formats` when prompted for a name for your command file. DB-Access creates a file called `formats.sql` in your current directory when you do this. You do not need to exit DB-Access to examine your directory; you can list its contents from where you are now.

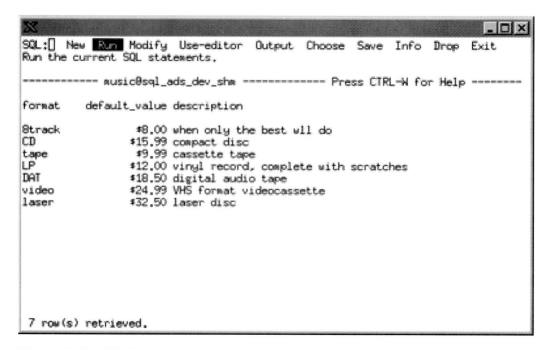

Figure 3–10 DB-Access `Query-language:Run` option.

A hidden option, the exclamation mark (!), exists on every DB-Access menu. It allows you to execute a single shell command without exiting DB-Access. For example, to use the `ls` command to list the contents of your current directory, type the following:

!ls

After you press Return, your current DB-Access menu resumes.

If you look in your current directory, you should now see the `formats.sql` file. Its entire contents are the four-word `select` statement you created.

The `Save` option overwrites—without warning—any existing file of the same name.

The Modify Option

Now modify your current SQL statement by selecting the Modify option. Using the arrow keys to navigate, type over formats and replace it with genres. You can see that certain editing options are listed at the top of the screen, such as the Ctrl-A keystroke combination that toggles your editing session between typeover and insert mode. Such options are useful if you choose to use the SQL editor to construct many of your SQL statements. You should not.

tip

Don't become dependent on the DB-Access editor, the one launched by the New and Modify options. Its limitations are severe. Instead, get in the habit of choosing the Use-editor option for all of your query creation and modification. Additionally, learn a UNIX editor, such as vi, if you do not already know one.

Press Esc to save your query. Save it as genres.sql. Remember that you do not need to add the .sql extension; DB-Access does it for you.

The Choose Option

With the Choose option you browse your command files and select one, whose contents then become your current SQL statements.

note

All of the files in your current directory that end with .sql are displayed in the Choose list. If you have placed the Appendix A command scripts, used to create the music database, in your current directory, those five files will appear in your Choose list along with the two you have already saved.

Use the Choose option to make the formats query your current SQL statement.

The Output Option

Table 3-4 summarizes the options available in the Output sub-menu.

Table 3-4 *DB-Access Output **submenu map.***

Menu Command	Command Description
Printer	Send query results to a printer
New-file	Send query results to a new file
Append-file	Append query results to an existing file
To-pipe	Send query results to the standard input of a program

For now, let's use the Output option to send the results of your current query to a file. At the New-file option prompt, enter formats.out. Notice that the following message appears at the bottom of your screen:

7 row(s) retrieved.

None of these seven rows are displayed on your screen; instead, the results are placed in the formats.out file.

caution

Before the New-file option executes, it creates your file if it does not exist, and empties it if it does. Old contents are overwritten. If you want to preserve the existing contents of your output file, be sure to use the Append-file option.

The Drop Option

Use the Drop option to delete an SQL command file permanently. Use it now to drop your genres.sql command file. Just as with the Save and Choose options, Drop supplies the .sql extension for you. Also, exactly as with Choose, only those command files that end with .sql are displayed for dropping. Notice that you must select Yes at the CONFIRM: prompt to effect the drop.

With your last commands, you've completed the guided part of the tour of the Query-language menu. You need to become familiar with the options on this menu, especially Use-editor and Run. You'll use them more than any other Informix commands.

Using DB-Access Shortcuts

You can instruct DB-Access to start at a specific menu or submenu. To use this type of shortcut, you include the letter or letters of the menu sequence as options when you run dbaccess. For example, to launch the Query-language menu directly, enter the following:

```
$ dbaccess music -q
```

You can start DB-Access at a submenu by including the sequence of letters required to reach that menu. For example, the following command brings up the Table:Info:albums: Columns menu:

```
$ dbaccess music -tic albums
```

If you do not include a database or table name as needed when you invoke DB-Access in this way, you must choose one from the appropriate screen. After you do, your requested menu appears.

Executing SQL Command Files from the Shell

So far, all of your SQL commands have been run from within DB-Access. You can also run them directly from the shell. There are numerous reasons you might want to do this, such as enabling

SQL operations from an automated process, timing a specific query, or simply avoiding having to navigate the DB-Access menu. To run a command script you first need to create it as a file that contains the SQL operations you want to perform. You can create the file directly with an editor, or use a command file you have saved from within DB-Access. In any case, the file must end with the extension `.sql`. Remember that when DB-Access saves command scripts it appends this suffix automatically.

Let's use your file called `formats.sql`, which contains the following `select` statement:

```
select *
  from formats;
```

To invoke this query directly from the command line, enter the following:

$ **dbaccess music formats**

Notice especially that you must specify the database name, and that you do not need to type the `.sql` extension for the command script; DB-Access fills it in. When you execute the previous command, the following results are directed to your terminal:

```
Database selected.


format    default_value description

8track            $8.00 when only the best will do
CD               $15.99 compact disc
tape              $9.99 cassette tape
LP               $12.00 vinyl record, complete with scratches
DAT              $18.50 digital audio tape
video            $24.99 VHS format videocassette
laser            $32.50 laser disc


7 row(s) retrieved.
Database closed.
```

If you like, you can also have DB-Access echo the SQL statements that were executed in a command file. To do so, add a -e option just before the database name, as in the following example:

```
$ dbaccess -e music formats
Database selected.
select *
  from formats
format    default_value description
...
```

UNIX File Redirection

A *megadweeb* is a pointy-headed geek who roams your office pontificating about relational calculus and theta-joins. His condescending demeanor is to be pitied; he has no real friends. *Don't be a megadweeb.*

A *dweeb* is you, unfortunately, after you have soaked up a few of the pearls in this tome. You are someone who has enough useful knowledge to be competent—even borderline boring—but without the esoterica that forebodes pretentiousness.

 *caution*

Some fine points about the UNIX concepts of file redirection follow. Use the data with care, lest you become a megadweeb.

When UNIX commands execute, they usually create some form of output. In a broad sense, UNIX divides that output into two categories: standard output and errors. Normally, both of these sets of output are interleaved and displayed on your terminal, but you can separate and redirect them. When you use the UNIX redirection operator (>) to send the output of a command to another location, only the standard output's destination is altered. The standard error output remains targeted to your terminal. You can also redirect the standard error by preceding the redirection operator with a 2, the file descriptor for standard error.

When you execute an SQL statement from a command line script, you can add these redirection operators to the end of the command. If you redirect the standard error output, only the data proper and the column headings remain. Enter the following command:

```
$ dbaccess music formats 2> /dev/null
format      default_value description

8track          $8.00 when only the best will do
CD             $15.99 compact disc
tape            $9.99 cassette tape
LP             $12.00 vinyl record, complete with scratches
DAT            $18.50 digital audio tape
video          $24.99 VHS format videocassette
laser          $32.50 laser disc
```

If, instead, you redirect the standard output, as in the following example, all that remain are the status messages.

```
$ dbaccess music formats > /dev/null
Database selected.
7 row(s) retrieved.
Database closed.
```

The /dev/null pseudo-file is a black hole that quietly ignores all data sent into it. Sending the data to /dev/null is a common tactic to use when you want to time a query, but do not want the delay that results from displaying all of the data to interfere with your timing test.

Entering SQL Commands Interactively

When you do not want to enter the Query-Language menu or build a command file just to run simple statements, you can use DB-Access's interactive session capability from the command line. To enter the interactive mode, just add a single - at the end of your dbaccess command.

The DB-Access Prompt

Invoke an interactive session with the following command:

```
$ dbaccess music -
```

This places you in interactive mode, already connected to the
music database. Notice that you must supply the database name
when invoking interactive DB-Access. You should see the DB-
Access prompt (>). Type in your query directly, as shown here:

```
Database selected.

> select *
>    from formats;

format    default_value description

8track           $8.00 when only the best will do
CD              $15.99 compact disc
tape             $9.99 cassette tape
LP              $12.00 vinyl record, complete with scratches
DAT             $18.50 digital audio tape
video           $24.99 VHS format videocassette
laser           $32.50 laser disc

7 row(s) retrieved.

> Ctrl-D
```

Within the interactive mode you use a semicolon to terminate
each SQL statement. To exit interactive mode, press the *end-of-file*
key, Ctrl-D.

*In interactive mode, any line that begins with an exclamation mark
(!) signals a shell escape. It allows you to execute a single shell
command without exiting DB-Access. You can intermix shell escape
lines with SQL statements as you wish.*

Using a Here Document

You can extend the interactive mode of DB-Access by embedding SQL statements within shell scripts. The method shown in Listing 3-1 uses a specialized type of file redirection called a *here document*. The << signals that all characters that follow are to be used as input to the command just preceding it. End of input is identified when the word that follows the << (in this case, EOF) is found on a line by itself.

Listing 3-1   Method for using dbaccess within a shell script.

```
dbaccess music - <<EOF

select count(*)

    from albums;

EOF
```

This method of embedding SQL statements in shell scripts is a versatile and useful tool. You'll see several examples of using here documents in Chapter 16, "Migrating Data."

Summary

DB-Access is the principal tool you use to execute SQL statements and to examine your database. Its use depends on your setting the proper environmental variables: identifiers that define your current operating environment. Environmental variables can be set either interactively within your current shell, or in your login script.

You can use DB-Access to execute SQL commands in several ways. From within the `Query-language` menu you can create, run, and drop SQL command scripts. You can also use `dbaccess` as an SQL driver to execute command files from the operating system prompt. Finally, you can use DB-Access interactively, both directly on the command line and from within here documents, often embedded in shell scripts. When you execute SQL commands from the shell, you can use shell redirection commands to limit the output that appears on your screen.

The DB-Access menu structure is a consistent and friendly interface especially useful for managing SQL command files and examining the structure of your tables and indexes. Throughout the remainder of this book, and for most day-to-day tasks you perform, you'll use those components of the DB-Access menu. Certain DB-Access menu shortcuts can make these operations easier.

In the next chapter, you'll examine the parts of the DB-Access menu that allow you to create databases and tables. You'll also learn some tasks for which building SQL command files directly is much easier than using the menu.

Extra Credit

Q&A

Question	**Answer**
These ring menus that DB-Access uses are swell. How can I create my own?	Aren't you ambitious! In Chapter 11, "Your 4GL User Interface," you'll learn how simple it is to make your own menus like this using Informix-4GL. In fact, the DB-Access menu structure is built using Informix-4GL's ring menu paradigm.
After I resized a window that had a DB-Access session in it, the display became mangled. What can I do?	From within DB-Access, the Ctrl-R keystroke redraws your screen.

Question	**Answer**
Is there any way to avoid having to type `vi` (or any editor of preference) at the `USE-EDITOR:` prompt from within the `Query-language:Use-editor` option of DB-Access?	Yes. The DBEDIT environmental variable defines your editor of choice. For example, the following Korn shell command declares `vi` to be your preferred editor: `export DBEDIT=vi` When `DBEDIT` is defined, DB-Access launches that editor automatically after you choose `Query-language:Use-editor`.
My SQL command file contains a `database` statement (a statement that declares a specific database to be my current one). Do I have to specify a database when I invoke `dbaccess` on this command file?	No. When your command file contains a `database` statement, you can substitute a hyphen (–) for the database name on the command line. If your command file were `my_script.sql`, your command would look like the following: `dbaccess - my_script`

Exercises

....

1. Launch DB-Access. Adjust your login file (`.profile` for the Bourne shell or Korn shell; `.login` or `.cshrc` for the C shell) to establish the correct environmental variables for your Informix environment.
2. Build the sample `music` database, if you haven't already.
3. Use the `Table Info` submenu to examine the `album_copies` table. Be sure to explore the `Defaults` option of the `Constraints` submenu.

Exercise Answers

1. The answer for this exercise varies with your environment.
2. Detailed instructions are found in Appendix A, "The Sample Database."
3. To view the `Defaults` option, choose the following menu sequence from within DB-Access:
   `Table:Info:album_copies:cOnstraints:Defaults`. Alternatively, launch the menu directly with `dbaccess music -tiod album_copies`.

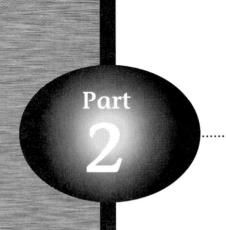

Part

2

SQL
Fundamentals

D rinks for everyone, Isaac! And while he's spinning a few upbeat tunes from "Zydeco Live!", Nathan Williams' latest, let's glance ahead. This part contains the fundamentals of working constructively with the Informix product line.

Where you start to get your hands dirty is Chapter 4, "Creating Databases and Tables." By then you will have created and explored the sample `music` database. Working without a net, you'll drop this database and create it again yourself.

Chapter 5, "Basic SQL," is heady stuff. You'll learn how to put data into and retrieve data from your rebuilt copy of the `music` database. The `select` statement is the key SQL statement in that chapter—in fact, in all of SQL. You'll begin to explore how you can construct `select` expressions that let you extract very specific result sets from your database.

The next chapter is a useful aside. Chapter 6, "ISQL Forms and Reports," introduces tools that help you build simple applications, usually with no coding. You'll find the Perform and Ace tools to be welcome additions to your toolkit: they allow for speedy data entry and reporting.

After all that, it will be no surprise if you're thirsty. There will be time to relax, with "Barrel Full of Monkees" queued up on the 8-track, and shrimp on the barbie. Be prepared to take the night off and sample the drinks in the coconut shells.

Chapter

4

Creating Databases and Tables

In the previous chapter you got off easy, riding in the tour bus all day. Starting with this chapter you have to get out and get your hands dirty. You need to learn how to make databases and tables. Even in an environment where a DBA maintains the database, you must still understand the table structures and constraints. Tables are the primal clay with which you mold Informix works of art (or something).

You can't be an effective Informix developer unless you have a clear understanding of these topics. This chapter may seem a little dry—more like a reference chapter than a tutorial—but the take-home lessons are crucial nonetheless.

Introduction

By now you've used the automated scripts in Appendix A to create the sample `music` database. In Chapter 3, "DB-Access," you used the DB-Access toolkit to tour this database. However, you can only learn so much by using automated scripts and examining a pre-built database. Now you'll start over, and this time recreate the database by hand.

By the end of the chapter, you'll have dropped and rebuilt the database, and rebuilt all of the tables and constraints that compose it. You'll not only understand how to create databases and tables, but which elements you should include in the creation of each. This is useful stuff—get comfortable.

Creating a Database with DB-Access

Let's start off this section by dropping a database. That way, you'll be working without a net, and you'll have to pay close attention.

Table 4-1 shows the components of the `Create Database` submenu from DB-Access. It's the road map you'll use to create a database after you drop the current one.

Table 4-1 ***DB-Access*** `Create Database` ***submenu map.***

Menu Command	Command Description
Dbspace	Select a dbspace for storing the database's data
Log	Specify the type of transaction logging
None	No transaction logging
Log	Unbuffered transaction logging
Buffered_log	Buffered transaction logging
log_Mode_ansi	Create an ANSI-compliant database with unbuffered transaction logging
Exit	Return to the Database Menu

(Continued)

Table 4-1 **DB-Access** `Create Database` **submenu map.**

Menu Command	Command Description
`Create-new-database`	Create the new database
`Discard-new-database`	Do not create the database; return to the Database Menu

First, though, look back to Table 3-2. On that main menu map, you see that the `Drop` option from the `Database` menu drops a database. Let's follow that path now. Launch DB-Access, being sure not to specify a database at the command line.

$ **dbaccess**

From the main menu, select `Database`, then `Drop`. Choose the `music` database. Confirm that you want to drop it by selecting `Yes` at the prompt. (Trust me: drop the database.)

Now, creating a database is a little trickier, but you are already in the right place to start the process:

1. Select the `Create` option from the `Database` menu.
2. At the prompt, enter `music`, the name of your new database. You should see the `Create Database` submenu, mirrored in Table 4-1.
3. The `Dbspace` option lets you choose the specific place on disk where your database will be stored. For now, skip the `Dbspace` menu. Informix supplies a default value (the root dbspace) that is adequate for the `music` database. Dbspaces are introduced in the "Storage Option Definitions" section later in this chapter.
4. Choose the `Log` option.
5. Select `Buffered_log` from the menu. This enables transaction logging—essential for data integrity—for your database. Transaction logs are explained in the following section.
6. Exit the `Create Database` submenu.
7. Select `Create-new-database`.

Your `music` database exists again. You still need to create each of your tables, but at least now they have a place to live. When you create a database, it automatically becomes your current database. You can confirm this by noticing that the database name is now displayed on the dashed line just below the DB-Access menu.

Creating a Database Manually

Using the DB-Access menu is not the only way to create a database, but it's usually the best way. Often with Informix you'll be presented with several methods of performing the same task. In this case, the choice is between using a native SQL command to create and drop your database, or using DB-Access.

 Create and drop your database with the DB-Access menus. It's easier than using the SQL commands, displays all of your choices for easy selection, and prompts you for confirmation.

Nonetheless, you still need to know the mechanics of the `create database` statement. You may need to embed the commands in an easily executable script, such as in the `makedb.sql` script from Appendix A, "The Sample Database." At the least, you need to be able to understand such commands when you encounter them.

The syntax for the `create database` statement is as follows:

```
create database database-name [in dbspace-name] [logging-mode]
```

where `database-name` is the name of the database you are creating, `dbspace-name` is the name of the dbspace where you want to store the data for this database, and `logging-mode` specifies the type of transaction logging associated with your database. If you do not specify `dbspace-name`, your database is stored in the root dbspace. If you do not specify `logging-mode`, no transactions are allowed in your database. The possible values for `logging-mode` are:

- `with log`—Use unbuffered transaction logging
- `with buffered log`—Use buffered transaction logging
- `with log mode ansi`—Use ANSI-compliant unbuffered logging

These different logging modes all dictate whether and to what degree your database will support *transactions*. A transaction is a logical sequence of database operations that must be performed entirely or not at all. For example, a bank transaction that debits one account should not be allowed without a corresponding credit to an offset account. The `begin work` SQL statement signifies the start of a transaction, and remains in effect until either a `commit work` or `rollback work` statement is encountered. Between these work delimiters, you place those SQL statements that you want treated as a whole.

Informix uses its logs to track transactions in progress. Thus, the logging mode you specify prescribes whether and how transactions are enabled for your database. Use the following decision tree to decide which logging mode to use:

If your business mandates ANSI compliance, then use

```
with log mode ansi
```

else if you do not want transactions at all
   do not specify any logging mode
else if you favor performance over a minor risk of data loss, use

```
with buffered log
```

else use

```
with log
```

For example, to create a nonlogging database named `coins` in the root dbspace, use the following syntax:

```
create database coins;
```

To create the `stamps` database in the `collection` dbspace using a buffered transaction log, enter the following:

```
create database stamps in collection with buffered log;
```

It's only proper that you clean up after yourself. You should know how to drop everything you create. To promote your tidy habits, learn the `drop database` syntax:

```
drop database database-name;
```

where `database-name` is the name of the database you wish to drop. You cannot drop the current database, or one that is in use by another user. To close your current database in anticipation of dropping it, first use the `close database` SQL statement.

caution   *When you drop a database you drop all of its tables, indexes, constraints, and stored procedures—everything about the database. The statement cannot be undone. You are not asked to verify your command. It's final. Be careful out there.*

Data Types

In Chapter 2, "Data Modeling 101," you learned the principles of effective relational database design. You were also introduced to the Informix data types in general terms, as the tools with which you begin to enforce a column's *domain*, or pool of legal values. In this chapter you'll examine all of the data types in detail, and learn exactly when to use each. In addition to dictating a column's domain, data types restrict the type of operation that you can perform on a column. For example, you cannot sum a character-based description field, or find the length of a date field.

You'll need to have a solid grasp of the data types available: they are the most basic specifiers of your table definitions. Table 4-2 summarizes the Informix data types, and includes all of the possible alternative names for each type.

The following sections explain each of these data types, how they are stored, and when to use them.

Table 4-2 Informix data types.

Data Type	Category	Subcategory	Stores
char, character	Character	Fixed length	Strings of letters, numbers, and symbols
varchar, character varying	Character	Varying length	Character strings of varying length
nchar	Character	Fixed length	Native strings of characters
nvarchar	Character	Varying length	Native character strings of varying lengths
int, integer	Numeric	Whole	Large whole numbers
serial	Numeric	Whole	Auto-incrementing integers
smallint	Numeric	Whole	Small whole numbers
money	Numeric	Real	Amounts of currency
dec, decimal, numeric	Numeric	Real	Numbers with a precision that you define
float, double precision	Numeric	Real	Double-precision floating point numbers
small-float, real	Numeric	Real	Single-precision floating point numbers
date	Chronological	Date	Calendar dates

(Continued)

Table 4-2 *Informix data types.*

Data Type	Category	Subcategory	Stores
datetime	Chronological	Date/time	Calendar dates and their associated times
interval	Chronological	Date/time	Spans of time
byte	Binary	Nonprintable	Any binary-format data
text	Binary	Printable	Any text data

Character Data Types

The character data types allow you to store arbitrary strings of characters: letters, numbers, and symbols. They are commonly used for descriptive fields such as names and addresses. For most applications, char is the most commonly used data type.

 note *The char type is pronounced like burnt toast: "char." Do not pronounce it like an automobile ("car") or like a concern ("care"). You need to know these things.*

You specify a length when you define a character data type. That length is the maximum number of characters the column may hold. Should you try to insert a string longer than a character field's length, all excess characters are truncated. The number of bytes required to store a character data type is equal to its defined length. That is, character columns are stored as fixed-width fields. When retrieved, character data is padded with spaces to fill the width of the column.

The varchar data type (character varying is the ANSI equivalent) is used for efficient storage of character values that have widely differing lengths. The amount of space required to store varchar types varies.

The `nchar` and `nvarchar` data types are used when you have enabled *Native Language Support (NLS)*. NLS is the mechanism by which you accommodate non-English characters in your data and object names, such as tables and columns. You activate NLS by setting the `DBNLS` and `LANG` environment variables (among others) as appropriate for your locale. Unfortunately, the proper values for these variables are not standard, and vary among operating systems. If you find that you wish to enable NLS, you'll need to refer to the documentation shipped with your Informix installation: specifically, the *Informix Guide to SQL, Reference*.

In Informix versions 7.2 and higher, NLS has been superseded by *Global Language Support (GLS)*. GLS adds Asian language support to the NLS features. For a complete reference, you'll need to refer Informix's *Guide to GLS Functionality*.

When NLS or GLS is activated, you ensure accurate storage and sorting of native character strings by using `nchar` in place of `char` and `nvarchar` rather than `varchar`.

Numerical Data Types

The numerical data types allow you to store your numbers with varying ranges and degrees of precision. Some are best used as counters, others to store currency, and the rest in engineering or scientific applications.

Whole Number Data Types

The `int`, `serial`, and `smallint` data types store whole numbers. Their properties are shown in Table 4-3.

Table 4-3   Whole number data types.

Data Type	Bytes to Store	Minimum Value	Maximum Value
int, serial	4	–2,147,483,647	2,147,483,647
smallint	2	–32,767	32,767

tip

Use the smallest data type that conforms to your column's domain. For example, if you're sure your whole number variable will not exceed the range of a smallint *variable, use that type rather than the* int *type. Less bytes equates to more efficiency.*

Real Number Data Types

The remaining numerical data types store real numbers: those that may contain a decimal point. In Table 4-4, p specifies a data type's precision, its total number of significant digits. The default is 16. Scale, or the number of digits to the right of the decimal point, is represented by s. Its default is 2. Notice that some of the real number data types may round your data if a value exceeds its maximum precision.

Table 4-4   Real number data types.

Data Type	Decimal Point	Bytes to Store	Maximum Digits	May Round
dec[(p)]	Floating	2 to 17	32	Yes
dec(p,s)	Fixed	2 to 17	32	No
float	Floating	8	16	Yes
money[(p[,s])]	Fixed	2 to 17	32	No
smallfloat	Floating	4	8	Yes

Chronological Data Types

Informix has two categories of chronological data types. The date data type represents only calendar dates. The datetime and interval types represent date and time values of varying precision.

The date Data Type

You use the date data type to signify calendar dates. Internally, a calendar date is stored as an integer: the number of days since December 31, 1899.

This means of storage alleviates any *Year 2000* concerns when using Informix native date operations. However, it forces Informix to format date fields whenever they are retrieved to your application. How the dates are formatted for display depends on the value of your DBPATH environmental variable. You can refer to Chapter 3 for a complete explanation of environmental variables.

Table 4-5 shows some possible values you can assign to the DBDATE variable. Its default is MDY4/, where M is the month, D represents the day, Y4 is the four-digit year, and slash (/) is the separator. The acceptable separator characters are a hyphen (-), a period (.), and a zero (0). Use a zero to indicate no separator. If you do not specify a separator, a slash is used.

Table 4-5   DBDATE ***patterns.***

DBDATE	September 29, 1998 Is Displayed as
MDY4/	09/29/1998
MDY2.	09.29.98
MDY20	092998
DMY2-	29-09-98
Y2DM/	98/29/09
Y4MD	1998/09/29

Remember: these values dictate how date columns are displayed, not how they are stored.

Date/Time Data Types

The date/time data types are datetime, which stores an instant in time, and interval, which stores a span of time. They are usually used in conjuction. For each, you specify the precision—from a year to a fraction of a second. Table 4-6 summarizes the units with which you can specify a `datetime` column's precision.

Table 4-6   Units of precision for date/time columns.

Unit	Valid Entries
year	1 to 9999 (A.D.)
month	1 to 12
day	1 to 31 (as allowed, by month)
hour	0 to 23 (0 is midnight)
minute	0 to 59
second	0 to 59
fraction[(n)]	Up to 5 digits of precision of fractions of a second; 3 is the default

You define a datetime variable by specifying the largest and smallest unit it can store, as follows:

```
datetime largest-unit to smallest-unit
```

All units between `largest-unit` and `smallest-unit` are included in the column's definition. For example, the following definition allows its column to store a moment that includes the calendar year, month, and day, as well as the hour, minute, second, and fractional second of an occurrence:

```
datetime year to fraction
```

A column defined in this way is often used to store a timestamp for an event's occurrence. Chapter 5 shows how the `current` keyword extracts the system time. You can store that time in a column defined as `datetime year to fraction` as a means of recording ing exactly when a row is inserted.

There are two types of `interval` data types: year-month and day-time. Each can store only spans of time in their range. This is because, given the differing numbers of days in months, a single `interval` value cannot combine months and days. Intervals are often generated as the difference between two `datetime` variables.

You define `interval` data types with the same units as `datetime` types, as follows:

```
interval largest-unit[(n)] to smallest-unit
```

where *n* is the precision of the largest unit. As `interval` data types are spans of time, they are not restricted to the valid entries shown in Table 4-6. Instead, you can specify how many digits the largest unit may be; the default is 2.

The storage space required for each date/time data type depends on its precision.

Binary Data Types

Binary data types are known collectively as *blobs*. A blob, or *binary large object*, is a data type that stores a stream of bytes of any length. It is typically used to store items like digitized sound or images, saved spreadsheets, word processing documents, and the like. You may not perform string or arithmetic operations on blobs, but you can generally otherwise manipulate them with standard database operations.

The two types of blobs are `byte` and `text`. The primary use of the `text` type is to store printable documents. A `text` column can contain any combination of printable characters and the following selected formatting characters:

- Tabs (Ctrl-I)
- Newlines (Ctrl-J)
- New pages (Ctrl-L)

The `byte` data type has no such restrictions, and can store any arbitrary stream of bytes. You can learn more about how blobs are stored and managed in Chapter 17, "Database Administration Fundamentals."

Creating Tables with DB-Access

So, what do you do with all those data types? You define columns, the primary elements of tables. The remainder of this chapter presents the various methods you can use to create, drop, examine, and alter your database's tables.

Within DB-Access, Informix provides a well-intentioned, structured, menu-driven means of creating tables. Table 4-7 shows you this Create Table submenu map.

Table 4-7   *DB-Access* Create Table *submenu map.*

Menu Command	Command Description
Add	Add columns to the table above the line with the highlight
Modify	Modify the column definitions
Drop	Drop the highlighted column from the table
Screen	Display the next screen of the table
Table_options	Dbspace, extent size, and lock mode menus
Storage	Define dbspace or fragmentation strategy for table storage
Dbspace	Select a dbspace in which to store the table
Fragment	Define a fragmentation strategy
eXtent_size	Specify an initial extent size for the table

(Continued)

Table 4-7   DB-Access `Create Table` **submenu map.**

Menu Command	Command Description
`Next_size`	Specify the next size for the table
`Lock_mode`	Specify the lock mode
`Page`	Locking is at page level; this is the default
`Row`	Locking is at the row level
`Constraints`	Primary, foreign, check, unique, and defaults menus
`Primary`	Define primary key constraint
`Foreign`	Define foreign key constraint
`Check`	Define column and table check constraints
`Unique`	Define unique column constraints
`Defaults`	Define column defaults
`Exit`	Leave the Create Table Menu
`Build-new-table`	Build a new table and return to the Table Menu
`Discard-new-table`	Discard changes and return to the Table Menu

Using the DB-Access `Create Table` Submenu

You need to know about the DB-Access menu-based means of table creation, but for most people using SQL commands is easier, faster, and less frustrating. I'll show you what I mean. We'll use the menus to create the `formats` table. Afterwards, we'll move on to the *real* method for creating tables: the SQL `create table` command.

First, traverse the DB-Access menus to reach the `Create Table` submenu. You can refer to Table 3-2, "DB-Access Main Menu Map," or use the following shortcut:

```
$ dbaccess music -tc formats
```

You should see a screen like Figure 4-1.

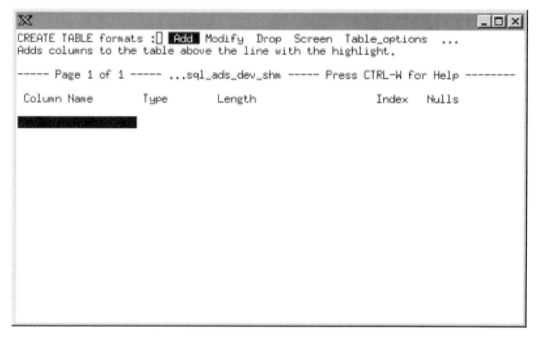

Figure 4–1   *DB-Access* `Create Table` *option.*

note   *The DB-Access `Create Table` and `Alter Table` submenus use a different means of screen navigation than the rest of DB-Access. The arrow keys no longer let you traverse the ring menu; instead, they allow you to navigate the column definitions. Additionally, you must use the Interrupt key (usually Ctrl-C) to return to the ring menu from the column definitions area of the screen.*

You need to watch the menu description line (just below the ring menu) closely. It often indicates which keys enable each option. Choose Add by pressing Return or a. You cannot use the arrow keys to make your menu selection, although the space bar remains an effective means of navigating the ring menu.

1. At the CREATE TABLE >> prompt, enter formats, the name of the table to create. You'll skip this step if you used the shortcut to jump straight to the table creation.
2. At the ADD COLUMN NAME >> prompt, enter the name of the first column in the formats table, format.
3. At the ADD TYPE formats : menu, choose Char.
4. At the ADD CHAR TYPE formats : menu, choose Char.
5. At the ADD LENGTH >> prompt, enter 6.
6. At the ADD INDEX formats : menu, choose No.
7. At the ADD NULLS formats : menu, choose No.

Your screen should now resemble Figure 4-2. If at some point you've entered an errant menu, or found yourself unable to manipulate the cursor properly, try pressing the Interrupt key until you return to the Create Table submenu. Not all menus have an Exit option.

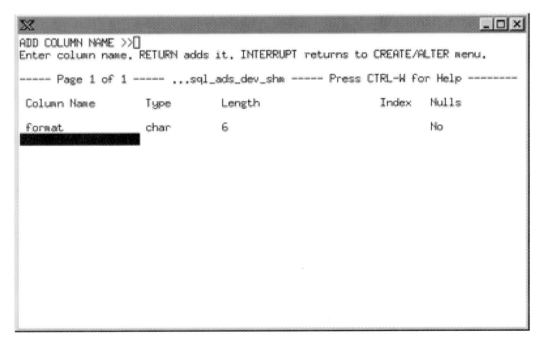

Figure 4–2 DB-Access Create Table:Add *option.*

Let's continue defining the columns in the formats table.

1. At the ADD COLUMN NAME >> prompt, enter the name of the second column in the formats table, default_value.
2. At the ADD TYPE formats : menu, choose Money.
3. At the ADD LENGTH >> prompt, press Return to accept the default precision.
4. At the ADD INDEX formats : menu, choose No.
5. At the ADD NULLS formats : menu, choose Yes.

Now, use the same means to add the description column, whose type is char(40) and which allows nulls. When you have completed this addition, press Interrupt to return to the Create Table submenu. You should see a screen like Figure 4-3, but I'll understand if you are having some difficulties. Try again; I'll wait right here.

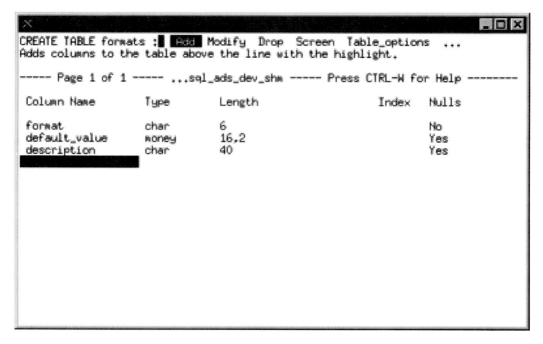

Figure 4–3   *The* formats *table defined with the DB-Access* Create Table *option.*

All that remains is to define the primary key constraint. The Table_options selection on this menu leads you to a panoply of physical implementation choices. The "Storage Option Definitions" section later in this chapter introduces the ideas that underlie these options. We'll skip those for now. Instead, choose the Constraints option by using the space bar to highlight it or pressing c. From within the Create Table:Constraints submenu, select Primary to define your primary key constraint. Your screen should resemble Figure 4-4.

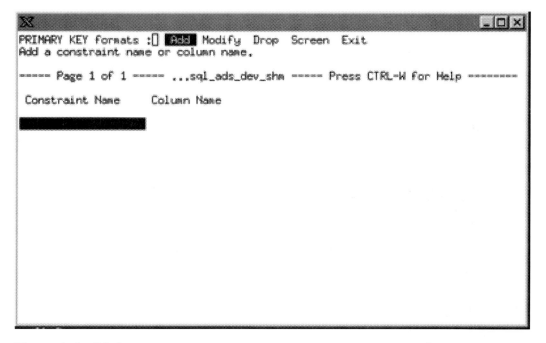

Figure 4–4 *DB-Access* Create Table:Constraints:Primary *option.*

To add the primary key constraint, follow these steps:

1. At the PRIMARY KEY formats : menu, choose Add by pressing Return or a.

2. At the ADD CONSTRAINT NAME >> prompt, enter pk_formats, the name you are giving to the primary key constraint.

3. At the ADD COLUMN NAME >> prompt, enter format, the column on which the primary key constraint is based.

4. Press Interrupt to return to the Create Table:Constraints submenu.

5. Use the space bar or press E to select Exit from the Create Table:Constraints submenu to return to the Create Table submenu.

Nearly done. Now exit the Create Table submenu, and choose Build-new-table. Perhaps, when you are done, you will have created the formats table. You can use DB-Access to check the table's structure.

This interface is admittedly awkward. Compare the steps from the previous pages to the following SQL statement, which also creates the formats table.

```
create table formats (
    format          char(6)   not null primary key
                              constraint pk_formats,
    default_value money,
    description     char(40)
);
Table created.
```

I rest my case.

Creating Tables Manually

You can and should use native SQL statements to create your tables. The create table command is one of the principal elements of the Data Definition Language (DDL) subset of SQL.

 Create and drop your tables with the create table SQL commands, rather than with the DB-Access menus. The command scripts are easier to use, and, when saved, provide a convenient means to recreate your tables when the need arises—and it will.

The syntax for the create table statement follows:

```
create [temp] table table-name (
column-name data-type [default default-value] [not null]
    [constraint-definitions]
[, ...]
[, table-constraint-definitions]
)
[storage-options];
```

where table-name is the name of the table you are creating, column-name is the name of the column you are creating, and data-type is the Informix datatype that defines this column. There may be any number of column definitions, each separated by commas. Only these three components are required. For example, the following syntax creates a simple table:

```
create table fruits (
     fruit_name char(10)
);
```

When specified, default-value defines the value to be supplied when no explicit value is given during an insert operation. Each of the remaining specifiers (constraint-definitions, table-constraint-definitions, and storage-options) are described by example later in this section.

If the temp specifier is included, the table lasts only for the duration of your SQL session.

Remember that the easiest way to enter and execute your SQL statements is via the DB-Access menu structures. In Chapter 3, the section titled "The Query-language Menu" explores this essential tool. You may want to refer to that section as you create the tables that follow.

Column-Level Constraint Definitions

It's easiest to understand the details of the table creation syntax by example. Use the following SQL statement to create the genres table.

```
create table genres (
     genre          char(10) not null primary key
```

```
                           constraint pk_genres,
    description    char(60)
);
Table created.
```

As it creates the `genres` table, this statement adds constraint definitions to the `genre` column. It adds a not null constraint and a primary key constraint. The primary key constraint is named `pk_genres`.

Table 4-8 describes the five types of constraints you can apply to your column definitions.

Table 4-8   Constraint definitions for columns.

Constraint Type	Enforces	Restrictions
not null	Existence of a value	
primary key	Uniqueness	No more than one per table
unique	Uniqueness	
references	Referential integrity	The table referenced must have a primary key or unique constraint in place
check	Domain validation	

In your table definitions, you can follow each constraint definition with the phrase `constraint constraint-name`. Such a declaration gives your constraint a friendly name. All constraints are named; the only question is whether you allow Informix to assign an arbitrary internal name, or whether you assign one yourself. You see these names when an attempt to violate the constraint occurs, and in DB-Access under the `Table:Info:cOn-straints` submenu. In the previous SQL statement, the primary key constraint is named `pk_genres`; Informix assigns an internal name to the not null constraint.

tip

Name your constraints. Except for the not null constraints, you should supply explicit names for your constraints. By doing so, you make later identification of constraint violations much easier. The pervasiveness of non-null constraints, and the adequate error message Informix supplies upon attempted violation of them, dictate that you need not name those.

Table-Level Constraint Definitions

The next example introduces check constraints and table constraint definitions. Use the following SQL statement to create the `performers` table.

note

Within your SQL statements, white space is irrelevant. DB-Access ignores your extra spaces, tabs, and carriage returns. Use them as you wish to align your definitions for readability.

```
create table performers (
    last_name       char(15) not null,
    first_name      char(15) not null,
    sex             char(1)  not null
                             check (sex in ('F', 'M'))
                             constraint
    ck_performer_sex,
    birth_date      date,
    death_date      date,
    primary key (last_name, first_name) constraint
    pk_performers
);
Table created.
```

This code includes a check constraint (named `ck_performer_sex`) being defined. It enforces that no values except F and M may be stored in the `sex` column. Any attempt to do so results in the runtime error "`530: Check constraint` (`informix.ck_performer_sex`) `failed`." When you see such an error—regardless of the source: DB-Access, Informix-4GL, ESQL/C, whatever—you know by your descriptive constraint name the nature of the violation. The next to last line introduces a table constraint definition. In general, you need to use a table constraint when your constraint involves more than one column, as in this composite primary key definition.

Check constraints can include most simple SQL comparison conditions. The most common ones use the `between`, `in`, and equality operators. You can also define check constraints at the table level. You might do this when you want to enforce a relationship between two columns. For example, you might consider adding the following constraint to the performers table:

```
check (birth_date < death_date) constraint ck_performer_age
```

Referential Constraint Definitions

Both column-level and table-level constraints may be referential constraints. Such constraints enforce referential integrity by ensuring that no values may be entered into the referencing column(s) that do not exist in the referenced table.

Use the following SQL statement to create the `albums` table. Notice that the `albums_fk_genres` referential constraint is defined.

```
create table albums (
    album_num       serial      not null primary key
                                constraint pk_albums,
    title           char(30),
    artist          char(20),
    issue_year      smallint,
    genre           char(10)  references genres
                              constraint albums_fk_genres,
    rating          smallint check (rating between 0 and 10)
                              constraint ck_album_rating,
    notes           varchar(80),
    unique (title, artist) constraint ak_albums
);
Table created.
```

The constraint on the `genre` column defines the referential constraint between `albums` and `genres`.

You can include several referential constraint definitions in your `create table` statement. Use the following statement to create the `album_copies` table, including its two referential constraints.

```
create table album_copies (
    album_num      integer   not null references albums
                             constraint ac_fk_albums,
    format         char(6)   default 'CD' not null
                             references formats
                             constraint ac_fk_formats,
    location       char(15)  default 'shelf 1',
    amount_paid    money,
    primary key (album_num, format) constraint pk_album_copies
);
Table created.
```

You may get an error like "`297: Cannot find unique constraint or primary key on referenced table`" while trying to execute this statement. Such an error will result if you have not created either the `formats` or `albums` table, or if you do not have primary keys defined for both of them yet. Given the circuitous means used to create the `formats` table and its primary key, such an ommission is likely.

caution   As with all SQL identifiers, constraint names may be no longer than 18 characters. Within that limit, you should make every effort to name your constraints consistently.

Referential constraints can also be defined at the table level. When you do so, you must introduce the constraint with the `foreign key` (*column-names*) clause. The following statement shows an example of a table-level referential constraint. Execute this SQL to create the `album_performers` table.

```
create table album_performers (
    last_name      char(15) not null,
    first_name     char(15) not null,
```

```
    album_num       integer  not null references albums
                             constraint ap_fk_albums,
    foreign key (last_name, first_name) references performers
                             constraint ap_fk_performers,
    primary key (last_name, first_name, album_num)
                             constraint pk_album_perfs
);
Table created.
```

You've now recreated all of your tables. You can refer to Appendix A, "The Sample Database," to see how to reload all of the original data.

Constraint Naming Recommendations

Be consistent. Adopt a scheme you'll always use when naming your constraints. Table 4-9 presents one such scheme.

Table 4-9   Constraint naming recommendations.

Constraint Type	Constraint Naming Pattern
Primary Key	pk_table-name
Unique (Alternate Key)	ak_table-name
Check (One Column)	ck_table-name_column-name
Check (Multiple Column)	ck_table-name_description
Foreign Key	referencing-table_fk_referenced-table

An example of the foreign key naming convention will help clarify these recommendations. Consider the ap_fk_performers foreign key constraint used in the previous example. The abbreviation ap represents the *referencing-table*, album_performers. The 18-character restriction on length forces you to abbreviate the table name. Connecting that abbreviation to the *referenced-table* name, performers, is the _fk_ connector, a convention identifying this as a foreign key constraint. You'll be forced to abbreviate some table and column names if you follow this scheme. Be consistent.

Storage Option Definitions

The following line defines the create table storage option choices, an optional set of clauses that dictate how your table is physically stored:

```
[in dbspace-name] [lock mode page | row ] [sizing-specifications]
    [fragmentation-strategy]
```

Each of these items is explained completely in Chapter 17, "Database Administration Fundamentals." For now, you need only have a broad understanding of each. You do not need to specify storage options explicitly; Informix supplies default values for each that are adequate for most tables.

A *dbspace* is physical section of disk space assigned by a system administrator to be available for your use. Often, an administrator creates several dbspaces, to either exploit hardware efficiently or segregate logically disparate databases. Every Informix-OnLine system must have a root dbspace, whose name can vary, but which Informix uses to manage internal operations. The default value for your tables is the dbspace in which your database was created.

The *lock mode* is the granularity at which items from this table are locked (say, for updates) in a multi-user environment. Tables are stored in physical units called *pages*, the building blocks of dbspaces. Several rows of data usually occupy any given page. Page-level locking is more efficient than row-level locking. By locking at the page level—the default—you increase the chance that you might lock a row needed by another user, but you gain some performance. The choice of which to use depends on your application type.

The sizing specifications are the extent size *initial-extent-size* and next size *next-extent-size* clauses. The extent size units are Kbytes. Extents are collections of contiguous pages within a single *chunk* (a subunit of a dbspace) that are allocated for the exclusive use of a single table. By creating your large tables with proper extent sizes, you can prevent excessive scattering of their data across disks. Scattered data can be inefficient to retrieve. The default size for your initial and next extents is eight pages (usually 32 Kbytes) each.

Finally, a *fragmentation strategy* is a set of rules you define that dictate how a table should be partitioned across several dbspaces. You can often enhance system performance considerably by fragmenting large tables across multiple dbspaces. The general benefit is a balancing of disk I/O, but you can also enable parallel scanning of the multiple table fragments. The default is no fragmentation: a table is stored in a single dbspace.

Dropping a Table

Remember: take only photographs; leave only footprints. The `drop table` statement allows you to erase all evidence of any `create table` mayhem you may have caused. When you drop a table, you permanently remove its structure and contents from the database. Use it with care. Its syntax follows:

```
drop table table-name [restrict];
```

where `table-name` is the name of the table you are dropping. When you use the default mode to drop a table, you also drop all other database elements that reference this table. These include the referential constraints with which you are familiar, as well as synonyms, triggers, and views (more advanced SQL constructs introduced later in this book) based on the table.

If you include the `restrict` clause, the table will not be dropped as long any referential constraints or views still reference the table.

Altering Tables

Let's say you have a table you are quite fond of, and you decide that you need to change it slightly. Perhaps your `albums` table has several hundred rows, but you find that you need to increase the width of the `title` column. So far, your current toolkit contains only the `drop table` sledgehammer. You need a more delicate `alter table` chisel. The `alter table` statement is what you use to modify a column's definition, as well as to add and drop constraints to an existing table.

The syntax for the `alter table` statement is, unfortunately, nearly as complex as the `create table` statement. However, you need not learn it completely. A few examples will suffice to show you the nature of the `alter table` operations. For example, to increase the width of the `albums.artist` column to 25 characters, type the following:

```
alter table albums modify (artist char(25));
```

If you find that the `ck_performer_sex` constraint is too confining, use the following statement to drop it:

```
alter table performers drop constraint ck_performer_sex;
```

If you want to ensure that you don't accidentally allow performers to be recorded as having died before they were born, add the following constraint:

```
alter table performers add constraint
check (birth_date < death_date) constraint
   ck_performer_age;
```

 You cannot modify a constraint. Instead, first drop a constraint, and then add it again with the new definition.

If you find that you want to make modifications more complicated than these, you should use DB-Access. Its `Alter Table` submenu allows you to make precise changes to specific column definitions, and to add constraints with some facility. Use the following shortcut to invoke this submenu:

```
$ dbaccess music -ta
```

You'll notice that the menu is the same as the Create Table submenu (see Table 4-7). Its interface, likewise, is just the same. Some of the difficulty in using this interface for table creation is that the work of defining each column is tedious. The more pinpointed action of altering a column or adding a constraint makes using DB-Access for altering tables reasonable.

Examining Your Database Structure

With Informix, there are often several ways to do the same thing. In addition to using the DB-Access options you learned in Chapter 3, you can also examine your database and table structures with the info SQL command and the dbschema UNIX utility.

The info SQL Command

Informix provides an SQL statement you can use to gather information on your tables. The info command has two flavors: the first shows you all the tables in your database; the second shows you a subset of a specific table's definition. The syntax for both forms of the info statement follows:

```
info tables;
info info-specifier for table-name;
```

where *table-name* is the table for which you are requesting data, and *info-specifier* is one of the following:

- columns
- fragments
- indexes
- references
- status

You use the `info` statement from within SQL to gather the same kind of data that is revealed by DB-Access's `Table Info` submenu. Use the following SQL statement to examine the columns in the `performers` table:

```
info columns for performers;
Column name            Type                                        Nulls

last_name              char(15)                                    no
first_name             char(15)                                    no
sex                    char(1)                                     no
birth_date             date                                        yes
death_date             date                                        yes
```

dbschema

An administrative utility that is supplied with your Informix system, `dbschema` allows you to examine your database *schema*, or data model. Generally, *schema* refers to the exact sequence of SQL statements required to create your database or objects within it. Although `dbschema` comprises several options, the following syntax summarizes the most useful ones:

```
dbschema [-ss] -d database-name [-t table-name] [output-file-name]
```

The `-ss` option generates server-specific output: the values you specify with the storage option definitions; otherwise, a site-independent schema is generated. If you include `output-file-name`, the schema is written to that file. If not, it is displayed on your screen.

From the UNIX prompt, try the following to view the schema for the `albums` table:

```
$ dbschema -d music -t albums
{ TABLE "informix".albums row size = 149 number of columns = 7
    index size = 114 }
create table "informix".albums
  (
    album_num serial not null constraint "informix".n103_13,
    title char(30),
```

```
    artist char(20),
    issue_year smallint,
    genre char(10),
    rating smallint,
    notes varchar(80),
    unique (title,artist) constraint "informix".ak_albums,
    chcck ((rating >= 0 ) AND (rating <= 10 ) ) constraint
    "informix".ck_album_rating,
    primary key (album_num) constraint "informix".pk_albums
  );
revoke all on "informix".albums from "public";

alter table "informix".albums add constraint (foreign key (genre)
    references
    "informix".genres  constraint "informix".albums_fk_genres);
```

Your output may vary slightly. For example, your user ID is probably shown as the owner of the table and its constraints, and if you altered the size of any columns during previous exercises, those changes will be reflected here. Worth noting as well is that all column-level constraints have been redefined to their table-level equivalents. Also, you get to see the internal name that Informix assigned to any not null constraints. Additionally, all table and constraint names are shown *fully qualified*; that is, with their owner included. Finally, the revoke all line hints at the permissions available for effective management of databases in a multi-user environment.

Summary

In this chapter, you learned how to create and drop databases and tables. Even for a developer, knowing how to do these things is essential.

When you create a database, you can specify its location (dbspace) and its logging mode. These are easy to do using DB-Access. Likewise, dropping a database using DB-Access is simple, and you are prompted for confirmation. The equivalent SQL statements—create database and drop database—are less friendly.

DB-Access provides a menu-driven means of creating tables. Don't use it. Using the SQL create table statement is not only easier, it also (when you save it) creates a schema file for the tables you create.

You use specific data types and constraints to enforce the domains of your columns. Constraints not only help you refine a column's domain, but also maintain a table's integrity. You should adopt a consistent naming scheme, and include constraints in every meaningful table you create.

Should you find that you need to change a table's structure, and you need to retain its data, you should use the `alter table` command. Its complementary DB-Access menu is a reasonable alternative when the syntax needed to effect the table modification is unclear. These same tools are used to add and drop constraints.

You can use the `dbschema` utility and the `info` command to view your tables' structures at a glance.

In the next chapter you'll finally get to manipulate the data in your tables, not just the tables themselves. You'll find, starting with Chapter 5, that the pace accelerates.

Extra Credit

Q&A

Question	**Answer**
All these data types frighten and confuse me. What is the minimum set that I need to remember?	Many applications make use of only the `char`, `integer`, and `date` data types. Start there.
Do I have to include constraints when I create my tables? They are so ... *constraining.*	I suppose you run with scissors too? Grow up: wear your seat belt, eat your vegetables, call your mother, and use constraints.
Can I use a table-level constraint definition when I'm defining a constraint on just one column?	Sure. Many people do. In fact, when Informix shows you a table's structure with the *dbschema* command, it translates all column-level constraints into table-level constraint definitions. In your table creation scripts, place the constraint definitions wherever they are most clear to you.

Exercises

1. Make sure that you have recreated all of the six tables in the music database.

2. Use the DB-Access menus to alter the size of the albums.title column from 20 characters to 30.

3. Use dbschema to save a copy of the music schema to a file named music.sch.

4. Use at least three different methods to show the columns that compose the albums table.

Exercise Answers

1. The SQL statements required for this are scattered throughout the current chapter.

2. Trace the following commands:

    2.1. `$ dbaccess -d music -ta albums`

    2.2. Use the arrow keys to position the cursor on the 20 in the Length column of the artist row.

    2.3. At the ALTER TYPE albums : menu, choose Modify.

    2.4. At the MODIFY LENGTH >> prompt, enter 30.

    2.5. At the ALTER TYPE albums : menu, choose Exit.

    2.6. At the CREATE TABLE albums : menu, choose Build-new-table.

3. Either of the following commands saves the music schema:

    ```
    $ dbschema -d music > music.sch
    $ dbschema -d music music.sch
    ```

4. Each of the following shows you the columns in the albums table:

    ```
    $ dbaccess music -tic albums
    $ dbschema -d music -t albums
    $ dbaccess music -
    > info columns for albums;
    ```

Basic SQL

SQL stands for Structured Query Language. Often pronounced *sequel*, it is a collection of standard commands with which to build and maintain relational databases. It was developed at IBM in the 1970s, and has since been updated and standardized several times. In 1986, a branch of the American National Standards Institute (ANSI) issued the first standardized core syntax for SQL, called SQL1. The standard was updated in 1992. Most major database vendors, including Oracle, Microsoft, Sybase, and Informix have adopted the majority of this SQL-92 standard. While each has its own extensions to the base standard, their similarities greatly outweigh their differences. Thus, the SQL principles taught in this book are generally applicable to all relational database systems; in general, the examples in this book are SQL-92 compliant.

Introduction

It is seldom essential to limit your toolset to those commands that are strictly ANSI-compliant. For example, the "Pattern Matching Expressions" section later in this chapter defines the distinctions between the ANSI-compliant operator `like` and the related Informix extension `matches`. In practice, you should use whichever statement more concisely and accurately performs the function you want.

SQL is a text-based language. Whereas some companies, including Informix, have created graphical front-ends that generate native SQL, at its core SQL is a text language. This core SQL is the *lingua franca* of relational databases, and is used for all of the examples in this book. Additionally, once you acquire a solid understanding of SQL, you will be able to modify the SQL that is automatically produced by graphical front-ends, such as Microsoft Access. Your ability to tweak the SQL will greatly enhance your facility with such products.

There are several categories of statements that make up Informix's SQL. Data definition language (DDL) includes the set of commands that define the tables, indexes, databases, and other objects that store and constrain the data. All of the previous chapters dealt primarily with DDL. Data manipulation language (DML) includes the very small set of commands (`delete`, `insert`, `load`, `select`, `unload`, `update`) that are used to view and alter the data stored in the database. Even though the list of DML commands is short, there are many variants within them. A facility with DML—especially the `select` statement—is the most important skill a database developer can have.

Besides DDL and DML, Informix includes several other categories of SQL statements. The most important of these are cursor manipulation statements, discussed in Chapter 13, "Cursors and Dynamic SQL."

Inserting Data

The `insert` statement is the basic way to populate the tables in your database. This section explains the different formats of the `insert` statement.

note *In the previous chapter, you dropped and recreated the music database. In this section, you'll selectively reload pieces of the database so that certain topics can be better illustrated. Start by referring to Appendix A, "The Sample Database," to see how to reload only the* genres *table.*

Supplying Data for Each Column

The most common way to insert a row of data is to use the insert statement in the following format:

```
insert into table-name
values (value-list);
```

where *table-name* is the name of the table into which you are inserting the data, and *value-list* is a comma-separated list of the values you are inserting into the table. The order of the values you supply must exactly match the order of the columns in the table.

Now try this yourself. Suppose you want to insert the data for one of your favorite albums. First, you need to open a DB-Access session for your music database. From the UNIX command line, enter the following:

$ **dbaccess music**

You should see the main DB-Access menu with which you are now familiar. If you encounter difficulties, you might need to refer back to Chapter 3, "DB-Access." You will perform the exercises for this chapter from within the Query-language option of this menu. Enter the following insert statement:

```
insert into albums
values (0, 'Cruisin', 'Village People', 1978, 'disco', 6,
        'Introduced Y.M.C.A, a gift to the world');
1 row(s) inserted
```

With this statement, you have inserted a single row into the albums table. You had to arrange the values in the order in which they were listed in the target table, and ensure that their data types matched those of the target columns. Table 5-1 shows how the values correspond to the respective columns and data types.

Table 5-1   *Insert values correspond to columns.*

Column	Data Type	Value	Notes
album_num	serial	0	Informix supplies the next number automatically for serial types, when a 0 is inserted.
title	char(30)	'Cruisin'	The quotes are essential for all character data types.
artist	char(25)	'Village People'	
issue_year	smallint	1978	No quotes are required, since this is a numeric field.
genre	char(10)	'disco'	This value must exist in the genres table to satisfy the referential constraint defined when you created the albums table.
rating	smallint	6	Not bad for a disco beat.
notes	varchar(80)	'Introduced ...'	

When you insert data with the insert statement, you must supply exact values for each column in the table. Each value you supply must be either a literal value appropriate for the data type, a null, or one of Informix's five predefined keywords. The following list enumerates these ten choices:

- A number
- A quoted string
- A literal date
- A literal datetime
- null
- `user`, your login id
- `today`, the current date
- `current`, the current date and time
- `sitename`, the database server
- `dbservername`, the database server (same as `sitename`)

These last five insert the current value for that keyword when used. Finally, you can explicitly supply an unknown value by identifying it as *null*. A null is an unknown value. It is not 0, or blank, or any other value. It is neither equal to, nor *not* equal to any value. It is absent of value. Generally, a null in a column means that it is inapplicable or unknown. Adding a value to a null yields another null. What is 37 plus *unknown*? It would be presumptuous to suggest that the answer is 37, so Informix does not presume so. Neither should you.

Listing Columns Explicitly

An alternative form for the `insert` statement calls for supplying the names of each column for which a value is supplied. The following shows the syntax for the `insert` statement, listing columns explicitly:

```
insert into table-name (column-list)
values (value-list);
```

where *table-name* is the name of the table into which you are inserting the data, *column-list* is a comma-separated list of the columns for which you are supplying values, and *value-list* is a comma-separated list of the corresponding values you are inserting into the table. The order of the values you supply must exactly match the order of the columns you list.

Try using this format to add a new row to the `genres` table. Enter the following:

```
insert into genres (genre, description)
values ('new wave', 'Synth pop of the 80s');
1 row(s) inserted.
```

When you use this format and exclude a column, Informix inserts a null into each unnamed column for which you have not defined a default value. Because Informix supplies default values when they are available, it is a good practice to explicitly insert nulls where you want them. Consequently, you should use this format of the `insert` statement only when you want to rely on defaults you have predefined.

Using Defaults

When you create a table, you can define a value that is supplied automatically as you insert a row into the table. This default value is inserted only when you do not explicitly supply another value.

note *Before proceeding, reload the* `formats` *and* `albums` *tables, as shown in Appendix A.*

Consider the `album_copies` table, which has default values of CD for the `format` column and `shelf` 1 for the `location` column. Enter the following set of SQL statements to see how defaults work. Notice that although each uses the same general form of the insert statement, the values they supply differ.

```
insert into album_copies
(album_num, format, location, amount_paid)
values (12, null, null, 14.95);

insert into album_copies
(album_num, amount_paid)
values (8, 15.95);

insert into album_copies
(album_num, format, location, amount_paid)
values (19, 'tape', 'car', 9.95);
```

```
select *
  from album_copies;

album_num format location      amount_paid
       12                          $14.95
        8 CD      shelf 1          $15.95
       19 tape    car               $9.95
```

Notice that the default values for `location` and `format` are generated only when the columns are not named in the `insert` statement. When you supply a null value, as in the third `insert` statement, you override the defaults.

Inserting Data from Another Table

The previous modes of the `insert` statement inserted only one row at a time. With an `insert-select` statement you can insert multiple rows by replacing the hard-coded values with data selected from other tables. The following shows this form of the `insert` statement:

```
insert into table-name [(column-list)]
select-statement;
```

where `table-name` is the name of the table into which you are inserting the data, `column-list` is an optional list of columns for which you are supplying values, and `select-statement` is a complete `select` statement that returns the values you are inserting into the table. The order of the values returned by the `select` statement must exactly match the order of the columns in the table, or, if you include `column-list` values, they must match the columns you list.

Imagine that you just accidentally deleted all the data from the `genres` table. Assuming each genre had at least one album of that type, you could enter the following statement to repopulate the keys in the table:

```
insert into genres (genre)
select distinct genre
  from albums;
```

The details of the `select` statement nested in this example are explained in the next section.

Even this form of the `insert` statement can be tedious. Subsequent chapters explain how to use forms, custom 4GL programs, and load scripts to enter large amounts of data.

Selecting Data

The `select` statement is the heart of SQL. It is the means by which you request that the database extract specific data and display that data to you. The queries you construct with the `select` statement can take from milliseconds to days to execute. They collect data for ad hoc requests, and for complicated mission-critical reports. You will probably spend most of your development time building and executing `select` statements, so it is important that you learn sound fundamentals.

 From this point on, Informix Basics uses all of the data in the sample database. Refer to Appendix A to see how to delete all of the data you've currently entered and reload the original sample data. Alternatively, you can use insert *statements like those shown in the previous section to create your own data.*

The `select` statement comprises several distinct clauses, as the following description shows:

```
[output to output-file]
 select expression-list
    from table-list
 [where condition-list]
 [order by order-list]
```

where each clause is described in more detail in its own section below. Briefly, `expression-list` is the columns or derived values you are extracting from the tables in `table-list`. The `condition-list` describes and restricts the rows returned, and `order-list` specifies the sort order of the result set. The clauses shown, in the order shown, constitute the fundamental elements of every `select` statement. Of these, only the `select` and `from` clauses are mandatory. For now, you need only recognize that the order of the clauses is important (for example, the `select` clause must precede the `from` clause).

Formatting Your `select` Statement

SQL imposes strict rules on the order of clauses within statements, and on the syntax of individual clauses, but has no actual formatting rules. For example, it is not case-sensitive. Also, all forms of white space—spaces, tabs, and newlines—are interchangeable. Finally, tables and columns can be assigned temporary names, or aliases, that last for the duration of the `select` statement. As a result, functionally identical SQL statements can appear quite different.

Which style you adopt is less important than that you pick one. The following guidelines are ones you might consider.

Some Formatting *Dos* and *Do Nots*

DO

Arrange the statement around a column gutter. In this format, the significant keywords are to the left of an empty column—the gutter—and all user-defined values are to the right of this column. The keywords are right-justified; the user values are left-justified. The visual effect created is

```
select  |  |  expression-list
  from  |  |  table-list
 where  |  |  comparison-condition
   and  |  |  more-comparisons
   and  |  |  join-conditions
 order  |     by order-list;
```

DO

Use lowercase keywords. It is important to set these keywords apart from other elements, but the gutter is sufficient. Besides, why add extra typing?

DO NOT

Combine clauses on a single line. Your friends will not respect you if you do not at least make this minimal effort to grant each clause its own line. Trust me. I've met your friends and felt their withering scorn firsthand.

DO

Use single quotes to set apart literal text. Double quotes, although legal, can acquire other meanings within Informix. Besides, single quotes are easier.

DO NOT

Create aliases for tables needlessly. Create them only when there is a compelling reason to do so. Generally, complete table names make a `select` statement clearer than aliases.

DO NOT

Prefix column names with table names unless the columns are otherwise ambiguous. Although more exact, the table names clutter the statement and make it more difficult to read.

To show how different styles can affect the appearance of a `select` statement, consider the following three statements, the third of which follows the Do/Do Not formatting guidelines:

```
SELECT Genres.genre,Genres.description
 FROM Genres WHERE Genres.genre = "reggae";


Select g.* From genres g Where genre = 'reggae';


select genre, description
  from genres
 where genre = 'reggae';
```

Each is functionally identical and produces the same result when executed:

```
genre       description
reggae      The sun-splashed Jamaican beat of Bob Marley.
1 row(s) retrieved.
```

Armed with the rudiments of style consciousness, you can proceed to understanding the individual clauses within the `select` statement. Look back to the list of clauses that compose a `select` statement above. That list shows nearly all the clauses valid in a `select` statement. The only other valid components are the following:

- `group by` clause
- `having` clause
- `into` clause
- `union` clause
- subqueries

These additional components will be covered in Chapter 7, "Intermediate SQL," and Chapter 8, "Advanced SQL Queries."

Selecting Database Columns

The expression list of the `select` clause is where you identify the values you want returned from the database. Usually, these are columns in the tables of interest, but can also be expressions or even constants. To select individual columns you list the column names explicitly, separated by commas. Try the following:

```
select format, default_value, description
   from formats;
```

This statement retrieves every row from the `formats` table. Your result set should resemble the following output:

```
format       default_value description

8track               $8.00 when only the best will do
CD                  $15.99 compact disc
tape                 $9.99 cassette tape
LP                  $12.00 vinyl record, complete with scratches
DAT                 $18.50 digital audio tape
video               $24.99 VHS format videocassette
laser               $32.50 laser disc

7 row(s) retrieved.
```

note

The rows returned by a `select` *statement are in no particular order. This is characteristic of relational databases, and in fact is part of their theoretical underpinnings. The rows are intrinsically unordered. You may, on occasion, notice that rows are displayed in the order in which they were entered, but you cannot rely on that. If you want your data to be sorted, you must explicitly use an* `order by` *clause. Refer to "The* `order by` *Clause" section for more details on this important* `select` *statement component.*

A shortcut exists for selecting all of the columns from a table. You can use an asterisk (*) instead of the individual column names. Enter the following:

```
select *
  from formats;
```

This statement generates the same output as the previous example.

Using Expressions in `select` Statements

In addition to the raw values stored in columns, you can also select expressions from tables. The following sections show a few of the most useful ones.

Selecting Constants

Constants include quoted literals, numbers, and Informix keywords. Except for nulls, this list is the same one used for inserting data above. The following SQL fragments are all legal `select` clauses, which when included as part of a complete `select` statement will display the given constants as if they were database values:

```
select current, *
select user
select 'The rating for the CD is:' || rating
```

note

The last example uses the concatenation operator (| |) to link two character expressions together. It is the string complement of the numeric + operator. When you concatenate expressions, their output is treated as a single field: a conjunction of two strings.

You might select a constant as means of timestamping a `select` statement, or adding an additional label to your output. Try the following example:

```
select current, *

  from genres

 where genre = 'polka';
```

It produces not only the polka description, but also a recording of when the query was executed, as the following output shows:

```
(expression)   1998-09-29 17:46:05.000

genre          polka

description    Beer barrel Bohemian sounds in 2/4 time


1 row(s) retrieved.
```

Of course, the date and time returned in your query will differ from the example. Notice also that the format of the data returned is different than on previous queries. When the total length of one output row exceeds 80 characters, Informix alters the format from columnar to this one-column-per-line mode. When calculating the length of a row for this conversion, Informix considers the maximum length of each column, even when the data does not fill the field. One of the advantages of *subscripting*, described in the next section, is to be able to trim the size of columns to retain a columnar display of the output.

Subscripting is selecting subscripts, or fragments of values, from the character-based data types: `char`, `varchar`, and `text`. To do so, you define the beginning and ending character positions within square brackets ([ ]).

Selecting Column Expressions

The following code shows how displaying only the first forty characters of a description field maintains the friendly columnar format and loses little of the data.

```
select current, genre, description[1, 40]
  from genres
 where genre in ('calypso', 'punk');


(expression)              genre       description


1997-09-29 17:51:12.000 calypso     Steel drums and coconut drinks
      with litt
1997-09-29 17:51:12.000 punk        Edgy, cacophonous anger, with
      instrument
2 row(s) retrieved.
```

The in operator used above tests whether the database column listed (genre) equates to any of the comma-separated values listed ('calypso' or 'punk'). It is described fully in "The Inclusion Operator" section later in this chapter.

Selecting Function Expressions

Informix provides many built-in functions that you can include in your expression list. Each of these requires an argument, as the following template shows:

```
select function(argument)
remainder-of-select-statement
```

where function is the operation you want to perform (see Table 5-2), argument is the expression or database column that the function operates on, and remainder-of-select-statement is any legal combination of clauses that completes the select statement.

Try the following example to see how you can find the length of a character field, in this case a specific description column in the genres table:

```
select length(description)
  from genres
 where genre = 'calypso';


(expression)


        52
1 row(s) retrieved.
```

Table 5-2 lists some of the most useful function expressions.

Table 5-2 Useful function expressions.

Type	*Function*	*Operates on*	*Evaluates to*
Hex	hex	Integer	Hexadecimal encoding
Length	length	Character field	Number of bytes, excluding trailing spaces
Math	abs	Any real number	Absolute value
	mod	Dividend, divisor	Remainder when the dividend is divided by the divisor
	pow	Base, exponent	Value of base, raised to the power of exponent
	round	Number, precision	Value of number, rounded to the precision specified
	sqrt	Numeric field	Square root
	trunc	Number, precision	Value of number, truncated to the precision specified
Time	day	Date or datetime	Numerical day of the month, as a number between 1 and 31
	month	Date or datetime	Month, as a number from 1 to 12

(Continued)

Table 5-2   Useful function expressions.

Type	Function	Operates on	Evaluates to
	weekday	Date or datetime	Day of the week, with 0 representing Sunday, 1 Monday, and so on.
	year	Date or datetime	Year, as a four-digit integer
Trim	trim	Character field	Significant characters, with all leading and trailing blanks removed

Selecting Aggregate Expressions

Whereas functions perform operations on a single row's argument, aggregate expressions evaluate a group of rows, and return a single value that satisfies the aggregate function. All aggregate expressions accept an argument, generally a single column, and perform the appropriate operation across all rows for that column. The aggregate expressions are:

- avg
- count
- max
- min
- sum

avg   The avg function returns the average value for every non-null value in the group selected. Enter the following query to show the average amount paid for LPs:

```
select avg(amount_paid)
  from album_copies
 where format = 'LP';


    (avg)


    $12.50
```

You can use the avg function only on numeric values.

count The `count` function returns a count of the number of rows that match the `where` clause, if there is one. Otherwise, it returns the number of rows in the table. Let's say you want to know how many different formats you have defined. Enter the following query:

```
select count(*)
  from formats;
```

```
(count(*))

       7
```

Notice that because `count` is an expression, it acts on an argument, and thus has parentheses to surround that argument. It is legal, but simply never done, to use a column name where the asterisk is used in the `count` expression above. The results would be the same, but the asterisk is a convenient and ubiquitous shortcut.

 tip *When you combine the `distinct` restriction with the `count` expression, you get a count of all of the unique occurrences of the columns selected. For example, the following statement returns the number of artists in your collection, regardless of how many albums of each you have:*

```
select count(distinct artist)
  from albums;
```

min and max The `min` and `max` functions return the minimum or maximum value for the column specified. The column need not be numeric; Informix sorts character fields alphabetically and date fields chronologically to determine minimums and maximums of those data types. Also, the following code shows you can select multiple aggregate functions at once. Let's say you want to show the range of ratings for all the Culture Club recordings. Enter the following query:

```
select min(rating), max(rating)
  from albums
 where artist = 'Culture Club';


       (min)          (max)


         1              2
```

You can also combine expressions, as in the next example. Suppose you want to find the longest description for any row in the genres table. Create and run the following query:

```
select max(length(description))
  from genres;


      (max)


       52
```

sum The final aggregate expression is the sum function. Only valid for numeric data, it totals the values in a column for all rows selected. Enter the following example to show the total paid for all music videos:

```
select sum(amount_paid)
  from album_copies
 where format = 'video';


      (sum)


      $39.00
```

Selecting Arithmetic Expressions

You can use any of the four basic arithmetic operators (+-*/) in an expression within a select statement. Let's say you want to calculate what effect a six percent sales tax would have on amounts paid for videos. Enter the following:

```
select amount_paid, amount_paid * 1.06
  from album_copies
 where format = 'video';
```

```
amount_paid        (expression)

  $21.50              $22.79
  $17.50              $18.55
```

Operations of this sort can let you examine the effect of proposed changes to the data without actually changing what is stored in the database.

Creating Display Labels for Selected Values

As you've seen, when Informix displays the results of a query, it labels the data with the names of the database columns from which they were derived. When it executes a function, it labels the column with the function name, such as `min` or `max`. However, when an expression is selected, as in the previous example, there is no meaningful column label that Informix can use. Instead, it supplies "(expression)" as an artificial column label. You can override this, or any, column label by introducing a *display label* in your `select` clause.

A display label is a temporary column label that overrides the default supplied by Informix. It lasts only for the duration of the current `select` statement. To create one, simply follow the expression, function, or column in your `select` statement with a space followed by any descriptive header you choose. As with column names, display labels may not contain spaces, and are limited to 18 characters.

Try the following example to make the previous `select` statement more readable by adding a display label:

```
select amount_paid, amount_paid * 1.06 amount_with_tax
   from album_copies
 where format = 'video';

      amount_paid   amount_with_tax

        $21.50           $22.79
        $17.50           $18.55
```

The `from` Clause

This part of a `select` statement is where you list the tables from which you will be selecting data. The examples so far have extracted data from a single table at a time, but much of the power of SQL resides in selecting from multiple tables at once. To select data from multiple tables, you separate each table name with a comma in the `from` clause. The order in which the tables are listed in unimportant. Although the following example shows the form of listing multiple tables, a detailed explanation must wait until Chapter 8.

```
select albums.*, album_copies.location
  from albums, album_copies
 where albums.album_num = album_copies.album_num;
```

When you select data from multiple tables, you need to indicate how these tables relate, or *join*. To join is to combine rows from multiple tables into composite related rows. You specify a column the rows have in common, and Informix constructs a virtual row that combines data from both tables where the rows share values for this join column. Chapter 8 describes in detail this key idea of joining.

Notice also that when you select data from multiple tables you sometimes have to reference column names more explicitly. In the previous example `album_num` is in both tables. To clarify which `album_num` is being referenced, you need to prefix each column name with its table name and a dot (`.`). This prefix can be used anywhere that a simple column name can be used.

In the same way that you can create display labels for columns, you can create aliases for table names. This is most often done to create table name shortcuts for complex SQL statements or to create self-joins (see Chapter 8). An *alias* is a temporary name for a table within a `select` statement. You create it by following the table name with a space and the alias name. When you alias a table, the change is effective only for the duration of that `select` statement. Within the statement, all other references to the table must also use the alias, not the original table name. As with table names, aliases may not contain spaces, and are limited to 18 characters.

The following statement shows a simple use of table aliases, where the table names from the previous example are temporarily replaced with simpler abbreviations:

```
select a.*, ac.location
  from albums a, album_copies ac
 where a.album_num = ac.album_num;
```

The where Clause

Within the where clause you define the rows that will be included or excluded by your select statement. A where clause can contain any combination of *comparison conditions* and *join conditions*. Comparison conditions, or *filters*, describe criteria your data must meet in order be selected. Each of the following are valid comparison conditions, explanations of which are in the sections that follow:

```
where genre = 'reggae'
where genre in ('calypso', 'punk')
where rating between 8 and 10
where genre not like 'rock%'
where notes is not null
where rating > 7 or genre = 'blues'
where format = '8track' and amount_paid >= 7.50
```

The full range of these and other comparison conditions are described in this section. Join conditions are those that relate two tables based on the values of certain columns in each, as in the following examples:

```
where album_copies.format = formats.format
where albums.album_num = album_copies.album_num
```

Joining tables in this way is described in Chapter 8. Comparison conditions comprise the following operators:

- Relational operators
- The between clause
- The inclusion operator

- Null comparisons
- Logical operators
- Pattern matching expressions

This list is not nearly as imposing as it may seem. Examples will help clarify each of these types of comparison conditions.

Relational Operators

The relational operators are listed in Table 5-3.

Table 5-3   Relational operators.

Operator	What It Tests
=	Equal to
!= or <>	Not equal to
>	Greater than
>=	Greater than or equal to
<	Less than
<=	Less than or equal to

Relational operators can be used on all numeric, character, and date data types. For character data types, greater than means that it sorts after alphabetically. For date types, greater than means it occurs chronologically after.

Many earlier examples have already used the equality operator. You can even combine relational operators with mathematical operators, Informix keywords, and column expressions, as in the following two examples. Suppose you want to see if there are any young rockers in your collections. First, remember that the year function, as explained in Table 5-2, returns the year of a date field. Then enter the following query:

```
select *
  from performers
 where year(today) - year(birth_date) < 18;
```

No rows found.

Or let's say you want to list all genres that begin with `rock`. Try the following statement:

```
select *
  from genres
 where genre[1,4] = 'rock';
```

```
genre        description


rockabilly High energy nascent country rock
rock        Tunes your kids (or your parents) hate
```

The between Clause

The between clause tests whether a column or expression is within a range of values. Let's say you want to list the `title` and `artist` for all albums issued in the '60s. Try the following query:

```
select title, artist, issue_year
  from albums
 where issue_year between 1960 and 1969;
```

```
title                     artist               issue_year


Abbey Road                Beatles                    1969
Help!                     Beatles                    1965
Revolver                  Beatles                    1966
Please Please Me          Beatles                    1963
```

Notice that rows that match `1960` or `1969` are included in your result set. Try the following example to show that the previous and following queries produce identical results:

```
select title, artist, issue_year
  from albums
 where issue_year >= 1960
   and issue_year <= 1969;
```

The Inclusion Operator

This operator (in) allows you to check whether a column or
expression is equal to any of the values you list. Try the following
example to see the descriptions for each of your favorite music
types:

```
select genre, description
  from genres
 where genre in ('ska', 'jazz', 'salsa');
```

genre	description
ska	Reggae plus six cups of coffee
jazz	From beatnik to new acoustic
salsa	Songs with irresistible Latin spice

Null Comparisons

Let's say you've lost your favorite Go-Gos CD. To reflect this,
you've set the value of album_copies.location for that recording to null, reflecting that the value is unknown or inapplicable.
Null values do not equal any other values. Therefore, it is apparent that a query like the following would fail to include this CD in
the result set:

```
select *
  from album_copies
 where location = 'car';   -- where the CD had been kept


No rows found.
```

note

Note the use of comments in the null comparison queries. In SQL, a double dash (--) denotes that the database engine should ignore everything that follows it on that line. You should occasionally use comments to make complicated queries easier for you and others to understand.

What is perhaps not so apparent about the treatment of nulls is that the following query will *also* not include the lost CD in the result set:

```
select *
  from album_copies
 where location != 'car';    -- show everything not in the car


No rows found.
```

By declaring the location to be null, you've indicated that it might be in your car, so the previous query dare not include it in its result set. The only way to check for a null value is to test for it explicitly. The is null comparison does this, as the following example shows:

```
select *
  from album_copies
 where location is null;    -- list the lost albums


album_num format location              amount_paid
       12 CD                                $9.50


1 row(s) retrieved.
```

You can also check for the converse: values that explicitly have contents, those that are not null. The following query provides an example:

```
select *
  from albums
 where rating is not null    -- list albums with evaluations
   and notes  is not null;    -- and descriptive text
```

Logical Operators

The logical operators are and, or, and not. They are used to combine multiple conditions in a where clause.

For the examples in this section, consider the following imaginary table, favorites:

```
artist              title           rating
Tito Jackson        Best of Tito         2
Terry Jacks         Greatest Hit         1
Leo Sayers          Greatest Hit         2
Billy Idol          The Ballads          4
```

Before proceeding, you should first create this table and insert the above rows into it. You should be able to do this on your own, but you can refer to the first exercise at the end of the chapter for one possible set of SQL statements that will suffice.

and The and operator between conditions signifies that only rows that satisfy each of the conditions will be returned. Suppose you want to list those rows that have a rating of 2 and are titled Greatest Hit. Enter the following query:

```
select *
  from favorites
 where rating = 2
   and title = 'Greatest Hit';
```

```
artist              title           rating

Leo Sayers          Greatest Hit         2
```

not The not operator reverses the truth of a given condition. Suppose you want to list those rows that have a rating of 2 and are *not* titled Greatest Hit. Enter the following query:

```
select *
  from favorites
 where rating = 2
   and not title = 'Greatest Hit';
```

artist	title	rating
Tito Jackson	Best of Tito	2

or The `or` statement can be trickier. You use it to return those rows that satisfy any of the selection conditions. Now imagine you want to list those rows that have a `rating` of 2 or are titled `Greatest Hit`. Enter the following query:

```
select *
  from favorites
 where rating = 2
    or title = 'Greatest Hit';
```

The following three rows each satisfy some part of the statement, and so are returned:

artist	title	rating
Tito Jackson	Best of Tito	2
Terry Jacks	Greatest Hit	1
Leo Sayers	Greatest Hit	2

When there are multiple comparison conditions, the evaluation of the `or` statement can be less clear. Examine the following statement:

```
select *
  from favorites
 where title = 'Best of Tito'
    or title = 'Greatest Hit'
   and rating = 1;
```

If the `or` operator is evaluated first, the only row returned is the following:

artist	title	rating
Terry Jacks	Greatest Hit	1

Conversely, if the and operator is evaluated first, both of the following rows satisfy the select statement:

```
artist              title          rating


Tito Jackson        Best of Tito      2
Terry Jacks         Greatest Hit      1
```

This confusion can result whenever it is unclear to Informix which operators are meant to be logically combined. You should use parentheses to make your meaning exact. The following two examples show how parentheses clarify the previous listing. Try the following statement to see the difference.

```
select *
  from favorites
 where (title = 'Best of Tito'
    or  title = 'Greatest Hit')
   and rating = 1;


artist              title          rating


Terry Jacks         Greatest Hit      1
```

Now try this one:

```
select *
  from favorites
 where title = 'Best of Tito'
    or (title = 'Greatest Hit'
   and rating = 1);


artist              title          rating


Tito Jackson        Best of Tito      2
Terry Jacks         Greatest Hit      1
```

Pattern Matching Expressions

Informix uses both like and matches to create pattern-matching comparisons that can be used on character strings. The like command conforms to ANSI standards, but `matches` has a little more functionality. With each, you embed special operators in a search string to identify the pattern to be matched. Table 5-4 summarizes these operators.

Table 5-4   Pattern-matching operators.

To Search For	Using `like`	Using `matches`
Any single character	_	?
Any number of characters	%	*
Any of a set of single characters	Not available	[character-list]

The following are valid examples of comparison conditions that use the pattern-matching operators:

```
where description like '%rhythm%'
where description matches '*rhythm*'
where genre like '_l%'
where description matches '?l*'
where title matches '[Kk]*'
```

Each of these is used in some example in this section. Let's say you want to list all rows from the `genres` table that have `rhythm` anywhere in the `description` field. Try the following two `select` statements, each of which produces the same result set.

```
select genre, description
  from genres
 where description like '%rhythm%';

select genre, description
  from genres
 where description matches '*rhythm*';
```

```
genre       description

soul        Earthy rhythm and blues
hip hop     Rap, and urban rhythmic screeds
genre       description

soul        Earthy rhythm and blues
hip hop     Rap, and urban rhythmic screeds

2 row(s) retrieved.
```

note *When you combine multiple SQL statements, the DB-Access status line (the line at the bottom of the screen) reflects the status of the last SQL statement only. In the previous example, the* `2 row(s) retrieved` *status applies only to the second* `select` *statement. The first statement also returned two rows, but its status was overwritten by the status of the second statement.*

Now let's suppose you want to find all genres that have an "l" as the second letter (I don't know why either; it's an example). Enter the following queries:

```
select genre, description
  from genres
 where genre like '_l%';

select genre, description
  from genres
    where description matches '?l*';

genre       description

blues       Chicago, Texas, and Memphis heartache
classical   Rock me, Amadeus
genre       description

blues       Chicago, Texas, and Memphis heartache
classical   Rock me, Amadeus

2 row(s) retrieved.
```

With the `matches` command you can also specify a list of characters to include or exclude in a pattern, by enclosing the character list in square brackets. To test for a match of any character *not* in the list, precede the character list with a caret (^). You can also include a range of characters within the brackets. Each of the following is a valid comparison condition using `matches`:

```
where location[1,1] matches '[a-z]'
where title matches '[^abcABC]*'
where artist not matches '*[0-9]*'
```

Try an example. Suppose you want to find all albums whose title begins with k, regardless of case:

```
select title, artist
  from albums
 where title matches '[Kk]*';
```

To create the equivalent statement using `like`, you are forced to include an `or` clause:

```
select title, artist
  from albums
 where title like 'K%'
    or title like 'k%';
```

The `order by` Clause

When you want to ensure that your result set is sorted, you must include an `order by` clause. In its simplest form, the `order by` statement sorts the result set according to the values in one of the columns you select. To produce a standard (or ascending) ordered list of all genres, try the following query:

```
select genre, description
  from genres
 order by genre;
```

```
genre       description

blues       Chicago, Texas, and Memphis heartache
calypso     Steel drums and coconut drinks with little umbrellas
classical   Rock me, Amadeus
country     Songs about trains, dogs, and trucks
disco       Do the hustle in your platform shoes
gospel      Inspirational voices from the choir
hip hop     Rap, and urban rhythmic screeds
jazz        From beatnik to new acoustic
metal       Loud and rebellious screeching guitars
polka       Beer barrel Bohemian sounds in 2/4 time
pop         Easy, catchy, even bubble gum tunes
punk        Edgy, cacophonous anger, with instruments
reggae      The sun-splashed Jamaican beat of Bob Marley
rock        Tunes your kids (or your parents) hate
rockabilly  High energy nascent country rock
salsa       Songs with irresistible Latin spice
ska         Reggae plus six cups of coffee
soul        Earthy rhythm and blues
world beat  Rhythms from the many corners of the globe
zydeco      Blackened Cajun beat, with pepper sauce
```

You can also reverse the default sort order by declaring the order by to be descending. Insert the word desc in your previous query to reverse the ordering of the above result set.

```
select genre, description
  from genres
 order by genre desc;
```

You can list multiple columns in the order by clause. Let's say you want to list all of your pop albums by artist, and within each artist by year, oldest first. Enter the following:

```
select artist, title, issue_year
  from albums
 where genre = 'pop'
 order by artist, issue_year desc;
```

artist	title	issue_year
Bay City Rollers	Absolute Rollers - The Best of	1995
Bay City Rollers	Once Upon A Star	1975
Culture Club	Colour by Numbers	1983
Culture Club	Kissing to be Clever	1982
Go-Gos	Beauty and the Beat	1981
Milli Vanilli	Girl You Know its True	1989
Monkees	Barrel Full of Monkees	1971

Informix allows a shortcut in the `order by` clause. Instead of listing the column names explicitly, you can replace any name with its *select number*, the position in which it is listed in the `select` clause. The following example produces the same results as the previous one:

```
select artist, title, issue_year
  from albums
 where genre = 'pop'
 order by 1, 3 desc;
```

Using select numbers is a handy trick to sort results based on a derived column, one generated via an expression.

Redirecting Query Output

Query results are normally displayed directly to the screen. You can specify instead that the result set be written to a file. To do this, you precede the `select` statement with an `output to` clause. You can also include the optional `without headings` clause to suppress the column names in the output. Let's say you want to save the results of an important query to a file called `/tmp/milli_albums`. Enter the following:

```
output to /tmp/milli_albums without headings
select *
  from albums
 where artist = 'Milli Vanilli';
```

If the filename does not exist, it will be created; if it exists, it will be overwritten. If you do not specify a directory, the output file will be created in your current directory. Wherever you specify, you need to be sure that you have operating system permissions to create a file in that directory.

Deleting Data

The delete statement permanently removes rows from a table. Its syntax is straightforward:

```
delete from table-name
[where condition-list]
```

where *table-name* is the name of the table from which you are deleting rows of data, and *condition-list* is an optional set of conditions that describe and restrict the rows deleted. The syntax of *condition-list* is identical to that for the select statement.

The simplest form, shown in the following example, removes all rows from the formats table:

```
delete from formats;
```

If you execute this statement from within DB-Access, it warns you that you are about to empty the table. (See Figure 5-1.)

 caution Be very sure of your intentions when executing a delete statement without a where clause. Such statements irreversibly delete all rows from the target table.

It is much more common to restrict the rows to those that meet conditions you specify. For example, the following statement deletes all of the *bad* disco albums:

```
delete from albums
  where genre = 'disco'
    and title != 'Cruisin';
```

Figure 5–1   *DB-Access ensures that you want to delete all rows.*

The operators available with which to define the deletion are the same ones used to create `select` statements. Therefore, you can always verify which rows will be deleted by first creating a `select` statement with the conditions of interest, and once only the rows you want to remove are returned, replace `select *` with `delete`. Sometimes, however, especially when you are deleting a large number of rows, selecting every row for this verification is unreasonable. A shortcut that often proves just as useful is to count the number of rows that will be deleted. The following example performs such a count:

```
select count(*)
   from albums
  where artist = 'Meat Puppets'
      or rating <= 2;
```

Once you see that the number returned is what you expected, you can replace `select count(*)` with `delete` to effect the deletion.

caution

Counting the rows you are about to delete is a foolproof verification method only when you are the exclusive user of the database. Otherwise, between the time you perform the select *statement and the* delete *statement, other users could alter the data.*

Updating Data

The update statement changes the value of specified columns for rows that match the search criteria. Its syntax can take either of two forms.

The first and easiest form is

```
update table-name
    set column-name = value
    [, column-name = value ...]
[where condition-list]
```

where *table-name* is the name of the table whose rows you are updating, *column-name* is the column whose contents you are replacing with *value*, and *condition-list* is an optional set of conditions that describe and restrict the rows updated. The new *value* can be a constant or an expression. The syntax of *condition-list* is identical to that for the select statement.

The alternative form is

```
update table-name
    set (column-list) =
        (value-list]
[where condition-list]
```

where *column-list* is a comma-separated list of the columns whose contents you will be changing, and *value-list* is a comma-separated list of the corresponding values you are supplying for those columns.

Just as with the delete statement, if you have no where clause and execute the update from within DB-Access, it prompts you for verification, as shown in Figure 5-2.

Figure 5–2 *DB-Access ensures that you want to update all rows.*

Let's say that you want to modify the rating and notes values for your favorite album. Enter the following:

```
update albums
   set rating = 10,
       notes  = 'A modern blues tour de force'
 where title  = 'Soul to Soul'
   and artist = 'Double Trouble';


1 row(s) updated.
```

Although this example updates two columns (rating and notes) for this row, you can include any number of column assignments in the set clause.

The alternative form of the update statement, as shown in the following example, is equivalent to the previous one. Alter your previous update statement to comply with the following format:

```
update albums
   set (rating, notes)
      = (10, 'A modern blues tour de force')
 where title  = 'Soul to Soul'
   and artist = 'Double Trouble';

1 row(s) updated.
```

Notice that even though you did not actually change the values of the two columns (they had been set with the previous SQL statement), the status line still shows that a row was updated. An update statement replaces the existing values, even when they do not change.

For most people, the second form is harder to read, and is used only when the data being assigned is derived from a subquery, as in the following example:

```
update albums
   set (rating, notes)
      = (select rating, notes
           from critiques
          where critiques.title = 'Soul to Soul')
 where title  = 'Soul to Soul'
   and artist = 'Double Trouble';
```

The critiques table does not exist in the sample database. This format is shown here for illustrative purposes only. This kind of subquery is explored in much greater depth in Chapter 8.

The following statement shows an example of using an expression in an update statement. Suppose you decide that your Bay City Rollers recordings are passé, and you want to reflect that assessment by downgrading your album ratings. Enter the following statement to decrement the proper rows:

```
update albums
   set rating = rating - 1
 where artist = 'Bay City Rollers'
   and rating > 0;

1 row(s) updated
```

The other math operators described in the `select` statement may also be used to construct expressions. Notice also that while a single `update` statement can only act on one table, it might update multiple rows within that table.

It is legal to update any column via an `update` statement, but as a general rule you should avoid updating a row's primary key.

tip

Don't update a row's primary key. Instead, delete the row and insert a replacement. This ensures that your operations conform to the design principle that a primary key is invariant. There is no good reason to violate this rule.

Summary

SQL is the standard language used to define and manipulate relational databases. In this chapter, you learned the fundamentals of the subset of SQL known as Data Manipulation Language. You learned the basic format and components of the `insert`, `select`, `update`, and `delete` commands.

You can insert one row of data at a time by listing the values to be assigned to each column. You can insert null values, or let the system assign defaults if they have been assigned. The `insert-select` form of the `insert` statement allows multiple rows of data to be extracted from one table and inserted into another.

The `select` statement is the most critical and fundamental component of SQL. With it, you extract data that meets your specified criteria. In this chapter you learned how to construct basic `select` statements and include comparison conditions to limit the rows returned.

The `update` and `delete` statements alter rows of data or remove them from the database. Each uses comparison conditions like those applicable for `select` statements to limit the rows on which they act. The values you can assign in an `update` statement are drawn from the same set used by the `insert` statement.

Extra Credit

Q&A

Question	**Answer**
How can I put multiline comments in my SQL script?	The curly braces (`{}`) delimit comments that span several lines.
How do I include an apostrophe (`'`) in a character field using an `insert` statement, since that is also the character used to quote text fields?	Use double quotes (`"`) to surround any text field that contains any apostrophes.
Can I sort my output by a column I haven't included in the `select` clause?	No. To include a column in an `order by` expression, you have to list it in your `select` clause.
I'd like to write a `select` statement that finds data regardless of case. I don't care whether the data is stored as "Smith," "SMITH," or even "sMiTH." How do I do this?	Sorry. This function isn't available from within SQL. What you want is a comparison condition that looks something like: `where upshift(last_name) = 'SMITH'`. This is only available from within Informix-4GL.
If the `avg` function returns the average value for every non-null value in the group selected, what happens when all of the values I try to average are null?	A null value is returned in that case.

Exercises

1. Create the `favorites` table if you have not done so already. Load it with the four rows of sample data presented in the chapter.
2. Insert a new row of data into the `genres` table. Add a row for folk music. One possible description is "Songs to roast marshmallows by."
3. Use a `select` statement to verify that the row was inserted into the `genres` table, and sorts in its proper place if you display all the rows in reverse alphabetical order.

4. Construct a query that selects your new row and the world beat row, but no others.

5. In preparation for updating the row, construct a `select` statement that retrieves only your new row.

6. Update the description for this row to "Songs to sing around the campfire," being sure not to change the `where` clause you wrote in Exercise 5.

7. Select the row again to verify that your update was effective.

8. Delete the row, again being sure not to change the `where` clause.

Exercise Answers

1. The following statements show one possible way to build and load the `favorites` table used in this chapter:

```
create table favorites (
    artist char(15),
    title  char(12),
    rating smallint
);


insert into favorites values ('Tito Jackson', 'Best of Tito', 2);
insert into favorites values ('Terry Jacks', 'Greatest Hit', 1);
insert into favorites values ('Leo Sayers', 'Greatest Hit', 2);
insert into favorites values ('Billy Idol', 'The Ballads', 4);
```

2. Execute the following statement from within DB-Access:

```
insert into genres
values ('folk', 'Songs to roast marshmallows by');
```

3. Execute the following `select` statement:

```
select *
  from genres
  order by genre desc;
```

4. One possible answer follows:

```
select *
   from genres
  where genre in ('world beat', 'folk');
```

5. The most direct answer follows:

```
select *
   from genres
  where genre = 'folk';
```

6. Use this `update` statement:

```
update genres
   set description = 'Songs to sing around the campfire'
 where genre = 'folk';
```

7. Repeat the query from Exercise Answer 5.
8. Use this `delete` statement:

```
delete from genres
  where genre = 'folk';
```

Chapter

6

ISQL Forms and Reports

In the previous chapter you learned how to use the standard SQL operators to insert, query, and update data. In practice, you will use those operators often—sometimes as direct SQL statements; occasionally embedded in programming languages such as Informix-4GL or Informix-ESQL/C. You need to understand how to use the core SQL operators, but you do not always have to rely on them to enter, manipulate, and display data.

Introduction

Informix-SQL (ISQL) is a tool that allows you to create simple forms, reports, and user-defined menus. Often overlooked in the Informix product line, and largely superseded by DB-Access, ISQL is exceedingly useful for quick data entry or speedy reporting. Launch ISQL from the UNIX command line as follows:

```
$ isql music
```

The database name (in this case, music) is optional, but it is easiest to enter it on the command line. Alternatively, ISQL will prompt you to select a database when necessary. You should see the main ISQL menu as in Figure 6-1.

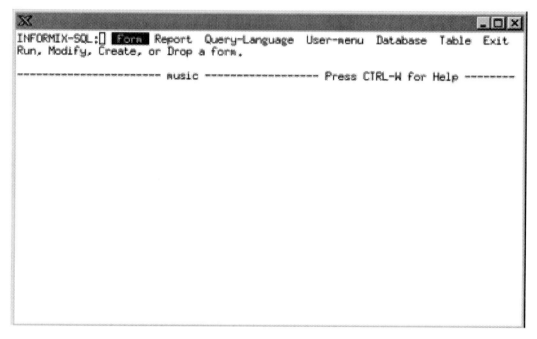

Figure 6-1 *ISQL main menu.*

Each of the options in this ring menu leads to a submenu that allows you to use that function. Use the space bar to move through the options and examine the descriptions for each menu selection. The list of options follows:

- Form: Create and run data entry forms.
- Report: Create and run custom reports.
- Query-language: Move to the Query-language menu. This is the same as for DB-Access.

- `User-menu`: Create and run user-defined menus.
- `Database`: Move to the database menu. This is essentially the same as for DB-Access.
- `Table`: Move to the table menu. This is a subset of the same menu in DB-Access.
- `Exit`: Return to the operating system.

The `Form`, `Report`, and `User-menu` options are the only functions in ISQL that are not available in DB-Access. In this chapter you will learn how to use each of these three tools.

Forms

Forms are user-created data entry and *query-by-example* screens. A *query-by-example (QBE)* is a method of using a form to return rows that match user-entered criteria. With a query-by-example you enter the values you want to match into the appropriate fields of the data entry form, then instruct the program to retrieve all of the rows whose values match those you have entered. This chapter shows many examples of QBE operations.

With forms you can enter data, query for data, and update data. From within the ISQL main menu, press f to display the `Form` submenu. Your screen should resemble Figure 6-2.

From within this menu you can do the following:

- `Run`: Use a form to alter data or query a table.
- `Modify`: Alter a form specification.
- `Generate`: Build a default form from the table's schema.
- `New`: Create a new form from scratch. In practice, this option is never used.
- `Compile`: Translate a form specification into an executable format.
- `Drop`: Delete a form.
- `Exit`: Return to the ISQL Main Menu.

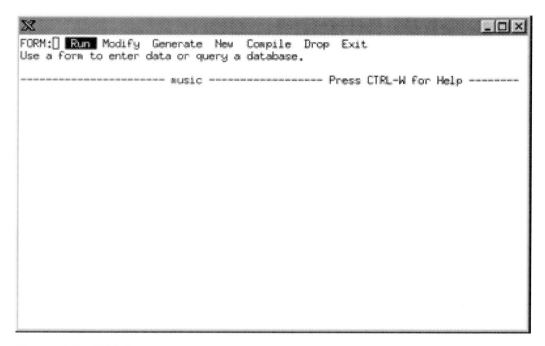

Figure 6–2 *ISQL Form menu.*

Generating a Default Form

The most useful feature of ISQL is its ability to generate default forms. Let's generate a form to manipulate the data in the `performers` table. From the `Form` menu, press g to begin the process of generating a default form. At the prompt, enter `performers` as the name to assign to your form.

Try to give your form the same name as the table it reflects. This will make your forms easier to manage. The 10-character limit on form names will make this occasionally impossible, but you should strive for consistency in any case.

You'll be shown a list of tables on which to base your form (see Figure 6-3).

Use the arrow keys to choose the `performers` table.

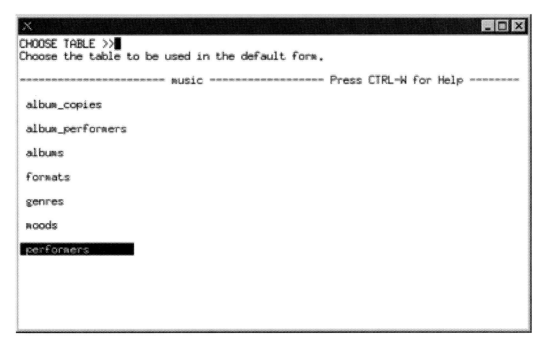

Figure 6–3 *Choosing a table for an ISQL default form.*

The tables displayed in Figure 6-3 are derived from the sample database. Your list may vary. Each table currently existing in your database is displayed for selection as the basis for your default form.

You'll be prompted to either select more tables or declare your list of tables complete. Choose `Table-selection-complete` and ISQL will build your form.

Executing Your Form

Now select `Run` from the ISQL `Form` menu. Select `performers` from the list of forms available. Figure 6-4 shows that only one form is currently available.

Figure 6-5 shows the default form ISQL generates. You can see that every column from the `performers` table is represented here. With this form, you can query, add, update, and remove data from the `performers` table.

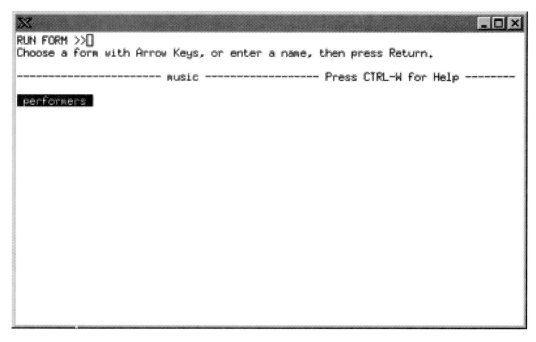

Figure 6–4 *Choosing a form to run.*

Although not all menu choices are currently visible on the PER-FORM menu, the complete list of operations follows:

- Query: Perform a Query-by-Example in the current table.
- Next: Go to the next row in the active set.
- Previous: Go to the previous row in the active set.
- View: Invoke an editor on any blob fields in the form.
- Add: Add a row to the current table.
- Update: Update the current row.
- Remove: Delete the current row.
- Table: In a multitable form, select the next table.
- Screen: In a multiscreen form, select the next screen.
- Current: Display the current row of the active table.
- Master: Select the master table of the current table, if defined.
- Detail: Select the detail table of the current table, if defined.
- Output: Send the current row or active set to a file.
- Exit: Return to the Form Menu.

The "User-Menu" section later in this chapter shows the use of a multitable form, but in practice the multiform and multiscreen

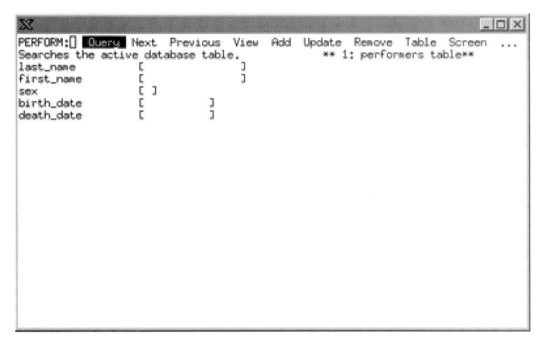

Figure 6–5 *The default* `performers` *form.*

options are used infrequently. Applications requiring that complexity are usually written in more robust languages like Informix-4GL.

Using Your Form for a Query-By-Example

First, let's use the `Query` option to find existing rows in the `performers` table. Enter `Jackson` in the `last_name` field, as the search criteria for a simple query-by-example. Your screen should look like Figure 6-6.

When you press the Esc key, ISQL searches the `performers` table to find all rows that match every value you enter. As with any query, it places those rows into an internal buffer called the *active set*.

The active set is the collection of rows that satisfy a query. Whether the query is created in DB-Access, through an embedded language program like Informix-4GL, or via an ISQL form, rows that Informix returns in response to a query are called the active set. One of the challenges facing the Informix developer is to address this set of data singly: one row at a time. ISQL places the

```
QUERY:  ESCAPE queries,  INTERRUPT discards query,  ARROW keys move cursor.
Searches the active database table.            ** 1: performers table**
last_name          [Jackson]        ]
first_name         [              ]
sex                [ ]
birth_date         [         ]
death_date         [         ]
```

Figure 6–6   *Using a form for a query-by-example search.*

active set into a structure called the *current list*, and allows you to traverse that list with the Next and Previous menu options.

After you execute the QBE, ISQL displays the first row of the active set, as in Figure 6-7.

Notice that the comment line at the bottom of the screen displays the number of rows in the active set. Use the Next and Previous options to traverse these rows.

The example in Figure 6-6 used an exact match to build a QBE. You can also use the operators listed in Table 6-1 to construct your QBE conditions.

The following are all valid examples of QBE expressions that could be applied in the performers form:

```
last_name    [D*                   ]
last_name    [Lennon|McCartney]
first_name   [Bo?                  ]
sex          [F]
birth_date   [<=01/01/1940]
birth_date   [>>                   ]
death_date   [=                    ]
```

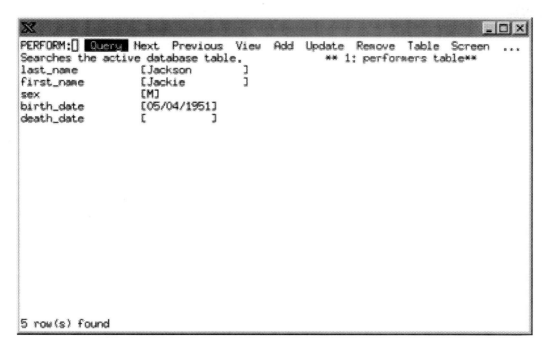

Figure 6–7   *Using a form to examine a QBE active set.*

Table 6-1   The ISQL form QBE operators.

Operator	What It Tests
=	Equal to
!= or <>	Not equal to
>	Greater than
>=	Greater than or equal to
<	Less than
<=	Less than or equal to
<<	Minimum value for that column
>>	Maximum value for that column
*	Match any number of characters

(Continued)

Table 6-1   The ISQL form QBE operators.

Operator	What It Tests
?	Match any single character
expr1:expr2	Between *expr1* and *expr2*, inclusive
expr1|expr2	True if either expression is true

Try various combinations of the above expressions—and some of your own—to see how the expressions and operators work in conjunction.

A QBE expression that is longer than its column width will de displayed on the status line at the bottom of the form.

Using Your Form to Modify Data

Using forms to select and view your data is useful. Equally useful is the ability to add, update, and delete rows via forms. Try adding a row to the `performers` table. From the ISQL Main Menu, press a to enter Add mode. Add yourself as a performer (it's easier than practicing). You can use the `Remove` option to delete data after you have entered it.

A brief overview of the editing commands is available online. From within any field on your form, press Ctrl-W to display the online help.

Because the form is based on a database table, it must comply with all of the constraints that are on the table. These include the not-null constraints, check constraints, and referential constraints discussed in Chapter 2, "Data Modeling 101." If you try to enter data that would violate one of these constraints, ISQL displays an error message and does not add the row. For example, try to add a new performer that violates the constraint that specifies that `performers.sex` may only be F or M. Figure 6-8 shows the error message returned.

Figure 6–8 *No data may be added that violates a constraint.*

You can see here the value of naming your constraints. As discussed in Chapter 4, "Creating Databases and Tables," it is important to name your constraints consistently and clearly so that you can easily identify the source of constraint violations.

In addition to adding data, you can also update and delete data with a form. However, you cannot invoke the Update or Remove options unless you have a current list of data, either from just adding a row, or as the active set returned from a QBE.

Removing a row is straightforward. Just press the r option when a row is displayed on your form. If you answer Yes at the ensuing confirmation prompt, the row will be permanently deleted from the table.

Updating a row is hardly more difficult. When the row you want to change is displayed in your form, press u to enter Update mode. Simply type over the data you want to change, and use the Esc key to commit your work. You can use the Tab key and arrow keys to move from field to field.

Customizing Your Form

Default forms are almost always adequate for simple querying and data entry. Nonetheless, you can customize your form specification in a number of ways. From the ISQL Form Menu, choose `Modify` to customize a form. The specifications for the `performers` form should resemble Listing 6-1.

Listing 6-1 *The default form specification for the* `performers` *table.*

```
database music

screen size 24 by 80

{

last_name          [f000          ]

first_name         [f001          ]

sex                [a]

birth_date         [f002     ]

death_date         [f003     ]

}

end

tables

performers

attributes

f000 = performers.last_name;

f001 = performers.first_name;

a = performers.sex;

f002 = performers.birth_date;

f003 = performers.death_date;

end
```

You can use your editor to customize the form specification. Listing 6-2 shows one example of a customized `performers` form specification file. Take a moment to compare the two.

Listing 6-2   *A customized* `performers` *form specification.*

```
database music


screen size 24 by 80

{


Performer Information:


Last Name              [f000            ]

First Name             [f001            ]

Sex                    [a]


Born on                [f002      ]

Died on                [f003      ]

}

end


tables performers


attributes

f000 = performers.last_name,

        comments = "Enter performer's last name";

f001 = performers.first_name;
```

(Continued)

Listing 6-2   *A customized* performers *form specification.*

```
a    = performers.sex, upshift, autonext, include = (F, M);

f002 = performers.birth_date;

f003 = performers.death_date;

end
```

The Parts of a Form

The form specification file is divided into four sections: database, screen, tables, and attributes. The database section identifies your database. The screen section, which starts and ends with curly braces ({ }), defines what the user sees. All characters not between square brackets ([ ]) are displayed literally to the user. Brackets enclose field tags, which are mapped to database columns in the attributes section. The tables section identifies which tables are used in the form. Finally, the attributes section specifies the database columns associated with each field tag, and allows you to define customized field attributes.

Setting Field Attributes

The attributes section of Listing 6-2 shows several of the attributes available to you. Table 6-2 describes these features. You should also notice that you can define multiple attributes for a single column by separating the attributes with commas, as in Listing 6-2.

Compiling Your Changes

Now edit your performers form specification with the changes shown in Listing 6-2, or with alterations of your own. To compile your changes, exit from the editor after making any changes and select the Compile option. If your change was successful, use the Save-and-exit option to save your work (see Figure 6-9).

If an error prevents your form from being compiled, ISQL will identify the error as best it can and allow you to correct it.

Table 6-2 Useful ISQL form attributes.

Attribute	Function
autonext	Causes the cursor to move automatically to the next field after the field is filled
comments	Generates a message on your form's comment line whenever your cursor is in the field
downshift	Converts each character you enter to lowercase
include	Defines the complete list of valid entries for a field; if you try to enter a value not in the include list, ISQL rejects it and leaves the cursor in the current field
required	Forces an entry; the cursor will not leave the field if no value is entered
reverse	Enables reverse video for the field
upshift	Converts each character you enter to uppercase

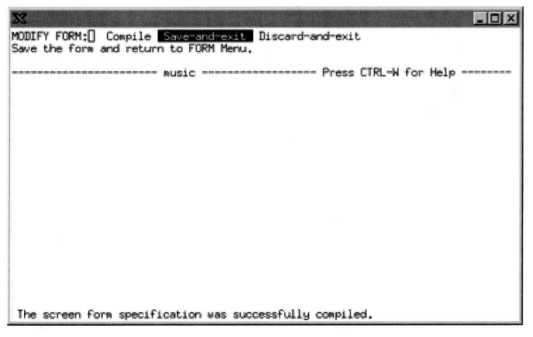

Figure 6–9 Saving your changes after a successful form compilation.

Don't be too ambitious with changes at first: make a small change, compile it, and test it. If you are satisfied with the change, modify your form again with another change. Improve your work incrementally without breaking it. Customization by this kind of stepwise refinement is a hallmark of effective applications development.

Behind the Scenes

Take a look in your current directory. You should see several new files. Those that end in .per are your form specification files. The .per extension reflects the fact that the form builder by itself is called Perform. Compiled forms gain the .frm suffix. You can edit the form specification files directly, but not the .frm files. If you wish, you can compile your forms from the command line with the command sformbld, as in the following example:

```
$ sformbld performers
The form "performers.per" will now be compiled.

     The form compilation was successful.
```

You can also run your forms directly from the command line with the command sperform, as in the following example:

```
$ sperform performers
```

Reports

Reports allow you to see related data at a glance. ISQL reports need not create only printed output. They can also direct the output to your screen or to a file. This section shows you how to generate default reports and how to customize those default report specifications.

As you proceed, you should notice the parallels between the Report and Form menus. Their methods of operation are almost identical. To begin building your first report, press r from within the ISQL main menu. The Report submenu will be displayed (see Figure 6-10).

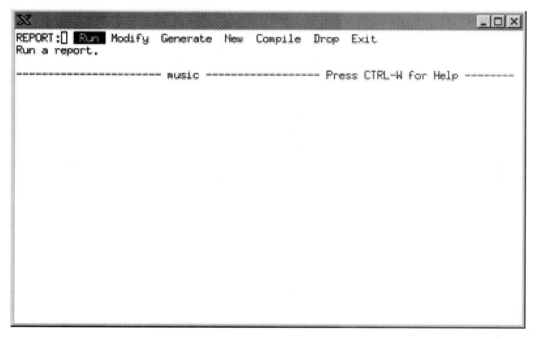

Figure 6–10   *ISQL Report menu.*

From within this menu, you can do the following:

- Run: Execute a report you have built.
- Modify: Alter a report specification.
- Generate: Build a default report from the table's schema.
- New: Create a new report from scratch. In practice, this option is never used.
- Compile: Translate a report specification into an executable format.
- Drop: Delete a report.
- Exit: Return to the ISQL Main Menu.

Generating a Default Report

Let's say you want to generate a report to show the data in the `performers` table. From the `Report` menu, press g to begin the process of generating a report. At the prompt, enter `performers` as the name to assign to your report. As with forms, you can assign any name you choose—up to ten characters—but you should strive for consistency. You'll then be shown a list of tables on which to base your report (see Figure 6-11). Choose the `performers` table.

ISQL builds your report from the table selected.

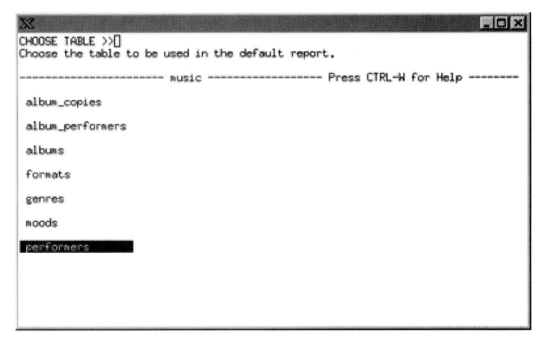

Figure 6–11   *Choosing a table for an ISQL default report.*

Executing Your Report

Now select Run from the ISQL `Report` menu. Choose `performers` from the list of reports available. The data will scroll through your screen and end with something like Figure 6-12.

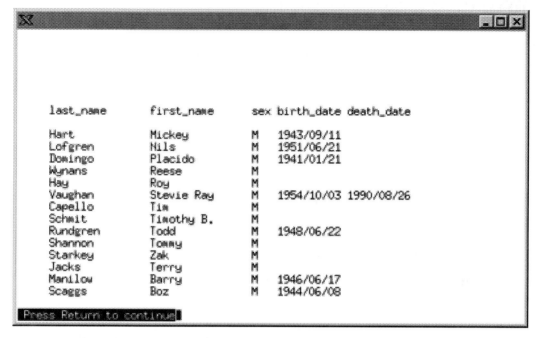

```
last_name        first_name       sex  birth_date death_date

Hart             Mickey           M    1943/09/11
Lofgren          Nils             M    1951/06/21
Domingo          Placido          M    1941/01/21
Wynans           Reese            M
Hay              Roy              M
Vaughan          Stevie Ray       M    1954/10/03 1990/08/26
Capello          Tim              M
Schmit           Timothy B.       M
Rundgren         Todd             M    1948/06/22
Shannon          Tommy            M
Starkey          Zak              M
Jacks            Terry            M
Manilow          Barry            M    1946/06/17
Scaggs           Boz              M    1944/06/08
Press Return to continue
```

Figure 6–12 *ISQL reports display to your screen.*

Notice that the rows are in no particular order, and the column headings are the same as the column names in the performers table.

Customizing Your Report

More than forms, reports usually require a small degree of customization to be most useful. From the ISQL Report menu, choose Modify to customize your report. The specifications for the performers report should resemble Listing 6-3.

You can use your editor to customize the report specification. Listing 6-4 shows one example of a customized performers report specification file. The customized listing adds significantly to the default specification. Take a moment to compare the two.

Listing 6-3   *The default report specification for the* performers *table.*

```
database music end


select

        last_name,

        first_name,

        sex,

        birth_date,

        death_date

from performers end


format every row end
```

Listing 6-4   *A customized* performers *report specification.*

```
database music end


output

    report to 'performers.out'

    top margin 0

    bottom margin 0

    left margin 0

    page length 60

end
```

(Continued)

Listing 6-4 *A customized* `performers` *report specification.*

```
select last_name, first_name, sex, birth_date,
       death_date
  from performers
 order by last_name, first_name
end


format
page header
    print column  1, 'Last Name',
          column 17, 'First Name',
          column 33, 'Sex',
          column 38, 'Born On',
          column 48, 'Died On'
    skip 1 line


on every row
    print column  1, last_name,
          column 17, first_name,
          column 34, sex,
          column 38, birth_date using 'mm/dd/yy',
          column 48, death_date using 'mm/dd/yy'


page trailer
    skip 1 line
    print column 25, 'Page: ', pageno using '##'
end
```

The output of this version will be placed in a file called `per-formers.out`. An excerpt from the first page of that output file follows:

```
Last Name          First Name        Sex   Born On     Died On

Avila              John              M     01/14/57
Bartek             Steve             M     01/30/52
Bostrom            Derrick           M
Briley             Alexander         M
Caffey             Charlotte         F
Capello            Tim               M
Carlisle           Belinda           F     08/16/58
Carreras           Jose              M
Craig              Michael           M
Cummings           Burton            M     12/31/47
Dolenz             Mickey            M     03/08/45
Domingo            Placido           M     01/21/41
Dylan              Bob               M     05/24/41
...
Nesmith            Michael           M     12/30/42
Orbison            Roy               M     04/23/36    12/01/88
Pavarotti          Luciano           M     10/12/35
Petty              Tom               M     12/31/53
Phipps             Sam               M     10/01/53
Pilatus            Rob               M                 04/03/98
Preston            Billy             M     09/09/46
Rose               Felipe            M
Rundgren           Todd              M     06/22/48
Scaggs             Boz               M     06/08/44
Schmit             Timothy B.        M

                    Page:    1
```

The Parts of a Report

The customized `performers` report specification shown in Listing 6-4 introduced the `output` section and greatly expanded the `format` section. The `database` and `select` sections are the same, respectively declaring the database to be used and describing the rows to be included in the report. Table 6-3 describes the components of the optional `output` section. The default value is used for any element you do not define explicitly.

Table 6-3   Components of the ISQL report `output` section.

Element	Default	Defines
`report to`	`screen`	Destination file for report's output
`top margin`	3	Number of blank lines at the top of each page
`bottom margin`	3	Number of blank lines at the bottom of each page
`left margin`	5	Number of blanks by which all output is indented
`page length`	66	Number of lines on each page

Formatting the Output

The `format` section is where you define how you want your data to be presented. It consists of any number of `print` statements and `skip x line` statements embedded in control blocks. The control blocks are:

- `first page header`
- `page header`
- `on every row`
- `before group of`
- `after group of`
- `page trailer`
- `on last row`

Each is optional, but you must include at least one control block within the `format` section. To see examples of the control blocks not included in Listing 6-4, look ahead to Chapter 14, "4GL Reports." It defines these constructs and shows the tight parallel between the ISQL Report Writer and the Informix-4GL Report Writer.

The `print` Statement

With the `print` statement you define exactly how your output is formatted across the page. Each `print` statement builds one line of your output, but may consist of several expressions separated by commas. The following are all valid expressions within the `print` statement:

- *column-name*: any column from your `select` statement
- `'literal text'`: any string of characters you choose, surrounded by quotation marks (`' '`)
- `column` *x*: where *x* is the column where the next expression in this `print` statement will begin
- *x* `space[s]`: where *x* is the number of blanks to print
- `today`: the current date
- `pageno`: the current page number
- `lineno`: the current line number

You can follow any of these expressions with a formatting qualifier. The two qualifiers are `clipped` and `using`. The `clipped` qualifier, only valid for character data types, trims any trailing spaces. Without it, trailing spaces are always included. The following report specification fragment shows how you might use `clipped` to generate a common name format:

```
print last_name clipped, ',', 1 space, first_name
```

Sample output would appear as follows:

```
Dolenz, Mickey
Domingo, Placido
Dylan, Bob
```

The `using` qualifier allows you to specify the format of numbers and dates. A complete list of the `using` strings is presented in Tables 14-5 and 14-7.

Compiling Your Changes

Now edit your `performers` report specification with the changes shown in Listing 6-4, or with alterations of your own. To compile your changes, exit from the editor after making any changes and select the `Compile` option. If your compilation is successful, use the `Save-and-exit` option to save your work. If an error prevents your report from compiling, ISQL identifies the error as best it can and allows you to correct it. For example, Figure 6-13 shows what happens if you misspell the word `page`.

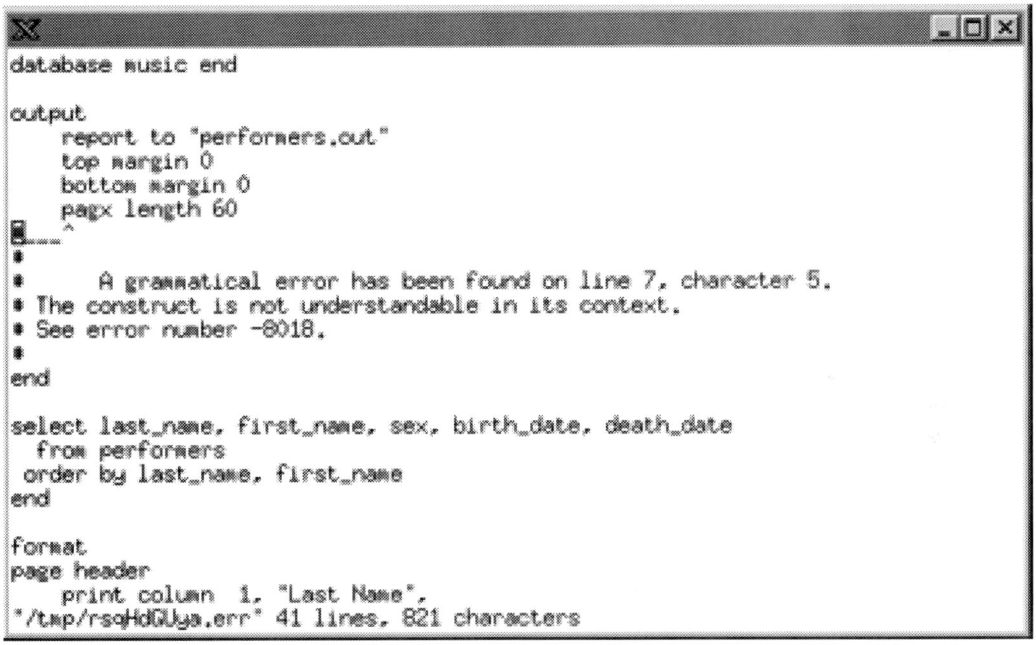

Figure 6–13 *ISQL identifies the location of a report specification error.*

As with forms, you should adhere to the principle of stepwise refinement: make incremental changes and ensure that each works before proceeding to the next change. By proceeding in this way you will more easily be able to identify the location of any errors you may introduce.

Behind the Scenes

Take a look in your current directory. You should see several new files. Those that end in .ace are your report specification files. The .ace extension reflects the fact that the report writer, when decoupled from ISQL, is called Ace. Compiled reports adopt the .arc (Ace Report Control) suffix. You can edit the report specification files directly; the .arc files are not editable. Should you choose, you can compile your reports directly from the command line with the command saceprep, as in the following example:

```
$ saceprep performers
The file "performers.ace" will now be compiled.


The compilation was successful.  The file that holds
the ACE Report Control tables, "performers.arc", has been created.
```

You can also run your reports directly from the command line with the command sacego. The following example shows how sacego is used in this way:

```
$ sacego performers
The reading of the database will now begin.
Select statement number 1 will now be processed.
The reading of the database has finished.
The report will now be written to file "performers.out".
```

User-menu

The third utility that makes ISQL useful is its menu-building tool. With this function, you can generate custom menus with which to organize and launch your ISQL report and forms, as well as queries and other programs. You can only have one main menu per database, but this menu can have nested submenus if you choose.

Figure 6-14 shows you the menu you will build in this section.

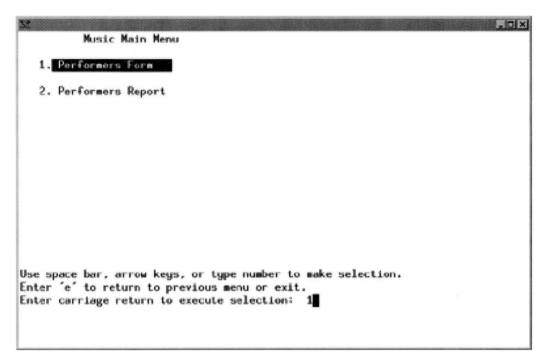

Figure 6–14 ISQL menus create an easy-to-use user interface.

To create your user menu, choose u from the ISQL main menu. From within this menu, you can do the following:

- Run: Run the user-defined menu for this database.
- Modify: Modify the menu definitions for this database. You also create the initial menu with this option.
- Exit: Return to the ISQL Main Menu.

Choose Modify to see a screen like Figure 6-15.

This kind of form should look familiar by now. Use the Add option to add a row with a Menu Name of main and a Menu Title of Music Main Menu. Each database with user menus must have exactly one main menu; you have just created that row for the music database.

Notice that your cursor does not move to the SELECTION SECTION part of the screen. This is because this form is used to manipulate two tables simultaneously. The top half of the form, the MENU ENTRY FORM section, manipulates the internal sysmenus table. The bottom half manipulates the related sysmenuitems

```
┌─────────────────────────────────────────────────────────────────────────────┐
│ ☒                                                                    _ □ ×    │
│ PERFORM:☐ █Query█ Next  Previous  View  Add  Update  Remove  Table  Screen  ...│
│ Searches the active database table.              ** 1: sysmenus table**       │
│                                                                               │
│ =========================MENU ENTRY FORM===================================== │
│                                                                               │
│ Menu Name:  [                        ]                                        │
│                                                                               │
│ Menu Title: [                                                              ]  │
│ ──────────────────────────SELECTION SECTION──────────────────────────────    │
│                                                                               │
│ Selection Number:                        Selection Type:                      │
│                                                                               │
│ Selection                                                                     │
│ Text:                                                                         │
│                                                                               │
│ Selection                                                                     │
│ Action:                                                                       │
│                                                                               │
│                                                                               │
│                                                                               │
└─────────────────────────────────────────────────────────────────────────────┘
```

Figure 6–15   *ISQL menus are built using standard forms.*

table. The `sysmenus` table stores each menu you create, whether the main menu or a submenu, and the `sysmenuitems` table stores the individual items that compose each of those menus. On the second line of the form the current table is shown between pairs of asterisks (**).

note   *ISQL stores the structure of your user menus in two system tables: `sysmenus` and `sysmenuitems`. After you create any menus, those tables will subsequently appear in your table selection lists.*

Now that you have created the main menu—a row in the `sysmenus` table—you need to add menu items to it. To do this you need to switch to the detail table for this form, the `sysmenuitems` table. Choose `Detail` from the `User-menu` submenu. Your screen should resemble Figure 6-16.

You should see that the current table has changed to `sysmenuitems`. To reflect this on the form, brackets appear around all of

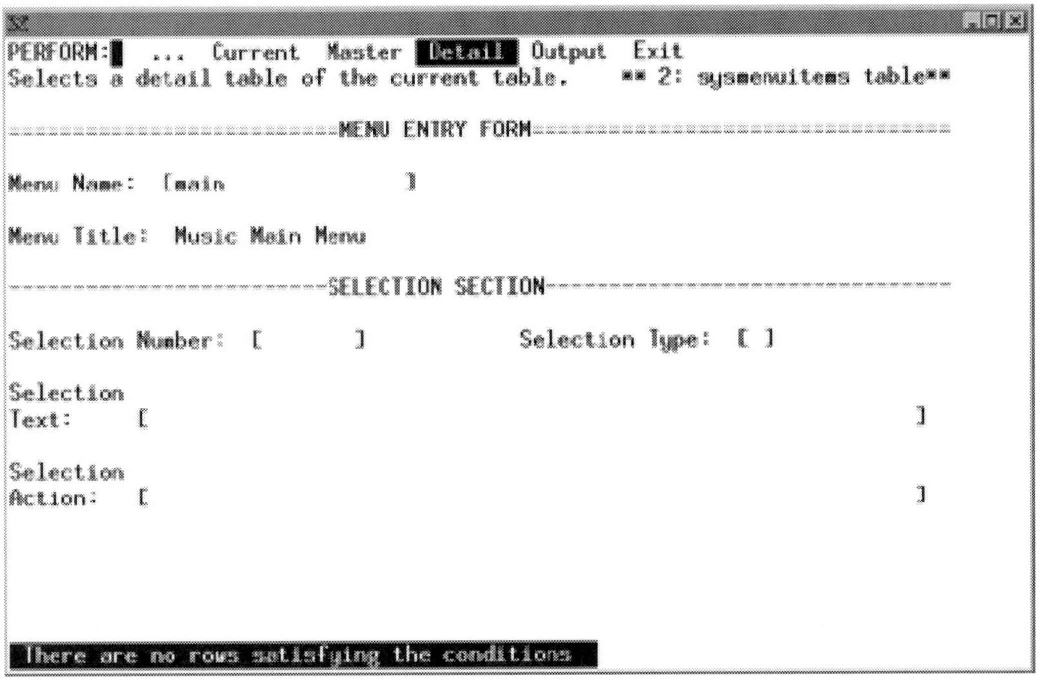

Figure 6–16 *ISQL menu items are each detail items for a specific menu.*

the columns for this detail table. This includes the Menu Name column, since it is the foreign key by which the menu items are related to the menus. Finally, notice the error message at the bottom. When you switch to a detail table, the form automatically queries the detail table for all rows that correspond to the current row of the master table. For now, you have no detail rows. The next step is to create them.

Choose Add and create the sysmenuitems row shown in Figure 6-17.

Notice that the Selection Type value (F) indicates that this Selection Action of performers is a form. Now add another detail row, this time representing the performers report. Its Selection Action will also be performers, but the Selection Type will be R to indicate that this action will launch a report. When you exit the menu creation form, choose Run from the User-menu submenu. You should see the menu shown in Figure 6-14. Try it out.

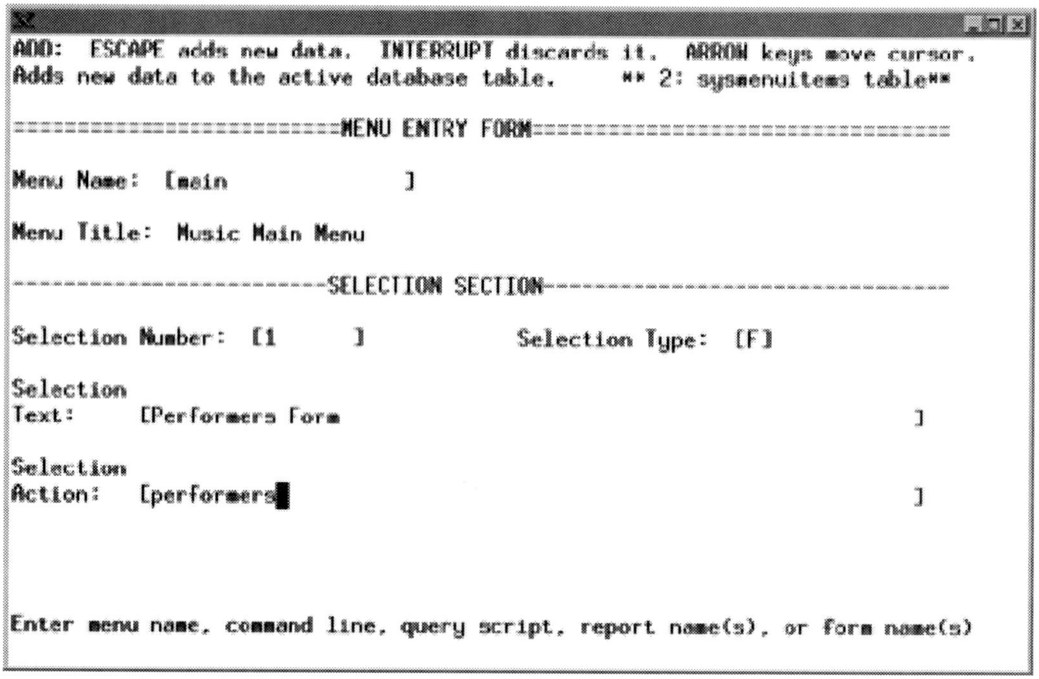

```
ADD:  ESCAPE adds new data.  INTERRUPT discards it.  ARROW keys move cursor.
Adds new data to the active database table.      ** 2: sysmenuitems table**

=========================MENU ENTRY FORM=========================

Menu Name: [main                ]

Menu Title:  Music Main Menu

---------------------------SELECTION SECTION--------------------------------

Selection Number: [1      ]           Selection Type:  [F]

Selection
Text:      [Performers Form                                        ]

Selection
Action:    [performers█                                           ]




Enter menu name, command line, query script, report name(s), or form name(s)
```

Figure 6–17 *Adding a menu detail item to the main menu.*

Summary

In this chapter you learned how to create simple forms, reports, and menus with ISQL. In each case you learned only the most useful fundamentals. Each of these tools has more features with which you can build increasingly sophisticated applications. In fact, many mission-critical business applications have been built with these three tools as the core. However, the limitations of these tools begin to hamper development as you use them to create applications of greater complexity. For that reason, most elaborate Informix applications instead use combinations of other development tools, such as Informix-4GL (Chapters 10 through 14) and Informix-ESQL/C (Chapter 15).

Nonetheless, for straightforward applications and simple data entry, you should not overlook the utility of the ISQL toolkit.

Extra Credit

Q&A

Question	Answer
When I use a form for QBE, how can I match an empty field?	Use = by itself in a field to instruct the form to return only those rows that have no value for that field.
In a report, can I select expressions of the kind available with native SQL, such as math operations and subscripts?	You can include `select` statements of any complexity in your report. If you choose to use expressions, you'll need to assign them aliases so that you can refer to those values in your `format` section by their alias names.

Exercises

1. Create a default form for each of your tables.
2. Use the `albums` form to enter your favorite album.
3. Update that row with a rating of 9.
4. Delete that album; it's overrated anyway.
5. Create a default report for each of your tables.
6. Package all of your forms and reports into a custom user menu. Create a forms submenu for your forms, and a reports submenu for your reports.

## Part 3

SQL Advanced Tools

Good morning. I hope you've recovered from last night's overindulgences. Isaac's got the coffee on, and the cassette player on high volume. Maybe a little "Help!" from the Beatles will get your circulation flowing. Now, follow along on your tour map as I preview this part's itinerary.

Chapters 7, "Intermediate SQL," and 8, "Advanced SQL Queries," complete the treatment of SQL proper. In the first of the two chapters you'll explore the set-based nature of SQL, and learn more about group and aggregate functions. Following that, Chapter 8 explains how to address multiple tables. It shows how to *join* tables, a critical operation for databases of any complexity. It also introduces views, synonyms, and subqueries. When you can master these, you'll save yourself plenty of procedural coding as you develop applications with Informix.

Chapter 9, "Stored Procedures and Triggers," explores the tools you'll need when even these advanced SQL components aren't sufficient for your application. Beth Popovich steps to the open mike to lend her dulcet voice to this important topic. Stored procedures allow you to capture sets of SQL and procedural statements within the database itself. Beth also explains triggers, mechanisms that activate stored procedures when certain database events occur. You learn how you can use stored procedures and triggers to develop efficient and reusable SQL functions.

Remember, there's a midnight dance on the Lido deck after that, so bring your platform shoes. You won't want to miss the Village People's "Cruisin'" crackling from the phonograph.

Chapter

7

Intermediate SQL

This is the second of three chapters devoted to SQL. The first half of this chapter covers all of the clauses in the `select` statement that were deferred in Chapter 5, "Basic SQL." Chapter 8, "Advanced SQL Queries," covers those remaining SQL statements that involve multiple tables.

Introduction

This chapter explores the SQL toolkit further, examining both the `select` statement in greater detail and the SQL operators that are applicable in a multi-user environment. Additionally, it presents the topic of index creation, whose only function is to enhance system performance in a large database.

More on the `select` Statement

....

Chapter 5 introduced the `select` statement, and showed by example how you use it to extract specific data from tables. You'll remember that the complete list of clauses was not explored in that chapter. The following components were specifically excluded:

- `group by` clause
- `having` clause
- `into temp` clause
- `union` clause
- subqueries

Although subqueries are explored in Chapter 8, the first four of these items are explained in detail in the sections that follow. The order in which each is used within a `select` statement follows:

```
select expression-list
  from table-list
[where condition-list]
[group by aggregated-column-list]
[having aggregate-comparison-conditions]
[union another-select-statement]
[order by order-list]
[into temp temp-table-name]
```

As before, only the `select` and `from` clauses are mandatory. Each of the other clauses may be combined or included separately.

The `group by` Clause

The `group by` clause in a `select` statement aggregates data into summary rows, which represent groups of rows that share values for each column listed in the `select` list. Usually, the `group by` clause is combined with aggregate functions: `count`, `min`, `max`, `sum`, and `avg`. In Chapter 5, the aggregates were applied to the whole table. This chapter shows how the aggregate functions are applied to groups of rows.

Without Aggregate Functions

Not all uses of the `group by` clause include an aggregate expression, but without one the result set is the same as produced when using the `distinct` qualifier. For example, the following two `select` statements, each designed to show all the genres that have albums defined, produce identical results:

```
select distinct genre
  from albums;

select genre
  from albums
 group by genre;

genre


blues
classical
disco
pop
rock
soul
zydeco
8 row(s) retrieved.
```

The `group by` clause combines multiple similar rows into a single row, which has the same result in this case as using the `distinct` keyword. Notice that of the eight rows returned in the previous example, only seven are seen. The eighth row is null, indicating that one album selected has no `genre` defined.

Using Aggregate Functions

When you use the aggregate functions with a `group by` clause, they are applied to each group of like data. After each group is formed, any aggregate functions are then applied to that group. Examine the following refinement of the previous example, where this time the number of occurrences of each genre is listed:

```
select genre, count(*)
  from albums
 group by genre;


genre                (count(*))


                          1
blues                     1
classical                 1
disco                     1
pop                       7
rock                      9
soul                      1
zydeco                    1
8 row(s) retrieved.
```

note *If your* select *list contains a mix of nonaggregate and aggregate expressions, you must group by every nonaggregate expression. That way, the aggregate expressions can act on groups of rows of similar data.*

If you want to sort the data, add the order by clause last, as in the following example that counts the number of albums by artist:

```
select artist, count(*)
  from albums
 group by artist
 order by 2;


artist                            (count(*))


Double Trouble                          1
Monkees                                 1
Go-Gos                                  1

 ...
```

```
Bay City Rollers                              2
Culture Club                                  2
Beatles                                       4
```

```
17 row(s) retrieved.
```

This query creates groups of `albums` rows that share artists, and to each of those groups applies the `count(*)` function. After the group totals are computed, the rows are sorted according to the `order by` clause. Notice the use of the `2` in the `order by` clause. Chapter 5 introduced the concept of applying a select number, the position of an expression in the `select` list, to the `order by` clause. Such a shortcut can also be used in the `group by` clause, as in the following example, which groups and sorts the result set by `artist`:

```
select artist, min(rating), max(rating)
   from albums
 where genre = 'pop'
 group by 1
 order by 1;
```

```
artist                        (min)    (max)

Bay City Rollers                0        4
Culture Club                    1        2
Go-Gos                          6        6
Milli Vanilli                   4        4
Monkees                         7        7
```

```
5 row(s) retrieved.
```

Just as with any other `select` statement, you can include display labels in your `select` list. These temporary column names last only for the duration of the current `select` statement. The following query, which calculates how much has been spent by format and sorts the results in descending order, shows how a display label creates friendly column headers:

```
select format, count(*) num_copies,
       sum(amount_paid) total_paid, avg(amount_paid) avg_paid
  from album_copies
 group by 1
 order by 4 desc;
```

format	num_copies	total_paid	avg_paid
laser	2	$29.99	$29.99
video	2	$39.00	$19.50
LP	2	$25.00	$12.50
CD	10	$90.30	$11.29
tape	4	$28.93	$9.64
8track	2	$14.95	$7.48

6 row(s) retrieved.

Notice that the avg_paid column's values do not match the average you would calculate if you divided the total_paid value by the num_copies value for each row. This happens because some of the data rows have a null amount_paid value. The avg function excludes any rows with null values from its calculations.

The having Clause

The having clause allows you to place conditions on the values that the group by clause returns. It is like the where clause, but instead of applying restrictions to individual rows, the having clause qualifies groups of rows. Its syntax is otherwise similar to the comparison conditions used in the where clause. The following example shows how the having clause can be used to refine a previous query to show only your most popular artists:

```
select artist, count(*)
  from albums
 group by artist
having count(*) > 1
 order by 2 desc;
```

artist   (count(*))

```
Beatles                              4

Bay City Rollers                     2

Culture Club                         2


3 row(s) retrieved.
```

It is legal, but almost never done, to use a `having` clause without a `group by` clause. In such cases, the qualifying conditions in the `having` clause are applied to the entire result set; that is, the results of the query are treated as a single group, and the `having` clause is applied once to that group. When you use a `having` clause without a `group by` clause, the `select` list can contain only aggregate expressions; otherwise, the result set could not be treated as a group. If the `having` clause is satisfied by the result set, one row is returned; otherwise, no rows are returned by the `select` statement. The following example illustrates a case where the `having` clause is satisfied by the result set:

```
select min(birth_date) oldest_born_on,
       max(birth_date) youngest_born_on
  from performers
 where last_name = 'Jackson'
having count(*) >= 5;


oldest_born_on youngest_born_on


05/04/1951     08/29/1958


1 row(s) retrieved.
```

In this example, the `having` clause acts like a conditional statement on the result set. If the `having` clause condition is met (there are at least 5 `Jackson` performers in the table), one row of data is returned; otherwise, no rows of data are returned.

I did say that this was almost never done.

The union Clause

The union clause allows you to combine the results of multiple select statements into a single result set after removing any duplicates. Consider the following example, which combines data from separate tables into a single *compound query*. In this case, the intent of the query is to find those performers who either perform on more than three albums or are deceased. Because one of these criteria calls for a group operation and the other does not, their results cannot be generated in a single select statement, except as follows:

```
select last_name, first_name
   from album_performers
 group by 1, 2
having count(*) > 3

union

select last_name, first_name
   from performers
 where death_date is not null
 order by 1, 2;


last_name          first_name

Garcia             Jerry
Harrison           George
Lennon             John
McCartney          Paul
Orbison            Roy
Pilatus            Rob
Starr              Ringo
Vaughan            Stevie Ray

8 row(s) retrieved.
```

Notice how the order by clause is applied to the combined set of rows returned from both parts of the select statement. Its placement at the end of the last component statement reflects the timing of when it is applied. When you use an order by clause with a compound query you must refer to any ordering columns by number, not by name.

note

When you use the union *keyword to create a compound query, the corresponding columns in the component* select *statements need not have the same names, but they must match in number and data type.*

Union All

When you include the all keyword in a union clause, any duplicates—which are otherwise removed by default—are instead included. It is rare that you will need to use the union all clause, but it is included here for completeness. Modify the previous query to add the all keyword after the union clause. Your results should resemble the following:

```
last_name          first_name

Garcia             Jerry
Harrison           George
Lennon             John
Lennon             John
McCartney          Paul
Orbison            Roy
Pilatus            Rob
Starr              Ringo
Vaughan            Stevie Ray

9 row(s) retrieved.
```

An additional row has been included, one that satisfies both of the component select statements.

The into temp Clause

Normally, the results of a select statement are displayed directly to the user. With the into temp clause, you instead capture those rows into a temporary table, one created implicitly by the select statement and which evaporates when the current session ends. You use the `into temp` clause to save the results of a query so that you can refer to that data repeatedly without having to reselect it.

Let's say that you want to perform some analysis on your favorite albums, those with a rating over 7. You create this initial result set with a statement like the following:

```
select *
  from albums
 where rating > 7
   into temp best_albums with no log;

6 row(s) retrieved into temp table.
```

tip

The optional `with no log` specifier of the `into temp` clause prevents Informix from incurring the overhead of a transaction log for the implicit temporary table created. This is a good thing. Unless your temp table will specifically be used for transactions, and thus require a log, use the `with no log` option to improve performance.

The columns in a temporary table inherit the names and data types of the columns from which they are derived. A consequence of this assignment is that if you include any expressions in your select list, you must assign display labels to them as names for the temp table to inherit.

Note that you cannot use an `order by` clause with an `into temp` clause. This is because the rows in a table, even a temporary one, are intrinsically unordered. Rows, by definition, cannot be stored in an ordered fashion within any table.

Now that the temporary table exists, you can perform SQL operations on it as you would on any other table. It has been populated with the data from your six best albums, so any subsequent `select` statements executed against it will choose from only those six rows. For example, to see which artists are most popular on those albums, execute the following statement:

```
select artist, count(*) num_albums
  from best_albums
 group by artist
 order by 2 desc, 1;
```

artist	num_albums
Beatles	4
Double Trouble	1
Three Tenors	1

3 row(s) retrieved.

The temporary table exists until your session ends, or until you explicitly drop it. Thus, you can execute multiple queries against this selected subset of data.

Improving Query Performance

As your `select` statements and databases become more complex, you may notice that the time it takes for queries to execute increases. One tool that you can create in an effort to reduce the query execution time is an index.

Indexes

You learned in Chapter 3, "DB-Access," that indexes are internal data maps that Informix uses to enhance performance and enforce constraints. Yet so far, all mention of indexes has been regarding their use as tools to enforce constraints. In addition to that function, indexes also enhance performance by storing the disk addresses of frequently accessed data. Imagine trying to find a person at home when you know only his or her neighborhood, but not the street address. You would need to stop at every house and inquire within, sequentially visiting every house until you found your target. Without an index, a database searches for columns that contain values of interest in just the same way, examining every row in a table in search of the values specified in the `where` clause.

When the tables are small, such as with the `music` database, sequentially scanning for data is fast enough. However, when a table contains tens or hundreds of thousands of rows, you should consider indexing columns you frequently use in your `where` or `order by` clauses. The syntax to create an index follows:

```
create [unique] index index-name on table-name (column-list)
```

where *index-name* is a unique name you supply, *table-name* specifies the table that contains the column(s) of interest, and *column-list* is a comma-separated list of columns that this index will map. When you use the `unique` keyword, Informix guarantees that no two rows for the table can share values for *column-list*. You need the `resource` privilege (see "Permissions: Database-Level" later in this chapter) to create an index.

Most tables usually have multiple indexes attached to them. For example, you saw in Chapter 3 that the `albums` table had three indexes associated with it, each in place to enforce a constraint. Indexes that Informix creates to support constraints serve two purposes. They are also used to enhance query performance.

Whether you need to create any indexes explicitly depends entirely on your system performance. If your music collection grew very large, for example, and you discovered that you were commonly performing queries based on the year in which albums were issued, you might issue the following SQL statement:

```
create index ix_album_issue_yr on albums(issue_year);
```

It is likely that the performance of statements like the following would execute faster with such an index in place.

```
select issue_year, title, artist
  from albums
 where issue_year = 1968
 order by 1;
```

 tip *Add an index. If a query is slow, and accesses a large table, consider adding an index on columns used in the `where` or `order by` clause. Performance increases can be dramatic.*

You can try this experiment on the `music` database, but because the `albums` table has so few rows the performance difference with or without the index will be negligible.

Indexes remain in place until you drop them explicitly, as follows:

```
drop index index-name
```

For best performance you should drop indexes that you no longer use, because Informix must update the index address maps any time the indexed contents of the table change. Likewise, too many indexes on a table that changes significantly can slow performance. However, you should not be timid about creating an index if you think one might help. They are easy to drop if ineffective, and the benefits of faster queries often outweigh the costs of slower updates.

Database Statistics

When Informix receives a query request, it has to choose how to find the data. For example, it needs to determine whether indexes exist, and if so, whether it should use them. When tables are very small, it is faster for the database engine to sequentially scan every row than to examine an index to find the address of rows of interest, and only then find the data. Informix generates its *query plan*, or exact method of how it will solve a query, based on statistics such as the number of rows in each table. However, Informix does not maintain this count of table rows automatically. Rather, it relies on diligent users or DBAs to periodically execute the statement that keeps these counts up to date. The syntax to do so follows:

```
update statistics
```

tip

When your database is large and the number of rows in a table changes dramatically, you should execute the update statistics *command to refresh Informix's internal table counts.*

Multi-User SQL

A few SQL operators exist to manage the database conflicts that can arise when multiple users attempt to access or update the same data simultaneously. The tools that handle these interactions deal with the extra overhead that the database must invoke to referee concurrent requests. Thus, in addition to developers in a multi-user environment, users concerned with system performance—ways to reduce unnecessary overhead—should also have an awareness of these SQL operators. If you are neither in a multi-user environment nor yet concerned with enhancing the performance of your database interactions, you can skip this section for now.

This treatment of multi-user SQL encompasses the following topics:

- Permissions
- Locking
- Isolation levels

Permissions

In some cases, you may want to restrict or allow certain users varying permissions in your database, or to specific items within it. For example, you may want to prevent certain users from updating the values in specific tables, or you may choose that another user should have complete permissions to modify your database structure. Although none of the examples in these sections refer to the `music` database, you'll be able to see by example how custom permissions schemes can help you manage sensitive data. With the `grant` and `revoke` SQL operators, you can manage these permissions at the following decreasing levels of granularity:

- Database
- Table
- Column

These permissions form a veto-based hierarchy. That is, a user first needs database privileges to see any tables within the database.

Without it, all privileges below it are superseded, or vetoed. By default, database permissions grant access to all tables within it, but you can revoke those permissions selectively. Finally, if a table-level permission is in effect, that privilege can be selectively revoked at the column level. Thus, if any position in the hierarchy has its privileges revoked, all levels below it are revoked as well.

Privileges are also applied to stored procedures (see Chapter 9, "Stored Procedures and Triggers"), sets of related SQL and procedural statements you create for custom purposes.

Database-Level

When you create a database, you are the only user with permission to access it. With the following statement, you, as de facto DBA, grant other users specific privileges in your database:

```
grant [connect|resource|dba] to user-name
```

where *user-name* is either a comma-separated list of user names or the keyword `public`, which is shorthand for the set of all users. The database-level privileges, in increasing order of authority, are `connect`, `resource`, and `dba`. The `connect` privilege allows a user to query and modify data, unless further restricted by table- or column-level restrictions. With the `connect` privilege, a user can also create temporary tables, views, and synonyms (see Chapter 8). The `resource` privilege subsumes `connect` privileges and grants a user the additional authority to extend a database: to add tables, indexes, and stored procedures. Finally, the `dba` privilege grants all authority on a database to a given user, including the ability to create and drop any object, regardless of the creator, and the authority to grant privileges to any other user.

 The `informix` user ID, which is present on every Informix installation, is automatically granted `dba` privileges on every Informix database. In this regard, it is a privileged superuser for all database interactions, similar to the `root` ID on UNIX systems.

What you give, you can also take away. The `revoke` statement withdraws the permissions the `grant` statement allows:

```
revoke [connect|resource|dba] from user-name
```

For example, the following sequence of SQL statements grants the `connect` privilege to all but three troublesome users:

```
grant connect to public;
revoke connect from curly, larry, moe;
```

Table-Level

Users with `connect` permission to a database are automatically granted permission to examine and change the data within all of its tables. That is, they are granted all table-level permissions except `alter` and `reference` (see the list that follows). So, while you can grant permissions on a table, more often you will revoke them instead, since table-level privileges are granted by default once a user has at least the `connect` privilege. The syntax for these statements follows:

```
grant table-level-privileges on object-name to user-name
revoke table-level-privileges on object-name from user-name
```

where *object-name* is the name of a table, view, or synonym; *user-name* is the keyword `public` or a comma-separated list of user or role names (see the "Roles" section); and *table-level-privileges* is either the keyword `all` or a comma-separated list of any of the following operations:

- `select`: View data, unless restricted at the column level
- `update`: Update data, unless restricted at the column level
- `insert`: Insert rows of data
- `delete`: Delete rows of data
- `index`: Create an index, as long as the user also has the `resource` privilege
- `alter`: Alter the table's structure, as long as the user also has the `resource` privilege
- `reference`: Create a referential constraint, as long as the user also has the `resource` privilege

For example, with the following sequence of SQL statements you can ensure that careless users cannot change important data.

```
grant connect to public;
revoke update, insert, delete on mining_plans from dopey, sleepy;
```

Note that this leaves only the `select` table-level privilege in effect for `dopey` and `sleepy` on `mining_plans`. This is because without the `resource` database-level privilege, the `index` table-level privilege is inactive, and the `alter` and `reference` privileges are not granted automatically with the `connect` privilege. You can achieve the same permissions structure with the following more explicit sequence of SQL statements:

```
grant connect to public;
revoke all on mining_plans from dopey, sleepy;
grant select on mining_plans to dopey, sleepy;
```

Column-Level

Column-level privileges can be granted to refine the `select`, `update`, and `reference` table-level permissions. To do so, use the following addition to the table-level syntax:

```
grant [select|update|references] (column-list)
    on object-name to user-name
```

where `column-list` is a comma-separated list of columns in `object-name`. You cannot revoke column-level privileges. Instead, you must revoke the entire table-level privilege, and then grant privileges on the appropriate columns.

You might use column-level privileges to restrict access to sensitive data, such as with the following sequence of SQL statements:

```
grant connect to public;
revoke all on players from public;
grant select on players to coach, assistant_coach;
grant select (player, position, start_date) on players to public;
```

Stored Procedures

Stored procedures are custom functions that you create and store within the database engine. In practice, they extend the built-in SQL statement set. Stored procedures by default are executable by any user with `connect` permission. With the following two statements, you can control which users can execute specific stored procedures:

```
grant execute on stored-procedure-name to user-name
revoke execute on stored-procedure-name from user-name
```

where *user-name* is the keyword `public` or a comma-separated list of user or role names, and *stored-procedure-name* is the name of a previously created stored procedure.

Roles

Roles are timesaving database devices that help you assign the same permission scheme to groups of users. A role is a pseudo-user you create, and to which you assign users who will share privileges. You create a role as follows:

```
create role role-name
```

where *role-name* is any name you assign. Only a DBA can create a role. The following statement drops a previously created role:

```
drop role role-name
```

After creating a role, you craft a custom series of table- or column-level privileges for it with the appropriate `grant` and `revoke` statements. You include or exclude users from a role with the following statements:

```
grant role-name to user-name
revoke role-name from user-name
```

For example, the following sequence of SQL statements creates a `top_secret` role, assigns three users to it, and gives all of those users expansive privileges.

```
revoke all on evil_plans from public;
create role top_secret;
grant top_secret to bond, helm, powers;
grant all on evil_plans to top_secret;
```

With judicious use of the various `grant` and `revoke` statements, you can ensure that only authorized activity will occur in your database.

Locking

In a multi-user database environment, certain controls must exist to prevent multiple users from trying to access or modify the same data at the same time. Consider, for example, if the following two SQL statements were launched by different users simultaneously:

```
update album_copies
   set location = 'truck'
 where location = 'car';
select *
  from album_copies
 where location = 'car';
```

Depending on how the timing of the statements interacted, the `select` statement might return any or none of the following rows:

album_num	format	location	amount_paid
6	CD	car	$14.95
2	8track	car	$6.95
16	8track	car	$8.00

3 row(s) retrieved.

Usually, returning all or none of the deleted data is harmless. The deletions could just as well have occurred days before or after the `select` statement. The potentially troubling circumstance is when only some of the updated rows are retrieved by the `select` statement. Imagine a month-end banking application, designed to increment multiple accounts based on the interest earned. Creating a bank statement that ran during these updates and produced a mix of updated and original data would be incorrect.

Other concerns arise when two processes both attempt to update the same set of data simultaneously with differing values.

How should the database engine decide which updates from each process take precedence? It needs guidance from the user. Locks are the controls with which you offer guidance for managing *concurrency*, where multiple processes want to use the same data at the same time. With a lock you place a reservation on certain data, which guarantees that the database server will allow no other process to modify it until you release the lock. Other programs that try to do so receive an error message, or must wait for your lock to be released.

Locks can be either *exclusive*, which grant you sole access to the locked object, or *shared*, which allow other processes to see the object, but not to change it. Although there can be only one exclusive lock on a given object at a time, there may be multiple simultaneous shared locks in effect. Exclusive locks are needed only when you intend to modify the locked object.

Database-Level

Locks are available at several levels of granularity or scope. At the highest level, you can lock an entire database when you open it with the following extension to the `database` statement:

```
database database-name exclusive
```

This statement grants you sole access to the database. When you exclude the `exclusive` keyword, as you do almost every time you open a database, you place an implicit shared lock on the database name. This ensures that no other user can rename or drop the database while you are using it. Database locking is often used in production environments when massive database changes are being applied during an off-peak maintenance period. Database locks are released when the database closes.

Table-Level

With the following syntax, you can lock an entire table:

```
lock table table-name in [share|exclusive] mode
```

You might use a shared table lock before executing a report, such as the bank statement example, that cannot afford to have a mix of original and modified data. Alternatively, if you are using INFORMIX-OnLine Dynamic Server, you can receive the same concurrency protection by setting the proper isolation level (see the "Isolation Levels" section later in the chapter). Incidentally, Informix implicitly locks a table in exclusive mode whenever it performs certain table maintenance operations such as `alter table` or `create index`.

If your database was created with transaction logging, you can execute the `lock table` statement only within a transaction.

You release a table-level lock with the following statement:

```
unlock table table-name
```

Be a polite programmer. Polite programmers explicitly release resources when they are through with them. Table locks are no exception.

Row- and Page-Level

The finest level of granularity available for locking depends on how you have defined your tables. You'll remember from Chapter 4, "Creating Databases and Tables," that you can specify a table's lock mode. Although the default is page-level, you can also specify row-level locking. Pages are physical units of disk storage that usually contain several rows of data. In cases when you would lock multiple rows on a single page, page-level locking is more efficient than row-level locking. However, by locking at the page level you increase the chance that you might lock a row needed by another user. In most applications, the default page-level lock mode provides a good balance between performance and concurrency.

You cannot explicitly lock a specific row or page. Instead, Informix creates an exclusive lock implicitly when it updates a row, and, depending on the isolation level, may place a shared lock on rows it reads.

Wait Mode

When a program encounters a lock, it either waits on the lock or fails and returns an error code. You determine which occurs with one of the following statements:

```
set lock mode to not wait
set lock mode to wait [wait-time seconds]
```

where `wait-time` is the number of seconds the process should wait on the lock. If `wait-time` expires and the lock has not been released, an error is returned just as if the lock mode were set to `not wait`. If you do not specify a maximum wait time, the process will wait on a lock indefinitely. The lock mode of `not wait` is the default. These statements remain in effect until another `set lock mode` statement is encountered or the current session ends.

Isolation Levels

With INFORMIX-OnLine, you can set the isolation level for your session, which determines how your reads from the database affect and are affected by other concurrent users. The different levels place increasingly stringent requirements on what changes other processes are allowed to make to rows you are examining and to what degree you can read data currently being modified by other processes. Isolation levels are meaningful only for reads, not for inserts, updates, or deletes. You set the isolation level for your session with the following statement:

```
set isolation to isolation-level
```

where `isolation-level` is one of the following, in decreasing order of permissiveness:

- `dirty read`
- `committed read` (the default)
- `cursor stability`
- `repeatable read`

Dirty Read is the most efficient and simplest isolation level. When it is in effect, your process neither places nor honors any locks. Regardless of whether data on disk is committed or uncommitted, a Dirty Read isolation level allows the data to be scanned. The danger is that a program using Dirty Read isolation might read a row that is later rolled back. Therefore, be sure that you account for this possibility or read only from static tables when this isolation level is set.

 For greatest efficiency, use the Dirty Read isolation level when your application permits.

The Committed Read isolation level ensures that only rows committed in the database are read. As it reads each row, OnLine checks for the presence of a lock. If one exists, it ignores the row. Because OnLine places no locks with this isolation level, using Committed Read is almost as efficient as using the Dirty Read isolation level.

The last two isolation levels are most important when you are using explicit cursors, database tools that allow you to treat sets of rows serially (see Chapter 13, "Cursors and Dynamic SQL"). Cursor Stability causes the database to place a lock on the current row as it reads the row. This lock ensures that the row will not change while the current process is using it. When the server reads and locks the next row, it releases the previous lock. The placement of locks suggests that processes with this isolation level will incur additional overhead as they read data.

With Repeatable Read, processes lock every row that has been read in the current transaction. This mode guarantees that reading the same rows later would find the same data. Consequently, Repeatable Read processes can generate many locks and hold them for a long time.

Knowing which isolation level to use is not always clear. Dirty Read offers the best performance, but Repeatable Read guarantees the most stability. You should discuss with your DBA which isolation levels are most appropriate for your application.

Summary

This chapter covered more of the SQL toolkit. The first half explored the `select` statement in detail, showing how to use the group by clause to create summary rows in SQL. With the having clause you can apply comparison conditions to those summary rows, just as you apply restrictions to single rows using the where clause.

Additional components of the select statement include the union operator, which allows you to combine the results of multiple select statements into a single result set, and the into temp specifier. With into temp, you store the results of a select statement for the duration of the current session.

The second half of the chapter introduced several topics relevant to operating effectively in a large or multi-user environment. The first of these was indexes, internal data maps that Informix uses to enforce constraints and enhance query performance. You can create your own custom indexes as system performance demands.

The remaining topics showed how you could include SQL statements for effective cooperation in a multi-user environment. With the judicious use of permissions, locking, wait modes, and isolation levels, you can instruct the database engine to gracefully handle database conflicts that might occur.

Extra Credit

Q & A

Question

I'm the DBA who was asked by a developer which multi-user settings should be used. The interactions of the various isolation levels and lock modes seem complex. My application must accommodate multiple users simultaneously and with strict data integrity. System performance is not a problem. What are the best settings?

Answer

Consider using the following statements at the beginning of any SQL-based application programs:

```
set lock mode to wait;
set isolation to repeatable read;
```

If performance problems do not arise, keep these settings and attend to more interesting topics.

Exercises

1. It is common that you need to know the sorted distribution of data in a column. Write a query that shows how many performers were born in each year, sorted from the highest frequency to the lowest.
2. Modify the previous query so it shows only those values that have duplicates.
3. Don't just do the previous exercises, learn them. Queries of the following form are so useful that they should roll easily off your fingertips:

```
select expression, count(*)
  from table-name
 group by 1
having count(*) > 1
 order by 2 desc;
```

Exercise Answers

1. Your query should resemble the following:

```
select year(birth_date), count(*)
  from performers
 group by 1
 order by 2 desc;
```

2. Add a having clause to the previous query, as follows:

```
select year(birth_date), count(*)
  from performers
 group by 1
having count(*) > 1
 order by 2 desc;
```

3. Really.

Chapter

8

Advanced SQL Queries

This is the last chapter devoted to SQL proper. SQL will continue to be the core command set on which future chapters are built, but this is the last chapter devoted to its fundamentals.

Introduction

This chapter covers the most advanced SQL topics, those involving multiple tables. The first and most fundamental multiple table operation is the join. It allows you to relate multiple tables dynamically, based on values they have in common. Views will follow. Views are permanent pseudo-tables; they are based on other tables, but have additional conditions applied. Synonyms are permanent alternative names for tables or views that exist on a local or networked database. Finally, we will address subqueries, those `select` statements that are nested within other SQL statements. Generally, each of these four constructs requires you to understand how multiple tables can act in concert.

Joining Tables

Joining is the method you use to select related data from multiple tables simultaneously. Remember that one important design principle was to reduce redundancy. With less redundancy, updates have to be performed in a single place only. The balancing disadvantage is that the data may seem scattered. Joining is the method used to paste the scattered data back together.

A *join* is an SQL operation that combines rows from two tables based on columns shared by each table. You declare the join by creating a *join condition* in your `select` statement that relates the tables. An example of a join condition is:

```
where albums.album_num = album_copies.album_num
```

When this `select` statement executes, Informix constructs a virtual row that combines data from both tables where the rows share values for this join column. That is, those `albums` rows are selected where their `album_num` value is equal to the value of `album_num` in any `album_copies` rows. The following sections explore this critical operation in detail.

Equijoins

Let's say that you want to list information about your Beatles CDs. The data about albums in general—their titles, issue dates, artists and such—is in the `albums` table; but the information about your copies of the albums (what format, how much you paid, where they are) is in a separate table, the `album_copies` table. The following two examples show how you can use two separate queries to find this data. Try the following queries to perform this "join-by-hand."

```
select album_num, title, issue_year
  from albums
 where artist = 'Beatles'
 order by 1;

album_num title                                issue_year

       3 Abbey Road                                  1969
       4 Help!                                       1965
       5 Revolver                                    1966
       6 Please Please Me                            1963
```

Once you have selected the `album_num` values, you can then build the second query to select data from the `album_copies` table. Enter and run the following statement, using the `album_num` values revealed by the previous query:

```
select album_num, format, location, amount_paid
  from album_copies
 where album_num in (3,4,5,6)
 order by 1;

album_num format location                 amount_paid

       3 CD     shelf 5                       $16.95
       4 tape   work                           $9,95
       4 CD     shelf 5                        $0.00
       5 CD     shelf 5                       $13.50
       6 CD     car                           $14.95
```

The result set accurately reflects that you have two copies of `album_num` 4, "Help!". You remember: one was a gift from your swell Uncle Marvin.

You can see that this two-step method of selecting data is inadequate. To retrieve the data from both tables at once you must join the tables with an equijoin. An *equijoin* is a join condition where rows from two tables are related based on a column or columns that are equal, as in the following query. It is possible to construct a join where the columns are not equal (*megadweebs* call this operation a theta-join; slowly back away from such people, they are unhealthy), but in practice you will never see it done. Most people simply use the term "join" to refer to an equijoin.

Enter the following query to select the related album information in a single operation:

```
select albums.album_num, title[1,20], issue_year, format,
     amount_paid
  from albums, album_copies
 where albums.artist = 'Beatles'
   and albums.album_num = album_copies.album_num
 order by 1;
```

album_num	title	issue_year	format	amount_paid
3	Abbey Road	1969	CD	$16.95
4	Help!	1965	CD	$0.00
4	Help!	1965	tape	$9.95
5	Revolver	1966	CD	$14.95
6	Please Please Me	1963	CD	$13.50

The equijoin clause in the previous query instructs the database to combine each row from the `albums` table with each matching row from the `album_copies` table where their values for `album_num` are equal. Notice that because `album_num` is in both tables, to avoid ambiguity you must reference the column explicitly by prefixing it with a table name each time it is referenced.

Composite Joins

Sometimes you need to join on a composite key; that is, one that requires more than one column to uniquely identify a row. The `performers` table has a composite primary key: the combination of `first_name` and `last_name`. To join on a composite key you construct an equijoin condition on every component of the key.

For example, let's say that in your role as President of the Bay City Rollers Fan Club, it is your responsibility to send birthday cards to each Roller who performed on `Once Upon a Star`, `album_num` 2 in your collection. The birthday data is in the `performers` table; the performers for that album are stored in the `album_performers` table. Use the following query to join these two tables together on a composite key:

```
select p.last_name, p.first_name, birth_date
  from performers p, album_performers ap
 where ap.album_num = 2
   and ap.last_name  = p.last_name
   and ap.first_name = p.first_name;
```

last_name	first_name	birth_date
Wood	Stuart Woody	02/25/1957
Longmuir	Derek	03/19/1952
Faulkner	Eric	10/21/1955
McKeown	Leslie	11/12/1955
Longmuir	Alan	06/20/1951

Multitable Joins

Each join can relate only two tables together, but by including multiple independent join conditions in a `select` statement, you can include data from several tables at once. Notice how the previous query specified an explicit `album_num`. It is likely that you do not know the value of `album_num` for `Once Upon a Star`. In general, there is no reason for you to remember the value of such item numbers. Instead, you can join `album_performers` to `albums` across `album_num` without ever having to know the specific `album_num`. Try this by adding another join condition to the previous query:

```
select p.last_name, p.first_name, birth_date
  from performers p, album_performers ap, albums a
 where ap.album_num = a.album_num
   and a.title = 'Once Upon a Star'
   and a.artist = 'Bay City Rollers'
   and ap.last_name  = p.last_name
   and ap.first_name = p.first_name;
```

Your output should be the same as for the previous query.

It is not necessary to select those columns that are used only to join tables. Merely include these join columns in the join condition and exclude them from the select *list.*

Figure 8-1 shows the relationships between the three tables. The columns used to join `album_performers` to `performers` are independent of the column that joins `album_performers` to `albums`.

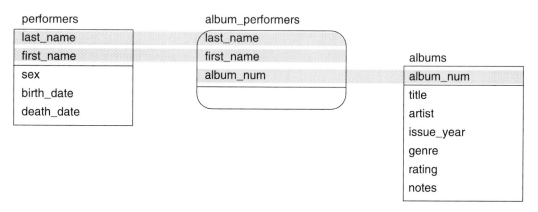

Figure 8–1   *Join columns relate multiple tables independently.*

Cartesian Products

A join creates a set of virtual rows by combining individual rows from multiple tables, based on a value held in common by column(s) from each table. What happens if you select data from multiple tables without including the join condition? For example, the following query is legal, but misleading:

```
select title, format
   from album_copies, albums
  where location = 'car'
  order by title;
```

```
title                          format
Abbey Road                     8track
Abbey Road                     CD
Abbey Road                     8track
```

```
Absolute Rollers - The Best of  8track
Absolute Rollers - The Best of  CD
Absolute Rollers - The Best of  8track
Barrel Full of Monkees          8track
Barrel Full of Monkees          CD
Barrel Full of Monkees          8track
...
Zydeco Live!                    8track
Zydeco Live!                    CD
Zydeco Live!                    8track
```

Only a fraction of the voluminous output is shown. This statement returns many more values than just the titles and formats of the music in your car. Because you did not specify which rows from the `albums` table match which other rows from the `album_copies` table, the database supplies values for *every* possible combination of the two tables. This is a bad thing.

caution

Always supply a join condition when selecting data from multiple tables. If you do not, the database will construct a Cartesian product and return many more rows than you want.

In fact, the number of rows returned is always the product of the number of rows in each table that meet the other criteria in your `select` statement. The term *Cartesian product* comes from a mathematical concept of combining sets, and is a term you need to know. If you don't learn it now, you will have to learn it from a dour database administrator when the DBA castigates you for producing one. This is something you should instead learn from a friend.

Let's revisit the previous query and alter it to examine more clearly the incongruity of the Cartesian product. Add the `album_num` columns to your `select` list, as shown in the following query:

```
select title, albums.album_num, album_copies.album_num, format
  from album_copies, albums
 where location = 'car'
 order by title;
```

title	album_num	album_num	format
Abbey Road	3	2	8track
Abbey Road	3	6	CD
Abbey Road	3	16	8track
Absolute Rollers - The Best of	1	2	8track
Absolute Rollers - The Best of	1	6	CD
Absolute Rollers - The Best of	1	16	8track
Barrel Full of Monkees	16	2	8track
Barrel Full of Monkees	16	6	CD
Barrel Full of Monkees	16	16	8track
...			
Zydeco Live!	22	2	8track
Zydeco Live!	22	6	CD
Zydeco Live!	22	16	8track

Notice especially how the two different album_num values do not match. Only one row in the output shown (where album_num is 16 for both tables) is reasonable.

To repair this query, you need to add the join condition that specifies that the album_num values from each table must equate. The following example includes such an equijoin:

```
select title, albums.album_num, album_copies.album_num, format
  from album_copies, albums
 where location = 'car'
   and album_copies.album_num = albums.album_num
 order by title;
```

title	album_num	album_num	format
Barrel Full of Monkees	16	16	8track
Once Upon a Star	2	2	8track
Please Please Me	6	6	CD

Self-Joins

There are occasions when you need to join a table with itself. Such an operation is called a *self-join*. This occurs when you need to use the same table in a single query to represent two independent instances simultaneously.

Let's say you want to list all of the performers who performed on any album with Ringo Starr. In this case, you need to use the `album_performers` table twice; once to find your albums on which Ringo performed; then independently to list the other performers on those same albums.

The key idea is that the `album_performers` table must be treated as two independent tables in this query. The tool you use to effect this independence is a table alias, introduced in Chapter 5, "Basic SQL." Remember that an alias is a temporary name assigned to a table; the alias lasts only for the duration of the `select` statement. With an alias, you can reference the same table twice in the same `select` statement. You create an alias by following the table name with the alias name you invent. In the following example, the aliases are `ringo_albums`, which represents the instance of `album_performers` on which Ringo performed, and `other_performers`, which represents a second instance of `album_performers` that identifies his co-performers. Try the following query:

```
select unique other_performers.last_name,
       other_performers.first_name
  from album_performers ringo_albums,
       album_performers other_performers
 where ringo_album.last_name = 'Starr'
   and ringo_albums.first_name = 'Ringo'
   and ringo_albums.album_num =
    other_performers.album_num
 order by 1;


last_name           first_name

Capello             Tim
Cummings            Burton
Edmunds             Dave
Harrison            George
Lennon              John
Lofgren             Nils
McCartney           Paul
Rundgren            Todd
Schmidt             Timothy B.
Starkey             Zak
```

```
Starr          Ringo
Walsh          Joe
```

Notice the use of the `unique` qualifier to strip out duplicate rows from the result set. Also, strangely enough, Ringo performed on every album that he was on. (If, instead, we had asked about Milli Vanilli....)

Restrictive Joins

Joins are intrinsically restrictive. That is, each row of data returned by a `select` statement must satisfy the entire set of conditions listed in the `where` clause. This restriction, or elimination of nonqualifying data, occurs not only for the comparison conditions such as `performers.first_name = 'Tito'`, but also for each join condition. Therefore, if a row does not exist in both joined tables with a matching value in the other, no row will be returned. Let's say you want to list all of the performers for every album that starts with `S`. First, use the following query to see which albums comply:

```
select title, artist
   from albums
 where title like 'S%';
```

```
title                            artist

Soul to Soul                     Double Trouble
Sounds of the Okefenokee Swamp   Ambient Sounds
```

Now modify the query by adding a join to the `album_performers` table. You should produce something like the following query:

```
select title, artist, last_name
   from albums, album_performers
 where title like 'S%'
   and albums.album_num = album_performers.album_num;
```

title	artist	last_name
Soul to Soul	Double Trouble	Vaughan
Soul to Soul	Double Trouble	Sublett
Soul to Soul	Double Trouble	Layton
Soul to Soul	Double Trouble	Wynans

No rows are returned for `Sounds of the Okefenokee Swamp` because there are no `album_performers` rows for that album. Those rows are eliminated by the restrictive nature of the join operator.

Outer Joins

For occasions where you want to get data from one table even when there is no corresponding row in the joined table—that is, when you want the join to not be restrictive—you need a construct known as an *outer join*. An outer join is a join condition that preserves all rows from one of the joined tables, the dominant table, even when no corresponding rows exist in the second table, the subservient table. Null values are substituted for all columns that would have been selected from the subservient table. You declare an outer join by inserting the keyword `outer` before the subservient table in the `from` list of the `select` statement.

Modify the previous query to create an outer join with `albums` as the dominant table. The following example shows what your query should look like:

```
select title, artist, last_name
  from albums, outer album_performers
 where title like 'S%'
   and albums.album_num = album_performers.album_num;
```

title	artist	last_name
Soul to Soul	Double Trouble	Vaughan
Soul to Soul	Double Trouble	Sublett
Soul to Soul	Double Trouble	Layton
Soul to Soul	Double Trouble	Wynans
Sounds of the Okefenokee Swamp	Ambient Sounds	

The `Sounds of the Okefenokee Swamp` row has returned. A null value is supplied for the `last_name` column. By including the outer join you allowed the preservation of all the rows from `albums` that met the comparison condition.

Views

Views are virtual tables you construct for specific purposes. They allow you to create custom means of applying conditions and restricting access to actual underlying tables. Informix maintains view definitions in the database, but does not maintain the data associated with a view. A view's data is always derived dynamically from its *base table(s)*, the table(s) from which the view is derived.

The Syntax for the `create view` statement follows:

```
create view view-name [column-list] as
select-statement;
```

where *view-name* is the name of the view you are creating; *column-list* is an optional list of column names for the view; and *select-statement* is any valid `select` statement except one with an `order by` clause, an `into temp` clause, or the `union` operator. The *view-name* must follow the conventions for all SQL identifiers: it must consist solely of characters, numbers, and the underscore character (_), and it can be no longer than 18 characters.

What Is a View?

In practice, a view acts like a table, but with additional conditions already applied to it. You can select data from it; join to it; and, within certain restrictions, perform `update` or `insert` operations against it. Generally the only operation you perform on a view is a `select`, and in this chapter you will learn four ways in which views can simplify certain of your `select` operations. These uses of views are:

- Include a hidden comparison condition
- Restrict the select list
- Present an aggregate as a column
- Hide a complex join

Include a Hidden Comparison Condition

In this example you will create a view called `veterans` that acts in all respects like the `performers` table—the base table—except that whenever you select data from it, certain comparison conditions are always applied in addition to any conditions your `select` statement contains. Create the following view, then select all of its data:

```
create view veterans as
select *
  from performers
 where birth_date < '01/01/1950'
   and death_date is null;

select *
  from veterans
 order by last_name;
```

last_name	first_name	sex	birth_date	death_date
Cummings	Burton	M	12/31/1947	
Dolenz	Mickey	M	03/08/1945	
Domingo	Placido	M	01/21/1941	
Dylan	Bob	M	05/24/1941	
Edmunds	Dave	M	04/15/1944	
Harrison	George	M	02/25/1943	
Hart	Mickey	M	09/11/1943	
Jones	Davy	M	12/30/1945	
Manilow	Barry	M	06/17/1946	
McCartney	Paul	M	06/18/1942	
Nesmith	Michael	M	12/30/1942	
Pavarotti	Luciano	M	10/12/1935	
Preston	Billy	M	09/09/1946	
Rundgren	Todd	M	06/22/1948	

```
Scaggs          Boz                 M    06/08/1944
Starr           Ringo               M    07/07/1940
Tork            Peter               M    02/13/1942
Turner          Dale                M    07/02/1941
Walsh           Joe                 M    12/31/1947
Weir            Bob                 M    10/06/1947
```

Notice that the view inherits the column names from its base table. Any further references to the `veterans` view combines the comparison conditions in the view with any in the current query. For example, if you display all of the performers whose last name starts with `S`, you find the eight rows shown in the following example:

```
select *
  from performers
 where last_name matches 'S*';

last_name         first_name       sex birth_date death_date

Scaggs            Boz              M   06/08/44
Schmit            Timothy B.       M
Schneiderman      Leon             M   01/25/54
Schock            Gina             F
Shannon           Tommy            M
Starkey           Zak              M
Starr             Ringo            M   07/07/40
Sublett           Joe              M
```

Now consider what happens when you, in effect, combine the two `select` statements. Try the following selection from the `veterans` view:

```
select *
  from veterans
 where last_name matches 'S*';

last_name         first_name       sex birth_date death_date

Scaggs            Boz              M   06/08/44
Starr             Ringo            M   07/07/40
```

Notice that the result set is the same as if you had included all the comparison conditions in a single `select` statement. Informix combined the criteria that is always applied whenever you address the `veterans` view

```
where birth_date < '01/01/1950'
   and death_date is null
```

with the new conditions from this listing

```
where last_name matches 'S*'
```

to produce this custom result set.

Restrict the `select` List

A common use of views is to limit the `select` list for a certain table. In this way you can make certain columns invisible when a base table is examined through a view. Consider your `veterans` view. Because you included only living performers, the `death_date` value is `null` for every row you select from the view. Therefore, there is no reason to include the `death_date` column in the view. Use the following example to modify the view creation to restrict the columns shown to only those that have values:

```
create view veterans as
select last_name, first_name, sex, birth_date
   from performers
 where birth_date < '01/01/1950'
    and death_date is null;
```

```
310: Table (informix.veterans) already exists in database.
```

This error message reminds you that Informix treats a view like a table. The view definition is stored permanently in the database, and no two views can have the same name.

First, you need to drop your current `veterans` view. The following statement shows how:

```
drop view veterans;
```

```
View dropped.
```

 **caution**   *If you drop the base table on which a view relies, Informix quietly
drops the view as well.*

Now recreate the `veterans` view and again select from it only
those veteran rockers whose last names begin with S. You should
see output like the following:

```
last_name        first_name      sex    birth_date

Scaggs           Boz             M      06/08/44
Starr            Ringo           M      07/07/40
```

Notice that the `death_date` column is no longer displayed.
Views are commonly used in this way with confidential data. By
using a view to restrict the `select` list, and granting certain users
access only to the view rather than to the base table, you can control which data fields they see.

Hide a Complex Join

More than comparison conditions may be included in a view's
definition; join conditions are also allowed. You might choose to
create a view that includes a join you commonly execute, thus
saving you the need to include the join explicitly when you select
from the view. Try creating the following view, which also restricts
the `select` list:

```
create view copy_details as
select format, location, amount_paid, artist, title, issue_year
  from albums, album_copies
 where albums.album_num = album_copies.album_num;
```

Now use the view to examine your Beatles albums and notice
how the two base tables are joined as the query is executed:

```
select title[1,20], issue_year, format, amount_paid
  from copy_details
 where artist = 'Beatles'
 order by 1;

title                  issue_year format amount_paid

Abbey Road                  1969 CD          $16.95
Help!                       1965 CD           $0.00
Help!                       1965 tape         $9.95
Revolver                    1966 CD          $14.95
Please Please Me            1963 CD          $13.50
```

This result set resembles the output of a similar query at the beginning of the chapter, where the same join was performed explicitly.

Present an Aggregate as a Column

One further use of views is to present an aggregate expression, such as count(*), as a database column. Let's say you commonly count the number of albums on which performers have appeared, with a query like the following, which shows those performers who appear on more than three albums.

```
select last_name, first_name, count(*)
  from album_performers
 group by 1, 2
having count(*) > 3;

last_name           first_name          (count(*))

Harrison            George                   5
Lennon              John                     4
McCartney           Paul                     4
Starr               Ringo                    5
```

You can create a view that presents the aggregate count as a column. The appearances view in the following example shows you how to do this.

```
create view appearances (last_name, first_name, num_albums) as
select last_name, first_name, count(*)
  from album_performers
 group by 1, 2;
```

 note   *If the `select` statement that defines a view contains an expression, you must include a complete list of column names for the view. This is because the column in the view that corresponds to the expression is a virtual column. There is no name it can inherit from the expression, so you must provide one. And, when you name any column in the view definition, you must name them all.*

With the `appearances` view, you can more easily select from and join to this list of popular performers than when you used the `group by` clause explicitly. The following example uses this simplifying view to show which performers have performed on more than three albums in your collection.

```
select *
  from appearances
 where num_albums > 3;
```

last_name	first_name	num_albums
Harrison	George	5
Lennon	John	4
McCartney	Paul	4
Starr	Ringo	5

Synonyms

Synonyms are permanent alternative names for tables or views. Unlike table aliases, which expire when their current `select` statement finishes, synonyms are stored as permanent table references in your database. Unlike views, synonyms may contain no additional conditions that are applied to the tables they reference.

Their primary utility is to reference a table or view in another database, perhaps even on another database server.

The syntax for the `create synonym` statement follows:

```
create synonym synonym-name for
[database-name[@database-server-name]:][table-owner.]table-name;
```

where `synonym-name` is the name of the synonym you are creating, `table-name` is the table or view for which you are creating the synonym, `database-name` is the name of the database that contains `table-name`, `database-server-name` is the name of the database server where `database-name` resides, and `table-owner` is the owner of `table-name`. The synonym can refer to any table or view that exists in your current database or in any online networked database.

Although synonyms can be especially valuable in a networked database environment, for your local `music` database there is no need to create them. Instead, synonyms will be revisited in the section titled "Networked Databases" in Chapter 17, "Database Administration Fundamentals."

Subqueries

A subquery is a `select` statement that is nested inside another SQL statement. In such a multipart statement, Informix uses the output of its subquery, or inner `select`, as criteria for evaluating its outer statement, usually an outer `select`.

Subqueries in `select` Statements

Before trying the following subquery example, take a moment to review the first two queries at the beginning of this chapter.

```
select album_num, format, location, amount_paid
   from album_copies
  where album_num in (select album_num
                        from albums
                       where artist = 'Beatles')
   order by album_num;
```

Your output should be the same as when you performed the *query-by-hand*. Let's examine the components of this `select` statement. Between the parentheses is an inner `select` statement. The parentheses around it instruct the system to perform that statement first. The inner `select` generates the list of `album_num` values used by the outer `select`. Then the outer `select` is executed using that `album_num` list as part of its comparison condition. The result is as if the `album_num` list had been defined explicitly, as it was at the beginning of the chapter.

In addition to the standard conditional operators, such as = and `in`, subqueries can be introduced in a `where` clause with any of the following operators, each optionally preceded by `not` to negate the search condition.

- `any`, used to determine if an expression is true for any of the values returned by the subquery
- `some`, a synonym for `any`
- `all`, used to determined if an expression is true for every value returned by the subquery
- `exists`, used to determine if any rows are returned by the subquery

In practice, the `in` and `exists` operators are the only ones you will see.

caution *If your subquery might return multiple rows, be sure to use an operator that can address a set of data (such as `in` or `exists`) when introducing it. If you use the equality operator (=), for example, and the subquery returns multiple rows, Informix will return the error message "284: A subquery has returned not exactly one row." Your statement will fail.*

Subqueries can be either *correlated* or *uncorrelated*. Uncorrelated subqueries execute exactly once; their value is not dependent on any value from the outer `select`. The previous example shows an uncorrelated subquery. Correlated subqueries, conversely, depend on some value from the outer `select` statement. As a result the subquery must execute once for each row returned by the outer `select`. This can be slow.

Suppose you want to list all of the `albums` for which there are no `album_performers`. One way to approach the search is to examine each album, and for each album look in the `album_performers` table for any matching entries. Finally, only return those `albums` for which no such rows were found. A correlated subquery is ideal for this task. Enter and run the following statement to find all rows of this kind.

note

The `exists` operator returns a `true` or `false` value to the outer `select`. Thus, any columns you include in the `select` list of the inner `select` are merely placeholders and are ignored.

```
select title, artist
  from albums
 where not exists (select album_num
                     from album_performers
                    where album_performers.album_num =
                          albums.album_num);
```

title   artist

Sounds of the Okefenokee Swamp Ambient Sounds

Notice that since the inner `select` depends on the `album_num` value from the outer `select`, you had to reference the outer `select`'s albums table from within the inner `select`. That join, on the last line of the query, is characteristic of a correlated subquery.

tip

The form of the previous subquery example, using the `not exists` comparison, is the most commonly used subquery. It is especially useful to check referential integrity. In a database where strict referential constraints have not been enforced, you can use queries of this form to see whether any rows in your table of interest have foreign key values that are not defined in their lookup table.

Subqueries in update Statements

An update statement may contain a subquery as part of its condition list. Suppose you recognize that music you don't own is intrinsically more attractive than music you already have. To reflect this, you want to increment the rating of each album that you have defined but do not own; that is, for each albums row with no album_copies. Before updating any such data, first use the following query to examine those albums.

```
select title, artist, rating
  from albums
 where not exists (select album_num
                     from album_copies
                    where album_copies.album_num =
                          albums.album_num);
```

title	artist	rating
Only a Lad	Oingo Boingo	2
Traveling Wilburys	Traveling Wilburys	5

2 row(s) retrieved.

To effect the rating upgrade, enter the following update statement:

```
update albums
   set rating = rating + 1
 where not exists (select album_num
                     from album_copies
                    where album_copies.album_num =
                          albums.album_num)
   and rating < 10;
```

2 row(s) updated.

If you query the data again, you will find that the ratings for your two unowned albums have increased. Your output should now resemble the following:

title	artist	rating
Only a Lad	Oingo Boingo	3
Traveling Wilburys	Traveling Wilburys	6

2 row(s) retrieved.

Subqueries in **delete** Statements

A delete statement may also contain a subquery as part of its condition list. Suppose you decide to delete all of the genres rows for which you have no albums of that type. The following statement shows one way to do this, using an uncorrelated subquery. Only try this if you actually want to delete these rows.

```
delete from genres
  where genre not in (select genre
                        from albums);
```

Summary

In this chapter, you learned ways to manipulate multiple tables simultaneously with SQL. Joins and subqueries are the principal means of addressing multiple tables. Joins are relationships between two tables that return a single row for every instance where the tables intersect across a joined column. Joining is a critical, fundamental component of SQL. It is the means by which you relate the intrinsically non-redundant data that is characteristic of a well-defined database.

Views are virtual tables. They are reflections of base tables, but with additional conditions applied. These conditions can restrict a select list, create virtual columns, or apply comparison or join qualifications.

Synonyms are permanent aliases for tables or views. They can reference not only local tables or views, but also those in databases that reside on networked database servers.

Subqueries allow you to include the result set of one query in the comparison condition of another SQL statement. They may be included in `select`, `update`, and `delete` statements.

This is the last lesson on SQL. Its limitations by now may start to be apparent as you consider areas where you want to perform more complicated tasks. In the next chapter you'll be introduced to the first of Informix's traditional programming languages, stored procedure language. With it, you can include operations such as procedural logic and looping. You'll be able to create reusable functions, and extend the base SQL operators. This next step is a big one; get some rest.

Extra Credit

Q&A

Question	Answer
These joins aren't clear. Is it really necessary that I understand them before proceeding?	Yes.
Every join example joins columns of the same name to each other. Can't I join columns with different names?	You can, but not in this database. As a design principle, it's a good idea to try to enforce joins only between those columns that share domains, or common pools of acceptable values. In the `music` database (except for `description`) only columns named the same share a domain, and may be reasonably joined.

I expected the following query to return no rows, because I have no DAT recordings:

```
select *
  from album_copies, outer formats
 where album_copies.format =
       formats.format
   and formats.format = 'DAT';
```

The `outer` keyword instructs Informix to return all rows from the dominant table even if it can find no matching rows in the subservient table. In this case, because the comparison condition is based on the subservient table, Informix can find no `formats` rows that both join and meet the comparison condition, so it instead supplies `null` values for each

Question	Answer
Yet it returned several rows. What happened?	`formats` column. If you change the last line to read `and album_copies.format = 'DAT'`, no rows will be returned. Alternatively, you can remove the `outer` keyword.
How do I alter a view to add more comparison conditions?	Views cannot be altered. This is one way in which views differ from tables. To change a view's definition, you have to drop the view and create it with your new definition.
Can I use a view as a base table when creating another view?	Yes you can, and should. See Exercise 5.
Can I update a base table's values through a view?	Yes, with certain restrictions. The view must be built on a single base table. Also, the `select` statement that defines the view may not contain a `group by` clause, the `unique` keyword, an aggregate value, or a derived value that was created using an arithmetic expression.

Exercises

1. Write a query that finds the `artist`, `title`, and `format` for every album for which you paid more than $13 for your copy.

2. Write a query that finds the `title` of every album with a performer over 55 years old.

3. Write a query that finds the `title` and `artist` for every album you have defined. Also include the `location` of each copy you have for every album, if you have any copies. Be sure to display the `title` and `artist` even if you have no copies of the album.

4. Create a view called `albums_owned` with the same format as the `albums` table, but that includes only those albums you own; that is, for which copies exists in the `album_copies` table.

5. Create a view called `best_albums_owned` that contains only `title`, `artist`, and `rating`. Include in the view only those albums you own, and with a `rating` over 6. Hint: do the previous exercise first.

6. Write a query that finds any `album_copies` with a `format` that is not defined in the `formats` table.

Exercise Answers

1. This query shows an example of joining two tables.

```
select artist, title, format
  from albums, album_copies
 where albums.album_num = album_copies.album_num
   and album_copies.amount_paid > 13.00;
```

2. The following query is a good general answer.

```
select unique title
  from albums a, album_performers ap, performers p
 where a.album_num = ap.album_num
   and ap.last_name = p.last_name
   and ap.first_name = p.first_name
   and today - p.birth_date > (365.25 * 55);
```

You can also base the query on the current date, in which case you would modify the last line of this query to resemble the following, depending on the current date.

```
   and p.birth_date < '1943/09/29';
```

3. The following answer shows how an outer join is appropriate.

```
select title, artist, location
  from albums, outer album_copies
 where albums.album_num = album_copies.album_num;
```

4. Any of the following three statements will do.

```
create view albums_owned as
select *
  from albums
 where album_num in (select album_num
                       from album_copies);

create view albums_owned as
select *
  from albums
 where exists (select album_num
                 from album_copies
                where album_copies.album_num =
                      albums.album_num);

create view albums_owned as
select unique albums.*
  from albums, album_copies
 where albums.album_num = album_copies.album_num;
```

5. For this answer to work, you must first successfully create the albums_owned view from the previous exercise.

```
create view best_albums_owned as
select title, artist, rating
  from albums_owned
 where rating > 6;
```

6. Either of the following subquery-based statements will suffice:

```
select *
  from album_copies
 where not exists (select format
                     from formats
                    where formats.format =
                          album_copies.format);

select *
  from album_copies
 where format not in (select format
                        from formats);
```

Chapter

9

Stored Procedures and Triggers

Are you tired of typing all those `select` and `insert` commands using DB-Access? Can you imagine maintaining an entire database by hand? The good news is that there are many more tools available to help you automate these processes. This chapter will introduce and explore Informix stored procedures.

With stored procedures, you can write SQL that resides in the database. You write it only once, store it in the database, then execute the stored procedure as many times as necessary. Stored procedures can help extend the power of your database utilities by allowing you to use input parameters. Also, you can code a stored procedure to make logic decisions based on data retrieved from database tables.

When coupled with triggers, stored procedures become even more powerful. You can write stored procedures, then direct Informix to execute those stored procedures whenever certain events happen to the database, such as when a row is deleted from a particular table.

In this chapter, we'll discuss how to write and execute stored procedures, how to write triggers, and how these two work together. We'll see a lot of new syntax and examples to help you leverage their power. But first, let's talk about why you might want to use stored procedures.

When SQL Just Isn't Enough

Stored procedures allow you to extend the power of SQL for your database application. You can use stored procedures to add business logic to your database, or just utilize SQL more efficiently than by using DB-Access or embedding SQL into your database application. Following are a few good reasons to use stored procedures:

- Improving database performance
- Sharing or reusing work
- Controlling access to data
- Making decisions based on data at runtime

Improving Database Performance

Stored procedures are processed by Informix, then stored in the database in executable format (see "Behind the Scenes" later in this chapter). A stored procedure, once stored, is more efficient to use than direct SQL because Informix can bypass parsing the SQL, checking the validity of referenced database objects, and optimizing the query. Once the stored procedure is prepared and stored in the database, the stored procedure can be executed any number of times without additional database overhead. This makes the use of stored procedures a good solution for performing repetitious tasks.

Stored procedures can also save on network traffic. Since the stored procedure resides in the database, its execution requires less information to cross the network. When executing SQL, the entire body of SQL moves from the client to the database server, but for a stored procedure only the procedure name and its arguments cross the network.

Sharing or Reusing Work

Stored procedures are a good solution for tasks that are called often in your application. They need be written only once, then stored in the database. Any application accessing the database can use any stored procedure in that database.

Controlling Access to Data

You can create stored procedures that can be run only by certain users, or only by DBAs. In this way you can control who has access to certain data in the database. Stored procedures, like other database objects, require privilege to create and execute. The two types of stored procedures are owner-privileged and DBA-privileged. By default, an owner-privileged stored procedure is executable by anyone who has the `connect` database privilege. A user with the DBA privilege can create stored procedures with more restrictive permissions so that they are executable only by other users with DBA privilege. In this way you can have some stored procedures executable only by DBAs, further enhancing your ability to control access to certain data in the database.

 An owner of a stored procedure can grant privilege to any database user to execute that stored procedure.

Making Decisions Based on Data at Runtime

Stored Procedure Language (SPL) is a superset of SQL. SPL allows you to control the flow of your stored procedure with conditional and looping statements such as `if`, `while`, and `foreach`. Using these flow control statements, you can use data from the database to make decisions at runtime in your stored procedure.

Defining SPL Variables

Variables can be defined and used in your stored procedure. You can use variables in any SPL statement similar to how you might use a variable in any programming language. You can also use a variable in any SQL statement where a constant can be used. SPL variables are defined as follows:

```
define [global] variable-name data-type [default default-value];
```

where *variable-name* is any SQL identifier and *data-type* describes the variable's type. If you define a variable `like` a `table.column`, the variable takes on the data type of that database column. For example, you can define a variable `album_format like formats.format`, which is the same as declaring it to be `char(6)`. You can easily keep track of which variables refer to database columns by declaring your variables using `like`.

If you wish to define a global variable, use the optional `global` keyword and the `default` phrase to assign the variable a default value. A variable that is not explicitly declared as global is instead local in scope.

Here are a few examples of variable declarations, just to give you an idea of the different ways to define variables.

```
define counter int;
define music_genre like genres.genre;
define global status int default 0;
define album_format char(6);
define album_format like formats.format;
```

caution   *You cannot declare a variable to be* `serial`, *nor can you declare a variable* `like` `table.column` *where* `table.column` *is of* `serial` *type. Instead, use the* `int` *data type.*

You can define variables in SPL to be either local or global. Table 9-1 describes the differences between local and global variables.

Now that we have variables defined, how do we assign them values? There are four ways to assign values to variables. Following is the syntax for the four ways to assign variables:

```
define variable data-type;
let variable = expression;
```

```
select columns
  into variables
remainder-of-select-statement;

call stored-procedure-name(input-arguments) returning variables;

execute procedure stored-procedure-name into variables;
```

Table 9-1 Local and global variables in stored procedures.

Variable Type	Available	Default Value
Local	Within the procedure where it is defined	None allowed
Global	To other procedures run by the same user session in the same database	Required

Now let's put some variables to good use in a stored procedure. Suppose you want to name your new dog using the initials of one of your favorite performers. The performer should have at least one album with a rating 5 or greater in order to be worthy of having a dog named after him or her. Enter the SQL in Listing 9-1 using DB-Access.

Listing 9-1 Using variables in a stored procedure.

```
create procedure list_perf_intls()

    returning char(5);

define l_first like performers.first_name;

define l_last  like performers.last_name;

define l_initials char(5);
```

(Continued)

Listing 9-1   *Using variables in a stored procedure.*

```
foreach

    select unique performers.first_name,

            performers.last_name

      into l_first, l_last

      from album_performers, albums, performers

     where album_performers.album_num  = albums.album_num

       and album_performers.last_name  =

           performers.last_name

       and album_performers.first_name =

           performers.first_name

       and albums.rating >= 5


    let l_initials = l_first[1] || '. ' || l_last[1] ||

        '.';

    return l_initials with resume;

  end foreach;

  end procedure;
```

With this `create procedure` statement, you have created a stored procedure that returns the initials of all performers who have at least one album with a rating of at least 5. The `foreach` statement used in this Listing is explained further in this section.

For consistency and ease of debugging, use `l_` *as a prefix for local variables,* `i_` *for input variables, and* `g_` *for global variables. This makes it easier to recognize how variables are being used in your stored procedure.*

Now, let's execute the procedure from Listing 9-1. Enter the following into a new Query, using DB-Access:

```
execute procedure list_perf_intls();
(expression)
A.  B.
B.  C.
B.  P.
...
L.  P.
...
R.  J.
...
V.  W.
Z.  S.
40 row(s) retrieved.
```

Well, I don't know about you, but I think I'll name the dog "R. J."

You cannot edit a stored procedure that you have stored in the database. Instead, you need to drop it and replace it with the corrected `create procedure` command. The SQL syntax used to drop a stored procedure follows:

```
drop procedure procedure-name
```

This removes the stored procedure from the database. As with any SQL statement, `create procedure` and `drop procedure` statements can be saved in script files for future execution.

Control Structures

You can control the flow of your stored procedure using branching and looping statements. These statements allow you to make decisions inside your stored procedure based on data that you query from the database.

Conditionals

Use the `if` statements described here to branch the logic in your stored procedure.

```
if condition1 then
    statement-block1
[elif condition2 then
    statement-block2 ...]
[else
    statement-block3]
end if;
```

If `condition1` is true, `statement-block1` will be executed; otherwise, `condition2` will be tested. If `condition2` is true, `statement-block2` will be executed. If neither `condition1` nor `condition2` is true, `statement-block3` will be executed.

Looping

You can also use looping structures to control the flow of your stored procedures. The three looping structures in SPL are:

- The `for` statement
- The `while` statement
- The `foreach` statement

The `for` Statement

The `for` statement executes a statement block a defined number of times. First, it sets the value of an index variable you define to the value of a starting expression. For each iteration of the loop, the index variable is incremented. The loop ends when the incremented variable's value reaches the value of the ending expression you define. The syntax of the `for` statement follows:

```
for variable in (start-expression to end-expression
    [step step-expression])
    statement-block
end for;
```

where *variable* is an SPL variable to index the loop, *start-expression* is an expression describing the initial value of *variable*, *end-expression* describes the ending value of *variable*, and *step-expression* describes how to increment *variable*. *Step-expression* is optional, and defaults to +1 or -1, depending on the values of *start-expression* and *end-expression*.

The while Statement

The while statement is similar to the for statement, but establishes an indefinite loop, and does not increment any variables explicitly.

```
while condition
    statement-block
end while;
```

where *condition* is evaluated at the beginning of the loop. The *statement-block* continues to execute until *condition* is no longer true. In practice this means that the statements within your while loop must set *condition* to be false at the appropriate time.

The foreach Statement

You use the foreach statement when you want to select multiple rows from a table and work with each row individually. This is equivalent to using a cursor with SQL. See Chapter 13, "Cursors and Dynamic SQL," for more information on treating multiple database rows singly. The syntax for the foreach statement is as follows:

```
foreach
    select-statement;
    spl-statements
    [return variable-list with resume];
end foreach;
```

The *spl-statements* block is executed once for every row retrieved by *select-statement*. The `foreach` loop terminates when no more rows are returned.

You must use a `return` *variable-list* `with` `resume` statement if your `select` statement returns more than one row. The `foreach` statement implicitly declares and opens a cursor. The `return` *variable-list* `with` `resume` phrase causes the selected values to be returned to the calling program. Then, execution of the stored procedure is resumed on the line after the `return` statement.

Also, there are four ways to exit any of these loops. Table 9-2 describes these statements.

Table 9-2 Exiting a loop in SPL.

Statement	Description
continue	Does not execute the remaining statements in the loop; restarts execution at the beginning of the next iteration of the loop
exit	Exits the loop; restarts execution at the first statement following the loop
raise exception	Exits the loop if the exception is not handled within the loop
return	Exits the procedure

Let's look at an example of using these structures. Listing 9-2 contains a stored procedure that assigns a performer an age status based on birth year. Enter this stored procedure using DB-Access.

Now, execute the stored procedure with the following SQL statement:

```
execute procedure get_perf_status();

(expression)    (expression)    (expression)
```

```
Eric              Faulkner            Aging Rocker
...
John              Lennon              Veteran
Ringo             Starr               Veteran
Paul              McCartney           Veteran
...
Belinda           Carlisle            Aging Rocker
...
```

Listing 9-2 *Assigning age status.*

```
create procedure get_perf_status()

    returning char(15), char(15), char(20);


define l_perf_status char(20);

define l_birth_year int;

define l_first like performers.first_name;

define l_last  like performers.last_name;


foreach

    select first_name, last_name, year(birth_date)

      into l_first, l_last, l_birth_year

      from performers


    if l_birth_year is null then

        let l_perf_status = 'Status unknown';

    elif l_birth_year > 1980 then

        let l_perf_status = 'Way too young to be cool';
```

(Continued)

Listing 9-2 Assigning age status.

```
    elif l_birth_year > 1970 then

        let l_perf_status = 'Groovy young star';

    elif l_birth_year > 1950 then

        let l_perf_status = 'Aging rocker';

    else

        let l_perf_status = 'Veteran';

    end if


    return l_first, l_last, l_perf_status with resume;

  end foreach;

  end procedure;
```

If you haven't dropped either of your stored procedures, you now have two procedures within the music database. You can examine these procedures from within DB-Access via the Data-base:Info:Procedures menu. Chapter 3, "DB-Access," also showed how you could use shortcuts at the command line prompt to proceed directly to a specific DB-Access screen. Execute the following shortcut to use this method to examine your newest stored procedure:

$ dbaccess music -dip list_perf_intls

Calling Other Procedures

You can use the call statement to execute another procedure from within your stored procedure.

```
call procedure-name(calling-arguments)
     returning return-variables;
```

where *procedure-name* is the procedure name you wish to call,
calling-arguments provides the called procedure with inputs,
and *return-variables* refer to the variables that will contain
the values returned from the called procedure.

Passing Arguments

You can pass arguments into a stored procedure, and receive
return values from it.

```
create procedure procedure-name
(variable-datatype-pairs)
     returning datatypes;


     spl-statements;


     return return-variables;
end procedure;
```

where *procedure-name* is the procedure being created, *vari-
able-datatype-pairs* is the list of input arguments and their
types, and *return-variables* refer to the variables that are
returned from the stored procedure.

Now try creating and executing a procedure with input and output arguments. Suppose you just want to print the value of a performer's age. Listing 9-3 lists a stored procedure to accomplish this.

Listing 9-3 *An example of stored procedures with input and output
arguments.*

```
create procedure get_age(

i_first like performers.first_name,

i_last  like performers.last_name)

     returning int;
```

(Continued)

Listing 9-3   *An example of stored procedures with input and output arguments.*

```
define l_age int;


select year(today) - year(birth_date)

  into l_age

  from performers

 where first_name = i_first

   and last_name  = i_last;


return l_age;

end procedure;
```

Execute this procedure to find out Ringo Starr's age. Use the Query-language menu in DB-Access. Notice that, just as with all other SQL statements, you need to enclose non-numeric data types within quotes.

```
execute procedure get_age('Ringo', 'Starr');
(expression)
58
```

This age procedure works well (except when they haven't had their birthdays yet this year; then it makes them one year too old), but what about performers who are deceased? Try creating a procedure that tells either that a performer is deceased, or tells his age if the performer is still living. We can call the get_age procedure from our new stored procedure. Use the Query-language menu in DB-Access to enter the procedure in Listing 9-4.

The if statements allow you to base your output on the values of birth_date and death_date for each performer. Notice the

```
create procedure get_perf_age_stat(

i_album_title like albums.title)

    returning char(60);


define status char(60);

define l_age int;

define l_birth_date like performers.birth_date;

define l_death_date like performers.death_date;

define l_first like performers.first_name;

define l_last  like performers.last_name;


foreach

    select p.death_date, p.birth_date,

            p.first_name, p.last_name

      into l_death_date, l_birth_date, l_first, l_last

      from performers p, albums, album_performers

    where albums.title = i_album_title

        and albums.album_num = album_performers.album_num

        and album_performers.first_name = p.first_name

        and album_performers.last_name  = p.last_name


    if l_death_date is not null then

        let status = trim(l_first) || ' ' || trim(l_last)
```

(Continued)

Listing 9-4 *Stored procedures can call other stored procedures.*

```
                    || ' is deceased.';

        elif l_birth_date is null then

            let status = 'The age of ' || trim(l_first)|| ' '

                || trim(l_last) || ' is unknown.';

        else

            call get_age(l_first, l_last) returning l_age;

            let status = 'The age of ' || trim(l_first) ||

                ' ' || trim(l_last) ||  ' is ' || l_age ||
'.';

        end if


        return status with resume;

    end foreach;

    end procedure;
```

use of the `trim` function, which helps us format the output into something easy to read. Also, we used an alias for the `perform-ers` table in the `select` statement, as you've seen in previous chapters.

Execute this stored procedure using DB-Access. Enter the following using the `Query-language` menu in DB-Access.

```
execute procedure perf_age_status('Help!');
(expression)

The age of George Harrison is 55.
John Lennon is deceased.
The age of Paul McCartney is 56.
```

The age of Ringo Starr is 58.

4 row(s) retrieved.

Exceptions

Handling errors is an important part of programming with SPL. There are two SPL statements that can be used to handle exceptions in your stored procedure:

on exception
raise exception

In concert, these two statements allow you perform robust error handling with SPL. Each integrates with Informix's general handling of errors, insofar as they allow you to populate and read the global SQL and ISAM variables that are used by all other SQL statements.

The on exception Statement

Unlike other SPL statements, which are executable, the on exception statement is declarative. That is, it indicates only what exception handling actions to perform when an error occurs, but does not actually execute those statements until a triggering error occurs. For this reason, in the body of a procedure the on exception clause follows all define statements and precedes all executable statements. Its syntax follows:

```
on exception [in (error-numbers)]
    [set sql sql-var[, isam isam-var[, data-var]]]
    statement-block
end exception [with resume];
```

The in clause is optional, and specifies the *error-numbers* that should be processed by this on exception statement. The optional set clause can be used to set the SQL error variables into local procedure variables. The SQL error code is placed in *sql-var*, the ISAM error in *isam-var,* and the error text in the optional *data-var*. Statements in the *statement-block* are executed if an exception occurs that matches the optional in clause. If no in clause is specified, the *statement-block* is executed for any error. The optional with resume clause forces the stored procedure to continue executing even if an exception occurs.

The first exercise at the end of this chapter illustrates the use of the on exception statement.

The raise exception Statement

The raise exception statement sets custom error conditions when your procedure fails in a way you define. When encountered during execution, these error states are displayed just as standard SQL errors are. Alternatively, if you have defined any on exception statements that trap the exceptions raised, you can use those statements to perform custom error handling,

```
raise exception sql-err-var

[, isam-err-var[, err-text-var]];
```

where *sql-err-var* is the SQL error you wish to raise, *isam-err-var* is the appropriate ISAM error, and *err-text-var* is the text of the error message. The *sql-err-var* must be a valid SQL error number. If no ISAM error applies to the *sql-err-var*, a zero should be provided.

In order to make these admittedly complex exception conditions comprehensible, try adding some exception handling to the stored procedure from Listing 9-3. For example, if the performer's birth date is greater than today, an error should be issued. Enter the procedure from Listing 9-5 into DB-Access.

tip

You can use the user-defined SQL error, -746, to specify a meaningful error message.

Listing 9-5 *SPL exception handling.*

```
create procedure get_age_exc(

i_first like performers.first_name,

i_last  like performers.last_name)

    returning int;


define l_age int;


select year(today) - year(birth_date)

  into l_age

  from performers

 where first_name = i_first

   and last_name  = i_last;


if l_age < 0 then

    raise exception -746, 0,

    'get_age: Error in birth date of performer.';

end if


return l_age;

end procedure;
```

A Useful Example: Evaluating Your Collection

Let's combine everything you've learned so far into an example. Suppose you want to know the current value of your music collection, and you've come up with some rules for determining its value. Following are the business rules for determining the collection's value:

1. Start with the amount paid for the item. If that information is not known, assume a default value of $8.37.
2. Music from the '70s is trendy right now; if the album was issued during the '70s, add 25%.
3. Of course, disco is even better. If the album is a disco album, add another 15%.
4. Vinyl is being sought after at garage sales everywhere. Add 10% if the format is LP.
5. Finally, add 4% for every year that has passed since the album's issue date.

Listing 9-6 contains a stored procedure to obtain the value of the music collection. After creating this stored procedure, be sure to save it in a script file. Future examples will refine this stored procedure.

Listing 9-6   Evaluating your collection.

```
create procedure get_coll_value()

    returning money;


define index int;

define l_coll_value money;     --value of collection

define l_album_value money;

define l_amount_paid like album_copies.amount_paid;
```

(Continued)

```
define l_format like album_copies.format;

define l_genre like albums.genre;

define l_issue_year like albums.issue_year;


let l_coll_value = 0.0;

foreach

    select album_copies.amount_paid,

            album_copies.format,

            albums.genre,

            albums.issue_year

      into l_amount_paid,

            l_format,

            l_genre,

            l_issue_year

      from albums, album_copies

     where album_copies.album_num = albums.album_num


    if l_amount_paid is null then

        let l_album_value = 8.37;

    else

        let l_album_value = l_amount_paid;

    end if
```

Listing 9-6 *Evaluating your collection.*

```
if l_issue_year between 1970 and 1979 then

    let l_album_value = 1.25 * l_album_value;

end if


if l_genre = 'disco' then

    let l_album_value = 1.15 * l_album_value;

end if


if l_format = 'LP' then

    let l_album_value = 1.10 * l_album_value;

end if


for index in (l_issue_year to year(today) - 1 step 1)

    let l_album_value = l_album_value * 1.04;

end for


    let l_coll_value = l_coll_value + l_album_value;
end foreach;


return l_coll_value with resume;
end procedure;
```

Now, execute the procedure in DB-Access:

```
execute procedure get_coll_value();
```

```
(expression)
$538.46
```

```
1 row(s) retrieved.
```

Behind the Scenes

What happens behind the scenes in Informix when stored procedures are created and executed? While you certainly don't need to know all this information just to begin using stored procedures, it can help you understand how Informix deals with stored procedures internally.

Four Informix system tables are involved in administering stored procedures:

* `sysprocedures` contains the name of the stored procedure and other administrative details.
* `sysprocbody` contains the Pcode for the parsed stored procedure.
* `sysprocplan` contains the query plan for the stored procedure, as well as a dependency list of database objects.
* `sysprocauth` contains security authorization information about privileges on the stored procedure.

When a `create procedure` statement is executed, Informix parses the SPL statements and builds a dependency list of database objects referenced in the stored procedure. The resulting Pcode and dependency list are stored in the `sysprocbody` table. The SQL in the stored procedure is optimized to create a query plan, which is stored along with the dependency list in the `sysprocplan` table.

When an `execute procedure` statement is executed, the object dependency list, the Pcode, and the query plan are extracted from the appropriate system tables and stored in the stored procedure cache. If that particular stored procedure is already stored in the cache, Informix uses that information instead of repeatedly retrieving it from the system tables.

Informix then verifies that all the database objects in the dependency list have not changed since the time the stored procedure was created. If necessary, the SPL is reoptimized and a new query plan is created and updated in the `sysprocplan` table. Then the stored procedure is executed.

Triggers

You can extend the power of your SQL by directing Informix to perform database actions that you specify whenever a table's data is modified. *Triggers* are used to define this behavior. A *trigger* is a database mechanism associated with a table that directs Informix to automatically perform specified actions when the table's data is modified by an `insert`, `update`, or `delete` statement.

Why Use a Trigger?

You may want to use a trigger for one of the following reasons:

- To embed business rules in the database. Instead of using a database application to administer business rules, use a trigger. The rules are then closely bound to the data and not dependent on one or more applications. Also, all the applications running against the database can benefit from the trigger without duplicating effort.
- To maintain a derived value. If a certain database value is derived from other data in the database, you can use a trigger to force the derived value to be updated whenever its defining data is updated.
- To keep an audit trail of database activity. You can use triggers, combined with audit tables, to keep records of database tables that are updated. We'll look at an example of this in the next section.

- To maintain referential integrity. If you decide to sell all the copies of your "Kissing to Be Clever" album, you might set up a trigger in the `albums` table, to first delete all "Kissing to Be Clever" rows in `album_copies` before deleting the row in the `albums` table.

Triggers are created with the `create trigger` SQL statement.

note

You must be the table owner or have the DBA privilege to create a trigger.

Creating a Trigger

The following SQL syntax is used to create a trigger:

```
create trigger trigger-name
trigger-event
trigger-timing
action-clause;
```

where *trigger-name* is the name of the trigger, *trigger-event* specifies the statement that activates the trigger, *trigger-timing* specifies when the triggered action should occur, and *action-clause* describes what actions should occur when the trigger is activated.

The syntax for the `create trigger` statement can be complicated. Let's take a look at the different components, then look at some examples to further clarify this statement.

The trigger-event clause describes the event that activates the action clause. Table 9-3 describes the possible values for the *trigger-event* clause.

The *trigger-timing* clause describes when the triggered action should be executed. Table 9-4 describes the timing clause.

The *action-clause* specifies what SQL actions will occur when the trigger is activated. Let's take a look at some examples.

note

Use the SQL `drop trigger trigger-name` to remove a trigger from the database.

Table 9-3 **The** `trigger-event` **clause.**

Value	Notes
`insert on` `table-name`	Activates the trigger whenever a record is inserted into `table-name`
`delete on` `table-name`	Activates the trigger whenever a record is deleted from `table-name`
`update of` `column-name` `on` `table-name`	Activates the trigger whenever `table-name.column-name` is updated

Table 9-4 **The** `trigger-timing` **clause.**

Value	Notes
`before`	Specifies the `action-clause` to be executed before the triggering statement executes
`after`	Specifies the `action-clause` to be executed after the triggering statement executes
`for each row`	Specifies the `action-clause` to be executed once for each row affected by the triggering statement

Creating an Audit Trail

Suppose you want to keep track of when genres are added to or removed from the `music` database, in order to maintain some historical perspective on styles of music through the decades. And suppose you also want to note when and how the genre description changes. You can use an audit table and a trigger to log this information. First, create a table to log genre history. Execute the following SQL statements:

```
create table genre_history (
    genre char(10),
```

```
    action_date date,
    action char(8) check (action in
    ('added', 'modified', 'removed')),
    old_descrip char(60),
    new_descrip char(60)
);
```

```
Table created.
```

Next, create some triggers to be activated whenever any of the following events happens to the genre table: insert, update, or delete. First, create the trigger associated with deleting a genre record.

```
create trigger del_genre
    delete on genres
    referencing old as old_genre
    for each row
        (insert into genre_history
         values(old_genre.genre, today, 'removed',
                old_genre.description, null));
```

```
Trigger created.
```

The trigger named del_genre will be triggered whenever a record is deleted from the genres table. The deleted row will be referenced using the *correlation-name* old_genre. The *correlation-name* allows the columns in the deleted record to be accessed by the SQL in the *action-clause*. For each row deleted, a record will be added to the genre_history table. The values added to the genre_history table are identified in Table 9-5.

Now, create a similar trigger to be activated whenever a record is inserted into the genres table.

```
create trigger ins_genre
    insert on genres
    referencing new as new_genre
    for each row
        (insert into genre_history
         values(new_genre.genre, today, 'added', NULL,
                new_genre.description));
```

```
Trigger created.
```

Table 9-5 *Values added to the* `genre_history` *table for a deleted genre.*

Column	Source	Notes
`genre`	`old_genre.genre`	The value of the column `genre` in the deleted record.
`action_date`	`today`	An SQL function returning today's date.
`action`	'removed'	Indicates the genre was removed.
`old_descrip`	`old_genre.description`	The value of the `description` column in the deleted record.
`new_descrip`	null	This field does not apply to a deleted record.

The trigger named `ins_genre` will be activated whenever a record is inserted into `genres`. For every record inserted into `genres`, a record will be added to the `genre_history` table. In this case, the `new_descrip` field is filled with the genre's description. The `old_descrip` field has no meaning for a newly inserted record, and is assigned a NULL.

Finally, create a trigger to be activated whenever the genre's `description` column is updated.

```
create trigger upd_genre
    update of description on genres
    referencing old as old_genre
              new as new_genre
    for each row
      (insert into genre_history
       values(old_genre.genre, today, 'modified',
              old_genre.description,
              new_genre.description));


Trigger created.
```

In this case, the `referencing` clause references both the old record in `genres` as well as the newly updated record. This allows us to log how a genre's `description` was modified.

You can use DB-Access to see the triggers that are applied to a table. Table 3-3 summarizes the menu where this information can be seen, but you can also use a shortcut like the following to see the triggers for a table:

```
$ dbaccess music -tig genres
```

Figure 9-1 shows the output for this shortcut. Notice that this menu option displays the triggers available on only the currently selected table.

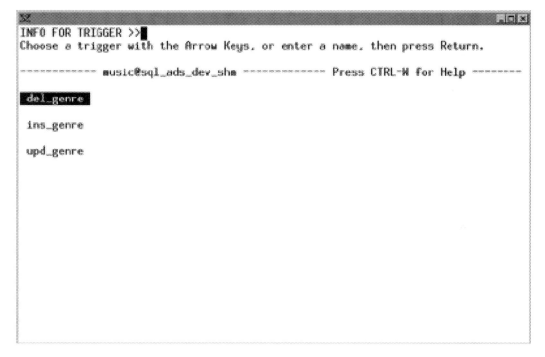

Figure 9-1 *Listing the triggers for a table.*

So, what happens when we modify the `genres` table? Enter the following SQL using DB-Access:

```
insert into genres values
    ('broadway', 'show tunes and Broadway soundtracks');
```

```
delete from genres
 where genre = 'rockabilly';

update genres
   set description = 'Trains, dogs, trucks, and broken hearts'
      where genre = 'country';
```

Of course, we didn't see anything being logged. But let's take a look at the `genre_history` table:

```
select *
  from genre_history;
genre          broadway
action_date 1998/09/29
action         added
old_descrip
new_descrip show tunes and Broadway soundtracks

genre          rockabilly
action_date 1998/09/29
action         removed
old_descrip High energy nascent country rock
new_descrip

genre          country
action_date 1998/09/29
action         modified
old_descrip Songs about trains, dogs, and trucks
new_descrip Trains, dogs, trucks, and broken hearts
```

Maintaining a Derived Value

Suppose you want to know the up-to-date value of your music collection any time a new album copy is added to the collection. You can use a trigger on the `album_copies` table and a stored procedure to attain this goal. You already have a stored procedure to calculate the value of your collection. The stored procedure needs to be modified a bit so that it places the collection value into your newly created `collection` table.

First, create and populate the `collection` table, with columns for the collector's name and the value of the collection.

```
create table collection (
    collector_first  char(15),
    collector_last   char(15),
    collection_value money
);


Table created.


insert into collection values
('your-first-name', 'your-last-name', 0.00);


1 row(s) inserted.
```

Next, modify your earlier stored procedure `get_coll_value` to update the `collection` table, and name your new stored procedure `upd_coll_value`. Listing 9-7 shows the SQL for creating the new procedure.

Listing 9-7 *SQL for procedure* `upd_coll_value`.

```
create procedure upd_coll_value()


define index int;

define l_coll_value money;      --value of collection

define l_album_value money;

define l_amount_paid like album_copies.amount_paid;

define l_format like album_copies.format;

define l_genre like albums.genre;

define l_issue_year like albums.issue_year;
```

(Continued)

Listing 9-7 *SQL for procedure* upd_coll_value.

```
let l_coll_value = 0.0;

foreach

    select album_copies.amount_paid,

            album_copies.format,

            albums.genre,

            albums.issue_year

        into l_amount_paid,

            l_format,

            l_genre,

            l_issue_year

        from albums, album_copies

        where album_copies.album_num = albums.album_num


    if l_amount_paid is null then

        let l_album_value = 8.37;

    else

        let l_album_value = l_amount_paid;

    end if


    if l_issue_year between 1970 and 1979 then

        let l_album_value = 1.25 * l_album_value;

    end if
```

(Continued)

Listing 9-7 SQL for procedure upd_coll_value.

```
if l_genre = 'disco' then

    let l_album_value = 1.15 * l_album_value;

end if


if l_format = 'LP' then

    let l_album_value = 1.10 * l_album_value;

end if


for index in (l_issue_year to year(today) - 1 step 1)

    let l_album_value = l_album_value * 1.04;

end for


    let l_coll_value = l_coll_value + l_album_value;

end foreach;


update collection

    set coll_value = l_coll_value;

end procedure;
```

Create this procedure in the database. Next, create a trigger to invoke this stored procedure whenever a new record is inserted into the album_copies table.

```
create trigger upd_value
    insert on album_copies
    after (execute procedure upd_coll_value());
```

```
Trigger created.
```

With this statement, you have created a trigger that will be activated whenever a row is inserted into the table `album_copies`. When this trigger is activated, Informix will automatically execute the stored procedure named `upd_coll_value`. The `after` keyword specifies that the procedure be executed after the new row is inserted into `album_copies`.

Now, let's insert a row into `album_copies` and see what happens. First, check the `collection` table:

```
select *
  from collection;
```

```
collector_first  collector_last  collection_value
John             Doe             538.46
```

Now add a new `album_copies` row, in this case a new vinyl version of "Please Please Me" that you just found at a garage sale:

```
insert into album_copies
values(6, 'LP', 'car', 10.50);
```

```
1 row(s) inserted.
```

Finally, take a look at the `collection` table again. The value of your collection has been increased by the value of the new album copy.

```
select *
  from collection;
```

```
collector_first  collector_last  collection_value
John             Doe             583.99
```

Summary

Stored procedures and triggers can help leverage the power of SQL and automate your database maintenance processes. They allow you to share database utilities among applications that access the database, embed business logic into the database, improve database performance, and control access to data.

Stored Procedure Language is a superset of SQL. Any valid SQL statement can be contained within a stored procedure. Additionally, SPL offers looping and branching statements, error handling statements, and variables to expand the capabilities of ordinary SQL.

You can use triggers in conjunction with either SQL or stored procedures to direct Informix to automatically perform database actions whenever certain events occur in the database. Examples of events that cause triggers to be activated are deleting a row, inserting a row, or updating a database column. You can use triggers to help maintain derived data in the database, maintain audit trails, and maintain referential integrity.

Extra Credit

Q&A

Question	Answer
Can I change the value of the indexing variable in a `for` loop?	No. This will generate an exception when the stored procedure is executed.
Can I use aggregate functions such as `count()` or `max()` in my stored procedure?	No. You can use any SQL function except aggregate functions.
What happens to my `delete` when a triggered action on the table causes an exception to be raised?	If your database uses logging, the triggered action as well as the trigger event will be rolled back. If not, then the trigger event will complete, but not the triggered action. For more information about logging, see Chapter 13.

Did I really need to use a stored procedure to print out the initials of performers, as in Listing 9-1?

No, not really. But it was a good way to show the use of subscripted variables in SPL. The following SQL would have worked just as well: `select first_name[1] || '. ' || last_name[1] || '.' from performers.`

Exercises

1. Create a table named `sp_errors` with the following columns: `err_num int, username char(20), err_date date`. Add the following exception handling to the `upd_coll_value` stored procedure: whenever the error -273 (No UPDATE permission) is encountered, insert a row into the table `sp_errors`. Use the `user` and `today` functions to log the user's name and error date.

2. We all know that some album formats are worth more than others. Write a stored procedure named `def_format_value` that assigns default album values based on format type. Modify the `upd_coll_value` stored procedure to call this new procedure instead of defining the default value to be `$8.37`. (You can use the `default_value` column in the `formats` table.)

3. Create a trigger that calls the stored procedure `upd_coll_value` whenever the `amount_paid` column in the `album_copies` table is updated.

4. Create a trigger that executes two different stored procedures for each row deleted in the `formats` table. Name the stored procedures `del_format1` and `del_format2`. Neither procedure takes input arguments. Note: you need to create dummy stored procedures in the database in order to create the trigger.

Exercise Answers

```
create procedure upd_coll_value_ex1()


define l_err_num int;

define index int;


define l_coll_value money;     --value of collection

define l_album_value money;


define l_amount_paid like album_copies.amount_paid;

define l_format like album_copies.format;

define l_genre like albums.genre;

define l_issue_year like albums.issue_year;


on exception in (-273)

    set l_err_num;

    insert into sp_errors values(l_err_num, user, today);

end exception;


let l_coll_value = 0.0;


foreach
```

(Continued)

```
select album_copies.amount_paid,

       album_copies.format,

       albums.genre,

       albums.issue_year

  into l_amount_paid,

       l_format,

       l_genre,

       l_issue_year

  from albums, album_copies

 where album_copies.album_num = albums.album_num


if l_amount_paid is null then

   let l_album_value = 8.37;

else

   let l_album_value = l_amount_paid;

end if


 if l_issue_year between 1970 and 1979 then

    let l_album_value = 1.25 * l_album_value;

 end if


 if l_genre = 'disco' then

    let l_album_value = 1.15 * l_album_value;
```

(Continued)

Listing E9-1 *Answer to Exercise 1.*

```
    end if


    if l_format = 'LP' then
        let l_album_value = 1.10 * l_album_value;
    end if


    for index in (l_issue_year to year(today) - 1 step 1)
        let l_album_value = l_album_value * 1.04;
    end for


    let l_coll_value = l_coll_value + l_album_value;


end foreach;


update collection
    set coll_value = l_coll_value;


end procedure;
```

Listing E9-2 Answer to Exercise 2.

```
create procedure upd_coll_value()


define index int;

define l_coll_value money;      --value of collection

define l_album_value money;

define l_amount_paid like album_copies.amount_paid;

define l_format like album_copies.format;

define l_genre like albums.genre;

define l_issue_year like albums.issue_year;


let l_coll_value = 0.0;


foreach

    select album_copies.amount_paid,

           album_copies.format,

           albums.genre,

           albums.issue_year

      into l_amount_paid,

           l_format,

           l_genre,

           l_issue_year

      from albums, album_copies

     where album_copies.album_num = albums.album_num
```

(Continued)

```
 if l_amount_paid is null then

    call def_format_value(l_format)

        returning l_album_value;

  else

     let l_album_value = l_amount_paid;

  end if



if l_issue_year between 1970 and 1979 then

     let l_album_value = 1.25 * l_album_value;

end if



  if l_genre = 'disco' then

    let l_album_value = 1.15 * l_album_value;

  end if



  if l_format = 'LP' then

     let l_album_value = 1.10 * l_album_value;

  end if



  for index in (l_issue_year to year(today)-1 step 1)

     let l_album_value = l_album_value * 1.04;

  end for



  let l_coll_value = l_coll_value + l_album_value;
```

(Continued)

Listing E9-2 Answer to Exercise 2.

```
end foreach;


update collection

   set coll_value = l_coll_value;


end procedure;
```

Listing E9-2a 2nd Part of Answer to Exercise 2.

```
create procedure def_format_value(

i_format like album_copies.format)

     returning money;


define l_def_value money;


select default_value

   into l_def_value

   from formats

 where format = i_format


return l_def_value;


end procedure;
```

Listing E9-3 Answer to Exercise 3.

```
create trigger upd_ac

    update of amount_paid on album_copies

    after (execute procedure upd_coll_value());
```

Listing E9-4 Answer to Exercise 4.

```
create trigger del_formats

 delete on formats

 for each row (

 execute procedure del_format1(),

 execute procedure del_format2());
```

Part
4

Informix Programming

Before the mirror ball starts spinning here on the Lido deck, let's preview this part's journey. Since the record player is already set up, we'll play the "Jackson 5 Christmas Album" in the background. Its tone is appropriately festive and solemn for exploring Informix's principal programming tools, Informix-4GL and Informix ESQL/C.

Chapter 10 begins the extensive study of Informix-4GL, a powerful programming language in which you can embed native SQL statements and stored procedure calls. In "Your First 4GL Program" you'll move quickly from writing a "Hello, World" program to learning the major components of this application development tool.

Chapter 11, "Your 4GL User Interface," shows you how to make your 4GL programs take visible shape. You'll learn how to include ring menus—just like DB-Access uses—in your programs. Additionally, you'll be introduced to forms, the primary means by which you enter and examine data in most 4GL applications. The user interface topic continues in Chapter 12, with "4GL Windows and Screen Arrays." You'll use these visual containers to develop a useful pop-up window: a pick list of values.

Chapter 13, "Cursors and Dynamic SQL," explores the crucial intersection of a set-based language (SQL) with a procedural language (4GL). Cursors—that intersection—come in several flavors. You'll sample each of them. You'll also need them to move on to Chapter 14, "4GL Reports," where you'll see one of the stars in the Informix firmament, its report writer. This versatile tool allows you to create custom reports in short order. You'll like it.

In the chapters that follow, I've arranged for some friends of mine to treat you kindly. Please, no tipping.

James Risinger completes the programming topic with Chapter 15, "ESQL/C." His treatment shows you how to embed your SQL statements within C code. You'll learn how to build advanced ESQL/C data structures, and when to use them. You'll also learn how to write dynamic SQL statements: those whose parameters can vary. Additionally, you'll see more attention paid to robust error checking, necessary in a production business environment. Be sure to bring your camera.

After that daunting look ahead, it's clearly time for a little high-energy release. As Isaac gets more ice, I'll spin up "Cruisin'"; "Y.M.C.A." is the first cut.

Your First 4GL Program

This is the first of several chapters devoted to Informix-4GL. Informix-4GL has been the workhorse programming language of Informix for over 10 years. As Informix's flagship development tool, it has been used for innumerable applications: from tracking hundreds of transactions per second, to storing hundreds of gigabytes of critical financial data, to, well, tracking your music collection.

It's a robust and friendly language. Its longevity, modular structure, and debugging capacity make it robust. You'll start to see over time how it's friendly (loosely typed, block structured, simple, handles the basics, doesn't complain much).

Informix-4GL is a general-purpose language, but is designed to make certain applications especially easy to create:

- Using complex procedural logic to process data returned from a database
- Using Query-By-Example (QBE) forms to find and display data

- Altering forms-based data and saving the changes in the database
- Generating multilevel reports

This chapter addresses the basics of effective 4GL program structure and development, and by the end of it you will have tackled the first of these bullet items. During the next several chapters, you'll create programs that showcase the rest of the topics, as well as other procedural and nonprocedural programs. The best way to learn to write programs in a language is to write programs in the language—so let's get started.

Hello, World

There are so many components to effective development that, to begin with, *what* you write is secondary to being able to write anything at all. In accordance with the principle of stepwise refinement, your first assignment is to write a very simple program. Only after you've mastered creating, compiling, and executing any program do you need to know more details about the language.

The first program you write in any language must display "Hello, world!" Now, play along. This won't hurt a bit. Launch the Informix-4GL Programmer's Environment.

```
$ i4gl
```

You should see a screen like Figure 10-1.

 note

The environmental variables that must be set for you to launch `i4gl` successfully are the same as for DB-Access. If `i4gl` won't start, review Chapter 3, "DB-Access," on the topic of environmental variables.

Use the following steps to create your first Informix-4GL program.

1. From within the INFORMIX-4GL: menu, select Module.
2. Choose New.

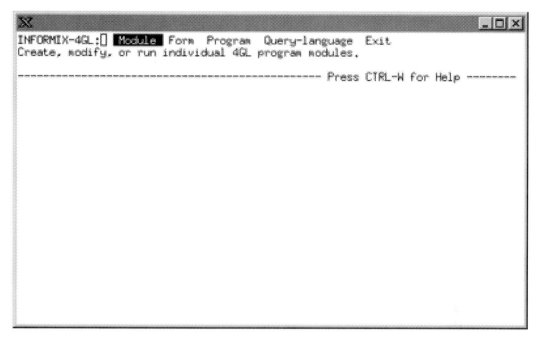

Figure 10–1 *Informix-4GL Interactive Editor.*

3. At the NEW MODULE >> prompt, enter hello.

4. If your DBEDIT variable is set, you'll find yourself in your favorite editor. Otherwise, enter your editor name at the USE-EDITOR >> prompt.

5. Create the program shown in Listing 10-1.

Listing 10-1 *Hello, world!*

```
main

    display "Hello, world!"

end main
```

Now follow these steps.

1. Exit your editor.

2. At the NEW MODULE: menu, select Compile, then Runable.

3. When it returns with the "A module was successfully compiled." message, select `Save-and-exit` from the `NEW MODULE:` menu.
4. From the `MODULE:` menu, select `Run`.
5. Choose `hello` from the `RUN PROGRAM >>` prompt.

At the top of your screen, you should see the following fruits of your labors:

```
Hello, world!
```

Let's view some of what you just did. First, you used the Informix Programmer's Environment. Table 10-1 shows its menu map.

Table 10-1 Informix-4GL Programmer's Environment menu map.

Menu Command	Command Description
Module	Create, modify, or run individual 4GL program modules
Modify	Change an existing 4GL program module
Compile	→ Compile submenu (see Table 10-2)
Save-and-exit	Save the 4GL module that was just modified and return to the `Module` menu
Discard-and-exit	Discard any changes and return to the `Module` menu
New	Create a new 4GL program module
Compile	→ Compile submenu
Save-and-exit	Save the 4GL module and return to the `Module` menu
Discard-and-exit	Discard the new module and return to the `Module` menu
Compile	→ Compile submenu

(Continued)

Table 10-1 Informix-4GL Programmer's Environment menu map.

Menu Command	Command Description
Program_Compile	→ Compile submenu
Run	Execute an existing 4GL program
Form	Create or modify 4GL screen forms
Modify	Change an existing form specification
Compile	Compile the form specification
Correct	Correct errors in the form specification
Save-and-exit	Save the form and return to the Form menu
Discard-and-exit	Discard all form changes and return to the Form menu
Generate	Generate and compile a default form specification
New	Create a new form specification (never used)
Compile	Compile an existing form specification
Program	Multimodule 4GL program specification menu
Query-Language	→ Query-language menu (see Table 3-2)

Table 10-2 shows the i4gl Compile submenu. It can be called from several menus within the Informix-4GL Programmer's Environment.

From within i4gl you created an Informix-4GL source module, compiled it into an executable program, and ran it. The remainder of this chapter expands on these fundamental steps. But first, let's take a look at the big picture.

Table 10-2 Informix-4GL Programmer's Environment `compile` **submenu map.**

Menu Command	Command Description
`Object`	Create an object file only; do not link an executable program
`Correct`	Correct errors in the 4GL module
`Runable`	Create an executable program
`Correct`	Correct errors in the 4GL module

What Is a 4GL?

So why is it called *4GL*? *4GL* stands for *fourth-generation language*. A *third-generation language* (*3GL*), such as C, COBOL, or Pascal, is a procedural language: one that dictates *how* a task is to be done. A fourth-generation language, ostensibly, indicates only *what* is to be done, but leaves the details to the development tool.

In broad terms, those details are the program's data structures and algorithms. Algorithms are what a program *does*; specifically, the exact steps required to perform a logical operation. Data structures are what algorithms are done *on*. They are the program variables, which can be simple variables or aggregate variables. Algorithms use the language's operators to manipulate the program variables to obtain the desired effect. Of course, it's theoretically possible to have programs without variables or operators (Listing 10-1 has no variables, for example), but the practical benefit of such endeavors is usually nil.

Part of what differentiates Informix-4GL from 3GLs is that you need not dictate the algorithms for all operations. These *4GL* operations, those in which you mandate only *what* occurs, but not *how*, primarily involve the following:

- Database access
- User interaction
- Report generation

With Informix-4GL, you can write programs that are explicitly procedural, as Listing 10-2 shows, but you can also use certain statements to write nonprocedural code (see Listing 10-3). Create and run the program shown in Listing 10-2. You can follow the same numbered steps you used to create your first program, only be sure to save the new module as fahr2cent instead of hello. You need not be concerned yet about exactly how each of these 4GL commands works. Each will be explored in sufficient detail as the chapter unfolds.

Listing 10-2 *Using procedural statements in Informix-4GL.*

```
main

    define fahrenheit decimal(4,1)

    define centigrade decimal(4,1)


  prompt 'Enter the temperature in Fahrenheit: '

    for fahrenheit

    let centigrade = ((fahrenheit - 32) * 5) / 9

    display 'The centigrade equivalent is: ', centigrade

end main
```

When you run your program, you are prompted to enter a temperature for conversion:

```
Enter the temperature in Fahrenheit: 212
The centigrade equivalent is:   100.0
```

Examine but do not write the program shown in Listing 10-3. It shows an example of nonprocedural code, insofar as it does not specify that this is a ring-type menu, where on the screen this menu should be displayed, how a user can navigate its elements, which hot-keys select a choice, when the descriptions for each item are shown, or how to display the help text. Informix-4GL supplies the defaults for each of these. Chapter 11, "Your 4GL User Interface," explores this rich toolkit in detail.

Listing 10-3 *Using nonprocedural statements in Informix-4GL.*

```
main

    menu 'Emergency'

        command 'Police' 'Dial the local police'

            help 101

            call DialPolice()

        command 'Fire' 'Dial the local fire department'

            help 102

            call DialFireDept()

        command 'Pizza' 'Dial the local delivery service'

            help 103

            call DialPizza()

        command 'Exit' 'Exit the Emergency menu'

            exit menu

    end menu

end main
```

Because you have not defined the functions called by this menu, you cannot run it—yet. Later, you'll learn how to create placeholder functions while developing Informix-4GL programs.

These *stubs* allow you to test the overall flow of prototype programs like Listing 10-3.

According to these 3GL and 4GL definitions, Informix-4GL has an effective mixture of both. Perhaps it should be called Informix-3-1/2GL.

Program Structure

The Informix-4GL code you write, the *source* code, is not directly executable by the operating system. As with most programming languages, it has to be prepared for execution.

Compiling Your Informix-4GL Program

With Informix-4GL, there are two ways you can prepare your source *modules* (the physical files that contain your source code). You can compile your source modules into executable programs, or you can translate them into *pcode*, a series of encoded commands that can be interpreted by Informix's pcode interpreter, *fglgo*. Figure 10-2 shows these sequences, and reveals the intermediate stages that are silently included when you choose the compile option.

 When you compile your source code through the Informix-4GL Interactive Editor, as you did with Listing 10-1, you are actually invoking the c4gl *compiler, albeit "behind the scenes." If you look in your current directory, you'll see files with each of the extensions shown in Table 10-3.*

Actually, the method of generating an executable program, or *executable*, is a little more interesting than shown in Figure 10-2. The file extensions identify the types of files they represent. Table 10-3 shows what each extension signifies, and the tool used to translate that file into an executable.

Each compile command comprises those below it. For example, when you execute the c4gl compiler, it only pre-processes the .4gl code into an .ec source file. Then it hands the processing off to the esql compiler. Likewise, the esql preprocessor creates

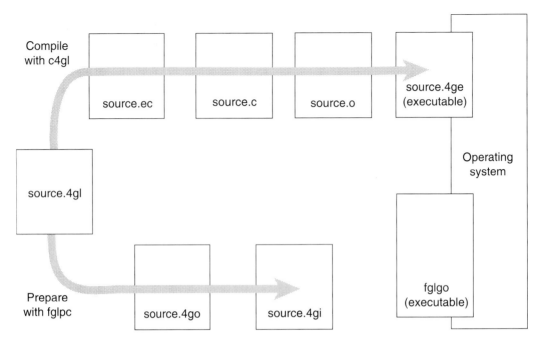

Figure 10–2 *Generating executable programs from Informix-4GL source modules.*

Table 10-3 The compilation stages of Informix-4GL source code.

File Extension	Compile with	Description
4gl	c4gl	Informix-4GL source file
ec	esql	Informix-ESQL/C source file
c	cc	C source file
o	ld	Object file, compiled from C source code
4ge		4GL executable program, linked from object file(s)

`.c` source files and passes control to `cc`. The C compiler subsumes the link editor (`ld`), or object code binder, so you generally never call that command directly. This handoff of processing is done quietly for you so that with a single `c4gl` command, you have Informix generate each of the intermediate stages, and link its own libraries with your object files to create an executable program. Figure 10-3 depicts this waterfall compilation method.

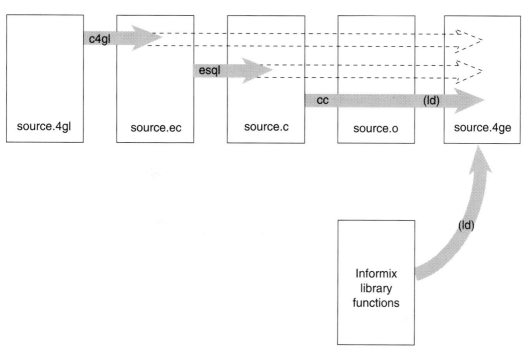

Figure 10–3   *Informix-4GL compilation is a series of processing hand offs.*

Even though for now you'll be using the Informix-4GL Interactive Editor to compile your programs, you need to understand this model since it's used for Informix-ESQL/C as well. In Chapter 15, "ESQL/C," you'll need to compile your `.ec` files directly from the command line. You can also invoke the `c4gl` compiler directly if you wish, with a command like the following:

```
$ c4gl hello.4gl -o hello.4ge
```

To execute the compiled program, type the name you assigned to the executable file:

```
$ hello.4ge
Hello, world
```

When you invoke c4gl from the command line, it inherits from C the default output file name of a.out for its executable. By adding the -o *file-name* you can dictate the name of the executable file that c4gl creates.

tip *For now, use the Informix-4GL Interactive Editor to compile your programs. Its menu-driven cycle of* Modify, Compile, Correct, Compile, Run *is more friendly than using the* c4gl *compiler at this stage. Later, when your programs become increasingly complex, you may consider switching to using the* c4gl *command directly.*

Multimodule Programs

Each source module you write can contain several independent program blocks, or functions. A *function* is a named block of logically related statements that perform a specific task. Functions contain definitions of variables and blocks of Informix-4GL statements. In every program you must include one special function, named main, so that Informix knows where to start the execution of the program. Listing 10-1 was a program with no variables and no functions other than main.

Although for small programs the source code is often contained entirely within one module, it need not be. The link editor can combine, or link, several object files into a single executable program. In fact, the c4gl compiler sends a silent directive to the link editor to have it link the Informix-4GL function libraries into every Informix-4GL executable.

No more than one of those object files may be generated from a special source file that contains *global* variable definitions (variables available to all functions that reference this source file; see "Global Scope" later in this chapter). Figure 10-4 shows how these multiple components are compiled into a single executable program.

The next four chapters rely on this multimodule compilation.

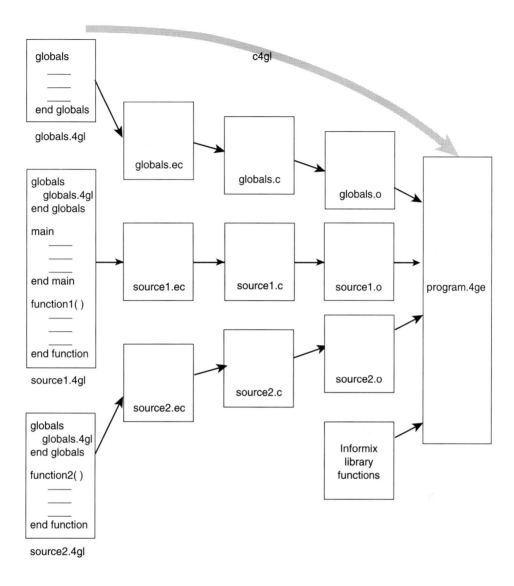

Figure 10–4 *Programs may include source code from multiple modules.*

Rapid Development System

The alternative method of preparing your programs for execution, the interpreted method, uses the Informix *Rapid Development System (RDS)*. The `r4gl` command invokes its Interactive Editor to prepare your programs. Try it.

```
$ r4gl
```

You should see a ring menu like you saw in Figure 10-1, with one exception. When you choose the `Module` option, you'll see a new `Debug` menu option. You should explore this option when you have time, but it is beyond the scope of this book.

The primary reasons you might choose to use the RDS method to prepare your 4GL programs for execution are to use the debugger and to allow faster preparation of your program; generating pcode is faster than compiling an executable. However, because pcode is interpreted rather than compiled, it runs a little more slowly than its compiled counterpart. For these reasons, developers often use RDS while developing their applications, then compile the final debugged version so that in *production*, the code executes most quickly.

Unless mentioned otherwise, the use of `i4gl` to compile your programs is assumed in this book.

The next two sections, "Defining Program Variables" and "Informix-4GL Statements," are admittedly dry. They explain how you define the variables for your 4GL programs, and which statements you can use to manipulate these variables. You needn't memorize these sections, but you must be familiar with their contents before you can write any substantive programs. You should read—not study—these sections before proceeding to the "Functions" section that follows. That section is where the hands-on tutorial resumes. Later, as needed, you can return to the next two sections for reference about the syntax explanations therein.

Defining Program Variables

You must declare your variables before you can use them. In a variable's declaration you name it and define its *scope* and data type. A variable's scope is the boundaries during which it comes into existence and maintains its value. Outside of its scope, a variable cannot be recognized. A variable declared local to one function cannot be referenced in a separate function. As a result, for example, you can use the same local variable name in different functions without conflict.

The placement and form of a variable's `define` statement declare its scope and data type.

Declaring a Variable's Scope

You can declare a variable in any of the following three places:

- Local, within a function
- Modular, within a source module
- Global, within a `globals` declaration module

The following sections describe how variables of different scope are treated.

Local Scope

A local variable is defined within a program block: between `function...end function`, `main...end main`, or `report ...end report` statements. The scope of reference is solely within that block of statements. All `define` statements declaring local variables must precede all executable statements within that block. Listing 10-2 uses two local variables, `fahrenheit` and `centigrade`.

Modular Scope

Variables declared outside of any program block, but not within a globals declaration, are modular in scope. Modular variables are available to all functions within that source module. The define statements that declare module variables must precede all executable statements within that file. Listing 10-15 uses the modular variables m_album_num and m_notes.

Global Scope

You use a globals declaration to make variables available across several source modules. To do so, you create a globals source module (*global-file-name*.4gl) whose only contents are variable definitions surrounded by the globals...end globals statements. All variables declared in the globals module are available not only in that module, but also in any module that has a globals '*global-file-name*.4gl' declaration.

Declaring a Data Type

You define variables with the define statement,

```
define variable-name[, variable-name …] data-type
   [, variable-name[, variable-name …] data-type …]
```

where *variable-name* is the name of the variable you are defining, and *data-type* is one of the SQL data types, the like statement, a record, or an array.

You can declare variables to be any of the SQL data types (see Table 4-2 back in Chapter 4) except serial; for that, use its equivalent type, integer. For example, each of the following is a valid declaration:

```
define hometown char(25)
define i,j,k smallint
define centigrade decimal(4,1)
define album_num  integer,
       birth_date date,
       lr_formats record like formats.*
```

Use a separate define *statement for each of your variables. Don't spread one* define *statement over several lines, and don't combine several variables' definitions into a single* define *statement. This practice simplifies editing, as each variable is self-contained, and can be copied or moved to other locations easier. Besides, it looks better.*

Declaring Variables like Database Columns

You can use the like notation to indicate that a variable's data type should copy that of a specific column in the database. For example, for the music database, the following two declarations are equivalent:

```
define l_rating smallint
define l_rating like albums.rating
```

The define *variable-name* like *equivalence is set at compile time. If you change data types in your database later, that change does not get reflected in your executable. You must recompile your source module to have the change in data type reflected in your variable's definition.*

Use define *variable-name* like *statements when your variables match database elements in name and data type. Such variables are easy to create, and easy to maintain when your schema changes.*

Declaring Records

A record is a set of related members, like a struct in C. The variables in this set, each with its own data type and name, are collected into a single declaration for easy reference. The following statement shows an example of a record declaration:

```
define track record
    track_number  smallint,
    song_name     char(20),
    song_length   datetime minute to second
end record
```

You reference a member in a record with the *dot* notation. For example, the following 4GL statement assigns a value to the `song_name` member of the `track` record.

```
let track.song_name = 'Karma Chameleon'
```

When you want to define a record whose members match every column in a table, you can use the `define` *record-name* `record like` *table-name*.`*` syntax, as in the following example:

```
define lr_performers record like performers.*
```

This shortcut creates a record called `lr_performers` that has one member for each column in the `performers` table. This declaration creates a record more easily than the following equivalent declaration:

```
define lr_performers record
    first_name    char(15),
    last_name     char(15),
    sex           char(1),
    birth_date    date,
    death_date    date
end record
```

Declaring Arrays

Whereas records are collections of (usually dissimilar) members, arrays are collections of identical elements. Those elements can be of any other Informix data type except arrays. Arrays can have up to three dimensions. Here are three examples of array declarations:

```
define ma_counts array[10]    of integer
define la_albums array[100]   of record like albums.*
define ga_screen_pos[24, 80] of char(1)
```

The last example shows a two-dimensional array, with a total of 1920 (24×80) elements. You reference an array's element by naming the array with a bracketed subscript, such as `ma_counts[3]` or `la_albums[19].rating` or `ga_screen_pos[1, 12]`. Array numbering starts at 1.

Naming Your Variables

What should you name your variables? As when naming tables and constraints, you should follow a clear, consistent scheme. Like all SQL identifiers, variable names are limited to 18 characters and are case-insensitive.

Dos and Do Nots When Naming Variables

DO

Use meaningful names. For example, a variable called `variable1` is viciously obtuse.

DO NOT

Abbreviate unnecessarily or arbitrarily. Especially don't remov vowls fr no gd resn.

DO NOT

Name variables the same as Informix keywords. Although legal, it invites confusion.

DO NOT

Use all uppercase letters. Instead, reserve such *loud* names for certain Informix global variables.

DO

Remember that another hapless programmer may need to modify your work. Be kind.

In this issue of style, you might consider prefixing your variable names with the first letter of their scope when your program has variables of differing scope. For example, each of the following names indicates its variable's scope:

`l_notes` (local)

`m_album_num` (modular)

`g_help_level` (global)

You can extend this scheme to indicate the complex data types `record` and `array`.

`lr_performers` (local record)

`ma_format` (modular array)

Consider using this type of notation when the complexity of your program starts to grow.

Informix Global Variables

Table 10-4 shows the global variables available in all Informix-4GL programs. These are always present in addition to any other local, modular, or global variables you may define. Later, you'll use the TRUE, FALSE, and STATUS global variables.

Table 10-4 Informix global variables.

Variable	Data Type	Value	Used For
FALSE	smallint	0	Any Boolean (true/false) comparison or assignment
INT_FLAG	smallint	TRUE or FALSE	Detecting when the Interrupt key has been pressed (see Table 10-5)
NOTFOUND	smallint	100	Comparing the STATUS of SQL select statements after they execute
NULL	Varies	null	Assigning null values to variables
QUIT_FLAG	smallint	TRUE or FALSE	Detecting when the Quit key has been pressed (see Table 10-5)
SQLCA	record	Varies	Determining the details of the most recent SQL operation (see Chapter 15, "ESQL/C")

(Continued)

Table 10-4 Informix global variables.

Variable	Data Type	Value	Used For
STATUS	smallint	Varies	Determining the success of the most recent SQL or forms-based operation: a value of 0 indicates success; a negative number indicates an error condition; a value of NOTFOUND indicates that an SQL statement returned no rows
TRUE	smallint	1	Any Boolean (true/false) comparison or assignment

By convention these names are in uppercase, but as with all variable names, they are case-insensitive.

Informix-4GL Statements

Informix-4GL is a full-featured programming language with a rich set of statements. This section classifies each of those into the following types:

- SQL statements
- Program blocks
- Declarations
- Compiler Directives
- Program flow control
- Assignment
- Screen interaction
- Report execution
- Operators

SQL Statements

One of the most useful features of Informix-4GL is its ability to execute native SQL statements directly. Effectively, all SQL statements can be embedded directly within Informix-4GL code. These statements can be either static, with a fixed form, or dynamic, where the form of the SQL statement is not known at compile time.

Static SQL

All of the SQL statements so far have been static. For example, the following `update` statement, a fixed-form SQL statement, is legal 4GL syntax:

```
update albums
   set notes =
       'Accordion to me, this is a good album.'
 where album_num = 22
```

The utility of embedding SQL is greatly expanded as a result of your being able to use 4GL variables as expressions in your SQL statements. Consider the following code fragment which, although it uses variables, still contains static SQL because the form of the SQL statement is fixed.

```
define l_album_num like albums.album_num
define l_notes     like albums.notes

let l_notes = 'Accordion to me, this is a good album.'
let l_album_num = 22

update albums
   set notes = l_notes
 where album_num = l_album_num
```

You can see how adding the flexibility of using variables in your SQL statements can make each statement more generic and reusable. In this case, you could have used any programming construct (such as `let`) to assign the values of l_notes and l_album_num. When modified to accept user-specified values (as in Listing 10-13), a code fragment such as this acquires significant versatility. You'll see by example in this chapter and the next four how the intermingling of variables and SQL statements can help you generate Informix-4GL programs of tremendous utility.

Dynamic SQL

In addition to static SQL statements, you can create dynamic SQL statements, those whose form is not known at compile time. The following three 4GL statements, described in Chapter 13, "Cursors and Dynamic SQL," allow you to create and manage SQL statements dynamically:

- execute
- free
- prepare

Cursor Manipulation

Chapter 13 also introduces the following cursor manipulation statements:

- close
- declare
- fetch
- flush
- open
- put

With the cursor manipulation and dynamic SQL statements, you can build and run SQL statements whose form is not known at compile time, such as those based on user-selected fields of a query-by-example form.

Program Blocks

Program blocks circumscribe other 4GL statements and organize them into discrete containers. The main and report blocks are functions with special traits. All processing starts at the main program block. The report block allows you to collate and summarize data in custom formats. The program blocks and their optional early exit statements are:

- `main ... exit program ... end main`
- `function ... return ... end function`
- `report ... exit report ... end report`

Be sure to include an end *statement to terminate your program blocks. If you commit the common oversight of excluding the proper terminator, the compiler becomes sorely confused, and may display deceptive and voluminous error messages.*

Declarations

The `define` statement is used to declare variables. When encountered at runtime, it instructs Informix to allocate memory for the defined variable, and to treat it as a certain data type. Its syntax was shown previously in the "Declaring a Data Type" section.

Compiler Directives

The statements listed in Table 10-5 direct the compiler to perform certain preprocessing operations.

Program Flow Control

Program flow control can be altered by branching or looping. Branching occurs when one of multiple processing paths is taken. Looping is when a series of statements is executed repeatedly until some condition occurs.

Branching

The branching statements are `if` and `case`. You use the `if` statement when you want your program flow to take one of two paths.

Table 10-5 Informix 4GL compiler directives.

Directive	Action
database database-name	Use database-name as a template for any define variable-name like statements.
defer [interrupt|quit]	Prevent 4GL from terminating program execution when the user presses the Interrupt key or the Quit key. By default any 4GL program exits when the Interrupt key (Ctrl-C) or Quit key (Crtl-\) is pressed. When the defer interrupt directive is included, instead of terminating, the program sets the global variable INT_FLAG to TRUE (see Table 10-4). The defer quit directive and QUIT_FLAG are similarly related. The defer statement may only appear in the main program block.
globals	Define or include variables of global scope.
whenever	Trap 4GL, ESQL, and SQL errors and warnings (see Chapter 15).

```
if (Boolean-expression) then
    4GL-statements
[else
    4GL-statements]
end if
```

where *Boolean-expression* is a 4GL statement that evaluates to TRUE or FALSE, and *4GL-statements* is any sequence of Informix-4GL statements, even other if blocks.

The case statement can take either of two forms. You use it to change your program flow based on the current value of an expression. Although it is identical to a series of nested if statements, when your program may take one of several paths, the case statement is usually easier to read. The first form of the case statement follows:

```
case

    when (Boolean-expression1)
        4GL-statements
        [exit case]
    [when (Boolean-expression2)
        4GL-statements
        [exit case]…]
    [otherwise
        4GL-statements]
end case
```

where *Boolean-expression* is a 4GL statement that evaluates to TRUE or FALSE, and *4GL-statements* is any sequence of Informix-4GL statements. The *Boolean-expressions* are evaluated in order, and only the *4GL-statements* following the first one that evaluates to TRUE are executed. If none of the *Boolean-expressions* evaluate to TRUE, then any statements in an otherwise block occur. There is an implicit exit case statement at the end of every when block, but you can also call the statement explicitly. The exit case statement transfers control to the next statement following the end case statement.

The following example shows this form of the case statement:

```
define response char(1)
…
case

    when (response matches '[yY]')
        let valid_response = TRUE
        let proceed = TRUE
    when (response matches '[nN]')
        let valid_response = TRUE
        let proceed = FALSE
    otherwise
        let valid_response = FALSE
end case
```

When a single expression may take one of several different values, you can use the second form of the case statement.

```
case (expression)
    when expression1
        4GL-statements
        [exit case]
    [when expression2
        4GL-statements
        [exit case]…]
    [otherwise
        4GL-statements]
end case
```

where *expression*, *expression1*, and *expression2* are 4GL statements or variables that evaluate to the same data type. This form is otherwise identical to the first form of the case statement.

The following example shows this form of the case statement:

```
define response char(1)
…
case (upshift(response))
    when 'Y'
        let valid_response = TRUE
        let proceed = TRUE
    when 'N'
        let valid_response = TRUE
        let proceed = FALSE
    otherwise
        let valid_response = FALSE
end case
```

Looping

The looping statements are for, while, and foreach. You use the for loop when you want to perform a set of statements a predetermined number of times, as shown in the following snippet. The while loop continues executing until its *test condition* is no longer true. A foreach loop is a specialized loop that executes once for each row returned from a select statement. It is described in Chapter 13. The syntax for the for loop follows:

```
for (counter = begin to end [step increment])
    4GL-statements
    [continue for]
    [exit for]
end for
```

where *counter* is an `integer` or `smallint` variable that indexes
the number of times the `for` loop executes; *begin* sets the initial
value of *counter*; *end* defines the value that, when equaled or
exceeded by *counter*, causes the loop to exit; *increment* is the
value by which *counter* is increased for each iteration of the
loop; and *4GL-statements* is any sequence of Informix-4GL
statements.

The default value for *increment* is 1. The `continue for` statement interrupts the current program flow, increments and tests
counter, and exits the `for` loop if *counter* now equals or
exceeds *end*. The `exit for` statement terminates the statement
block immediately, and passes control to the next statement after
the `end for` keywords.

The following example uses a `for` loop to initialize every element of a ten-element array to 0.

```
define idx smallint

for idx = 1 to 10
    let ma_counts[idx] = 0
end for
```

The `while` statement loops until its test condition is met. Its
syntax follows:

```
while (test-condition)
    4GL-statements
    [continue while]
    [exit while]
end while
```

where *test-condition* is a Boolean expression that evaluates to
TRUE or FALSE, and *4GL-statements* is any sequence of Infor-
mix-4GL statements. Generally, the *4GL-statements* change the
value of *test-condition*; otherwise, the loop might never exit.

The `continue while` statement interrupts the current program flow and reevaluates *test-condition*. If the value is FALSE, it exits the `while` loop. The `exit while` statement terminates the `while` loop immediately, and passes control to the next statement after the `end while` keywords.

The following example repeats its processing loop until the user no longer answers y.

```
define response char(1)


let response = 'y'
while (response = 'y')
    call UpdateNotes()
    prompt 'Update more album notes?' for response
end while
```

Assignment

There are several ways that you can assign values to variables. The following two statements are the most direct:

- `let` *variable-name* `= expression`
- `initialize` *variable-list* `to null`

The *variable-list* can be either a record or a comma-separated list of variables.

Additional ways of assigning values are consequences of other 4GL statements. For example, the following 4GL statements each assign a value to a variable:

- `prompt 'Enter the name of your llama: ' for`
  `como_se_llama`
- `select notes into l_notes from album where`
  `album_num = 22`
- `call ChooseAlbum() returning l_album_num`

Incidental assignments such as these will be introduced as their commands are described.

Screen Interaction

The following statements control screen displays and interaction with the user. They are described in Chapters 11, "Your 4GL User Interface," and 12, "4GL Windows and Arrays."

- clear
- display
- error
- menu
- message
- prompt
- sleep
- Forms control statements
- Window manipulation statements

Report Execution

The following four statements may be used only within the `format` section of a `report` program block:

- need
- pause
- print
- skip

These statements are defined in Chapter 14, "4GL Reports."

Operators

The following operators are not statements themselves, but rather are components of 4GL expressions. You use these operators on other expressions, or *operands*, to produce a resultant expression.

- + - / *: math operators, as in SQL
- = < > >= <= <> !=: comparison tests, as in SQL
- is null, is not null: null comparison tests, as in SQL
- and, or, not: Boolean operators, as in SQL
- like: string comparison, as in SQL
- matches: string comparison, as in SQL
- mod: modulus operator, returns the remainder of one value divided by another
- **: exponentiation operator, raises one value to the power of another

- `clipped`: operator to delete trailing blanks from a character expression
- `using`: operator to format a numeric or date expression

Functions

You'll see many program listings scattered through the rest of the chapter. Starting with Listing 10-5 you need to type in the code and test it yourself, because many exercises after that build on previous examples.

Informix-4GL programs begin executing at the first statement within the `main` program block, and stop when they reach the `end main` statement (or the `exit` statement, if you include one). Earlier, you learned ways of changing the procedural flow of a program with statements such as `if` and `while`. *Functions* offer another way to branch a program's control flow.

A *function* is a named block of logically related statements that perform a specific task. You begin a function definition with the `function function-name()` statement, and end it with the `end function` statement. Listing 10-4 shows a simple function, `RepeatGreeting()`, being defined only once but called twice.

Listing 10-4 Functions execute each time they are called.

```
main

    call RepeatGreeting()

    call RepeatGreeting()

end main


function RepeatGreeting()

    display 'Hello, again'

end function
```

The statements within a function execute only when the function is called, not when it is defined. Therefore, this program displays the "Hello, again" greeting twice.

After a program executes a function call, control returns to the point in the program at which the function was called.

Why Use Functions?

Functions allow you to partition complex programming tasks into discrete, understandable pieces. Their use in creating effective real-world code is not optional. By allowing you to create components that you can call repeatedly in one program and share between programs, they are the fundamental tools of software reuse.

In most applications, practically all of the work is done in functions. The `main` program block is merely the driver, the top level of control that organizes the real workhorse units: the functions. Although not executable because it lacks the function definitions, the following example shows this type of program structure:

```
main
    -- Basics of a handy robot control program
    call GoToTheFridge()
    call GetMeABeer()
    call StepAwayFromTheTV()
end main
```

 note   *Include a single-line comment in your 4GL program by preceding it with two hyphens (--).*

Notice in this example that the details of how each function performs its task are hidden. That is, when you look at the `main` program block, you can understand the program's intent at a glance without being immersed in the details of each operation. In fact, the actual source code that constitutes each of these functions may be in other files altogether. Each function may, in turn, consist of little more than other function calls, thus continuing to keep each program block's purpose clear. At some point in this functions-call-functions tree, when your functions can elucidate their tasks in a few lines of Informix-4GL code, you actually include the code for the task.

In accord with this stepwise approach, you should begin your development efforts at the highest level of abstraction, even going so far as to create your program with the `main` and `end main` statements only, or at most an additional comment line. Compile and run the program. Verify that your environment is properly configured to compile and execute programs. Only then should you proceed to add the custom statements that make your program unique.

This model is especially useful for you to use when writing programs from scratch. Let's say you want to write a program that allows you to update the notes for some of your albums. First, write an empty shell of a program: an empty `main` block. Save the program in Listing 10-5 as `fix_notes.4gl`. Compile and run it.

Listing 10-5 The most abstract main program block for the fix_notes.4gl program.

```
main

    -- Get an album's notes and update them

end main
```

This program has no input or output, but provides a framework from which to add functions. The fact that it compiles verifies your development environment.

Now, in the `main` block you can organize the program flow by indicating with function calls the operations you will soon define, and leave the details for later. Modify `fix_notes.4gl` to look like Listing 10-6, and try to compile it.

Its syntax is correct; its intent is clear; but something is missing. You should receive an error that includes the following:

```
Unresolved or undefined symbols detected:
.choosealbum
.displaynotes
.enternewnotes
.savenotes
```

Listing 10-6 *The main program block for* `fix_notes.4gl` *shows the program flow.*

```
main

    -- Get an album's notes and update them

    call ChooseAlbum()

    call DisplayNotes()

    call EnterNewNotes()

    call SaveNotes()

end main
```

Stub Functions

This error tells you that you must define the four functions called by your `main` program block. However, you need not create them fully formed, like Athena from the brow of Zeus. Add the lines from Listing 10-7 to the end of your program. If you are using `i4gl` to develop your programs (and you should be), you'll see the above errors embedded in your source module. You can leave the errors there while you correct your program. The Interactive Editor strips them out when it next compiles your program.

Listing 10-7 *Stub functions serve as placeholders.*

```
function ChooseAlbum()

    display 'Choosing album'

end function
```

(Continued)

Listing 10-7 *Stub functions serve as placeholders.*

```
function DisplayNotes()

    display 'Displaying notes'

end function




function EnterNewNotes()

    display 'Entering notes'

end function




function SaveNotes()

    display 'Saving notes'

end function
```

Use the `Runable` option from the `Compile` menu to create an executable program, then choose `Save-and-exit` and `Run`. You should see the following:

```
Choosing album
Displaying notes
Entering notes
Saving notes
```

Placeholder functions such as those shown in Listing 10-7 are known as *stubs*. These *stubbed out* functions are called by your `main` program block, and help verify its completeness and accuracy. Until you finally replace each `display` statement with the function's actual statements, each stub function still indicates that its place in the overall program flow is intact. In the process, your `main` program block remains relatively unchanged.

When developing programs in this way, you can treat each function as its own private *black box* of statements. You can write each without worrying that you might interfere with another. By repeatedly combing through your program as you develop it, each time replacing another stub's contents with its fleshed-out function, you can more easily identify the effect of each change. All the while, you can maintain the program's integrity, ensuring that it continues to compile and execute front-to-back without error. This method of stepwise refinement simplifies the development of complex applications.

Writing a Function

Let's continue to refine the `fix_notes.4gl` program by fleshing out its functions. Notice especially that the `main` program block changes little while you write each function, and that you write each function independent of the others. The syntax of a function block follows:

```
function function-name([input-variable-name-list])
[input-variable-definitions]

    [local-variable-definitions]

    [4GL-statements]
    [return[return-value-list]]
end function
```

where *function-name* is the name you invent for this function, unique within this program; *input-variable-name-list* is a comma-separated list of the names of any function *arguments*, or values to be received by the function; *input-variable-defini-tions* are the `define` statements that declare each of the variables in the *input-variable-name-list*; *local-variable-definitions* are the `define` statements that declare each of your local variables; *4GL-statements* is any set of legal Informix-4GL statements; and *return-value-list* is a list of comma-separated expressions whose values are sent back to the calling program from this function.

Functions can have any number of `return` statements, but only the first one encountered is executed, since then control has returned to the calling program. For each `return` statement a return value is optional, but all `return` statements within a function should return the same number and type of values.

You execute a function by calling it, either explicitly with the `call` *function-name*`()` statement, or implicitly by using the function name in an expression.

The Syntax to Call a Function

The following syntax shows an explicit function call:

```
call function-name([argument-value-list])

    [returning return-variable-name-list]
```

where *function-name* is the function you are calling, *argument-value-list* is a comma-separated list of the expressions supplied as arguments to the function, and *return-variable-name-list* is a list of comma-separated variables that becomes populated with the values returned from the function.

Your *argument-value-list* must match in number and type the *input-variable-name-list* defined in the function. Likewise, the *return-value-list* must match your *return-variable-name-list*. Thus, the `returning` clause may only be used when the function actually returns any values.

When your function returns exactly one value, you can use the function name itself wherever you can use an expression of its return value's type. The following examples show both explicit and implicit function calls:

```
call ChooseAlbum() returning l_album_num

let l_album_num = ChooseAlbum()

if (MoreUpdates()) then
```

Naming Your Functions

How should you choose appropriate names for your functions? As with table names, variable names, and constraint names, you should pick a clear, consistent naming scheme. One possible scheme is to try to follow a *Verb[Adjective]Noun*() format, such as with `DisplayNotes()` and `EnterNewNotes()`. As with variable names, function names are not case-sensitive. For example, the function names `DisplayNotes()` and `displaynotes()` are equivalent.

As a word separator in function names, a change of letter case is effective, but many programmers find underscores (_) to be more aesthetic: `display_notes()`, or `enter_new_notes()`. Still others never bother upshifting the first character of a mixed-case function name: `enterNewNotes()`.

This is an issue of style. Try a few formats, but eventually stay with the one that is most pleasing to you.

Passing Arguments to a Function

Let's explore passing arguments to, and returning values from, your `fix_notes.4gl` functions.

Update your `DisplayNotes()` function to accept an argument: the `album_num` whose notes you want to display. Replace the existing function with the statements from Listing 10-8.

Listing 10-8 The `DisplayNotes()` function accepts an argument.

```
function DisplayNotes(l_album_num)

define l_album_num integer


    define l_notes char(80)


    select notes

      into l_notes
```

(Continued)

Listing 10-8 *The* `DisplayNotes()` *function accepts an argument.*

```
    from albums

    where album_num = l_album_num

    display l_notes



end function
```

Now, try to compile your program. You should get an error message that includes the following:

```
The function "displaynotes" has already been called
    with a different number of parameters.
```

Of course it has. Your `main` program sends it no arguments, yet the function expects exactly one, the value of which it will assign to the local variable `l_album_num`. For now, change the `main` program to use a sample album number, as follows:

```
call DisplayNotes(11)
```

This time, when you compile and run the program, you should see the following output:

```
Choosing album
Program stopped at fix_notes.4gl, line number 22.
SQL statement error number -349.
Database not selected yet.
```

This error message is different than earlier ones. Those were compile-time errors, ones so syntactically incorrect or incomplete that an executable program could not be built. This one, conversely, is a runtime error. The program compiles properly, but as it executes it encounters an error and is forced to exit prematurely. Your inclusion of the stub functions allows you to easily tell that the `ChooseAlbum()` function has been called (its `display` is part of the output), whereas neither the `EnterNewNotes()` nor `SaveNotes()` functions have executed. Informix's inclusion of the line number where the error occurred also helps identify the problem.

At this point you might be getting frustrated at encountering so many errors. Cut it out. These are very gentle error messages, and each has guided you toward identifying what was wrong or missing. You'll see messages like these many times as you develop Informix-4GL programs, and should not consider them inimical.

The most recent error suggests that you need to declare your database somewhere within your `fix_notes.4gl` program. The first line in your source module, above the `main` program block, is where you should declare the database that your program uses. Add the following line to the top of your program:

```
database music
```

Now compile and run it. Your output look like the following:

```
Choosing album
Quite possibly the worst album by either Bob Dylan or
    the Grateful Dead.
Entering notes
Saving notes
```

Of course, the program still isn't very useful, given that you have to recompile it to see the notes for any album other than "Dylan and the Dead." But it has proven its ability to connect to a database and extract a value from it; no mean feat.

The next section shows how you can overcome the static argument limitation by having a function return a value. It also shows how the `main` program block acts as the coordinator, taking values from one function and supplying them as arguments to another.

Returning Values from a Function

Both the `ChooseAlbum()` and `EnterNewNotes()` functions should return values. The first should return the `album_num` whose notes you wish to update; the second should return the new notes you enter. Listing 10-9 shows a new `ChooseAlbum()` function, one that this time returns the chosen `album_num` to the calling program. Replace your `ChooseAlbum()` stub with the following statements.

Listing 10-9 The `ChooseAlbum()` *function returns an integer value.*

```
function ChooseAlbum()


    define l_album_num like albums.album_num


    prompt 'Enter album number: ' for l_album_num

    return(l_album_num)

end function
```

This time, you need to modify your `main` program block to accept a value returned from the `ChooseAlbum()` function, and pass it as an argument to the `DisplayNotes()` function. Listing 10-10 shows what your new `main` should look like.

Listing 10-10 *The main program block shuttles values between functions.*

```
main

    -- Get an album's notes and update them

    define l_album_num like albums.album_num


    call ChooseAlbum() returning l_album_num

    call DisplayNotes(l_album_num)

    call EnterNewNotes()

    call SaveNotes()

end main
```

Compile and run your latest version of `fix_notes.4gl`:

```
Enter album number: 13

Michael at his holiday best.
Entering notes
Saving notes
```

This form of the program now actually has some small value, as it can display the notes for a dynamically entered album number.

 note

The `l_album_num` *variables in each of the functions you have written (`ChooseAlbum()`, `DisplayNotes()`, and `main`) are different instances—separate variables. They are out of each other's scope, as each is a local variable. Thus, their separate assignments and uses cannot conflict with each other. That they share the same name is entirely inconsequential.*

Use the `ChooseAlbum()` function as a model for creating the `EnterNewNotes()` function. Listing 10-11 shows the completed function. Replace your stub function with this code.

Listing 10-11 *The* `EnterNewNotes()` *function returns a character value.*

```
function EnterNewNotes()


    define l_notes like albums.notes


    prompt 'Enter new notes: ' for l_notes

    return(l_notes)

end function
```

As before, you need to modify your `main` program block to receive the value returned by this function. Listing 10-12 shows these changes. You need a new variable to receive the value returned from the `EnterNewNotes()` function, and you need to assign that value to the variable. Notice in this case the use of an implicit function call with the `let` statement.

Listing 10-12 *The main program block coordinates the variables used between functions.*

```
main
    -- Get an album's notes and update them
    define l_album_num like albums.album_num
    define l_notes      like albums.notes


    call ChooseAlbum() returning l_album_num
    call DisplayNotes(l_album_num)
```

(Continued)

Listing 10-12 *The main program block coordinates the variables used between functions.*

```
    let l_notes = EnterNewNotes()

    call SaveNotes()

end main
```

You know the drill by now: compile and run your new program before proceeding. Verify that its flow is still intact, and that you've introduced no new errors. If you get stuck, you can peek ahead to Listing 10-14 for an example of the completed fix_notes.4gl program.

Now replace your final stub function with its functional equivalent. The SaveNotes() function needs to update a specific row in the albums table with the notes you've entered. Listing 10-13 shows one way you might write this function.

Listing 10-13 *The SaveNotes() function accepts multiple arguments and returns a value.*

```
function SaveNotes(l_album_num, l_notes)

define l_album_num like albums.album_num

define l_notes      like albums.notes


    update albums

       set notes = l_notes

     where album_num = l_album_num


    return(STATUS)

end function
```

note

The STATUS *variable is a global variable universally accessible to all Informix-4GL programs. Its value reflects the success of the most recent SQL operation;* 0 *indicates success. Its use in this program is only to show how a single function can both accept arguments and return values.*

Now, fix the `main` routine to interact properly with the `SaveNotes()` function. Additionally, have it display the value of STATUS that was returned by `SaveNotes()`. For the complete solution, see Listing 10-14, but first work on it yourself.

Meanwhile, the following section describes Informix's built-in functions.

Informix Built-In Functions

Informix-4GL includes a number of built-in functions. These behave exactly like functions you define, but are automatically linked with every program you write, and so are always available to you. Table 10-6 shows the most useful of these built-in functions, the data type of their arguments, and where each is described.

The following built-in functions are only valid in control blocks of `report` functions and some SQL statements.

- [group] avg (*numeric*)
- [group] count (*)
- [group] max (*numeric*)
- [group] min (*numeric*)
- [group] percent (*)
- [group] sum (*numeric*)

In reports, each may be preceded with the `group` specifier. These functions are described in Chapter 14.

Table 10-6 *Informix built-in functions.*

Function	Definition or Chapter Where Described
arg_val(int)	11, "Your 4GL User Interface"
arr_count()	12, "4GL Windows and Screen"
arr_curr(char)	12
downshift(char)	Returns a lowercase copy of its argument
fgl_getenv(char)	11
length(char)	Returns the length of its argument
num_args()	11
scr_line()	12
set_count(int)	12
showhelp(int)	12
upshift(char)	Returns an uppercase copy of its argument

Example: The `fix_notes.4gl` Program

Listing 10-14 shows one possible version of the completed
`fix_notes.4gl` program.

Listing 10-14 *The complete* fix_notes.4gl *program.*

```
database music


main

    -- Get an album's notes and update them

    define l_album_num like albums.album_num

    define l_notes      like albums.notes

    define l_status     integer


    call ChooseAlbum() returning l_album_num

    call DisplayNotes(l_album_num)

    call EnterNewNotes() returning l_notes

    call SaveNotes(l_album_num, l_notes)

        returning l_status

    display 'Update status is: ', l_status

end main



function ChooseAlbum()


    define l_album_num like albums.album_num


    prompt 'Enter album number: ' for l_album_num

    return(l_album_num)
```

(Continued)

Listing 10-14 *The complete* fix_notes.4gl *program.*

```
end function



function DisplayNotes(l_album_num)

define l_album_num like albums.album_num


    define l_notes like albums.notes


    select notes

      into l_notes

      from albums

     where album_num = l_album_num


    display l_notes
end function



function EnterNewNotes()


    define l_notes like albums.notes


    prompt 'Enter new notes: ' for l_notes

    return(l_notes)
```

(Continued)

Listing 10-14 *The complete* `fix_notes.4gl` *program.*

```
end function



function SaveNotes(l_album_num, l_notes)

define l_album_num like albums.album_num

define l_notes      like albums.notes


    update albums

        set notes = l_notes

       where album_num = l_album_num


        return(STATUS)

end function
```

After you compile this program, run it twice in succession. This way you can see that the notes you enter are saved in the database.

```
Enter album number: 21

Loony!
Enter new notes: The barred owl (Strix varia) steals the show.

Update status is:      0

Enter album number: 21

The barred owl (Strix varia) steals the show.
```

```
Enter new notes: But the red-cockaded woodpecker is also
     impressive.


Update status is:       0
```

> Notice especially how the first set of notes entered ("Strix varia") was saved, overwriting the original notes ("Loony!").

Scope Revisited

Before ending this chapter, let's revisit the issue of scope. So far, all of the variables in `fix_notes.4gl` have been local variables. As such, you've had to define similar variables in several places so that you could shuttle values between functions. Now let's use modular variables to avoid some of this work. You'll remember that modular variables must be defined before any executable statements, and outside of any program blocks.

In Listing 10-15, two variables have been elevated to modular scope. Notice also that their names have changed to reflect their new status. The `l_status` variable has been removed entirely, since STATUS is already global.

Listing 10-15 *The complete* `fix_notes.4gl` *program with modular variables.*

```
database music



define m_album_num like albums.album_num

define m_notes       like albums.notes



main

    -- Get an album's notes and update them
```

(Continued)

```
      call ChooseAlbum()

      call DisplayNotes()

      call EnterNewNotes()

      call SaveNotes()

      display 'Update status is: ', STATUS

end main




function ChooseAlbum()

      prompt 'Enter album number: ' for m_album_num

end function




function DisplayNotes()


      select notes

        into m_notes

        from albums

       where album_num = m_album_num


      display m_notes
```

(Continued)

```
end function




function EnterNewNotes()

    prompt 'Enter new notes: ' for m_notes

end function




function SaveNotes()

    update albums

       set notes = m_notes

     where album_num = m_album_num

end function
```

Is this form of the program better? Well, it's a little simpler—the
`main` block is especially clean—and a lot less robust. Each function has become dependent on others. You can no longer tell by
looking at the `main` program block which functions set values and
which use the values that were set. Also, nonlocal (modular and
global) variables are subject to unintended alteration by other
functions, and in a complex program the exact location of where
a nonlocal variable changes may be murky.

Additionally, you may eventually want to extract certain utility
functions for reuse in function libraries or in other programs.

Certainly none of these functions could be extracted from this source module and work as written, since then they would fall outside of the scope of the modular variables they use.

For clarity, you must hide certain programming details *within* functions, but it is often confusing when you hide the details of the interfaces *between* functions. This does not mean that you should never use modular or global variables; only that you should use them with care.

Over the next four chapters you'll have the chance to explore not only program scope in greater detail, but also ways to enhance your user interface, generate reports, and make your programs more robust.

Summary

You've come a long way, from "Hello, world!" to developing a top-down, structured, function-based application program. Along the way, you learned that the Informix-4GL source code you write has to be prepared for execution, either by compilation or via RDS. Your source code can comprise one or several modules, and they can all be linked by the compiler into a single executable.

The `define` statement declares variables and indicates their scope and data type. It, and the remainder of the 4GL statements, were introduced in this chapter. You place these statements inside program blocks to dictate a program's procedural flow and any compile-time directives you wish to include. You learned how to use branching and looping to indicate program flow control.

Most important, you learned about functions, named blocks of logically related statements that perform a specific task. By defining, passing arguments to, and returning values from functions, you developed an Informix-4GL program of some usefulness. The key principle of stepwise refinement made the transition from stub functions to actual functions smooth and iterative.

Extra Credit

....

Q&A

Question	**Answer**
Building all these functions seems like a lot of work. Can't I just do all my processing in the `main` program block?	O.K. Deep Breath. Not everyone sees the light at first. Trust me—learn to use functions and to use them well. Your friends will admire you, and you'll feel good about yourself. Here's a quote from earlier in this chapter, regarding functions: "Their use in creating effective real-world code is not optional."
Some codger in a trenchcoat tried to sell me something called a `goto` statement to perform what he called "unconditional branching." It looks harmless enough. Should I buy it?	Slowly back away. Just say "No" to the `goto` statement.
My source module has several functions. Does is matter how I order those functions within the module?	If your source module includes a `main` program block, that must come before any other functions. Otherwise, the ordering of functions within a module makes no difference.
I've built a handy function that I'd like to include in many of my 4GL programs. What's the best way to do that?	First: congratulations! Function reuse is what elevates programming from the tedious to the creative. Starting with the next chapter you'll learn how to create your own function libraries.

Exercises

1. Change the `fix_notes.4gl` program (Listing 10-14) to update notes only when a value is entered with the `EnterNewNotes()` function. That is, if an empty string is returned from `EnterNewNotes()`, do not update the album's notes. Modify only the `main` program block.

2. Keep the change from Exercise 1. Add a program control loop to `fix_notes.4gl` that allows you to continue prompting for new albums and entering new notes until you choose to exit. Do not alter any existing functions except `main`. You may add new functions if you wish.

Exercise Answers

Listing E10-1 *Answer to Exercise 1.*

```
database music


main
    -- Get an album's notes and update them
    define l_album_num like albums.album_num
    define l_notes     like albums.notes
    define l_status    int


    call ChooseAlbum() returning l_album_num
    call DisplayNotes(l_album_num)
    call EnterNewNotes() returning l_notes
    if (length(l_notes) > 0) then
        call SaveNotes(l_album_num, l_notes)
            returning l_status
        display 'Update status is: ', l_status
    else
        display 'Notes unchanged'
    end if


end main
```

```
database music


main

    -- Get an album's notes and update them

    define l_album_num like albums.album_num

    define l_notes      like albums.notes

    define l_status     int


    while (MoreUpdates())

        call ChooseAlbum() returning l_album_num

        call DisplayNotes(l_album_num)

        call EnterNewNotes() returning l_notes

        if (length(l_notes) > 0) then

            call SaveNotes(l_album_num, l_notes)

            returning l_status

            display 'Update status is: ', l_status

        else

            display 'Notes unchanged'

        end if

    end while
end main
```

(Continued)

Listing E10-2 *Answer to Exercise 2.*

```
function MoreUpdates()


    define l_more char(1)


    prompt 'More updates to perform? ' for char l_more
    if (upshift(l_more) = 'Y') then
        return(TRUE)
    else
        return(FALSE)
    end if
end function
```

Chapter

11

Your 4GL User Interface

Informix-4GL is designed to be effective at allowing you to create flexible *forms* for viewing, entering, and updating data. Forms are custom data entry templates that you design. Informix-4GL forms are merely an extension of the forms concepts you learned in Chapter 6, "ISQL Forms and Reports." You've also already been introduced to some of Informix's line-based user interface commands (`prompt` and `display`). In this chapter you'll learn how to use these and more components of Informix's user interface toolkit, including its ring-menu builder.

Table 11-1 shows an overview of these components and some ways in which they differ. This chapter is devoted to explaining this table, and showing you when you should use each of these interface methods.

Attributes are custom display options you define, such as `bold`, `yellow`, or `blink`. Also, by using the `options` command (see the next section), you can change the starting display line for most of these methods.

Table 11-1 User interface methods.

Method	Display starts on line #	Number of lines displayed	Can include attributes	Type of input accepted
display	1	1	Sometimes	None
menu	1	2	N	Menu selections
prompt	1	1	Y	One line of text
message	2	1	Y	None
input	3	5–24	By field	Varies by field
comment	23	1	N	None
error	24	1	Y	None
arg_val()	n/a	0	N	Command line arguments
fgl_getenv()	n/a	0	N	Environmental variables
run	n/a	0	N	Varies

The Screen, According to Informix

There is a default screen, the 4GL screen, that Informix-4GL uses as a grid for displaying messages, menus, and forms to the user. It is 24 lines long and 80 characters wide. On this screen are *reserved lines*, lines predefined as the location where certain types of displays occur. Figure 11-1 shows the default definitions for each of the reserved lines. The line numbers are shown for reference only; they are not displayed on your screen.

When you use any of the methods in Table 11-1 to put text onto the screen, Informix displays the text *within* its 4GL screen

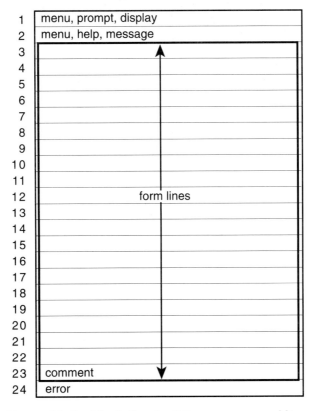

1	menu, prompt, display
2	menu, help, message
3	
4	
5	
6	
7	
8	
9	
10	
11	
12	form lines
13	
14	
15	
16	
17	
18	
19	
20	
21	
22	
23	comment
24	error

Figure 11–1   *The Informix-4GL screen reserved lines.*

grid. In Chapter 12, "4GL Windows and Screen Arrays," you'll learn how to add windows, online help, and screen arrays *on top of* this screen.

You can alter the location and appearance of the various user interface methods. The primary ways to do this are with the `options` statement and the `attributes` clause. These sections are included for completeness, but you can create robust and attractive applications without them. The example programs in *Informix Basics* use `options` and `attributes` sparingly.

The `options` Statement

Normally, a 4GL statement like the following has its text displayed on line 2 (the default `message` line):

```
message 'Please wait while the report is generated'
```

If, instead, you execute the following two statements, the text appears on line 6:

```
options message line 6
message 'Please wait while the report is generated'
```

You use the `options` statement to specify new default features of certain screen interaction statements, including the reserved lines for the 4GL screen.

```
options statement line [[first [+ offset]|
    last [- offset]]|line-number]
    [, statement line [[first [+ offset]|
    last [- offset]]|line-number] ...]
```

where *line-number* is a screen line number, from 1 to 24, *offset* is a relative number of lines from the top or bottom of the current window, and *statement* is one of the following:

* comment
* error
* form
* menu
* message
* prompt

For example, the following are both valid `options` statements:

```
options message line 6
options menu     line 20,
       prompt    line last - 2,
       form      line first
```

You can't use `options` to redefine the location for the `display` statement, since that command can specify its own location.

The `options` statement is a runtime specifier. That is, each program begins execution with the default reserved line values. If a program encounters an `options` statement, it uses any values therein to overwrite the current defaults for those user interface statements. Should the program encounter subsequent `options` statements, each one supersedes the previous ones.

There are many ways in which the various types of screen interaction statements interact and occasionally conflict. As one simple example, when you move from field to field on a form, the `comment` and `error` lines are cleared. If you redefine the `message` line to be line 24 (the default `error` line) without redefining the `error` line, your messages will get cleared whenever you navigate between fields.

tip

Don't redefine your reserved lines—at least not yet. Their complex interactions make redefinitions tricky. The defaults are adequate for most applications.

Defining Display Attributes

Certain screen interaction commands (see Table 11-1) allow you to customize their display by including an `attribute` clause when you invoke the specific statement. For example, on a color monitor the following statement changes the display attribute of the prompt string to reverse-video `yellow`, and the user response to `blue`.

```
prompt 'Enter a file name: '
    attribute (yellow, reverse)
    for file_name attribute (blue)
```

On a monochrome monitor, the attributes are mapped to other visual equivalents. Table 11-2 shows the various keywords you can include in an `attribute` clause.

You can include any number of comma-separated *custom* specifiers between the parentheses of an `attribute` clause, but at most one of any *color* or *intensity* specifier. Where the `attribute` clause is allowed for any specific 4GL statement, its use is noted in that statement's syntax box.

caution

Don't use the `blink` attribute unless you want to torment your users. It's not cute; it's annoying. Find a more gentle way.

Table 11-2 *The attribute specifiers.*

Specifier	Type	Monochrome Display	Color Display
black	Color	Dim	Black
blue	Color	Dim	Blue
cyan	Color	Dim	Cyan
green	Color	Dim	Green
magenta	Color	Bold	Magenta
red	Color	Bold	Red
white	Color	Normal	White
yellow	Color	Bold	Yellow
bold	Intensity	Bold	Red
dim	Intensity	Dim	Blue
invisible	Intensity	Invisible	Invisible
normal	Intensity	Normal	White
blink	Custom	Blinking	Blinking
reverse	Custom	Reverse	Reverse
underline	Custom	Underline	Underline

Line-Based Interfaces

Now that you've suffered through discovering how to make these screen interaction statements complex, you'll find that they are actually simple. To learn these statements, you should create a new 4GL program for this purpose only. Try the various sample statements that follow in this section. For those examples that include variable names, you should invent your own and assign them values. You already know how to do this; you won't see sample listings for such simple tasks.

One of the reasons you need to do this is that individual systems differ in how they display certain values. You need to discover what works on your system, and note in this chapter—yes, write in the book!—any local idiosyncrasies you encounter.

The message Statement

The message statement displays a single line of text to the message line,

```
message message-string [attribute-clause]
```

where message-string is any combination of quoted strings and variables separated by the string concatenation operator (,), and attribute-clause is any valid attribute clause. If the length of message-string exceeds the screen width, it is truncated to fit. The message-string is displayed at the current value of the message reserved line. You can include the clipped, using, and substring operators in message statements.

For example, the following are all valid message statements:

```
message 'You may find yourself living in a shotgun shack.'
message l_info_string
message 'Output will be sent to ', l_file_name clipped, '. Please
    wait.' attribute (reverse)
```

Informix-4GL ignores the invisible attribute if you include it in an attribute clause. (Well, of course it does. Of all the—*Invisible messages!* The cold war is over.)

The error Statement

The error statement displays a single line of text to the error line, and rings the terminal bell. By default, the error text is displayed in reverse video. The error line is also where system error messages are displayed. These include the kinds of diagnostic information you see when developing Informix-4GL programs as well as runtime error messages such as constraint violations.

```
error error-string [attribute-clause]
```

where *error-string* is any combination of quoted strings and variables separated by the string concatenation operator (,), and *attribute-clause* is any valid attribute clause. If the length of *error-string* exceeds the screen width, it is truncated to fit. The *error-string* is displayed at the current value of the error reserved line. You can include the clipped and using operators in error statements.

For example, the following are all valid error statements:

```
error 'This is not my beautiful house.'
error l_error_msg attribute (red)
error 'Cannot insert album number ', l_album_num using '<<<<', '.'
```

The display Statement

The display statement is the all-purpose command you use to display data values to the screen. It has three forms, one of which, dealing with forms, is described in the section "More on the display Statement" later in this chapter. The other two forms are *line mode overlay* and specified line display.

The first of these two forms shows the line mode overlay syntax; the second shows how to display text at a specific line and column.

```
display display-string
display display-string at line-number, column-number
    [attribute-clause]
```

where *display-string* is any combination of quoted strings and variables separated by the string concatenation operator (,), *line-number* and *column-number* are literals or variables that specify the line and column number on the screen at which the display starts, and *attribute-clause* is any valid attribute clause. If the length of *display-string* exceeds the screen width, it is truncated to fit. You can include the `clipped`, `using`, and substring operators in `display` statements.

In the first form, the *display-string* is actually displayed in a new window that opens on top of the current screen. It is a *line-mode* display that *overlays* the current screen. When all of the line mode overlay display statements in a set have finished executing, that window disappears and the underlying screen is restored.

With the second form, you indicate a specific line and column of the current screen at which to display text. Existing text there is overwritten. Notice that you can only use the `attribute` clause with the second form.

For example, the following are all valid `display` statements:

```
display 'This is not my beautiful wife.'
display l_msg at l_line_no, l_column_no attribute (bold)
display 'The first three characters of the last name are: ',
    l_last_name[1,3] at 8, 1
```

The **prompt** Statement

The `prompt` statement is the easiest way you can get input from the user. It operates much like the previous three line-based interfaces, but adds a twist: your program's operation suspends until the user enters a response. That response is assigned to the *response variable* you indicate.

```
prompt prompt-string [attribute-clause]
    for [char] response-variable
    [help help-number] [attribute-clause]
```

where *prompt-string* is any combination of quoted strings and variables separated by the string concatenation operator (,), *attribute-clause* is any valid `attribute` clause, *response-variable* is the name of the variable in which the user response is stored, and *help-number* is a help message number you define (see Chapter 12). The total length of *prompt-string* plus the user response must be less than 80 characters. If you include the `char` keyword, the user need not press the Return key after entering a single-character response.

The *prompt-string* is displayed at the current value of the prompt reserved line, unless a previous display statement has placed the program in line mode overlay. In that case, the prompt statement maintains the line mode overlay window. You can use the clipped and using operators to help build *prompt-string*.

For example, the following are all valid prompt statements:

```
prompt 'How did I get here? ' for l_answer help 205
prompt 'Press any key to continue: ' for char l_any_key attribute
    (invisible)
prompt 'Delete all rows from ', l_table_name clipped, '?'
    attribute (magenta)
    for l_response
```

Building Ring Menus

Ring menus are one of the most automated features of Informix-4GL. They are easy to create, easy to navigate, consistent, useful, and generally swell. Use them.

The Musical Therapy Ring Menu

Let's start by doing. Save the code from Listing 11-1 as ther-apy.4gl. Compile and run it.

Listing 11-1 *The Musical Therapy ring menu program.*

```
main


    -- Create a menu that suggests a cure for certain
ills

    options message line 4
```

(Continued)

Listing 11-1 The Musical Therapy ring menu program.

```
menu 'Musical Therapy'

    command 'Melancholia'

        'Pick an album to cure sadness.'

        message 'Beauty and the Beat'

        attribute (yellow)

    command 'Claustrophobia'

        'Pick an album to evoke the outdoors.'

        message 'Sounds of the Okefenokee Swamp'

        attribute (green)

    command 'Two left feet'

        'Pick an album to make you dance.'

        message 'Cruisin' attribute (magenta)

    command 'Squareness'

        'Pick an album to make you hip.'

        error 'Sorry, squareness is terminal.

        Try to cheer up.'

        next option 'Melancholia'

    command 'Exit' 'Exit the Musical Therapy menu'

        exit menu

    end menu


end main
```

When you run the program, you should see a screen like Figure 11-2.

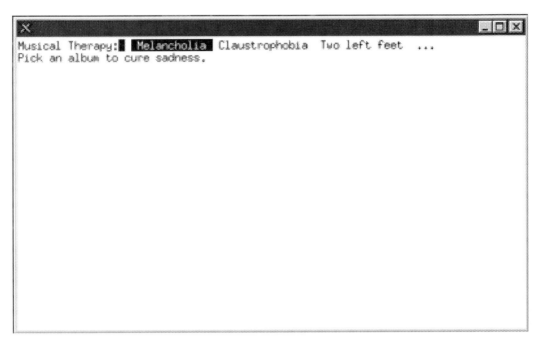

Figure 11–2   *The Musical Therapy ring menu.*

Use the various ring-menu navigation commands you've seen. Try the space bar, the arrow keys, and the first letters of each of the menu choices. They all work exactly the same as for the *official* ring menus that are an integral part of the Informix tools. DB-Access, ISQL, the Informix Programmer's Environment—they are all built with Informix-4GL and its ring menus. The syntax for the menu statement follows:

```
menu menu-title
    command-block
    [command-block ...]
end menu
```

where *menu-title* is a variable or quoted string that names the menu and *command-block* consists of the following clauses:

```
command [key (key-value)]
[option-name] [option-description]
    [help help-number]
    [4gl-statements]
    [next option option-name]
```

key-value is a single letter; *option-name* is a variable or quoted string that names the menu option; *option-description* is a variable or quoted string that describes this menu option; *help-number* is a help message number you define; *4gl-statements* is any sequence of 4GL statements, even another menu; and *option-name* is any option in this menu.

When you use the `next option` statement, that menu option becomes highlighted after the current statement completes, but it is not executed.

Using Command Keys

Command keys are individual keys you define as alternative single keystrokes the user can press to activate a menu option. There are two chief reasons you might want to do this:

- Changing *hot-keys*
- Creating invisible options

Changing Hot-Keys

You've already noticed that the first letter of a menu option (its hot-key) selects the option immediately. What happens when several options share the same first letter? Let's find out.

Alter your `therapy.4gl` program. Change `Two left feet` to `Clumsiness`; change `Squareness` to `Creepiness`. Compile and run it, then press `c`. You should see something like Figure 11-3.

Notice how the ring menu help line changes to show you the menu options that match your most recent keystroke. Now press `l`. The one option whose *second* letter fails to match this keystroke (`Creepiness`) disappears. Now, by pressing `a` you can select `Claustrophobia` or with `u`, `Clumsiness`.

This method of differentiating options based on their noninitial spelling is Informix's default method for ring menus. Many people find it unfriendly. You can instead use the `key (key-value)` clause to define your own hot-key. In `therapy.4gl`, replace your `Clumsiness` option name with the following line, and run it:

```
command key ('L') 'cLumsiness'
'Pick an album to make you dance.'
```

Figure 11–3 *The ring menu help line shows all nondistinct options.*

Notice the change in case of the `cLumsiness` option name. This reflects its hot-key's change from the `clu` sequence to `l`. This case change is not mandatory, but is conventional. Without the visual clue, a user would not know that this option's hot-key had changed.

Create hot-keys for all of your ring menu options that do not have unique initial letters. Better yet, choose creative option names so that you need not redefine their hot-keys.

Creating Invisible Menu Options

If you include in your option definition a `command key` clause but exclude an option name and description, the menu option is invisible. This is not as sinister as it may seem. In Chapter 3, "DB-Access," you learned that each standard Informix ring menu includes a hidden *shell escape* command, invoked with an exclamation mark (!). Such a handy escape allows you to run a single shell command without having to exit your ring menu. You can add a similar feature to your own ring menus. Add the following code fragment to your `therapy.4gl` program:

```
define l_shell_cmd char(80)
...
command key ('!')
    options prompt line last
    prompt '!' for l_shell_cmd
    run l_shell_cmd
    prompt 'Press return to continue'
        attribute (reverse) for char l_shell_cmd
    options prompt line first
```

You can insert this menu option anywhere within your `menu` command. The `run` command executes a single operating system command from within a 4GL program. It is described in the "Running Operating System Commands" section at the end of this chapter.

Using Forms

Line-based interfaces and menu statements are convenient and useful, and may even be sufficient interface tools for many simple applications. However, for significant data entry you need to use forms, custom input screens you define for field-based data entry. There are three 4GL statements that interact with forms:

- `display`, for showing program values in form fields
- `input`, for allowing data entry via forms
- `construct`, for using forms to build query-by-example (QBE) expressions

Here, you'll learn how to use the `input` statement and the forms-based `display` options. Chapter 12 adds the useful `construct` statement.

Form Specifications

You'll remember from Chapter 6 how the forms model works. Table 11-3 summarizes the how those ISQL steps compare to the Informix-4GL model.

Table 11-3 The steps involved in creating and running forms.

Operation	ISQL	Informix-4GL
Create a form	Text editor	Text editor
Create a default form	`sformbld -d`	`form4gl -d`
Compile a form	`sformbld`	`form4gl`
Run a form	`sperform`	Custom program

With ISQL, you create a form specification file (with a `.per` file name extension) by using a default form generator or with an editor. This file dictates where on the screen individual fields are placed, what literal text surrounds them, how these fields relate to database columns, and what display attributes apply to each field. This model is maintained for Informix-4GL forms. In fact, you can use your ISQL form specification files for your Informix-4GL programs.

In either model, you then use a screen compiler to prepare your form for execution. With ISQL, the screen compiler is `sformbld`; for Informix-4GL, it is `form4gl`. Each creates a compiled form (with a `.frm` extension), but neither compiled form can be used with the other application. With each application, you can also use its form builder (from `isql` or `i4gl`) to compile the form specification files. Table 10-1 shows how the Informix-4GL form builder fits into the Programmer's Environment.

Finally, you must run a program that references the compiled form, and allows you to navigate it field by field. With ISQL, this program is the same for all forms: `sperform`. The largest difference between ISQL-based forms and Informix-4GL forms is that

4GL forms must be driven by custom programs that you write. There is no default forms driver program for Informix-4GL.

The heart of any forms driver program is the `input` statement, the nonprocedural Informix-4GL statement that controls your program's interaction with your form. The following sections describe how you create form specification files, open them from within your 4GL programs, define screen records for your form interaction, display values to the form fields, and use the `input` statement to bind program variables to screen fields.

Generating Default Forms

Let's create a form that allows you to choose, view, and update rows in the `albums` table. If you already have an `albums.per` form specification file that you built in Chapter 6, you can use it. Otherwise, you can use the Programmer's Environment ring menu, or use the very convenient default form generation method that follows:

```
$ form4gl -d
Enter desired name for the form: albums
Enter the name of the database used by the form: music


You will now enter the names of the database tables which will
    appear on
the form.  You may enter a maximum of 14 table names.
Enter a carriage return alone to terminate the sequence.


Enter a table name: albums
Enter a table name:
The form "albums.per" will now be compiled.



The form compilation was successful.
```

Listing 11-2 shows the default form specification file.

Listing 11-2 *The default form specification file for the albums table.*

```
database music

screen size 24 by 80

{

album_num          [f000        ]

title              [f001                            ]

artist             [f002                    ]

issue_year         [f003   ]

genre              [f004        ]

rating             [f005   ]

notes              [f006                                    ]

                   [f007                                    ]

}

end

tables

albums

attributes

f000 = albums.album_num;

f001 = albums.title;

f002 = albums.artist;

f003 = albums.issue_year;

f004 = albums.genre;

f005 = albums.rating;

f006 = albums.notes[1,40];

f007 = albums.notes[41,80];

end
```

Customizing Your Forms

Now, you can use your favorite text editor to rearrange the form to make it a little more palatable. Listing 11-3 shows one possible customization method. You should alter the `albums.per` file so that it is similar to this.

Listing 11-3 *A customized form specification file for the albums table.*

```
database music


screen

{

                          Music Collection


                      Album Number      [f000        ]
    Title         [f001                            ]

    Artist        [f002                    ]

    Issue Year    [f003]


    Genre         [f004      ]      Rating           [f5]


    Notes         [f006                              ]

                  [f006                              ]

}


tables

    albums
```

(Continued)

Listing 11-3 *A customized form specification file for the albums table.*

```
attributes

    f000 = albums.album_num;

    f001 = albums.title;

    f002 = albums.artist;

    f003 = albums.issue_year;

    f004 = albums.genre;

    f5   = albums.rating, comments =

           'Enter a value from 1 to 10';

    f006 = albums.notes, wordwrap;


instructions

    screen record sr_albums (albums.title thru

        albums.notes)
```

You'll need to make the following changes to complete the transformation from the default form specification file to the customized one:

- Add a screen title (e.g., `Music Collection`).
- Rearrange the location of the display fields.
- Change the column names to be more English-like.
- Reduce the size of the `rating` and `issue_year` display fields, and change the field tag for `rating` to fit into the smaller field.
- Combine the two `notes` fields into a single data entry field, connected by the `wordwrap` attribute.
- Add the `comments` attribute to the `rating` field so that these comments are displayed when the cursor enters the `rating` field. The `comment line` is set to `last - 1` by default, but you can change it with the `options` statement.

- Remove the (unnecessary in 4GL) end keywords that separate each section of the form specification file.
- Add some white space to the various sections to enhance readability.
- Remove the optional size 24 x 80 specifier for the screen section. Without it, the number of lines defaults to 24 and the width of the screen becomes the maximum width of any line in the screen layout.
- Add an instructions section in which the sr_albums screen record is defined.

Screen Records

Screen records are convenient mechanisms through which your 4GL programs communicate with your 4GL forms. In your display, input, and construct statements you *bind*, or temporarily associate, program variables with screen fields. Just as records in a 4GL program collect related elements into a single container, screen records associate multiple form fields under one name for easier handling.

For example, each of the following 4GL statements bind records or simple program variables to the sr_albums screen record, or to individual screen fields:

```
input lr_albums.* from sr_albums.*
display by name lr_albums.*
display lr_albums.* to sr_albums.*
display l_album_num to sr_albums.album_num
construct query_string
    on lr_albums.title, lr_albums.artist
    from sr_albums.title, sr_albums.artist
```

Field Attributes

Just as with ISQL forms, you can include attributes in your field descriptions to customize the behavior of individual fields during input and construct statements. The rating and notes attribute definitions of Listing 11-3 show two such examples. Because of the flexibility of Informix-4GL, you generally limit the use of form attributes, and embed needed logic within the appli-

cation code instead. Nonetheless, Table 11-4 shows the most useful field attributes. When you separate them with commas, you
can include multiple attributes for a single field.

Table 11-4 Field attributes in 4GL forms.

Specifier	Effect
autonext	Force the cursor to the next field when the current field is full.
color = color-name	Display field text with a specified video attribute. Any of the custom or color attributes shown in Table 11-2 can be used as color-name.
comments = 'message-string'	Display message-string on the screen's comment line when the cursor moves into the field.
default = default-value	Assign a default value to a field during data entry. This attribute is ignored during an input statement declared without defaults.
downshift	Convert each uppercase letter to lowercase as it is entered.
include = (legal-value-list)	Prevent the cursor from leaving the field until one of the values in the comma-separated legal-value-list is entered. Include NULL as one of the legal values to prevent this attribute from forcing an entry in this field.
invisible	Do not echo user-entered data.
noentry	Prevent data entry during an input statement.
required	Force data entry during an input statement. If a default value is specified for this field the required attribute has no effect, since the default value satisfies the required attribute.
reverse	Display any value in the field in reverse video. The reverse attribute disables any color attribute for the same field.

(Continued)

Table 11-4 Field attributes in 4GL forms.

Specifier	Effect
upshift	Convert each lowercase letter to uppercase as it is entered.
wordwrap	Treat multiple-segment fields (those that occupy several lines and share the same field tag identifier) as a single field for editing.

Opening and Closing Forms

Your 4GL program can interact with a form only after the program has opened and displayed it. Listing 11-4 shows the simplest version of a program that uses forms. Save it as `albums.4gl`, then compile and run it. You'll need this programmatic scaffolding on which to add the `display` and `input` statements dictated by the exercises that follow.

Listing 11-4 The albums.4gl program, first pass.

```
main


    open form f_albums from 'albums'

    display form f_albums

    sleep 2

    close form f_albums


end main
```

The syntax for the `open form` statement follows:

```
open form form-name from 'file-name[.frm]'
```

where *form-name* is an identifier you assign here as the name of the form, and *file-name* is the name of a file that contains the compiled screen form. The scope of *form-name* is global to your entire 4GL program.

After you have declared a form name by opening it, you can display it as follows:

```
display form form-name [attribute (attribute-list)]
```

where *form-name* is the name of the screen form to be displayed, and *attribute-list* is a comma-separated list of attributes from Table 11-2. A previous `open form` *form-name* must already have been executed in this 4GL program to declare *form-name*.

Any attributes you specify are applied to each field in the form. If you assign display attributes in other places, those assignments override any `display form` attributes.

Finally, when you are through with a form you should close it:

```
close form form-name
```

where *form-name* is the name of a previously opened screen form. The statement releases the memory required for a form. Although all open forms are closed automatically when your program exits, it is polite and tidy to close any form after you are finished with it.

More on the `display` Statement

The `display` statement has three varieties. In addition to the *line mode overlay* and specified line display described earlier in "The `display` Statement," the `display` statement can also display values to the fields of a screen form. Listing 11-5 shows one (not yet very useful) example of displaying data to a form. Enter and run this version of `albums.4gl`.

Listing 11-5 The `albums.4gl` *program, second pass.*

```
database music


main


    define lr_albums record like albums.*


    open form f_albums from 'albums'

    display form f_albums


    select *

       into lr_albums.*

       from albums

      where album_num = 22


    display lr_albums.* to sr_albums.*

    close form f_albums


end main
```

Notice especially the use of the `into` clause to assign the selected column values to local program variables, and the `display` statement to show those values on the screen an entire record at a time.

When you run this version of the program, your screen should resemble Figure 11-4.

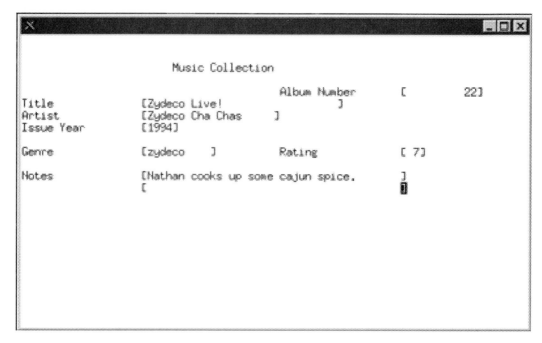

Figure 11–4 The `display` *statement displays values to fields of a screen form.*

You can use either of the following two methods to display program values to screen fields:

```
display value-list
    to form-field-list [attribute-clause]
display by name variable-list [attribute-clause]
```

where `value-list` is a comma-separated list of quoted strings and program variables, `form-field-list` is a comma-separated list of screen fields, `variable-list` is a comma-separated list of program variables, and `attribute-clause` is any valid `attribute` clause. The number and type of elements in the `value-list` must match the associated `form-field-list`. When you use the `by name` clause, the variables in `variable-list` are bound to screen fields of the same name. Informix-4GL ignores any record prefix when matching the names.

In place of an explicit comma-separated list of variables or screen fields, you can also use the `record.*` notation. It expands to a comma-separated list of all the elements, in order. You can also use the `thru` notation to expand `variable-list` or `value-`

list. For example, for this chapter's examples the following statements are equivalent:

```
display by name lr_albums.*
display by name lr_albums.album_num thru lr_albums.notes
display by name lr_albums.album_num, lr_albums.title,
             lr_albums.artist, lr_albums.genre,
             lr_albums.rating, lr_albums.notes
display lr_albums.* to sr_albums.*
display lr_albums.album_num thru lr_albums.notes to sr_albums.*
```

You can't use the `thru` notation to expand a screen record in a `display` statement.

Now let's expand the `albums.4gl` program to accept some user input. The next version will add `prompt` and `error` statements to make the program more useful; following that, the next version will include the `input` statement. Revise your program to reflect the significant additions represented by Listing 11-6. Run it several times, examining various albums in your collection.

Listing 11-6 *The* `albums.4gl` *program, third pass.*

```
database music


main


    define l_more_albums smallint

    define lr_albums record like albums.*


    open form f_albums from 'albums'

    display form f_albums


    let l_more_albums = TRUE
```

(Continued)

Listing 11-6 The `albums.4gl` *program, third pass.*

```
    while l_more_albums

        call GetAlbum() returning lr_albums.*

        display by name lr_albums.*

      let l_more_albums =

          YesNoPrompt('Do you want to see another album?')

      end while


    close form f_albums


end main



function GetAlbum()


    define lr_albums record like albums.*


    prompt 'Enter album number: ' for lr_albums.album_num


    select *
      into lr_albums.*

      from albums

    where album_num = lr_albums.album_num


    if (STATUS != 0) then
```

(Continued)

Listing 11-6 The `albums.4gl` *program, third pass.*

```
            error 'Sorry, album number ',

                lr_albums.album_num using '<<<',

                ' does not exist.'

            initialize lr_albums.* to null

        end if


        return lr_albums.*


end function



-- Return a TRUE or FALSE value to the question supplied.

function YesNoPrompt(l_prompt_string)

define l_prompt_string char(60)


    define l_response    char(1)


    while TRUE

        prompt l_prompt_string clipped, ': '

            for char l_response

        case (upshift(l_response))

            when 'Y'

                return TRUE

            when 'N'
```

(Continued)

Listing 11-6 *The* `albums.4gl` *program, third pass.*

```
                    return FALSE

            otherwise

                error 'Please enter Y or N'

        end case

      end while


    end function
```

This program incorporates some of the Informix-4GL constructs that are necessary in real-world programs. It makes more use of functions, using expressions as arguments, looping, branching, and user interaction, than you've seen before. Make sure that you understand this program thoroughly before proceeding.

The `input` Statement

The `input` statement lets you navigate your form field by field, entering values as you wish. The values that you enter in screen fields are stored in the program variables to which they are bound. You can use the stored values in these program variables to interact with the database. For example, the bare-bones `UpdateAlbum()` function from Listing 11-7 allows you to update albums based on values you enter. Add the function to your `albums.4gl` source module. You'll also need to add the following fragment to your `main` program block, just after you display the album record.

```
if (YesNoPrompt('Update this album?')) then

    call UpdateAlbum(lr_albums.*)

end if
```

Listing 11-7 The `albums.4gl` *program, fourth pass.*

```
function UpdateAlbum(lr_albums)

define lr_albums record like albums.*


    input by name lr_albums.* without defaults


    if (YesNoPrompt('Update current row with these
    values?')) then
        update albums
            set * = lr_albums.*
            where album_num = lr_albums.album_num
        end if


end function
```

 Informix exempts any serial columns from updates when you use the `set * = record-name.*` *clause, as in Listing 11-7.*

When you've made these changes, run the program several times, changing some of the `albums` values. The purpose of this example is to exercise the `input` statement, so don't be afraid to alter your data. You'll likely discover that it's easy to make the program crash, say, by entering an invalid rating—one outside the range of the `ck_album_rating` check constraint. Although the database prevents your saving values that violate constraints, it does so ungracefully. One of the challenges facing the developer of any user interface is to notify the user, as early as possible, that some value just entered is invalid. Generally, the bulk of any `input` statement consists of these field-by-field validity checks.

The next several sections introduce some such checks, but leave others as exercises for the reader.

The syntax for the `input` statement follows:

```
input binding-clause [attribute-clause]
[help help-number] [input-blocks end input]
```

where *attribute-clause* is any valid `attribute` clause, *help-number* is a help message number you define, and *binding-clause* and *input-blocks* are described below.

The *binding-clause* relates program variables to screen variables and defines the order of input. It can take either of the following two forms:

```
variable-list [without defaults] from form-field-list
by name variable-list [without defaults]
```

where *variable-list* is a comma-separated list of program variables and *form-field-list* is a comma-separated list of screen fields. The number and type of elements in the *variable-list* must match the associated *form-field-list*. When you use the `by name` clause, the variables in *variable-list* are bound to screen fields of the same name. Informix-4GL ignores any record prefix when matching the names.

The `without defaults` clause specifies that the current values of *variable-list* should be used as the initial values for each of your fields. The `without defaults` clause is appropriate for update operations, whereas excluding it is often reasonable when accepting values that will be used in an `insert` statement.

As with the `display` statement, you can also use the *record.** notation. It expands to a comma-separated list of all the elements, in order.

The *input-blocks* describe specific actions the program takes when certain events occur: before or after a field is entered, before or after the user is allowed to input any data, or upon pressing a special key. It can be introduced by any of the following five statements:

- `before input`
- `before field` *form-field-name*
- `after input`
- `after field` *form-field-name*
- `on key` (*special-key*)

Within an input block you can include any of the following statements:

- Any 4GL statements
- `next field` *form-field-name*
- `continue input`
- `exit input`

Refer to Listing 11-8 to see how input blocks are used to customize your input statement.

Navigating Form Fields

You'll notice that when you updated your rows using the `albums.4gl` program, the cursor always traversed the form fields in the same order. That order is the order in which the form fields are listed in the binding clause of the `input` statement.

Before the cursor enters any form field during an `input` statement, 4GL executes any code you have defined in a `before field` *form-field-name* block. Commonly, you display messages or initialize variables in such locations. Likewise, the `after field` *form-field-name* block contains statements to be executed as your cursor is leaving a form field. Such statement blocks usually contain the code that verifies the value just entered, and force the user to try again if the entry is invalid.

The code from Listing 11-8 guarantees that neither an invalid `rating` nor an invalid `genre` can be entered. Replace your existing `UpdateAlbum()` function with this version.

Listing 11-8 The `albums.4gl` program, fifth pass.

```
function UpdateAlbum(lr_albums)

define lr_albums record like albums.*


        input by name lr_albums.* without defaults


            after field genre

                select genre
```

(Continued)

Listing 11-8 The `albums.4gl` *program, fifth pass.*

```
            from genres

          where genre = lr_albums.genre

        if (STATUS = NOTFOUND) then

           error 'Genre must exist in the genres table'

             next field genre

        end if


     after field rating

         if (lr_albums.rating < 1 or

             lr_albums.rating > 10) then

             error 'Rating must be between 1 and 10'

             next field rating

         end if


   end input


   if (YesNoPrompt('Update current row with these

   values?')) then

       update albums

          set * = lr_albums.*

        where album_num = lr_albums.album_num

     end if


   end function
```

In data entry programs it is common that the bulk of the program is contained in `before field` and `after field` input blocks. Or, more correctly, it is common that you call data validation functions from those blocks. The range of operations that you can perform from within the `input` statement is extensive. Consider investing considerable time in customizing your 4GL programs' `input` statements.

The `clear` Statement

The `clear` statement is straightforward: it erases the screen display of some item. Its syntax follows.

```
clear target
```

where `target` is any one of the following:

- screen
- window *window-name*
- form
- *form-field-list*

window-name is the name of any open window, and *form-field-list* is a comma-separated list of screen fields. You may clear a window even if it is not the current window. Creating and managing windows is described in Chapter 12.

note   *The `clear` statement has no effect on program variables: it only affects what is displayed on the screen.*

More on the `options` Statement

In addition to specifying reserved lines, as shown in the section "The `options` Statement" earlier in this chapter, you can also use the `options` statement to modify other program settings. For the most part, these program settings affect the behavior of the `input` statement.

```
options setting setting-value
```

```
[, setting setting-value …]
```

where *setting* is one of the values listed below, and *setting-value* is the new value you assign to that setting. The settings and their default values (in parentheses) follow:

- `accept key` *key-name* (Esc)
- `input wrap|no wrap` (no wrap)
- `help file` *help-file-name* (default not supplied)
- `sql interrupt on|off` (off)

The `accept key` ends your current `input` statement and accepts the current values. The `input wrap` setting defines what happens when your cursor moves past the last field in an `input` statement. If it is set to `no wrap`, the `input` statement is terminated, just as if you had pressed the `accept key`. When it is set as `input wrap`, the cursor moves to the first field in the form instead, and your `input` statement is not terminated.

The *help-file-name* defines the location of any online help messages you have defined.

With `sql interrupt on`, you allow the user to terminate any SQL statements prematurely by pressing the interrupt key. This option is a useful one whose default is generally not preferred.

Communicating with the Operating System

Not all user interfaces need to interact with the user in realtime. There are also occasions where your programs may benefit from interacting with their own environment. Such interfaces could allow your program to run differently based on the values you supply as arguments or set in the environment. You might toggle a debug flag, turn on SQL monitoring with the `set explain` statement, vary menus based on the identity of the user, or pre-define certain report parameters. The options are limitless. Informix-4GL provides mechanisms that enable you to perform the following kinds of operating system interactions:

- Read command line arguments

- Read environmental variables
- Run operating system commands

Reading Command Line Arguments

One way of accepting input from the user is to read *command line arguments*. These are values you enter at the command line when you invoke your program from the operating system. Imagine in the following example that list_genres is a report program that lists all the genres you've defined, and sends the sorted list to a file (You'll actually create this program in Chapter 14, "4GL Reports"). With a command line argument, you can supply the output file name at runtime, as the following statement shows:

```
$ list_genres /tmp/genres_list.out
```

From within your program, you use the Informix built-in function arg_val(*argument-number*) as an expression that retrieves the value of a specific command line argument. Thus, you could assign the value of the first command line argument (/tmp/genres_list.out) to a local variable with 4GL statements like the following:

```
define l_rpt_dest char(18)
let l_rpt_dest = arg_val(1)
```

 You cannot use command line arguments when you launch your 4GL program with the Informix-4GL Programmer's Environment.

Reading Environmental Variables

Sometimes you may find a need to change how your program executes based on a user's environment. For example, you might want to create a switch inside your program that displays diagnostic information, but only when a certain environmental variable is set. In this way you can customize how your program runs based on a user's preferences. Unlike command line arguments, environmental variables *can* be used from within programs invoked with the Informix-4GL Programmer's Environment.

You use the Informix built-in function `fgl_getenv(`*environ-mental-variable-name*`)` to read the value of an environmental variable. It returns a string that contains the value of the variable you supply as an argument. The following code fragment activates an SQL diagnostic feature—at runtime—only when the EXPLAIN_MODE environmental variable has been set to the value ON:

```
if (fgl_getenv('EXPLAIN_MODE') = 'ON') then
    set explain on
end if
```

The `set explain on` SQL command appends the query plan (Informix's internal path used to satisfy a query) of all subsequent queries to a file named `sqexplain.out` in the user's current directory. This type of runtime directive allows the same code to act differently based on how the current user's environment is defined.

Running Operating System Commands

The final way to interact directly with the operating system is to run commands from within your Informix-4GL program. You use the `run` statement to execute a single operating system command in this way. For example, the following 4GL statement displays the system date to your screen, then returns control to your 4GL program:

```
run 'date'
```

Although this example is perhaps not so very useful, you can use the `run` statement to execute any executable program, regardless of its source: a C program, another Informix-4GL program, a shell script, or just an operating system command.

```
run shell-command [without waiting]
```

where *shell-command* is a variable or quoted string containing a command for the operating system to execute.

When that command executes, your current 4GL program suspends operations momentarily. Any output from the operating system command is displayed in a temporary window that overlays your current screen. When the command completes, that window closes and your previous screen is restored.

The optional `without waiting` clause specifies that the *shell-command* should be run in the background, with control returning to your 4GL program immediately.

In the Extra Credit exercises, you'll use the `run` command to enable the `ShellEscape()` function. This library function will let you include an invisible menu option in each Informix ring menu you create.

Summary

In this chapter you learned how to use the various 4GL user interaction statements. With them, you can accept user input of various kinds, and display data to the screen in a variety of ways. The four classes of user interfaces are:

- Line-based interfaces
- Ring menus
- Forms-based interfaces
- Operating system interactions

By combining these methods as needed, you can begin to develop 4GL programs of considerable utility. Chapter 12 extends this utility even further by adding windows, on-line help, and screen arrays to your 4GL user interface.

Extra Credit

Q&A

Question	**Answer**
How can I clear a message off the message line?	Display an empty message, by using the following 4GL statement: `message ''`
That `attribute (invisible)` clause in a `display` statement seems strange. When would I ever use it?	A common place to use an invisible entry is in a password field. You don't want to echo a password as the user enters it.
Explain again about screen records and program records and records (rows) in a database table. They all seem to melt together.	A screen record is a collection of names of form fields. These are placeholders on your screen that can accept user input and display program values. You can *bind*—temporarily associate—screen fields or entire screen records to program variables. Program variables store local copies of values and often act as intermediaries between database values and screen fields. For example, Listing 11-5 shows how a database row's values are temporarily stored in a program variable, the `lr_albums` record. Those values are then displayed to the screen record (`sr_albums`) to which the program variable is bound. The screen record cannot store values; it can only identify where program values are seen.

Exercises

1. Throughout the chapter you've already done enough exercises concerning user interfaces. This next task is to begin building a library of your own re-usable functions that can make your future 4GL programs more consistent and easier to write. You can't afford to skip these exercises, as later chapters refer to

these utility functions and will expect you to have already created your own `infxlibs.4gl` module.

Create a function called `ShellEscape()` that replaces the statements you used to create an invisible menu option. See Listing 11-1 and the section "Creating Invisible Menu Options" earlier in this chapter. Put this function into its own module, called `infxlibs.4gl`. Update your `therapy.4gl` program to call the `ShellEscape()` function, and link the `infxlibs.4gl` module into your `therapy.4ge` executable program.

Hint: the `c4gl` compiler script can take multiple Informix-4GL modules as command line arguments.

2. Extract the `YesNoPrompt()` function from your `albums.4gl` program and include it in your `infxlibs.4gl` module in the same way.

Exercise Answers

1. One possible listing for `therapy.4gl` is as follows.

Listing E11-1 *First part of answer to Exercise 1.*

```
main


    options message line 4


    menu 'Musical Therapy'

        command 'Melancholia'

            'Pick an album to cure sadness.'

            message 'Beauty and the Beat'

            attribute (yellow)

        command 'Claustrophobia'

            'Pick an album to evoke the outdoors.'
```

(Continued)

```
               message 'Sounds of the Okefenokee Swamp'

               attribute (green)

       command key ('L') 'cLumsiness'

           'Pick an album to make you dance.'

               message 'Cruisin' attribute (magenta)

       command 'Creepiness'

           'Pick an album to make you hip'

               message ''

               error 'Sorry, squareness is terminal.

               Try to cheer up.'

               next option 'Melancholia'

       command key ('!')

           call ShellEscape()

       command 'Exit' 'Exit the Musical Therapy menu.'

               exit menu

       end menu


end main
```

The `infxlibs.4gl` module should resemble the following.

Notice especially that there is no `main` block in the `infx-libs.4gl` module. You link the multiple source modules into a single executable as follows:

```
$ c4gl therapy.4gl infxlibs.4gl -o therapy.4ge
```

Listing E11-1a *Second part of answer to Exercise 1.*

```
function ShellEscape()


    define l_shell_cmd char(80)


    options prompt line last
    prompt '!' for l_shell_cmd
    run l_shell_cmd
    prompt 'Press return to continue' attribute (reverse)
         for char l_shell_cmd
    options prompt line first


end function
```

2. Your `infxlibs.4gl` module should now resemble the following.

Listing E11-2 *Answer to Exercise 2.*

```
function ShellEscape()


    define l_shell_cmd char(80)


    options prompt line last
    prompt '!' for l_shell_cmd
    run l_shell_cmd
    prompt 'Press return to continue' attribute (reverse)
         for char l_shell_cmd
```

(Continued)

```
    options prompt line first


end function



-- Return a TRUE or FALSE value to the question supplied.
function YesNoPrompt(l_prompt_string)
define l_prompt_string char(60)


    define l_response    char(1)


    while TRUE
        prompt l_prompt_string clipped, ': '
            for char l_response
        case (upshift(l_response))
            when 'Y'
                return TRUE
            when 'N'
                return FALSE
            otherwise
                error 'Please enter Y or N'
        end case
    end while


end function
```

4GL Windows and Screen Arrays

This chapter builds directly on the foundation you learned in Chapter 11, "Your 4GL User Interface," by adding two new types of visual containers to your user interface toolkit. These new containers are *windows* and *screen arrays*.

Introduction

A window is an independent operational screen that overlays your 4GL screen or other windows. In Informix-4GL, all windows are rectangular and no larger than your base screen. If you've pressed the Ctrl-W option from within DB-Access to see its online help screens, you've already seen windows in action. The online help appears in a full-screen window on top of your DB-Access screen, hiding it completely. When you exit the online help, your DB-Access session is again revealed, unchanged. In this chapter you'll learn how to create and manage Informix-4GL windows that act in just this way. Additionally, you'll learn how to construct your own online help windows.

Screen arrays are areas on your form that can display multiple rows of similar data. This chapter also describes the use of *display arrays*, which allow you to scroll through many rows of data via a small screen array. By the end of the chapter, you'll create a scrolling array inside a window, in the process creating a *pick list* function.

Using Windows

You can have any number of windows that overlay each other. By default your 4GL program has an initial full-screen window, named `screen`, that is opened automatically and can never be closed. Until you open any other windows, all of your screen interactions are conducted from the `screen` window. All other windows are superimposed. Figure 12-1 shows an example of overlapping windows.

A Sample Window Manipulation Program

You'll use Listing 12-1 to build the program that creates these windows. It uses each of the window manipulation statements, the complete list of which follows:

- `open window`: create a new window and make it the current (topmost) window
- `close window`: close a window and restore its underlying display
- `clear window`: erase the contents of a window
- `current window`: make a specified window the topmost in the window stack

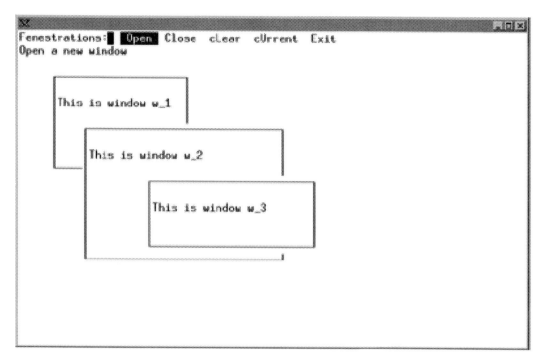

Figure 12–1 *Informix-4GL programs can create overlapping windows.*

Enter the code in Listing 12-1 to create the `voyeur.4gl` program, and use that program's menu to look through the 4GL windows it creates. After you've gotten comfortable manipulating windows in this way, we'll make your windows even more useful by adding forms to them.

Listing 12-1 *The* `voyeur.4gl` *program looks through 4GL windows.*

```
-- Test the various window manipulation statements


define ga_win_is_open array[3] of smallint


main
```

(Continued)

Listing 12-1 *The* voyeur.4gl *program looks through 4GL windows.*

```
    call InitWinArray()


    open window w_menu at 1, 1 with 2 rows, 78 columns
    menu 'Fenestrations'
        command 'Open' 'Open a new window'
            call OpenNextWin()
        command 'Close' 'Close a specific window'
            call CloseWin()
        command key ('l')
            'cLear' 'Clear a specific window'
            call ClearWin()
        command key ('u') 'cUrrent'
            'Make a specific window current'
            call CurrentWin()
        command 'Exit' 'Enough of this win-doodling'
            exit menu
    end menu


end main


function InitWinArray()


    define i smallint
```

(Continued)

Listing 12-1 The voyeur.4gl *program looks through 4GL windows.*

```
for i = 1 to 3

    let ga_win_is_open[i] = FALSE

end for



end function



function OpenNextWin()


    define win_num smallint


    let win_num = FindNextWin()
    case (win_num)
        when 1
            open window w_1 at  5,  7 with 6 rows,
                20 columns attribute (border)
        when 2
            open window w_2 at  9, 12 with 9 rows,
                30 columns attribute (border)
        when 3
            open window w_3 at 13, 22 with 4 rows,
                25 columns attribute (border)
    end case
```

(Continued)

Listing 12-1 The `voyeur.4gl` *program looks through 4GL windows.*

```
    if (win_num > 0) then

        message 'This is window w_', win_num using '#'

            let ga_win_is_open[win_num] = TRUE

    end if


end function



function FindNextWin()


    define i smallint


    for i = 1 to 3
        if (not ga_win_is_open[i]) then

            return i

        end if
    end for


    error 'All windows are already open'
    return 0


end function
```

(Continued)

Listing 12-1 *The* `voyeur.4gl` *program looks through 4GL windows.*

```
function CloseWin()


    define win_num smallint


    let win_num = ChooseWin()
    case (win_num)
        when 1
            close window w_1
        when 2
            close window w_2
        when 3
            close window w_3
    end case


    if (win_num > 0) then
        let ga_win_is_open[win_num] = FALSE
    end if


end function



function ClearWin()


    case (ChooseWin())
```

(Continued)

Listing 12-1 The `voyeur.4gl` *program looks through 4GL windows.*

```
            when 1

                clear window w_1

            when 2

                clear window w_2

            when 3

                clear window w_3

        end case


end function



function CurrentWin()


    case (ChooseWin())

        when 1

            current window is w_1

        when 2

            current window is w_2

        when 3

            current window is w_3

    end case


end function
```

(Continued)

Listing 12-1 *The* voyeur.4gl *program looks through 4GL windows.*

```
function ChooseWin()

    define win_num smallint

    prompt 'Choose a window number: ' for win_num

    -- If the chosen window is not open, send an error
    if (win_num >= 1 and win_num <= 3) then
        if (not ga_win_is_open[win_num]) then
            error 'Window', win_num using '#',
                ' is not open'
            let win_num = 0
        end if
    else
        error 'Window ', win_num using '&',
                ' is not a valid window'
        let win_num = 0
    end if

    return win_num

end function
```

This is the largest program so far, but still comprehensible, because each operation is segregated into distinct functions. This program makes extensive use of some Informix-4GL constructs. Much of the bulk of this program is mandated by the unfortunate fact that you cannot use a variable name as your window name. Near the program's beginning, the Fenestrations menu is opened in its own window, w_menu. If it were not, and the menu were created in the default window, screen, whenever screen were made current it would overlay and hide each of your new windows. This is not what you want.

It is interesting to note that since the ChooseWin() function returns exactly one argument, it is used both in an assignment statement (in the CloseWin() function) and directly as an expression (in the ClearWin() and CurrentWin() functions). Also, this program adds a little more error checking than previous programs, but is still incomplete (what happens if you enter xyz in response to the ChooseWin() prompt?).

The Syntax for the Window Manipulation Statements

The previous program showed the window manipulation statements by example. This section details their syntax.

The open window Statement

When you open a window, you can either include a form or not. The open window statements in Listing 12-1 do not use forms, whereas those in the "Using Screen Arrays" section later in this chapter explicitly do use forms. The formats for each of these variants of the open window statement follow:

```
open window window-name
    at row-position, column-position
    with num-rows rows, num-columns columns
    [attribute (attribute-list)]
open window window-name
    at row-position, column-position
    with form [form-file-name]
    [attribute (attribute-list)]
```

where *window-name* is the name of the window to be opened (this may *not* be a variable name), *row-position* and *column-position* are expressions that describe the position of the top left corner of the window, *num-rows* and *num-columns* are expressions that describe the height and width of the window, *form-file-name* is a variable or quoted string that identifies the form file to use when opening the window, and *attribute-list* is a comma-separated list of window attributes. Those attributes are the list of display attributes from Table 11-2, the keyword `border`, and the subset of the `options` command that resets the reserved lines.

If you open a window using the `with form` option, the form is opened automatically. You need not execute the `open form` and `display form` statements. The window is sized to fit the form. You can display at most one form in a 4GL window.

Informix maintains an ordered set of open windows, called the *window stack*. When you open a window, it becomes the current window on the top of the window stack. When your 4GL program starts, the default window, `screen`, is the current window.

The `clear window` Statement

Once you've opened a window you can clear it, close it, or make it current as needed. The syntax for clearing a window is straightforward:

```
clear window window-name
```

where *window-name* is the name of the window to be cleared, and may also include the keyword `screen`. The `clear window` statement only erases the screen display, but leaves the border, if the window has one, intact. It changes no program variables, nor does it affect the order of the window stack. A window need not be current for you to clear it.

The `current window` Statement

Only the current window is used for data entry; that is, by the `menu`, `construct`, and `input` statements. Use the `current window` statement to make a window current. Its syntax is as follows:

```
current window is window-name
```

where *window-name* is the name of the window to be brought to the top of the window stack. This may not be a variable name, but may be the name of the default 4GL window, `screen`.

The current window is always completely visible on your screen, and may obscure windows beneath it on the window stack. If the window contains a form, that form becomes the current form when you execute the `current window` statement on that window.

The `close window` Statement

After you are finished with any window, you should close it to erase it from the screen and to release the memory associated with that window. The syntax to do so follows:

```
close window window-name
```

where *window-name* is the name of the window to be closed. This may not be a variable name, nor the name of the default 4GL window, `screen`.

When you close a window, Informix clears the window from the screen and restores any underlying display. If you close the current window, the remaining topmost window on the window stack becomes the current window. Finally, if you close a window that was opened with the `with form` clause, the form is closed automatically as long as it is not currently being used for input.

caution   *If you close a window that is currently being used for input, Informix generates a runtime error.*

Creating Online Help Screens

One special kind of window that is available within Informix-4GL is the online help window. A user can request to see this help whenever the program is waiting for user input and help has been defined. The user-input types of statements are `menu`, `input`, and `prompt`, all described in Chapter 11. When you define those statements, you can indicate that a specific help message should appear whenever the user presses the help key (Ctrl-W). This help message appears in a new window that becomes current and overlays the entire screen. Figure 12-2 shows an example of a user-defined help screen. When you choose Resume from the help screen menu, the window is closed.

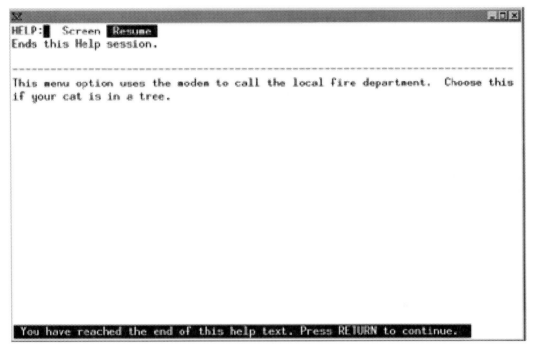

Figure 12–2   *The Informix-4GL help window.*

In the description of the syntax for the user-input types of statements, you saw that by adding the help *help-number* clause to a menu, input, or prompt statement you could indicate which error message should appear when the user presses the help key. You define the text for those custom messages in a help text file, and then use Informix's mkmessage utility (described in this section) to make these messages available in your applications. You specify the location of the output file created by the mkmessage utility with the options statement. Refer to the "More on the options Statement" section in Chapter 11 for details on how to indicate the location of this file.

The contents of the help text file are a series of numbered help messages that you define using the following format:

```
.num
help-text
```

where `.num` is a period followed by an integer, and `help-text` is the message you define for that help number. If `help-text` exceeds 20 lines, the online help window splits the message into 20-line pages for easier display.

Listing 12-2 shows what the contents of the help text file referenced in Listing 10-3 in Chapter 10, "Your First 4GL Program," might contain.

Listing 12-2 *A sample help message file.*

```
.101

This menu option uses the modem to call the local police.
Choose this if a crime is occurring.

.102

This menu option uses the modem to call the local fire
department.  Choose this if your cat is in a tree.

.103

This menu option uses the modem to call for immediate
pizza delivery.  Get onion and extra cheese--deep dish.
```

Once you have created your help text, you use the following command line syntax to process it for use:

```
$ mkmessage help-text-file out-file
```

With the `options` statement, you specify `out-file` as the current help file.

Although the most common use of help files is in the context just mentioned, where the user presses the help key in a user-input type statement, you can also summon the online help window explicitly with Informix's built-in Informix-4GL `showhelp()` function. Its syntax follows:

```
call showhelp(help-number)
```

where `help-number` is a numeric expression that identifies the specific help text to be displayed.

Using Screen Arrays

So far, this chapter has discussed only windows, but another type of visual container—the screen array—is also very useful. A screen array is an area on your form that you can use to browse through a list of data, viewing multiple rows at a time.

Why Screen Arrays Are Useful

Databases often contain large lists of data that you want to see. Screens are small. Screen arrays help ameliorate this mismatch by allowing you to scroll through a list, several rows at a time. They model the device shown in Figure 12-3, which displays subsets of a paper list as seen through a cardboard cutout.

Defining a Screen Array

Building a screen array requires two components: the form that contains the array specification, and the Informix-4GL program that controls the display of the list. Listing 12-3 shows the screen specification form for the `arr_genres.per` form. In the section "The `display array` Statement, by Example" that follows, you'll use this form to implement a scrolling array of all genres that allows you to select one from the list.

In this specification file, `sr_genres` is defined as a six-element screen array. This size determines how many records from the program array can be displayed at one time. With the `display`

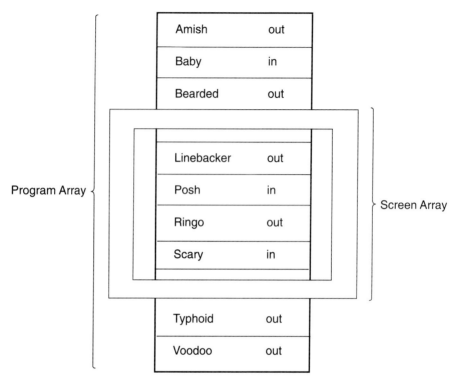

Spice Girl Auditions

Amish	out
Baby	in
Bearded	out
Linebacker	out
Posh	in
Ringo	out
Scary	in
Typhoid	out
Voodoo	out

Program Array

Screen Array

Figure 12–3 *A screen array shows a subset of a list, and allows scrolling.*

Listing 12-3 *The screen specification for the* genres *pick list.*

```
database music


screen

{

  Genre           Description


  [f000           ][f001                      ]
```

(Continued)

Listing 12-3 *The screen specification for the* genres *pick list.*

```
    [f000                    ][f001                      ]

    [f000                    ][f001                      ]

    [f000                    ][f001                      ]

    [f000                    ][f001                      ]

    [f000                    ][f001                      ]

    }


tables

    genres


attributes

    f000 = genres.genre;

    f001 = genres.description;


instructions

    delimiters ' '

    screen record sr_genres[6] (genre, description);
```

array statement you can bind this screen array to a program
array to create a scrolling window. Notice also the delimiters
instruction. This command replaces the default square brackets
([ ]), which normally delimit screen fields, with spaces, thus making the delimiters invisible. You can include any character
between quotes with the delimiters instruction, but spaces are
often appropriate for display-only fields such as these.

The `display array` Statement, by Example

The `display array` statement displays a scrolling window of program array values to a screen array. It is one of the most *4GL* of the built-in Informix-4GL statements. However, gaining the benefit of the `display array` statement requires that you pay a small price in administrative overhead. In order to use the `display array` statement, you need to perform the following steps:

1. Define a screen array in your form (Listing 12-3).
2. Open and display the form. You can use either the `open form` and `display form` combination or the `open window with form` statement. It is best to also display some instructions for the user (this, and all of the remaining steps, are in Listing 12-4).
3. Define a program array whose elements match the screen array in number, name, and data type. Its size can—and usually does—exceed the size of the screen array. You should declare it large enough to hold all the data rows you will select.
4. Fill the program array with the data to be displayed. This usually entails creating a cursor and a `foreach` loop (described in Chapter 13, "Cursors and Dynamic SQL"). These mechanisms allow you to treat the set of data returned from a `select` statement one row at a time.
5. Indicate to Informix the number of data rows you have populated. You do this by calling the built-in Informix function `set_count(array-count)`.
6. Display the program array to the screen array with the `display array` statement. This statement includes built-in operators for scrolling forward and backward, and for selecting the row of interest.
7. Find the element number of the program array that was selected by the user. You do this with the Informix built-in function `arr_count()`.
8. Use that element number as a subscript into the program array to determine the value the user selected.
9. Close and free the cursor.
10. Close the screen array form or window.

Listing 12-4 shows all the steps involved in using the `display array` statement.

Listing 12-4 *The code to create a scrolling array of all genres.*

```
database music


main


    define l_genre like genres.genre


    call PickGenre() returning l_genre

    display 'You picked ', l_genre


end main




function PickGenre()


    define lr_genres array[100] of record like genres.*

    define l_count     smallint

    define l_picked    smallint


    open window w_genres at 4, 3 with form 'arr_genres'

        attribute (border)

    display 'Use Esc to choose a genre. Use the arrow

keys to navigate.'

        at 1, 2 attribute (red)
```

(Continued)

Listing 12-4 The code to create a scrolling array of all genres.

```
declare c_genres cursor for

select *

  from genres

 order by genre


let l_count = 0

-- fill the program array with database values

foreach c_genres into lr_genres[l_count + 1].*

    let l_count = l_count + 1

end foreach


call set_count(l_count)

display array lr_genres to sr_genres.*

    attribute (blue)

let l_picked = arr_curr()


close c_genres

free  c_genres

close window w_genres


return lr_genres[l_picked].genre


end function
```

Create and run the above program. You should see something like Figure 12-4.

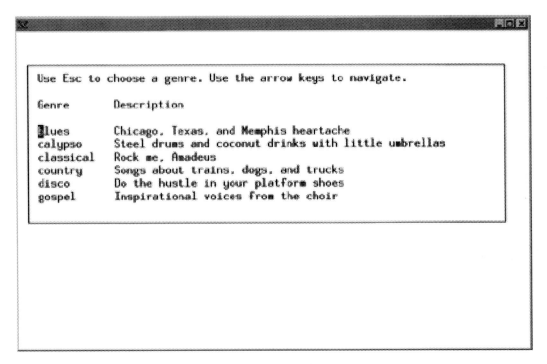

Figure 12–4 *A screen array is a scrolling list of values.*

Details of the `display array` Statement

The following section explores some of the finer points of the display array statement.

Syntax

The syntax for the display array statement follows:

```
display array program-array to screen-array.*
    [attribute (attribute-list)]
```

where *program-array* is the name of the program array you have defined, *screen-array* is the name of the screen array in your form, and `attribute-list` is a comma-separated list of `display array` attributes. Those attributes are the list of display attributes from Table 11-2 except `invisible`, and apply to all of the fields in `screen-array`.

Special Keys

The default keys for navigating the screen arrays are shown in Table 12-1.

Table 12-1 The keys used to navigate a screen array.

Key	Effect
↓ , →	Move the cursor to the next row of data in the program array.
↑ , ←	Move the cursor to the previous row of data in the program array.
F3, Page Down	Scroll the display forward to the next screenful of data.
F2, Page Up	Scroll the display backward to the previous screenful of data.
Esc	End the `display array` statement, and make the number of the current record of the program array available to the built-in function `arr_curr()`.
Ctrl-C	End the `display array` statement, and set the global variable INT_FLAG to TRUE. Unless you have executed the `defer interrupt` statement, pressing this interrupt key also exits the entire 4GL program. For more information on these topics, refer to Tables 10-4 and 10-5 in Chapter 10.

Summary

In this chapter you learned how to use windows and screen arrays, two visual containers helpful for creating friendly real-world applications. You also learned how to add online help to your 4GL applications.

Windows are overlapping rectangular areas of your screen that obscure the windows below them. They allow you to manage your limited screen space, segregating operations into independent working areas. They are arranged in a top-down order, with the topmost identified as the current window, and the entire series of windows known as the window stack. Included in this stack is Informix's default full-screen window, called `screen`, which is treated like any other window, except that it cannot be closed. You manage windows with the `open window`, `close window`, `clear window`, and `current window` statements.

You can use Informix's built-in utility, `mkmessage`, to make your application-specific text available to to your user interfaces. Within your `menu`, `input`, and `prompt` statements, you add the `help` keyword to identify a context-specific help screen that appears when a user presses the help key. You can also call the `showhelp()` function directly to summon a specific help message.

Screen arrays are forms-based sections of a screen that allow you to view multiple rows of similar data at once. They let you scroll through the contents of a program array using the built-in screen navigation commands of the `display array` statement.

Extra Credit

Q&A

Question	Answer
Hey, my head hurts. You've got program arrays, screen arrays, and display arrays. What gives?	There, there now. Let's revisit these one at a time. A program array is a data type. It is a kind of variable that holds repeating groups of similar data. A screen array is a forms-based device that you use to display such repeating groups of similar data. Usually, the values in a program array are what the screen array displays to a user. The `display array` statement is the Informix-4GL construct that lets you conveniently marry the many rows of data in a program array to the generally smaller screen array. It includes built-in tools for navigating the program array. You often have program arrays without screen arrays—not all program data should be displayed—but seldom will you have a screen array without a program array.
The Informix manual mentions something called an `input array`. Should I be using that for data entry?	Shh. Yes, Virginia, there is an `input array`. But in practice, its use is so complex that even experienced programmers seek alternatives. For almost all applications, using standard forms (without screen arrays) for data entry is preferred.

Exercises

1. Add the function `PickGenres()` to `infxlibs.4gl`.
2. Modify the `UpdateAlbums()` function from Chapter 11 to include a call to the `PickGenres()` function if the user enters an invalid genre. Call this function instead of displaying an error, as the function currently does. Showing the legal values in a lookup table like this is an important step toward making any application user-friendly.

Exercise Answers

1. Although this exercise is straightforward, you'll find that you need to add the database declaration line (`database music`) to the beginning of your `infxlibs.4gl` module. Without it, the declarative statement `define lr_genres array[100] of record like genres.*` would be unable to find the `genres` table.

2. The new `UpdateAlbums()` function should resemble the following.

Listing E12-2 Answer to Exercise 2.

```
function UpdateAlbum(lr_albums)

define lr_albums record like albums.*


        input by name lr_albums.* without defaults


            after field genre

                select genre

                  from genres

                 where genre = lr_albums.genre

                if (STATUS = NOTFOUND) then

                    let lr_albums.genre = PickGenre()

                    display by name lr_albums.genre

                end if


            after field rating

                if (lr_albums.rating < 1 or

                    lr_albums.rating > 10) then
```

(Continued)

Listing E12-2 *Answer to Exercise 2.*

```
                    error 'Rating must be between 1 and 10'

                    next field rating

              end if



       end input



       if (YesNoPrompt('Update current row with these val-
ues?')) then

            update albums

                set * = lr_albums.*

                where album_num = lr_albums.album_num

            end if



end function
```

Chapter

13

Cursors and Dynamic SQL

This chapter introduces cursors, a key procedural language construct that allows sets of data to be handled on a row-by-row basis. We'll also explore the related arena of building Dynamic SQL statements. As the fourth of five consecutive chapters on Informix-4GL, it continues to build on the function library and programs introduced by the previous three chapters.

Introduction

SQL is a set-based language. Data is stored in tables, which are sets of related rows. Date is extracted from these tables, via the `select` statement, to create other sets. That is, when you execute a `select` statement, the entire set of rows in the table is restricted to some smaller number of rows: that set of rows that satisfies each of the comparison conditions and join conditions. The result set may be further grouped or sorted, but remains a set. Although the set occasionally contains zero or one rows, it usually comprises multiple rows.

Conversely, the programming languages—Informix-4GL, ESQL/C—used to interface with these sets act on exactly one row at a time. Most parts of the language are procedural, and in any case *not* set-based. Yet Informix-4GL is a superset of SQL: it incorporates the set-based features of SQL within its overall language framework. Somehow Informix-4GL must marry its set-based and non-set-based elements. The tool it uses to overcome this paradigm mismatch is a *cursor*.

What Is a Cursor?

A *cursor* is a procedural-language construct that allows a set of values to be treated one at a time. It is a pointer to the current row of an SQL statement's active set—those rows that satisfy a `select` statement's `where` clause. Just as the cursor on a video terminal points to text or some other current object, a database cursor points to rows retrieved by a `select` statement. You *declare* a cursor for a target `select` statement, after which you can then perform the following procedural steps to treat each row in the result set singly. These steps are shown by example in Listing 13-1 in the beginning of the next section.

1. Define the cursor with the `declare` statement. This specifies the cursor name and allocates storage for the `select` statement.
2. Initiate the cursor with the `open cursor` statement. This parses the `select` statement, evaluates its syntax, and checks certain user permissions. The cursor is set to point to a place just before the first row in the active set. No rows are yet returned that satisfy the `select` statement.
3. Using some looping feature (often the `foreach` statement), `fetch` the active set rows one at a time, usually into program variables. Upon a fetch, the cursor points at the row just fetched.

4. Within the loop, perform any row-based processing required.
5. Exit the loop, usually after the last row in the active set.
6. Use the `close` statement to terminate the `select` statement, releasing all resources that may have been allocated to the active set.
7. Deallocate the resources that the cursor holds with the `free` statement.

The rest of this chapter elaborates on this model and describes the Informix-4GL tools with which you can manipulate cursors and the SQL statements for which they are declared.

Sequential Cursors

Sequential cursors are those in which the rows are fetched serially. That is, retrieved in the order dictated by the `select` statement. Listing 13-1 shows an example of using a sequential cursor to display every row of the `formats` table from within an Informix-4GL program. With the Informix-4GL Programmer's Environment (`i4gl`), create this program as `format.4gl`, then compile and run it.

Listing 13-1 Using a sequential cursor.

```
database music


main


    define lr_formats record like formats.*


    declare c_formats cursor for

      select *
```

(Continued)

Listing 13-1 Using a sequential cursor.

```
    from formats

  order by default_value


open c_formats


while (TRUE)

    fetch c_formats into lr_formats.*

    if (STATUS = NOTFOUND) then

      exit while

    end if

    display lr_formats.*

    sleep 1

  end while


  close c_formats

  free  c_formats


end main
```

 Listing 13-1 refers to the STATUS global variable. Informix includes it automatically in every Informix-4GL program, and sets its value after every SQL-based or forms-based statement, indicating that statement's success or failure. A value of NOTFOUND is assigned when a cursor tries to fetch past the last row in its active set, or when

a singleton `select` *statement returns no rows. A value of 0 indicates success, while a negative value indicates that an error occurred.*

Your output, displayed one line at a time, should resemble the following not-so-pretty results:

```
8track          $8.00when only the best will do
tape            $9.99cassette tape
LP              $12.00vinyl record, complete with scratches
CD              $15.99compact disc
DAT             $18.50digital audio tape
video           $24.99VHS format videocassette
laser           $32.50laser disc
```

Remember that the `open` statement returns no rows. Only the `fetch` and `foreach` statements (described below) actually retrieve any rows from the database.

The `declare` Statement

The `declare` statement associates a cursor name with an SQL statement. Its syntax is

```
declare cursor-name [scroll] cursor for target
```

where *cursor-name* is the name you give the cursor, and *target* is one of the following:

- *select-statement*
- *statement-id*

When the target is a `select` statement, you include any `select` statement directly. You use *statement-id* to refer to a dynamic SQL statement that you have previously prepared. See the section "Dynamic SQL Statements" later in this chapter for a full explanation of this construct, used mostly to manipulate `select` statements whose values are supplied at runtime.

Cursors by default are sequential cursors. Include the `scroll` keyword to identify the cursor as one that may be traversed back and forth. The "Scroll Cursors" section explores this extension.

The open Statement

To pass the SQL statement associated with a cursor to the database engine, you use the `open` statement. It begins the execution of the `select` statement, and passes to the engine any runtime values that you supply. Its syntax is

```
open cursor-name [using variable-list]
```

where `cursor-name` is the name of a previously declared cursor, and `variable-list` is a comma-separated list of program variables and constants that supply values for any placeholders that were included in the prepared `select` statement. The use of such placeholders is described in "Dynamic SQL Statements," later in this chapter. If you open a cursor that is already open, Informix will close the cursor and reopen it with any new values in your `variable-list`.

The close Statement

As a general programming maxim, you should clean up after yourself. If you open something, close it. If you allocate a resource (open a window, declare a cursor, prepare a statement ID, or the like), free it when you are done. As a matter of course, your program closes and frees its various resources when it exits, but you should adopt the habit of closing and freeing your resources explicitly.

You'll appreciate this habit as your programs grow in complexity. The number of unintended side effects you can introduce programmatically will be lessened because the only resources that can be modified are those you've explicitly kept available. Performance may marginally improve, since you'll have no memory dedicated to maintaining unneeded resources. Finally, it's simply polite and tidy.

The syntax is straightforward:

```
close cursor-name
```

where *cursor-name* is the name of a previously opened cursor. When you close a cursor, the database engine releases all resources that may have been allocated to the active set, such as a temporary table it might have built to hold an ordered set. If you try to close an unopened cursor, a runtime error will result.

If you close a cursor, you will need to reopen it before you may use it to fetch rows again.

The **free** Statement

The free statement is similar to the close statement.

```
free cursor-name|statement-id
```

where *cursor-name* is the name of a previously declared cursor, or *statement-id* is a previously prepared SQL statement. When you free an item, you deallocate all resources devoted to it, including program memory. Thus, you will be unable to declare a cursor for a freed statement until you prepare it again. If you try to free an unallocated item, you will get a runtime error.

The **foreach** Statement

The following cursor-based steps are so common in application programs that Informix has created a single looping construct, the foreach statement, to replace them.

1. Open a cursor
2. Within a loop, sequentially fetch rows that this cursor addresses until there are no more rows
3. Close the cursor

The foreach statement performs these statements on your behalf, and allows you to include other 4GL statements within your processing loop. Its syntax is

```
foreach cursor-name [into variable-list]
    4GL-statements
end foreach
```

where *cursor-name* is the name of a previously declared cursor, *variable-list* is a comma-separated list of program variables that will receive the values retrieved (it may include program records), and *4GL-statements* are any valid program statements as well as the following two procedural directives:

- `continue foreach`
- `exit foreach`

The `continue foreach` statement skips any remaining 4GL statements in the `foreach` loop and retrieves the next record referenced by the cursor. With `exit foreach`, processing control is passed to the next statement following the `end foreach` clause. It exits the loop.

Listing 13-2 shows how the `foreach` statement replaces several lines of 4GL code. It is functionally the same program as `format.4gl`. Create this listing as `foreach.4gl`, and execute it to see for yourself that it is similar.

Listing 13-2 *The* `foreach` *statement replaces other 4GL commands.*

```
database music


main


    define lr_formats record like formats.*


    declare c_formats cursor for

      select *

        from formats
```

(Continued)

Listing 13-2 The `foreach` *statement replaces other 4GL commands.*

```
    order by default_value


foreach c_formats into lr_formats.*

    display lr_formats.*

    sleep 1

end foreach


free c_formats


end main
```

tip *Use the* `foreach` *statement to collect all rows that a sequential cursor identifies. It is simpler and clearer than other looping constructs.*

Scroll Cursors

Whereas a sequential cursor allows rows to be fetched only in the order specified by the `select` statement, a scroll cursor lets you traverse back and forth through the result set. You can imagine a scroll cursor as a viewscreen that only ever reveals, or points to, one row in the active set at a time, but can be positioned dynamically at any location in the active set. Figure 13-1 illustrates this idea.

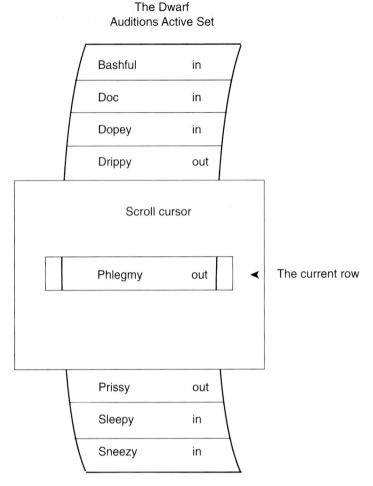

The Dwarf
Auditions Active Set

Bashful	in
Doc	in
Dopey	in
Drippy	out

Scroll cursor

Phlegmy	out

◄ The current row

Prissy	out
Sleepy	in
Sneezy	in

Figure 13–1 *A scroll cursor points to a single row in the active set.*

The `fetch` Statement

The fetch statement is the tool with which you navigate a cursor. Its syntax follows:

```
fetch [positioning-clause] cursor-name
    [into variable-list]
```

where *cursor-name* is the name of a previously declared cursor, and *variable-list* is a comma-separated list of program variables that will receive the values retrieved, and may include program records.

The default for *positioning-clause* is next, which is also the only legal value for a sequential cursor. When *cursor-name* has been declared as a scroll cursor, *positioning-clause* may be any of the following:

- next
- previous
- prior
- first
- last
- current
- relative *relative-offset*
- absolute *absolute-offset*

The previous and prior keywords are synonymous. You may use any numeric expression to indicate *relative-offset* or *absolute-offset*. A fetch relative statement fetches a row position relative to the current row in the active set; fetch absolute retrieves an absolute row position in the active set.

A Scroll Cursor, by Example

Now let's use a scroll cursor to improve the albums.4gl program under development from Chapter 11, "Your 4GL User Interface," and Chapter 12, "4GL Windows and Screen Arrays." This time, replace the main program block with the statements from Listing 13-3.

caution

Use a scroll cursor only when you must traverse your active set nonsequentially. The statement commandeers extra system resources to allow dynamic positioning of the cursor. Don't use such resources needlessly.

Notice that only the main program block changed. No modifications were needed in UpdateAlbum(), ShellEscape(), YesNoPrompt(), or PickGenre(). Continuing to limit incremental changes to isolated functions while maintaining consistent interfaces to related functions is a hallmark of effective program development—of stepwise refinement.

Listing 13-3 The albums.4gl *program, sixth pass.*

```
database music


main


    define item_num   smallint

    define lr_albums record like albums.*


    open form f_albums from 'albums'

    display form f_albums


    declare c_albums scroll cursor for

     select *

       into lr_albums.*

       from albums

      order by rating desc, title

    open c_albums

    initialize lr_albums.* to null


    menu 'Albums'

        command 'Next'

            'Fetch the next row in the active set'

            fetch next c_albums

            display by name lr_albums.*
```

(Continued)

Listing 13-3 The `albums.4gl` program, sixth pass.

```
command 'Previous'

    'Fetch the previous row in the active set'

    fetch previous c_albums

    display by name lr_albums.*

command 'Absolute'

    'Fetch a specific element in the active set'

    prompt 'Enter element number: ' for item_num

    fetch absolute item_num c_albums

    display by name lr_albums.*

command 'Relative'

    'Fetch a relative item in the active set'

    prompt 'Enter offset (may be negative): '

    for item_num

    fetch relative item_num c_albums

    display by name lr_albums.*

command 'Update'

    'Change the values for this album'

    if (lr_albums.album_num is not null) then

        call UpdateAlbum(lr_albums.*)

    else

        error 'No current album. You must select
an album first.'

    end if

command key ('!')
```

(Continued)

Listing 13-3 *The* `albums.4gl` *program, sixth pass.*

```
              call ShellEscape()

          command 'Exit' 'Exit the menu'

              exit menu

      end menu



      close form f_albums

      close c_albums

      free c_albums



  end main
```

A Little Error Checking

As you experiment with the new albums program, you'll find that it's still not bulletproof. For example, if you type a non-numeric entry as an absolute or relative value, the program will crash. Try it. Also, if you try to fetch beyond the active set, the program quietly ignores you. Let's modify the program to be friendlier when such fetches are attempted. The error checking needed to avoid a non-numeric program crash is added as the first exercise at the end of this chapter.

You'll notice that the first four menu entries in the `albums.4gl` `main` program block perform similar functions. That is, each tries to fetch data from the `c_albums` cursor and display the values returned. In every case, it is possible that the user could try to fetch a value outside of the active set. For example, trying to fetch a row previous to the first one, or with an absolute number larger than the program array, will fail. When you want to perform a similar series of operations in several places in a program, you should consider creating a function for this purpose. In this case, we'll create one called `DisplayAlbum()`, which each menu option will call as appropriate.

Add the function from Listing 13-4 to your `albums.4gl` module.

Listing 13-4 *Creating a function that is called from several places.*

```
function DisplayAlbum(lr_albums)

define lr_albums record like albums.*


    if (STATUS = NOTFOUND) then

        error 'There are no more rows in the direction
you are going'

    else

        display by name lr_albums.*

    end if



end function
```

Now modify the `main` program block to reflect the inclusion of this function. The beginning of your `menu` statement should now resemble the code excerpt from Listing 13-5.

Listing 13-5 *The* `albums.4gl` *program, seventh pass.*

```
menu 'Albums'

    command 'Next' 'Fetch the next row in the active set'

        fetch next c_albums

        call DisplayAlbum(lr_albums.*)
```

(Continued)

Listing 13-5 The `albums.4gl` *program, seventh pass.*

```
command 'Previous'

    'Fetch the previous row in the active set'

    fetch previous c_albums

    call DisplayAlbum(lr_albums.*)

command 'Absolute'

    'Fetch a specific element in the active set'

    prompt 'Enter element number: ' for item_num

    fetch absolute item_num c_albums

    call DisplayAlbum(lr_albums.*)

command 'Relative'

    'Fetch a relative item in the active set'

    prompt 'Enter offset (may be negative): '
        for item_num

    fetch relative item_num c_albums

    call DisplayAlbum(lr_albums.*)
```

Behind the Scenes

If you've used this program to update values in your `albums` table, you may have noticed a strange occurrence. And if you haven't—get off the sidelines. Programming is not a spectator sport! The disconcerting effect you may have seen is that if you update a row, then view another row, and then return to the modified row, it appears as if the row has not been modified. It's as if your update didn't *take*. What's up with that?

It turns out that in order for Informix to maintain an active set you can scroll through, it has to ignore certain database changes. Consider if, after you've fetched five rows, you or another user were to delete the first four rows. What should happen if you try to fetch those (now missing) rows again with your scroll cursor? One option is that Informix could reread each row from the database as you scroll back to previously fetched rows. A drawback is that such an approach is slow: the database must execute another fetch operation for data that probably hasn't changed. Another is that newly inserted rows might now satisfy your query and suddenly appear as you scroll backward. These data integrity and performance drawbacks turn out to be so severe that Informix has elected to have scroll cursors ignore database changes to rows that have already been fetched, and instead merely store images of those rows in memory, or in implicit temporary tables. As a result, when you revisit rows that you have changed, you don't see the changes (which were stored in the database), but rather the original images of the rows. To view any changes, you must close and reopen the cursor, which erases the active set and any stored fetch images. With this small sample program, it means that you must exit the application and restart it.

Dynamic SQL Statements

SQL statements can be static or dynamic. Static statements are those that are defined completely by your Informix-4GL code, and do not change upon successive iterations of the program. Conversely, dynamic SQL statements can change based on values supplied at runtime. The two broad categories of dynamic SQL are those for which you supply only values of variables and those in which you build custom SQL statements piecemeal. Supplying the value of placeholder variables is the easiest kind of dynamic SQL, but not the only kind. The second kind of dynamic SQL allows you to construct fully dynamic SQL statements on the fly, by building a character string that contains all the elements of a `select` statement. In the following sections, we'll build both types of SQL statements.

Using Placeholders

Why are placeholders useful? One reason is for proper modularity—to segregate your database operations from your user interface functions. Another, and more important, reason is for performance. The `prepare` operation that is implicit in any `select` statement takes some time to execute. It parses the statement and creates a statement identifier that identifies it. When a cursor is declared for this statement, the database further checks the statement for proper syntax, and verifies that the user has permissions to access the database. When the same `select` statement is to be performed many times, the accumulated performance drain of all these redundant steps can be noticeable. In such cases, isolating the preparation of the `select` statement so that those operations are performed only once can enhance performance dramatically. Note that for a `select` statement that is performed exactly once, explicitly preparing the `select` statement has no performance impact.

tip

To improve performance, prepare `select` statements that your program will execute repeatedly.

In our small application, you'll be unable to notice any performance improvement from explicitly preparing and declaring a cursor for a `select` statement that gets executed more than once. Nonetheless, you need to understand this important tactic. The following changes to the `albums.4gl` module show how you could declare a cursor to determine whether a `genre` is valid. Currently, the program executes the singleton `select` statement for this purpose in the `after field genre` block of the `UpdateAlbum()` function. The entire `select` statement gets executed for every row you try to update. With this modification the `select` statement will be prepared only once.

The `prepare` Statement

The syntax for the `prepare` statement follows:

```
prepare statement-id from SQL-statement
```

where *statement-id* is an identifier for the statement that a subsequent `declare` or `execute` statement will reference, and *SQL-statement* is a character variable or quoted string that contains a valid SQL statement. The SQL statement may include question mark placeholders (?), indicators that values will be supplied when the cursor declared for *statement-id* is opened.

The first step is to declare a cursor in your main program block that includes a placeholder. Add the following three lines above the current declaration of the c_albums scroll cursor, around line 11 of albums.4gl.

```
prepare genre_stmt from
    'select genre from genres where genre = ?'
declare c_genre cursor for genre_stmt
```

Extra credit if you remembered to add the following polite line at the end of your main program block:

```
free c_genre
```

Now add the following function to your albums.4gl module (Listing 13-6). It opens this cursor with a specific genre, and returns TRUE if the genre exists.

Listing 13-6 *Using a prepared cursor.*

```
function ValidGenre(l_genre)

define l_genre like genres.genre


    define l_found smallint


    open c_genre using l_genre

    fetch c_genre

    if (STATUS = 0) then

        let l_found = TRUE

    else

        let l_found = FALSE
```

(Continued)

Listing 13-6 *Using a prepared cursor.*

```
     end if

     close c_genre


     return l_found


  end function
```

All that remains is to modify your UpdateAlbums() function to call the ValidGenre() function as needed. This call not only simplifies the UpdateAlbums() function, but can improve performance marginally as described above. Your new after field genre program block should resemble the following:

```
after field genre
    if (not ValidGenre(lr_albums.genre)) then
        let lr_albums.genre = PickGenre()
        display by name lr_albums.genre
    end if
```

Compile and run your program with these changes in place. It should work just as before.

If you need clarifications on how all of the modifications fit together, you can peek ahead to the solution to Exercise 2 at the end of this chapter. Although that listing also includes the functions described in the following sections, you'll still be able to recognize the recommended changes to date.

The execute Statement

Although you can prepare almost any SQL statement, you most commonly to prepare dynamic select statements, as shown in the previous example. Later in this chapter we'll return to this more common usage, but first let's explore the full range of the execute statement. The execute statement is the alternative to using declare, open, and fetch on a prepared select statement. It is used to force execution of a prepared statement without the overhead of a cursor, and is most often seen when the statement being prepared is not a select statement. Its syntax follows:

```
execute statement-id

    [into receiving-variable-list]

    [using supplied-variable-list]
```

where *statement-id* is an identifier for a previously prepared statement, *receiving-variable-list* is a comma-separated list of program variables that will receive the values retrieved (it may include program records), and *supplied-variable-list* is a comma-separated list of program variables and constants that supply values for any placeholders (question marks) that were included in the prepared statement. For each placeholder you must supply a value that is compatible with the values the prepared statement requires.

caution *Although you can execute any prepared statement, if the prepared statement is a* select *statement that will return multiple rows, you must instead use the* declare, open, *and* fetch *sequence of statements. If instead you try to execute a prepared* select *statement that returns more than one row of data, you will receive an error message.*

The following sample lines show how you might prepare and execute an insert statement:

```
prepare inst_stmt from 'insert into formats values (?, ?, ?)'
execute inst_stmt using 'DVD', '27.99', 'the wave of the future'
execute inst_stmt using 'bits', '0.00', 'digitized sound clips'
```

Notice how the same prepared statement can be executed multiple times with separate values supplied each time.

A Query-by-Example

Informix-4GL has a built-in function—the `construct` statement—that allows you to build query-by-example forms easily. With such forms, you can navigate screens field by field, entering values to be used in query generation. These forms behave much like the ISQL forms you used in Chapter 6, "ISQL Forms and Reports."

The `construct` Statement

The `construct` statement allows you to build the `where` clause of a `select` statement based on values entered by the user. Just like the `input` statement, it allows the user to navigate a form according to parameters you define. When you press the `Escape` key, Informix-4GL generates a string containing all of the criteria you entered. It is then your responsibility to assemble and execute a `select` statement containing that string. Although the `construct` statement can be almost as complex as the `input` statement, the breadth of its options is unnecessary for most applications. A simplified form of its syntax follows:

```
construct by name selection-criteria on column-list
    [attribute (attribute-list)]
    [before construct 4GL-statements]
    [before field field-list 4GL-statements]
    [after field field-list 4GL-statements]
    [after construct 4GL-statements]
[end construct]
```

where *selection-criteria* is a character variable that will store the *where*-clause string, and *column-list* is a comma-separated list of database column names, but may also include the *table-name.** syntax. The now familiar *attribute-list* is a comma-separated list of screen display attributes, those listed in Table 11-2. Items in the optional `before construct` block are executed after all of the fields in *column-list* have been cleared, but before any screen navigation is done. The statements in the `after construct` block are executed immediately after the `construct` statement is terminated, but before the *selection-criteria* string is built. The `before` and `after field` blocks are where statements can be placed so that they are executed just when the user's cursor enters or leaves a field. The `end construct` statement is required only when any of the optional blocks are included. Finally, `4GL-statements` are any valid program statements as well as the following three procedural directives:

- `next field` *field-name*|next|previous
- `continue construct`
- `exit construct`

When a `next field` statement is encountered, the cursor moves to *field-name*, or to the `next` or `previous` screen field, as indicated, allowing certain fields to be skipped as desired. The `continue construct` statement skips any remaining 4GL statements in the `construct` statement, whereas with the `exit construct` statement processing control is passed to the next statement following the `end construct` clause.

Assembling an SQL Statement

Let's use the `construct` statement as the cornerstone to build a `FindAlbum()` function, one that allows the `albums` form to be used for QBE. Note especially that you must assemble the SQL statement piecemeal, using the `l_where_clause` variable as one component of the `select` statement. Add the function from Listing 13-7 to your `albums.4gl` module.

Now enable the function by adding the following three lines to your calling menu, in the `main` program block of `albums.4gl`:

```
command 'Search'
    'Find an album using Query-by-Example'
    call FindAlbum() returning lr_albums.*
    call DisplayAlbum(lr_albums.*)
```

Run this program several times. Experiment with the metacharacters that are allowed in the selection criteria—the same ones applicable when using ISQL forms. Consider displaying the value of `l_where_clause` during development so that you thoroughly understand how the `construct` statement functions. Especially curious is the value that is generated when no criteria are entered.

Listing 13-7 *Using the* `construct` *statement to create a QBE function.*

```
function FindAlbum()


    define lr_albums      record like albums.*

    define l_select_stmt  char(320)

    define l_where_clause char(160)


    construct by name l_where_clause on albums.*

        attribute (reverse)

        before construct

            message 'Press ESC to begin search.'

        before field album_num

            -- Don't search by album_num

            next field next

    end construct


    let l_select_stmt =

    'select * ',

      'from albums ',

      'where ', l_where_clause clipped


    prepare find_stmt from l_select_statement

    declare c_find cursor for find_statement
```

(Continued)

Listing 13-7 Using the construct *statement to create a QBE function.*

```
open c_find

fetch c_find into lr_albums.*

if (STATUS = NOTFOUND) then

    error 'No rows found'

    initialize lr_albums.* to null

end if


return lr_albums.*


end function
```

Summary

Cursors are essential components of Informix-4GL programming. They allow you to bridge the set-based nature of SQL with the row-at-a-time nature of most procedural programming constructs. In fancy terms, they allow you to manage the impedance mismatch between these two paradigms.

With a sequential cursor, you traverse a select statement's active set in the forward direction only. At the cost of some additional resource and performance overhead, scroll cursors let you traverse the active set directionally, or access any row that you specify.

The prepare statement lets you build dynamic SQL statements, often to allow for runtime creation of custom select statements. One common use of such customized select statements is to incorporate the where clause of a query-by-example (QBE). The `construct` statement lets you use screen forms to build QBE-based applications.

Prepared statements can also be used when you want to improve the performance of an SQL statement that is executed repeatedly. By saving the overhead of allocating system resources repeatedly, you can realize significant performance gains.

Finally, you were admonished to be a polite programmer by cleaning up after yourself: close what you open, and free what you prepare.

Extra Credit

Q&A

Question	**Answer**
Who can turn the world on with her smile? Who can take a nothing day, and suddenly make it all seem worthwhile?	Well it's you girl and you should know it. With each glance and every little movement you show it.
Would you like fries with that?	Sure. And super-size it.

Exercises

1. The latest version of the `albums.4gl` program still crashes if you enter a non-numeric value as an absolute or relative positioning value. Create a function called `NumberPrompt()` in your `infxlibs.4gl` module that accepts one argument (the text string to use as the prompt) and returns a valid number. Its nature will therefore be somewhat similar to the `YesNoPrompt()` library function. Alter the `main` program block to call this function where appropriate.

2. Compare your `albums.4gl` and `infxlibs.4gl` modules to those provided in the solution to this exercise. Take whatever time is necessary to understand each of the functions therein.

3. You've probably noticed that after you use the `Search` menu option to find a row, the active set from the scroll cursor is still operative. That is, if you use the `Next` menu option, you see the

next row in the scroll cursor's active set, not the next row that might have satisfied your search criteria. This counterintuitive performance is not generally preferred. Alter your `albums.4gl` program to avoid this disjunct behavior.

Exercise Answers

1. The following is one possible answer. The first few lines represent the small changes needed in the `menu` statement of the `main` program block.

   - Replace this line:

     ```
     prompt 'Enter element number: ' for item_num
     ```

   - with this line:

     ```
     let item_num = NumberPrompt('Enter element
       number')
     ```

   - And replace this line:

     ```
     prompt 'Enter offset (may be negative): ' for
       item_num
     ```

   - with this line:

     ```
     let item_num = NumberPrompt('Enter offset (may be
       negative)')
     ```

   - Add the following function to the `infxlibs.4gl` module.

   Listing E13-1 *Answer to Exercise 1.*

   ```
   function NumberPrompt(l_prompt_string)

   define l_prompt_string char(50)


       define l_number      smallint

       define l_response    char(6)


       let l_number = null
   ```

   (Continued)

```
while (l_number is null)

    prompt l_prompt_string clipped, ': '

        for l_response


        -- This assignment quietly fails if l_response

        -- is non-numeric

        let l_number = l_response

        if (l_number is null) then

            error 'Please enter a number'

        end if

    end while


    return l_number


end function
```

2. Listings E13-2 and E13-2a show the current versions of the albums program that has been developed throughout Chapters 11 through 13.

Listing E13-2 *The* albums.4gl *module.*

```
database music


main
```

(Continued)

```
define item_num  smallint
define lr_albums record like albums.*


open form f_albums from 'albums'
display form f_albums


prepare genre_stmt from
    'select genre from genres where genre = ?'
declare c_genre cursor for genre_stmt


declare c_albums scroll cursor for
  select *
    into lr_albums.*
    from albums
  order by rating desc, title
open c_albums


initialize lr_albums.* to null


menu 'Albums'
    command 'Next'
        'Fetch the next row in the active set'
        fetch next c_albums
        call DisplayAlbum(lr_albums.*)
    command 'Previous'
```

(Continued)

```
                    'Fetch the previous row in the active set'

                    fetch previous c_albums

                    call DisplayAlbum(lr_albums.*)

               command 'Absolute'

                    'Fetch a specific element in the active set'

                    let item_num =

                         NumberPrompt('Enter element number')

                    fetch absolute item_num c_albums

                    call DisplayAlbum(lr_albums.*)

               command 'Relative'

                    'Fetch a relative item in the active set'

                    let item_num = NumberPrompt

                         ('Enter offset (may be negative)')

                    fetch relative item_num c_albums

                    call DisplayAlbum(lr_albums.*)

               command 'Search'

                    'Find an album using Query-by-Example'

                    call FindAlbum() returning lr_albums.*

                    call DisplayAlbum(lr_albums.*)

               command 'Update'

                    'Change the values for this album'

                    if (lr_albums.album_num is not null) then

                         call UpdateAlbum(lr_albums.*)

                    else

                         error 'No current album. You must select
```

(Continued)

```
                        an album first.'

                end if

        command key ('!')

                call ShellEscape()

        command 'Exit' 'Exit the menu'

                exit menu

    end menu


    close form f_albums

    close c_albums

    free c_albums

    free c_genre


end main




function DisplayAlbum(lr_albums)

define lr_albums    record like albums.*


    if (STATUS = NOTFOUND) then

        error 'There are no more rows in the direction you
are going'

    else

        display by name lr_albums.*
```

(Continued)

```
        end if


    end function




function UpdateAlbum(lr_albums)
define lr_albums    record like albums.*


    input by name lr_albums.* without defaults


        after field genre
            if (not ValidGenre(lr_albums.genre)) then
                let lr_albums.genre = PickGenre()
                display by name lr_albums.genre
            end if


        after field rating
            if (lr_albums.rating < 1 or
                lr_albums.rating > 10) then
                error 'Rating must be between 1 and 10'
                next field rating
            end if


    end input
```

(Continued)

```
    if (YesNoPrompt

        ('Update current row with these values?')) then

        update albums

            set * = lr_albums.*

            where album_num = lr_albums.album_num

    end if


end function




function ValidGenre(l_genre)

define l_genre like genres.genre


    define l_found smallint


    open c_genre using l_genre

    fetch c_genre

    if (STATUS = 0) then

        let l_found = TRUE

    else

        let l_found = FALSE

    end if

    close c_genre
```

(Continued)

```
    return l_found


end function




function FindAlbum()


    define lr_albums       record like albums.*
    define l_select_stmt  char(320)
    define l_where_clause char(160)


    construct by name l_where_clause on albums.*
        attribute (reverse)
        before construct
            message 'Press ESC to begin search'
        before field album_num
            -- Don't search by this field
            next field next
    end construct


    let l_select_stmt =
    'select * ',
      'from albums ',
```

(Continued)

```
     'where ', l_where_clause clipped


   prepare find_stmt from l_select_stmt

   declare c_find cursor for find_stmt


   open c_find

   fetch c_find into lr_albums.*

   if (STATUS = NOTFOUND) then

       error 'No rows found'

       initialize lr_albums.* to null

   end if


   return lr_albums.*


end function
```

Listing E13-2a *The* `infxlibs.4gl` *module.*

```
database music


function ShellEscape()


   define shell_cmd char(80)


   options prompt line last
```

(Continued)

```
    prompt '!' for shell_cmd

    run shell_cmd

    prompt 'Press return to continue' attribute (reverse)

        for char shell_cmd

    options prompt line first


end function




function YesNoPrompt(l_prompt_string)

define l_prompt_string char(60)


    define l_response    char(1)


    while TRUE

        prompt l_prompt_string clipped, ': '

            for char l_response

        case (upshift(l_response))

            when 'Y'

                return TRUE

            when 'N'

                return FALSE

            otherwise

                error 'Please enter Y or N'
```

(Continued)

```
        end case

    end while


end function



function PickGenre()


    define lr_genres array[100] of record like genres.*
    define l_count    smallint
    define l_picked   smallint


    open window w_genres at 4, 3 with form 'arr_genres'
        attribute (border)
    display 'Use Esc to choose a genre. Use the arrow
        keys to navigate.'
        at 1, 2 attribute (red)


    declare c_genres cursor for
    select *
      from genres
     order by genre


    let l_count = 0
```

(Continued)

```
    -- fill the program array with database values

    foreach c_genres into lr_genres[l_count + 1].*

        let l_count = l_count + 1

    end foreach


    call set_count(l_count)

    display array lr_genres to sr_genres.* attribute

        (blue)

    let l_picked = arr_curr()


    close c_genres

    free  c_genres

    close window w_genres


    return lr_genres[l_picked].genre


end function




function NumberPrompt(l_prompt_string)

define l_prompt_string char(50)


    define l_number      smallint

    define l_response    char(6)
```

(Continued)

```
let l_number = null

while (l_number is null)

      prompt l_prompt_string clipped, ': '

            for l_response


            -- The following assignment quietly fails if

            -- l_response is non-numeric

            let l_number = l_response

            if (l_number is null) then

                  error 'Please enter a number'

            end if

      end while


      return l_number


end function
```

3. There are several effective approaches here, left as a substantial exercise for the reader. Each must include the key tactic of combining the current `c_albums` cursor with the dynamic nature of the `c_find` cursor. At the end, there can only be one cursor that populates the `lr_albums` record for display.

4GL Reports

Reports are programs that extract data from the database, format it according to rules you define, and display the output. Although this output is commonly sent to a printer or saved in a file, it can also be directed to the screen, or, in UNIX systems, used as the input (*piped*) to another command. Here are some pointers to follow when reading this chapter:

- Do the examples in this chapter in order, because they build on each other
- Do not try to memorize the many tables in this chapter. Instead, learn by example how the different pieces of a report program work in concert.
- Use those same tables for reference later

A Simple Report Example

Create and run the report program shown in Listing 14-1. As with the previous four chapters, you'll use the Informix-4GL Programmer's Environment (i4gl) to do the exercises in this chapter.

When the report runs, its output should scroll to your screen, finishing with something like Figure 14-1.

Let's examine each of the report components in detail.

Listing 14-1 *The* list_genres.4gl *report illustrates a report program's structure.*

```
database music


--This main block serves as the report driver

main


    define lr_genres record like genres.*


    declare Sgenres cursor for

    select *

       from genres

      order by genre


    start report GenresRpt

    foreach Sgenres into lr_genres.*
```

(Continued)

```
        output to report GenresRpt (lr_genres.*)

    end foreach

    finish report GenresRpt



end main



--This program block is the report formatter

report GenresRpt (lr_genres)

define lr_genres record like genres.*


    output

        left margin 0

        page length 24


    order external by lr_genres.genre


    format every row


end report
```

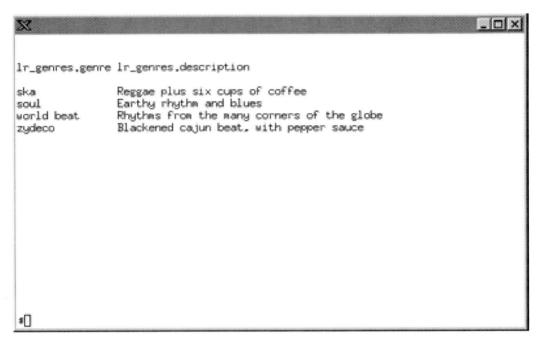

```
lr_genres.genre lr_genres.description

ska          Reggae plus six cups of coffee
soul         Earthy rhythm and blues
world beat   Rhythms from the many corners of the globe
zydeco       Blackened cajun beat, with pepper sauce
```

Figure 14–1 *By default, reports display on your screen.*

The Structure of a 4GL Report

There are two major components in an Informix report program: a *report driver* and a *report formatter*. The driver selects the data and sends it to the formatter one row at a time. The formatter generates the output, assembling the rows according to the printing specifications you define. The formatter also adds any page headers and trailers, as well as group and report totals.

The report driver is generally part of a standard function, usually using a `foreach` loop as its data-gathering mechanism, but the report formatter component must use the `report` program block. Although the `report` program block is a function, it is a very specialized one. As a function, it accepts arguments from a calling program and returns control when it finishes. However, its interface is otherwise unique, and the statements allowed within its control blocks are limited.

The Report Driver

You need to perform the following steps when building a report driver.

1. Declare a cursor for the `select` statement that generates the data used by the report. Although most reports use this construct, it is not required. Actually, the data sent to a report need not come from database rows at all; it can be calculated, invented, or can come from any source whatsoever.
2. Execute the `start report` statement. This initializes the report formatter.
3. Execute a `foreach` loop that generates the rows of data sent to the report driver. Again, the `foreach` loop is not required, but is very common.
4. For each row of data, pass its values to the report driver with the `output to report` statement.
5. Execute the `finish report` statement. This instructs the report formatter that no more rows of data will follow, and final report processing may occur.

You'll see several examples of report drivers throughout this chapter.

The Report Formatter

The following list shows the four sections that are allowed in a report formatter function. Only the `report` and `format` sections are mandatory, but any sections you include must be in the order shown. Listing 14-1 includes all four sections.

- The `report` declaration section
- The `output` section
- The `order by` section
- The `format` section

Each of these sections are detailed in the following paragraphs.

The `report` Declaration Section

As with any function, the `report` programming block must have its arguments declared; that is, the values that are sent to it must be assigned to named, typed variables. Notice that if you define a record to receive the report's row values (`lr_genres`, in this case), then all references to those variables must explicitly reference the record.

The `output` Section

The optional `output` section defines both the destination of your report and the overall page formatting; Table 14-1 describes its components. The default value is used for any element that you do not define explicitly.

Figure 14-2 shows how these margins affect the report page layout.

Table 14-1 Components of the 4GL report* output *section.

Element	*Default*	*Defines*
report to *dest*	Screen	Destination for report's output, where *dest* is one of the following three destinations:
file '*file-name*'		Send output to *file-name*, overwriting the file if it already exists
pipe '*UNIX-command*'		Send report output as an input stream to *UNIX-command*
printer		Send output to the UNIX `lp` command, or to the value of the DBPRINT environmental variable if it is set
top margin *n*	3	Number of blank lines at the top of each page

(Continued)

Table 14-1 *Components of the 4GL report* output *section.*

Element	Default	Defines
`bottom margin` *n*	3	Number of blank lines at the bottom of each page
`left margin` *n*	5	Number of blanks by which all output is indented
`page length` *n*	66	Number of lines on each page

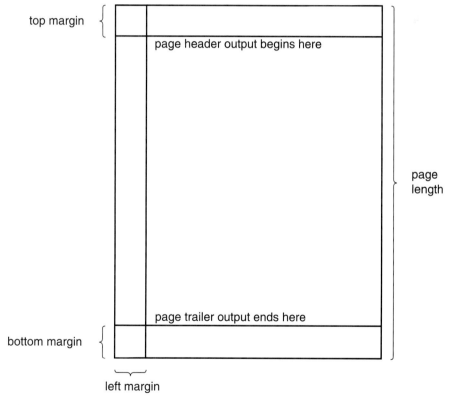

Figure 14–2   *Report margins customize your page layout.*

The order by Section

In the optional `order by` section you define the sort order of the rows that are sent to the report. You need to include this section if you want to include any `before group of` or `after group of` control blocks (you'll see examples of these in Listing 14-3). You can only group by the variables that are in your `order by` statement. For example, let's say you have the following `order by` section:

```
order external by artist, title
```

You can then include either or both of the following control blocks in your report formatter:

```
after group of artist
after group of title
```

You may include the optional keyword `external` in your `order by` section. When you do so, you are indicating that the rows have been presorted so that these grouping operations can aggregate rows properly. In such cases, the report formatter does not have to sort the rows. If you exclude the `external` keyword, the formatter itself sorts the rows, even if they are already sorted.

Sort your rows in your report driver function whenever possible. Although you can use the `order by` section of your report formatter to sort your rows, using the `order by` clause of a `select` statement is more efficient.

The format Section

The `format` section usually constitutes the bulk of any report program. The brief `format every row` line near the end of Listing 14-1 is anomalous. This shortcut generates default formatting, using the report variable names as column headers, and basing column widths on the column's data types. Generally, these `every row` keywords are only useful for the first prototype of a report; after that, you usually create a more explicit `format` section, comprising any number of the program blocks shown in Table 14-2.

Update your `list_genres.4gl` program, replacing the `GenresRpt()` function with the code from Listing 14-2. Then compile and run your new `list_genres.4gl` program.

Listing 14-2 *An expanded* `list_genres.4gl` *report function.*

```
report GenresRpt (lr_genres)

define lr_genres record like genres.*


    output

        left margin 0

        report to 'genres.out'


    order external by lr_genres.genre


    format

        page header

            print column 30, 'GENRES LIST'

            print column 31,  today using 'mm/dd/yy'

            skip 1 line

            print column  1, 'Genre',

                column 16, 'Description'

            print column  1, '-----',

                column 16, '-----------'

            skip 1 line


        page trailer

            print column 31, 'Page: ', pageno using
```

(Continued)

Listing 14-2 An expanded `list_genres.4gl` *report function.*

```
                          '<<<<'



            on every row

                print column   1,  lr_genres.genre,

                        column 16,  lr_genres.description



        end report
```

Now, from the operating system use the following command to examine the output file you have created. Your results should resemble those shown.

$ **cat genres.out**

```
                        GENRES LIST
                         07/05/98


Genre             Description
-----             -----------


blues             Chicago, Texas, and Memphis heartache
...
soul              Earthy rhythm and blues
world beat        Rhythms from the many corners of the globe
zydeco            Blackened Cajun beat, with pepper sauce


...


                        Page:  1
```

Notice especially that the `format` section of the `GenresRpt()` `report` program block has been expanded to include three of the seven possible formatting control blocks. The next section describes all seven of the program blocks.

Formatting Control Blocks

All procedural statements within a report must be inside some control block. Table 14-2 explains all of the report control blocks. Generally, what goes in these blocks are formatting directives like `print` and `skip`, but you may also include expressions and procedural logic. Your `format` section must include at least one report control block.

Although you can arrange the control blocks within your `format` section in any order, the order shown in Table 14-2 has proven to be easy to follow. The following sections clarify three of the report control blocks that merit special explanation.

Table 14-2 The report control blocks.

Control Block	When the Block's Statements Execute
first page header	At the beginning of the first page; if present, it suppresses the standard `page header` for the first page
page header	At the beginning of every page
page trailer	At the bottom of every page
on every row	As each row of data is processed
before group of *variable-name*	Before the first row of a group indicated by a change in the value of *variable-name*
after group of *variable-name*	After the last row of a group indicated by a change in the value of *variable-name*
on last row	After the last row of data is processed

The `first page header` Control Block

This block executes before the first input record is processed. Therefore, you can use it to initialize any variables that you use in the `format` section.

note *The `first page header` control block supersedes any `page header` block. Thus, if you use the `first page header` to initialize variables, and you want any titles that are defined in your `page header` control block to be included on the report's first page, you must duplicate those title definitions in the `first page header` control block.*

The `before group of` Control Block

The `before group of` block actually occurs once the report formatter receives the first row of a new group. Until then, it does not know that a new group is starting. Thus, it may be helpful for you to think of this block as "on first row of group." Likewise, the `after group of` control block can be considered "on last row of group." This consideration clarifies how the value of the variable that defines a group is known in a `group of` block. The `after group of l_artist` control block in Listing 14-3 shows how you might use a variable in a `group of` block.

Remember that you cannot have a `before group of` or `after group of` report control block for any variable that you have not included as a sort key in the `order by` section.

The `after group of` Control Block

The `after group of` block is commonly where you place subtotals and aggregate functions that apply to the group that was just processed. You precede aggregate functions with the keyword `group` in an `after group of` block to have those aggregates applied to the current group only. For example, the following code fragment (from Listing 14-3) shows how to print subtotals by artist:

```
after group of l_artist
    print column 57, '-------'
    print column 23, 'Total for ', l_artist,
        column 56, group sum(l_amount_paid) using '$,$$&.&&'
```

When you don't use the `group` restriction, the aggregates are generated from all the rows in the report. Usually, you use such statements in the `on last row` control block. Compare the previous example to the following code fragment from the same program:

```
on last row
    print column 57, '======='
    print column  1, 'Total for all albums',
          column 56, sum(l_amount_paid) using '$,$$&.&&'
```

A More Complex Report Example

Listing 14-3 generates a report that summarizes the amounts you paid for albums, by artist. It includes six of the seven possible formatting control blocks (there is no `first page header` block). You should create and run this report. A later example adds to its functionality, refining it from a useful but static report into an even more useful dynamic report.

Listing 14-3 The `artist_value.4gl` *report.*

```
database music


main


    define l_artist       like albums.artist

    define l_title        like albums.title

    define l_amount_paid  like album_copies.amount_paid


    declare Sartist cursor for

    select artist, title, amount_paid
```

(Continued)

Listing 14-3 *The* `artist_value.4gl` *report.*

```
   from albums, album_copies

  where albums.album_num = album_copies.album_num

  order by artist, title


start report ArtistRpt

foreach Sartist into l_artist, l_title,

                    l_amount_paid

    output to report ArtistRpt (l_artist, l_title,

                               l_amount_paid)

end foreach

finish report ArtistRpt


end main



report ArtistRpt (l_artist, l_title, l_amount_paid)

define l_artist       like albums.artist

define l_title        like albums.title

define l_amount_paid  like album_copies.amount_paid


    output

       report to 'artist.out'

       left margin 0
```

(Continued)

Listing 14-3 *The* `artist_value.4gl` *report.*

```
order external by l_artist, l_title


format

    page header

        print column 26, 'AMOUNTS PAID BY ARTIST'

        print column 33,  today using 'mm/dd/yy'

        print

        print column  7, 'Artist',

                column 34, 'Title',

                column 55, 'Amount Paid'

        print column  1, '--------------------',

                column 23, '-------------------------
----',

                column 55, '-----------'


    page trailer

        print column 33, 'Page: ', pageno using

            '<<<<'


    on every row

        need 3 lines

        print column  1, l_artist,
```

(Continued)

Listing 14-3 The `artist_value.4gl` *report.*

```
                        column 23, l_title,

                        column 56, l_amount_paid using

                                '$,$$&.&&'


        before  group of l_artist

            skip 1 line


        after group of l_artist

            print column 57, '-------'

            print column 23, 'Total for ', l_artist,

                    column 56, group sum(l_amount_paid)

                            using '$,$$&.&&'


        on last row

            skip 1 line

            need 2 lines

            print column 57, '======='

            print column  1, 'Total for all albums',

                    column 56, sum(l_amount_paid) using

                            '$,$$&.&&'


    end report
```

From the operating system, examine the output file:

```
$ cat artist.out
```

```
                        AMOUNTS PAID BY ARTIST
                             09/29/97

        Artist                    Title                   Amount Paid
------------------------  -----------------------------   -----------

Ambient Sounds            Sounds of the Okefenokee Swamp      $9.99
                                                            -------
                          Total for Ambient Sounds            $9.99

Bay City Rollers          Absolute Rollers - The Best of
Bay City Rollers          Once Upon A Star                    $6.95
                                                            -------
                          Total for Bay City Rollers          $6.95

Beatles                   Abbey Road                         $16.95
Beatles                   Help!                               $0.00
Beatles                   Help!                               $9.95
Beatles                   Please Please Me                   $14.95
Beatles                   Revolver                           $13.50
                                                            -------
                          Total for Beatles                  $55.35

Culture Club              Colour by Numbers                  $29.99
Culture Club              Kissing to be Clever
                                                            -------
                          Total for Culture Club             $29.99

Double Trouble            Soul to Soul
Double Trouble            Soul to Soul                        $8.99
                                                            -------
                          Total for Double Trouble            $8.99
...
Zydeco Cha Chas           Zydeco Live!                       $17.50
                                                            -------
                          Total for Zydeco Cha Chas          $17.50

                                                            =======
Total for all albums                                       $228.17
```

Take some time to compare the report output to the code that generates it. For example, the report driver (the `main` program block) defines a `select` statement that includes a join. Your report drivers' `select` statements can be of any complexity. Also, certain lines in the report output reveal that some albums have a null `amount_paid` value. Accordingly, no amount is printed. When it sums values that include nulls, the report writer ignores the nulls in its calculations. Compare the printing of null amounts to the printing of zero-value amounts (one of the Beatles' albums, `Help!`). In this report, the `using` operator is used to format a date string, an integer, and several money fields. For the money-field formatting, the ampersand symbol (`&`) forces three digits of zeroes to be printed when the value is zero. Tables 14-5 and 14-6 provide a reference for the versatile `using` operator. Notice the use of the `need` statement in the `on every row` block—it ensures that no row of data will be printed if its group totals (two lines) could not be printed on the same page. Table 14-3 explains the `need` statement and the rest of the formatting directives. Finally, compare the `after group of` and `on last row` blocks to see the clear distinction between a report aggregate and a group aggregate.

Formatting Directives

Formatting directive statements, sometimes called report execution statements, are only valid within the `format` section of a `report` function. You've seen them by example throughout this chapter's listings. Table 14-3 shows the formal list.

Table 14-3 The report formatting statements.

Statement	Effect
skip *n* line[s]	Print *n* blank line(s)
skip to top of page	Print enough blank lines to reach a new page
need *n* line[s]	Skip to top of page unless the following *n* lines can also be printed on this page

(Continued)

Table 14-3 The report formatting statements.

Statement	Effect
pause ['user-message']	If the report output is sent to the screen, display user-message, if present, and wait until the user hits any key before proceeding
print arguments	Print the arguments supplied (see Table 14-4)
print file-name	Print the contents of file-name

The print Arguments

The print statement is the *sine qua non* of any report program. You use it to direct what values are printed where, and, combined with the using operator, how they are formatted. Each print statement formats and prints its arguments, if any, and then prints a newline. Thus, a print statement without arguments acts just like a skip 1 line statement.

Experiment with the print and using statements. Several tables explaining these statements follow, but the best way to learn is to experiment on your own. Don't feel constrained by the sample listings in this chapter.

Table 14-4 shows the complete list of arguments you can supply to the print statement.

The using Operator

The using clause allows you to customize the appearance of the numeric, money, and date expressions in your report. Although shown here as part of the print statement, the using operator is

Table 14-4 *The* `print` *arguments.*

Argument	Effect
`expression` [using `format-string`]	Print the expression, with optional `format-string` specifications (see Table 14-5)
`character-expression` `clipped`	Print the `character-expression`, trimming all trailing spaces
n `space[s]`	Print *n* space(s)
`column` *n*	If the current column is less than *n*, print enough spaces to reach column *n*
`ascii` `ascii-value`	Print the ASCII equivalent of `ascii-value`
`,`	Concatenate the argument that follows to the current expression
`;`	Suppress the newline normally generated by the `print` statement

also used to format expressions in `display` statements, and, less frequently, in `let` statements.

Formatting Numeric Expressions

Table 14-5 shows the most useful symbols available for applying the `using` `format-string` to numeric and money values.

This is so much easier to show than to explain. Table 14-6 shows the effect some different format strings have on sample numerical values.

You can see the difference between the < and # symbols most clearly in statements like the following:

```
print 'Page: ', using '####'
print 'Page: ', using '<<<<'
```

Table 14-5 *The* using *format specifications for numeric and money values.*

Specifier	Effect on Expression
#	Right-justify, retaining blanks
<	Left-justify
&	Replace any blanks with zeros
,	Print this comma character only when any numbers are to its left
.	Print this decimal point
$	Print this dollar sign just left of the number being printed; otherwise, act like the # symbol (the dollar sign *floats*)
–	Print this floating minus sign just left of the number being printed when the number is less than zero; otherwise, act like the # symbol
( )	Print parentheses around the number being printed when the number is less than zero
+	Print this floating plus sign just left of the number being printed when the number is greater than or equal to zero, and as a minus sign when the number is less than zero; otherwise, act like the # symbol

which produce output like the following, respectively:

```
Page:    12
Page: 12
```

Table 14-6 Sample using **_format specifications outputs._**

Format String	Value	Output
'$$,$$&.&&'	0	$0.00
'$$,$$&.&&'	.03	$0.03
'$$,$$&.&&'	.31	$0.31
'$$,$$&.&&'	3.14	$3.14
'$$,$$&.&&'	31.42	$31.42
'$$,$$&.&&'	314.16	$314.16
'$$,$$&.&&'	3141.59	$3,141.59
'$$,$$&.&&'	31415.93	********* (overflow)
'$$$,$$&.&&'	31415.93	$31,415.93
'<<<<<'	123	123
'#####'	123	123
'+++++'	123	+123
'-----'	123	123

Formatting Date Expressions

Table 14-7 shows the most useful symbols available for applying the using `format-string` to date values.

All other characters in a date value format string are displayed literally. Table 14-8 shows some examples of using different date format strings.

*Table 14-7 **The** using **format specifications for date values.***

Specifier	Date Value Displayed	Range of Values
dd	Day of the month	01-31
ddd	Day of the week	Sun-Sat
mm	Numeric month	01-12
mmm	Abbreviated month	Jan-Dec
yy	Year in the 1900s	01-99 (for 1900–1999)
yyyy	Year	0000–9999

Table 14-8 Sample date formats.

Format String	September 29, 1998 Displayed As
'mm/dd/yyyy'	09/29/1998
'mm.dd.yy'	09.29.98
'mmddyy'	092998
'yy-mm-dd'	98-09-29
'mmm dd, yyyy'	Sep 29, 1998
'ddd, mmm. dd, yyyy'	Mon, Sep. 29, 1998

Changing the Report Destination Dynamically

I've been holding out on you. The `start report` clause that
you've used in your report driver functions can also accept a destination argument. The same values shown in Table 14-1 for the
`report to` clause may be applied to the `start report` statement. For example, the following are all legal ways to initialize a
report:

```
start report GenresRpt

start report GenresRpt to 'genres.out'

start report GenresRpt to l_file_name

start report GenresRpt to printer

start report GenresRpt to pipe 'more'
```

What makes this interesting is that, although the `output` section in the report formatter is declarative, the `start report`
statement in the report driver is procedural. In plain terms, this
means that you can base the report's destination on interactive
feedback from the user when you use a destination with the
`start report` statement.

You can see how the `case` statement in Listing 14-4 would redirect your report's output based on the value of `l_rpt_dest`.

This fragment would work especially well in conjunction with a
function that prompts the user for a report destination, and returns
values for `l_rpt_dest`, `l_file_name`, and `l_pipe_cmd`. Listing
14-5 is such a function, and besides, it is generic; that is, it can be
linked with any Informix-4GL program. Nothing about it is specific to the `list genres.4gl` or `artist_value.4gl` programs.
Add the `ChooseRptDest()` function to your `infxlibs.4gl` module, the one you created in Chapter 11, "Your 4GL User Interface."

Now you'll need to modify the `main` block of
`artist_value.4gl` to call this function. Use Listing 14-4 as a
guide; when you are finished, your `main` program block should
resemble Listing 14-6. Remember to remove the `report to`
`'artist.out'` statement from your report formatting function
(line 30, Listing 14-3).

Listing 14-4 *A* case *statement allows you to set a report destination dynamically.*

```
case (l_rpt_dest)

    when 'S'

        start report ArtistRpt           -- to screen

    when 'F'

        start report ArtistRpt to l_file_name

    when 'P'

        start report ArtistRpt to printer

    when 'I'

        start report ArtistRpt to pipe l_pipe_cmd

end case
```

Listing 14-5 *The generic* ChooseRptDest() *function.*

```
function ChooseRptDest()


    -- select a destination for a 4GL report


    define l_rpt_dest   char(1)

    define l_file_name char(18)

    define l_pipe_cmd   char(18)


    let l_rpt_dest  = 'S'

    let l_file_name = null
```

(Continued)

Listing 14-5 *The generic* `ChooseRptDest()` *function.*

```
let l_pipe_cmd   = null


open window Wchoose_dest at 4, 7 with 2 rows,

    44 columns

    attribute (border)


menu 'Destination'

    command 'Screen' 'Send the results to the screen'

        let l_rpt_dest = 'S'

        exit menu

    command 'File' 'Send the results to a file'

        let l_rpt_dest = 'F'

        prompt 'Enter destination file: '

            for l_file_name

        exit menu

    command 'Printer'

        'Send the results to the default printer'

        let l_rpt_dest = 'P'

        exit menu

    command key ('I') 'pIpe'

        'Use the results as input to a UNIX command'

        let l_rpt_dest = 'I'

        prompt 'Enter command: ' for l_pipe_cmd

        exit menu
```

(Continued)

Listing 14-5 *The generic* `ChooseRptDest()` *function.*

```
   end menu

   close window Wchoose_dest

   return l_rpt_dest, l_file_name, l_pipe_cmd

end function
```

Listing 14-6 *The* `main` *block of* `artist_value.4gl` *now calls the generic* `ChooseRptDest()` *function.*

```
main

   define l_artist       like albums.artist
   define l_title        like albums.title
   define l_amount_paid  like album_copies.amount_paid
   define l_rpt_dest     char(1)
   define l_file_name    char(18)
   define l_pipe_cmd     char(18)

   declare Sartist cursor for
   select artist, title, amount_paid
     from albums, album_copies
    where albums.album_num = album_copies.album_num
    order by artist, title
```

(Continued)

Listing 14-6 *The* main *block of* artist_value.4gl *now calls the generic* ChooseRptDest() *function.*

```
message 'Please choose a destination for the Artist
    Value report'
call ChooseRptDest() returning l_rpt_dest,
    l_file_name, l_pipe_cmd
case (l_rpt_dest)
    when 'S'
        start report ArtistRpt
    when 'F'
        start report ArtistRpt to l_file_name
    when 'P'
        start report ArtistRpt to printer
    when 'I'
        start report ArtistRpt to pipe l_pipe_cmd
end case


foreach Sartist into l_artist, l_title,
                    l_amount_paid
    output to report ArtistRpt (l_artist, l_title,
                                l_amount_paid)
end foreach
finish report ArtistRpt


end main
```

The only changes were the addition of three more `define` statements, a message to the user, the call to the `ChooseRptDest()` function, and the new `case` statement supporting the multiple `start report` options.

Remember that an easy way to compile a multimodule program is to use `i4gl` to create object files (`.o`) from each of the source modules, and then to link the object files (and the informix libraries) with the `c4gl` compiler at the command line, as with the following:

```
$ c4gl artist_value.o infxlibs.o -o artist_value.4ge
$ artist_value.4ge
```

When you run the `artist_value.4ge` program, the first output you see should resemble Figure 14-3. After that, your output will depend on which report destination you choose.

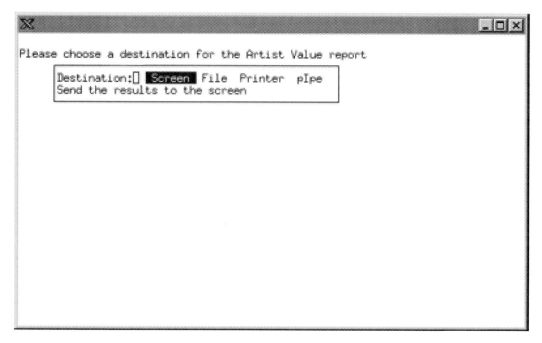

Figure 14–3   *The* `ChooseRptDest()` *function displays a ring menu.*

Notice again how a working version of a program is continually revised and enhanced, with the changes never being so major as to allow you to stray too far from a functional program. Stepwise refinement and modular programming combine to create an effective incremental development environment.

Summary

In this chapter you learned how to write reports with the Informix-4GL report writer. You saw how the two components of every report, the report driver and the report formatter, logically divide the processing. The driver assembles the data and sends it to the formatter; the formatter arranges the data and inserts whatever headers, groupings, and totals you define.

The report formatter includes up to four sections: `report`, `output`, `order by`, and `format`. You probably noticed how similar the `output` and `format` sections are to their Ace report equivalents that you used in Chapter 6, "ISQL Forms and Reports."

You saw the many flavors of the `print` and `using` statements, and how they can be used to customize your report output. Tables 14-3 through 14-8 provide useful reference on these commands for future reports you may write.

By the end of the chapter, you had added another generic function, `ChooseRptDest()`, to your own growing library of Informix-4GL utilities.

Extra Credit

Q&A

Question	Answer
Why should I use the Informix-4GL report writer when the Ace reports from Chapter 6 are easier to create?	You should use the right tool for the job. Simple, especially default, reports should be created with Ace. When you want to include more complex logic, such as is typified by the inclusion of the `ChooseRptDest()` function, Informix-4GL is the best choice.

If I include a destination with a `start report` statement in my report driver, and also have an `output to` statement in my report formatter, which wins?

When your destination in the `start report` statement includes a `to` clause, it takes precedence and the formatter's `output to` section has no effect. If your `start report` statement has no `to` clause, and would thus otherwise send its output to the screen, the destination in the `output to` section is used.

I'm printing a date field in a report. If I have the DBDATE environmental variable set to one format, and include a `using` specifier for a different format, what happens?

The `using` specification takes precedence.

Exercises

1. Write a report that prints all of the performers, and on which album each performed. After the list of albums for each performer, print a count of the number of albums on which he or she performed.
2. Expand your report to include your `ChooseRptDest()` library function.

Exercise Answers

1. No answer is provided for this exercise question because there are numerous ways you could write a program to perform this task. There is no *right* answer; rather, your tackling the project grants you necessary experience. If you peeked ahead to here before starting, get back to work.
2. See the answer to exercise 1.

Chapter 15

ESQL/C

The previous five chapters explored Informix-4GL, Informix's custom application programming language. Yet that programming language, while it has certain advantages, is not as widely known or as versatile as C. In this chapter, you'll see how you can combine the universal features of C with the database interaction features of SQL.

caution

Quicksand Chapter. The material in this chapter, although meaty, useful, and downright illuminating, can be dense. Clear your desk, put the dog out, and get an icy cold drink. You'll be here a while. Take your time—there's plenty to learn, and you shouldn't think that you can appreciate it all in one sitting.

Introction

Embedded Structured Query Language, more commonly known as ESQL/C, is a mechanism that provides access to Informix databases from within programs written in the C language. ESQL stands for Embedded Structured Query Language. The "/C" specifier in ESQL/C indicates that the SQL is embedded in C programs rather than, say, COBOL programs. ESQL/C programs are sometimes referred to as E/C programs or EC programs.

Embedded SQL syntax is specified by the ANSI standard. The embedded SQL standard provides a basic standardized subset for interfacing SQL databases with C programs, but the ESQL standard is usually embellished with extensions by different database vendors. Although all of the major database vendors provide an ESQL implementation, there are enough differences between them to make a program written for one vendor's database not necessarily portable to another's. The good news is that the differences between the vendors' ESQL implementations are not major, so a program written for one can easily be ported to another. You can also be very diligent about conforming to the ANSI standard when writing your E/C programs.

 This chapter assumes a basic familiarity with the C programming language and the process of compiling and linking a C program. The examples in this chapter are directed toward a UNIX environment. Details of compiling and linking an ESQL/C program are provided in the chapter. Although the method of turning the ESQL/C program into an executable is geared toward a UNIX environment, the ESQL/C examples are the same on platforms other than UNIX.

Why Use ESQL/C?

There are several reasons for needing to interface the Informix database with the C language. Programming in C allows for greater flexibility and control than is provided by native Informix applications such as DB-Access or 4GL. C is also by far the most widely used language, with many libraries and platforms already in existence that provide interfaces to other software. For example, it may be necessary to provide a custom graphical user interface to an Informix database with a system such as Microsoft Windows or X-windows for UNIX. There may be other libraries you want to use with your database, such as scientific or statistical libraries, that require special C coding.

ESQL/C also provides a mechanism for determining the specifics of an SQL statement dynamically at runtime. This is necessary if the SQL statement is not known at runtime. The need for dynamically determining the SQL query presents itself in applications such as ad hoc query applications where the user can select any tables or columns from the database when forming a query. In fact, this is the mechanism that the Informix DB-Access program uses to process SQL.

How Does It Work?

ESQL/C programs are written by *embedding* SQL statements into C programs, thus effectively extending the C language to provide a convenient interface to an SQL database. SQL statements in an EC program are prefixed with `exec sql`. Since these embedded statements are obviously not part of the C language, they must be translated into C before they can be compiled into a working program. This translation is accomplished by a precompiler program called `esql`. ESQL/C source code modules typically have an `.ec` suffix instead of the usual `.c` suffix for C program source. The `esql` program's primary task is to translate the `.ec` sources into `.c` sources. This is very similar to how 4GL programs are translated into ESQL/C and then into C.

Some vendors provide a nonembedded method of interfacing to SQL databases that consists of only C function calls. Each method has its advantages and disadvantages. The X/Open standards organization defines a standard for embedded interfaces to SQL databases that is language-independent. It is possible to write Informix ESQL/C programs that are entirely X/Open-compliant. However, a purely C function call interface to SQL databases is not X/Open-compliant, since it is tied to a specific language.

The ESQL/C interface to C programs is provided by embedding text in a C program that is converted to C calls by the `esql` precompiler. The intermediate output of the precompiling process is a C program with the original ESQL/C extensions converted to the appropriate C functions to interface with Informix. The ESQL/C extensions are prefaced with the text `exec sql`. Before continuing with our discussion of ESQL/C, let's go through a simple example to see how the various components work.

A Simple ESQL/C Program

Create a source file called `15_1.ec` that contains the program
shown in Listing 15-1. You'll use this listing to explore the basics
of compiling and running an ESQL/C program.

*The ESQL/C keywords are not case sensitive. Feel free to use
whichever case suits your coding style best. In accordance with the
Informix-4GL standards, lowercase keywords are used in this
chapter.*

Listing 15-1 *A simple* `insert` *statement.*

```
int

main()

{

    exec sql connect to 'music';

    exec sql insert into albums

            values (0, 'Couldn\'t Stand The Weather',

                'Stevie Ray Vaughan', 1984, 'blues', 10,

                'The blues, with a shot of tequila');

    return 0;

}
```

This simple program connects to the database and inserts one
row into the `albums` table. Notice that the `insert` clause that follows the `exec sql` prefix is exactly as it would appear in DB-
Access. One of the advantages of having the `esql` preprocessor

translate the embedded SQL statements into C is that the syntax of the embedded statements is consistent with the SQL you already know. However, some extensions to SQL are provided explicitly for the embedded C interface. These extensions are necessary to loop through the rows that are retrieved from a `select` statement. We will deal with these extensions when we cover multirow `select` statements in the section "Executing `select` Statements" later in this chapter.

Let's go through the steps of turning the simple program into an executable that can be run. The `esql` program does this task for you.

```
$ esql 15_1.ec
$ a.out
```

 Since C++ is backward compatible with C, you can also use C++ to compile your EC programs. Adding object-oriented extensions to your basic C ESQL/C program is a very effective programming methodology. Some vendors already offer C++ object-oriented extensions to ESQL/C that provide a convenient object-oriented interface to ESQL. This chapter, however, is restricted to C.

If the program compiles and executes correctly, there will be no output from the commands.

The `esql` program first translates the `.ec` module with the embedded SQL statements into a C file. It then invokes the C compiler to compile and link the `15_1` program. When this command finishes, provided there were no compilation errors, there will be a file in your directory named `a.out`. This is the default name that the C compiler names your executable. Typing `a.out` at the UNIX command line executes your new program. Since there is no error checking, there is no way to tell if the program ran successfully without using DB-Access to check for the record.

 Notice that there is also a `15_1.c` file in your directory. This C file is an intermediate file that `esql` generated from `15_1.ec`. You should examine the C code that the precompiler program produces to get an idea of how the translation process looks. Be forewarned that the resulting C code is ugly.

Adding Error Checking to Your ESQL/C Programs

ESQL/C does not perform any error checking or exception handling by default. Every embedded SQL statement can potentially result in a runtime exception that can range in severity from a warning to a fatal error. If you do not provide explicit error checking in your code, the program will continue execution after an error has occurred.

The first example ESQL/C program has two ESQL/C statements, and therefore two places where a runtime exception may occur. The first one would occur if the program could not connect to the `music` database. The second one would occur if, for some reason, the record could not be inserted into the `albums` table. The following are some examples of how to add exception handling to the first program.

There are two varieties of errors that can occur within a program: recoverable errors and nonrecoverable errors. Recoverable errors are those that occur when something goes wrong, but the program continues running and is able to react to the error, even if only to exit with a nonzero status. Nonrecoverable errors occur when some disaster has caused the program to be unable to execute. These nonrecoverable exceptions include such things as dividing by zero, memory corruption, and illegal instruction execution. In UNIX-speak, nonrecoverable errors cause a *core dump*. The UNIX operating system writes the runtime image of the program to a file called *core* so that it can later be analyzed with a debugger to determine what may have caused the error.

Error Status Codes

ESQL/C provides two different strategies for handling recoverable runtime exceptions. Since Informix sets an error status code after any runtime error, the first method involves checking the value of the such status codes after every embedded SQL statement. There are two different variables Informix uses to reflect the status of a statement: SQLSTATE and SQLCODE. The SQLSTATE variable is a five-character string and SQLCODE is an integer variable. Informix recommends the use of SQLSTATE over SQLCODE, since the SQL-STATE variable conveys more information than the SQLCODE variable. Both the SQLCODE and SQLSTATE variables are available in an ESQL/C program without having to make any special arrangements such as including a header file or declaring them as extern variables at the top of the program. This is something that the esql precompiler does for you.

The first two characters of the SQLSTATE variable record the class of the error; characters 3–5 record the subclass of the error. Table 15-1 shows a list of the basic SQLSTATE class codes.

Table 15-1 Classes of SQLSTATE **errors.**

Class	Meaning
00	Success
01	Success with a warning
02	No data found
07	Dynamic SQL error

For the SQLCODE variable, things are much simpler. An SQL-CODE of 0 indicates success, a negative number is a runtime error, and 100 indicates that no data was found for a select. Warnings are indicated by the sqlca.sqlwarn.sqlwarn0 variable being set to W. Details about the warning are provided in the variables sqlca.sqlwarn.sqlwarn1 through sqlca.sqlwarn.sqlwarn6.

The get diagnostics Statement

The following snippet shows a simple way to check for a runtime error occurring when attempting to connect to the music database.

```
exec sql connect to 'music';
/* For a connect statement, "01" reflects success. */
/* The warning describes the type of database that
   was opened. */
if (strncmp(SQLSTATE, "01", 2) != 0) {
    exec sql get diagnostics exception 1
        :message = message_text;
    fprintf(stderr, "Error in CONNECT: SQLSTATE=%s,
        %s\n", SQLSTATE, message);
    exit(1);
}
```

The previous lines show an example of the first strategy of checking for runtime exceptions: explicitly checking the status code after every SQL statement. The details of the error are discovered by using the get diagnostics statement, an SQL extension available within ESQL/C. Although this statement can be used to gather a variety of system data, in practice its use is almost always restricted to the following format:

```
get diagnostics exception 1 host-variable = MESSAGE_TEXT
```

where host-variable is a char[256] host variable you define, and the value 1 indicates that the most recent error's diagnostics are to be read. Listing 15-2 shows a small but complete program that uses the get diagnostics statement.

The whenever Statement

The statement-by-statementis method of error checking, like almost all methods of error checking, is tedious. ESQL/C provides as an alternative a method for automatically having the error codes checked after each SQL statement. This method is provided by the whenever statement in ESQL/C. Using the whenever statement in your program causes the esql precompiler to place the error checking code in the generated C program for you. Thus, using whenever is equivalent to placing error checking routines after each SQL statement. The syntax for the whenever statement follows:

```
whenever sqlerror|not found|sqlwarning
    exception-action
```

where *exception-action* is one of the following choices:

```
goto :label
call function-name
continue
stop
```

By using `whenever`, the program can be made to perform various actions (`goto`, `call`, `continue`, `stop`) if a runtime exception is encountered. You can use another `whenever` clause to override the action of a previous `whenever` clause. Each `whenever` clause is in effect until it is replaced by a new `whenever`, or to the end of the program module. For example, a `whenever...continue` statement turns off checking that was activated by a previous `whenever` statement.

You will make use of `whenever` throughout the programs in this chapter, since it provides convenient exception handling.

tip

The `whenever` statement is a very useful and convenient way to add exception handling to your programs. The `whenever` statement is robust enough to handle most of your basic needs. However, if you find that you need more flexibility and control over exception handling, it is acceptable to mix the `whenever` method with explicit error handling. If you provide explicit error handling for a section of code that already has a `whenever` declared, you can turn it off with `whenever...continue`.

Let's redo our the previous example by using `whenever` instead of explicitly checking `SQLSTATE` after the call to `connect`. Listing 15-2 includes `print_error()`, a simple function that will be called automatically whenever an error is encountered. When called, it prints the Informix diagnostic information found in `MESSAGE_TEXT`.

note

An alternative to using the `get diagnostics` statement is to use the `sqlca` structure. However, since the `sqlca` structure is a C-specific entity, it is not X/Open-compliant.

Listing 15-2 *An error reporting function.*

```
#include <stdio.h>


void
print_error(void)
{
    exec sql begin declare section;
    char        message[256];
    exec sql end declare section;
    exec sql get diagnostics exception 1
        :message = MESSAGE_TEXT;
    fprintf(stderr, "Error: %s, %s\n", SQLSTATE,
        message);
    exit(1);
}


int
main()
{
    exec sql whenever sqlerror call print_error;
    exec sql connect to 'music';
    exec sql insert into albums
        values (0, 'Couldn\'t Stand The Weather',
        'Stevie Ray Vaughan', 1984, 'blues', 10,
        'The blues, with a shot of tequila');
    return 0;
}
```

You can quickly see that using the `whenever` method of exception handling involves much less work on your part. However, one disadvantage of using the `whenever...call` statement is that no parameters can be passed to the function to be called. It would be useful to have the called error function print out the precise statement that caused the exception, and possibly other useful information like the line number of the statement.

Behind the Scenes

If you examine the `esql`-produced C module for a program that uses `whenever`, you can see how `esql` converts the `whenever` statement to C code. For example, if the program has the statement `exec sql whenever sqlerror stop;`, then the following lines are added after every SQL-based statement:

```
/* Some 'exec sql' statement */
if (SQLCODE < 0)
{
    _iqstop();
    exit(0);
}
```

 Notice that Informix uses the SQLCODE variable to check for exceptions, rather than the SQLSTATE—which is what Informix recommends. This is probably because the SQLCODE variable is easier to test than calling `strcmp()` *on the SQLSTATE variable. The SQLCODE variable is sufficient to determine whether an exception has occurred, and SQLSTATE can provide more information about the exception.*

The built-in `_iqstop()` function prints out verbose Informix diagnostic information, like the simple `print_error()` function in Listing 15-2.

Program Variables and Host Variables

Now that you have an error checking framework in place, you can move on to less mundane topics. All of the previous EC examples did not use any program variables, and consequently were limited to performing only the actions that were hard-coded in the SQL string. A program without variables is certainly not very useful.

C program variables that are used in an embedded SQL statement are called *host variables*. A host variable serves as an interface between the C program and the SQL statements in the program. Host variables get their name from the fact that the C language is *hosting* the SQL language, which serves as a guest.

Host variables are set apart from normal C program variables by being declared within the ESQL `declare section`:

```
exec sql begin declare section;
/* c program host variables go here. */
exec sql end declare section;
```

 An alternative to declaring host variables inside of the `declare section` *is to simply place a $ in front of host variable declarations. The $ character can also be used in place of* `exec sql`. *This is an Informix extension and is not ANSI standard.*

Host variables can be declared local to a subroutine or global to an entire module, as can normal C variables. Declaring a variable as a host variable lets the `esql` preprocessor know to handle the variable specially. There is no difference between using a host variable and any other variable in a C statement. When using the host variable in the embedded SQL text, it must be prefixed with a colon (`:`) so that `esql` can tell that it is a variable and not a constant.

Let's look at an example that uses a host variable (Listing 15-3). This program adds a new genre so that your George Clinton CDs will have a home.

Compile and run this program. This time, use the `-o` option of the `esql` program to specify an executable name other than `a.out`.

```
$ esql 15_3.ec -o 15_3
$ 15_3
```

Listing 15-3 *Insert example with a host variable.*

```c
/* Insert example with a host variable. */


int main()

{

    exec sql begin declare section;

    string          genre[11];

    string          description[61];

    exec sql end declare section;


    exec sql whenever sqlerror call print_error;

    /* Be sure to include the print_error function */


    exec sql connect to 'music';


    strcpy(genre, 'funk');

    strcpy(description, 'Heavy, thumping beat with

        plenty of wah');

    exec sql insert into genres

        values(:genre, :description);


    return 0;

}
```

If this program runs correctly, there will be no output from the command line. You can, however, use DB-Access to verify that the `funk` record was added to the `genres` table.

Host Variable Data Types

Since Informix supports various data types, it is necessary to have host variables that can be mapped to a matching Informix variable in a convenient way. Host variables are divided into three categories:

* Host variables for character data.
* Host variables that have a standard C data type representation.
* Host variables that are not directly supported with C standard data types.

Picking the Correct Host Variable Data Type

Choosing the proper data type for a host variable is a matter of matching the SQL data type of the database attribute with an ESQL/C predefined type or a C language data type that corresponds to that type. While some choices are obvious and straightforward, others can lead to some confusion. For instance, if the attribute being selected from the database is of type `serial`, there is no alternative but to declare the host variable to be of type `long int`. However, suppose that the SQL data type is of type `date`. You have already seen that `date` attributes are displayed in DB-Access as a familiar character string, like "mm/dd/yy". The host variable that matches `date` types is not a string, but is a `long int`! This is because—as you may recall from Chapter 4, "Creating Databases and Tables"—Informix stores the date as an integer. Luckily, there are Informix functions that can convert the `long int` date format into a string that is a little easier for humans to read. As an example, the `rfmtdate()` function converts a `long int` to a date string formatted according to a pattern you specify. Its use is illustrated in Listings 15-8, 15-9, and 15-14. For the complete list of these specialized ESQL functions, you'll need to refer to the *INFORMIX-ESQL/C Programmer's Manual*, shipped with the product.

Another confusing aspect of host variable data types surrounds the representation of character data. Depending on how the host variable data type is declared, the same character data can be fetched from the database in one of four different representations, explained in the following three sections.

Character Data Types

There are four data types available for representing character data: `char`, `string`, `fixchar`, and `varchar`. The primary differences between these data types involve the use of trailing blanks and null termination. The correct character data type to use in any particular instance depends on whether null termination and/or trailing blanks are desired.

Remember that the standard method for representing an array of character data, or string, in C is by a null terminator character appended to the end of the characters. The null terminator is represented as a zero character, usually written in C programs as `'\0'`.

Table 15-2 shows the correspondence between Informix native data types, ESQL data types, and C data types.

Table 15-2 SQL and C data type equivalencies for character data.

SQL Type	ESQL/C Predefined Type	C Type
char (n)	fixchar array[n] or string array[n + 1]	char array[n + 1] or char *
nchar (n)	fixchar array[n] or string array[n + 1]	char array[n + 1] or char *
nvarchar (n)	varchar[n + 1] or string array[n + 1]	char array[n + 1]
varchar (m, x)	varchar array[m + 1] or string array[m + 1]	char array[m + 1]

So, which data type is best to use? It turns out that `string` is probably the best choice for most situations. Declaring a host variable of type `string` causes the retrieved data to be null terminated and have no trailing blanks. Having the character string be null terminated is usually desirable, since that is how strings are naturally represented in C.

caution

A non-null terminated string can be very dangerous in a C program. All of the C standard library string functions, such as `strlen()`, `strcpy()`, `strcat()`, and even `printf()` will not work properly if they are given a non-null terminated string.

Trailing blanks can sometimes be useful for formatting purposes, since the correct amount of trailing spaces can make column data line up properly when printed with `printf()`. Table 15-3 shows the attributes of the four different character host variable types.

Table 15-3 Character data type attributes.

ESQL/C Data Type	Trailing Blanks?	Null Terminated?
char	Yes	Yes
fixchar	Yes	No
string	No	Yes
varchar	Yes	Yes

caution

Although the `fixchar` data type is not null-terminated, it is possible to put a null termination character into a `fixchar` string. You should avoid this, since the null terminator character is not interpreted as a null terminator by Informix. If a `fixchar` variable with a null terminator is inserted into the database, the null terminator will be placed into the table, making it impossible to search for the data value later.

C Standard Data Types

The C standard data types are the simplest to deal with because they have a direct mapping from SQL database variables to C. Also, the C standard data types are the only data types that are directly supported in C. To say that data types are directly supported means that operations on those data types are performed without making a function call. For example, adding two integer or floating point numbers in C is accomplished with the + operator. The related idea of concatenating two strings together must be accomplished by calling the C standard library function `strcat()`.

There isn't much guesswork about which host variable type to use with these SQL types, since there is only one available choice. Table 15-4 shows the mappings between the SQL and C standard data types.

Table 15-4 SQL and C data type equivalencies for C standard data.

SQL Type	C Type
float, double precision	double
integer	long int
serial	long int
smallfloat, real	float
smallint	short int

ESQL/C Special Types

Some Informix data types don't have a natural mapping to any predefined C data type. These data types are declared as predefined ESQL types and are converted into C data structures by the `esql` precompiler. The only exception is the `date` data type, which can be properly represented by a C `long int` variable. Table 15-5 shows the data type mappings for these special data types.

Table 15-5 SQL and C data type equivalencies for SQL special types.

SQL Type	ESQL/C Predefined Type	C Type
byte	loc_t	
date	date	long int
datetime	datetime	
dec, decimal, numeric, money	decimal	
interval	interval	
text	loc_t	

The ESQL/C predefined types are translated by the esql pre-compiler into an appropriate data structure to represent the SQL data. Since the predefined data types are not C elemental data types, you have to make special arrangements to perform operations on these types. For example, passing a decimal data value to the C square root function would not do what you expect, unless you expect your application to abort with a runtime exception. However, Informix provides many custom functions that allow you to work with these data types.

C Data Structures and Host Variables

ESQL supports the ability to declare arrays of host variables and to declare host variables as members of a C structure. While this is not always necessary, it can be a convenient method to simplify some programming tasks.

Arrays of Host Variable

Storing data in an array is often a convenient way to process and access that data. Although you could use scalar host variables to hold data elements while they are copied to an array, Informix provides a more direct method. Host variables can be declared as an array, which allows you to select or insert data directly from the array. Listing 15-4 shows how you can use an array of host variable to receive the results of a cursor-based `select` statement. Chapter 13, "Cursors and Dynamic SQL," introduced the idea of cursors and dynamically prepared SQL statements within Informix-4GL code. Here, the same tools are applied in an ESQL/C program. Save this listing as `15_4.ec`, then compile and run it.

Listing 15-4 *Using an array of host variables.*

```
/* Uses arrays of host variables. */


#include <stdio.h>


exec sql define ARRAY_SIZE 100;

exec sql define TITLE_LEN 30;


int

main()

{

    exec sql begin declare section;

    $ long int       album_num[ARRAY_SIZE];

    $ string         titles[ARRAY_SIZE][TITLE_LEN + 1];

    exec sql end declare section;

    int              num_selected;

    int              i;
```

(Continued)

Listing 15-4 *Using an array of host variables.*

```
exec sql whenever sqlerror call print_error;

/* Be sure to include the print_error function */


exec sql connect to 'music';


exec sql prepare sel_id from
    'select album_num, title from albums';
exec sql declare sel_curs cursor for sel_id;


exec sql open   sel_curs;
for (num_selected = 0, i = 0; i < ARRAY_SIZE; ++i)
{
exec sql fetch sel_curs into
    :album_num[i],  :titles[i];
if (SQLCODE == SQLNOTFOUND)
    break;
    ++num_selected;
}


exec sql close  sel_curs;


printf("%d records selected\n", num_selected);
for (i = 0; i < num_selected; ++i)
{
```

(Continued)

Listing 15-4 *Using an array of host variables.*

```c
        printf("%d\t%s\n", album_num[i], titles[i]);

    }


    exec sql free sel_curs;

    exec sql free sel_id;


    return 0;

}
```

Compile the listing with the following command:

$ **esql 15_4.ec -o 15_4**

Execute the newly created program:

```
$ 15_4
22 records selected
1    Absolute Rollers - The Best of
2    Once Upon A Star
3    Abbey Road
4    Help!
5    Revolver
6    Please Please Me
7    Live from Montreux: Vol. 2
8    Colour by Numbers
9    Kissing to be Clever
10   Soul to Soul
11   Dylan and the Dead
12   Beauty and the Beat
13   Jackson 5 Christmas Album
14   Huevos
15   Girl You Know its True
```

```
16   Barrel Full of Monkees

17   Only a Lad

18   In Concert

19   Traveling Wilburys

20   Cruisin

21   Sounds of the Okefenokee Swamp

22   Zydeco Live!
```

Host Variables as C Structures

Another convenient method for storing data is the C structure. Since much of the SQL data that you need to represent is record-based, representing this data in EC programs as a structure is especially useful. ESQL/C supports the ability to use the structure as a whole without having to independently specify each component in an ESQL statement. You will be using this feature in Listing 15-5 to select records from the `albums` table.

Listing 15-5 *Using a structure as a host variable.*

```
#include <stdio.h>


exec sql begin declare section;


typedef struct

{

    long int        album_num;

    string          title[31];

    string          artist[21];

    short           issue_year;

    string          genre[11];
```

(Continued)

Listing 15-5 *Using a structure as a host variable.*

```
    short          rating;

    varchar        notes[81];

}

albums;

exec sql end declare section;


int

main()

{

    exec sql begin declare section;

    /* Declare album of type album struct. */

    albums          album;

    exec sql end declare section;


    exec sql whenever sqlerror stop;

    exec sql whenever not found goto :finished;


    exec sql connect to 'music';


    exec sql prepare sel_id from

        'select * from albums order by rating desc';

    exec sql declare sel_curs cursor for sel_id;
```

(Continued)

Listing 15-5 *Using a structure as a host variable.*

```
exec sql open sel_curs;

for (;;)

{

        /* Fetch the record into the album struct. */

        exec sql fetch sel_curs into :album;


        /* Print the individual components of album. */

        printf("%*s %s\n", 12, "title:", album.title);

        printf("%*s %ld\n", 12, "album_num:",

            album.album_num);

        printf("%*s %s\n", 12, "artist:",

            album.artist);

        printf("%*s %d\n", 12, "issue_year",

            album.issue_year);

        printf("%*s %s\n", 12, "genre:", album.genre);

        printf("%*s %d\n", 12, "rating:",

            album.rating);

        printf("%*s %s\n", 12, "notes:", album.notes);

        printf("\n");

    }


finished:

    exec sql close sel_curs;
```

(Continued)

Listing 15-5 Using a structure as a host variable.

```
     exec sql free sel_curs;

     exec sql free sel_id;



     return 0;

}
```

Save this program as 15_5.ec, and then compile and execute it.

```
$ esql 15_5.ec -o 15_5
$ 15_5
      title: Please Please Me
  album_num: 6
     artist: Beatles
 issue_year 1963
      genre: rock
     rating: 10
      notes:

      title: Abbey Road
  album_num: 3
     artist: Beatles
 issue_year 1969
      genre: rock
     rating: 9
      notes: Paul is not dead.

      title: Soul to Soul
  album_num: 10
     artist: Double Trouble
 issue_year 1985
      genre: blues
     rating: 9
      notes:
```

The rest of the output has been trimmed off.

Arrays of Structures of Host Variables

Let's merge the last two example programs into a program that declares an array of structs as a host variable. Listing 15-6 shows how, with an array of structures, you can store and manipulate the cursor-based data with much more facility than was possible with just the single struct declared in Listing 15-5. Also, an alternative form of the whenever statement is included for illustrative purposes. Likewise, in this listing, $ is used as the Informix shorthand for exec sql.

Listing 15-6 *Array of structures of host variables.*

```
#include <stdio.h>


exec sql begin declare section;

typedef struct

{

     long int          album_num;

     string            title[31];

     string            artist[21];

     short             issue_year;

     string            genre[11];

     short             rating;

     varchar           notes[81];

}

albums;

exec sql end declare section;


void
```

(Continued)

Listing 15-6 *Array of structures of host variables.*

```
print_album(albums * album)

{

    printf("%*s %s\n", 12, "Title:", album->title);

    printf("%*s %ld\n", 12, "album_num:",

        album->album_num);

    printf("%*s %s\n", 12, "artist:", album->artist);

    printf("%*s %d\n", 12, "issue_year",

        album->issue_year);

    printf("%*s %s\n", 12, "genre:", album->genre);

    printf("%*s %d\n", 12, "rating:", album->rating);

    printf("%*s %s\n", 12, "notes:", album->notes);

    printf("\n");

 }


int

main()

{

    $ albums        *album_array;

    $ long int      num_rows;

    int             i;


    $ whenever sqlerror stop;

    $ whenever not found goto:finished;
```

(Continued)

Listing 15-6 *Array of structures of host variables.*

```
$ connect to 'music';


$ prepare sel_num_rows from

    'select count(*) from albums';

$ execute sel_num_rows into:num_rows;


album_array = (albums *) calloc(num_rows + 1,

    sizeof(albums));


$ prepare sel_id from

'select * from albums order by rating desc';

$ declare sel_curs cursor for sel_id;


$ open sel_curs;

for (i = 0; i <= num_rows + 1; ++i)

{

    $ fetch sel_curs into :album_array[i];

}


finished:


for (i = 0; i < num_rows; ++i)

{

    print_album(&album_array[i]);
```

(Continued)

Listing 15-6 Array of structures of host variables.

```
    }


    $ close          sel_curs;

    $ free           sel_curs;

    $ free           sel_id;

    $ free           sel_num_rows;


    return 0;

}
```

The input and output is the same as for program 15_5.

Host Variables as Function Parameters

Host variables can be used as parameters to functions. A host variable must be prefixed with the `parameter` keyword to declare it as a function parameter. Listing 15-7 shows this `parameter` keyword in use to declare the value passed to a custom ESQL `db_connect()` function.

Listing 15-7 Using a host variable as a function parameter.

```
int

db_connect(db_name)

    exec sql begin declare section;

    parameter char *db_name;

    exec sql end declare section;
```

(Continued)

Listing 15-7 *Using a host variable as a function parameter.*

```
{

    exec sql connect to :db_name;

    if (SQLCODE < 0)

        display_sqlstate();


    return SQLCODE;

}
```

Null Values in Host Variables

As you learned in Chapter 5, "Basic SQL," nulls represent unknown values. This presents a particular problem for host variables because C variables do not support the concept of an unknown value. Informix offers two distinct methods of overcoming this problem. The first is by using a special host variable known as an *indicator variable*. The other method uses the Informix functions `risnull()` and `rsetnull()` on the actual host variable to determine whether it is null or to set it to a null state.

Using Indicator Variables

An *indicator variable* is a host variable that is used to indicate whether another host variable is null. Indicator variables are declared within the ESQL `declare` section and are of type `short`. Indicator variables have the value `-1` if the matching host variable is null, and the value `0` if the host variable is not null.

Indicator variables are used in the `fetch` statement. If a host variable has a matching indicator variable, use the variables like this:

:host-variable indicator *:indicator-variable*

Listing 15-8 selects all artists who have a birth date that is not null. Depending on whether or not the death date is null, you will either print out Not dead yet or the actual date of their death. Save this listing as 15_8.ec.

Listing 15-8 *Handling null values with indicator variables.*

```
#include <stdio.h>


exec sql begin declare section;


char            sel_str[] = "\
select last_name, first_name, sex, death_date \
  from performers \
 where birth_date is not null \
 order by last_name";


exec sql end declare section;


int
main()
{
    exec sql begin declare section;
    string          last_name[16];
    string          first_name[16];
    fixchar         sex;
```

(Continued)

Listing 15-8 *Handling null values with indicator variables.*

```
/* Here is the indicator variable for death_date */

short           date_ind;

date            death_date;


exec sql end declare section;

char            date_str[32];

int             chars_printed;


exec sql whenever sqlerror stop;

exec sql whenever not found goto :finished;


exec sql connect to 'music';


exec sql prepare sel_id from :sel_str;

exec sql declare sel_curs cursor for sel_id;


exec sql open    sel_curs;

for (;;)

{

    exec sql fetch sel_curs into :last_name,

        :first_name,

        :sex,

        :death_date indicator :date_ind;
```

(Continued)

Listing 15-8 *Handling null values with indicator variables.*

```
            chars_printed = printf("%s, ", last_name);

            printf("%-*s\t%c  ", 32 - chars_printed,

                first_name, sex);

            if (date_ind < 0)

                printf("Not dead yet");

            else

            {

                rfmtdate(death_date, "ddd, mmm.dd, yyyy",

                    date_str);

                printf("%-15.18s", date_str);

            }

            printf("\n");

        }


    finished:

        exec sql close sel_curs;

        exec sql free sel_curs;

        exec sql free sel_id;


        return 0;

    }
```

Compile and run the program.

```
$ esql 15_8.ec -o 15_8
$ 15_8
Avila, John                          M  Not dead yet
Bartek, Steve                        M  Not dead yet
Carlisle, Belinda                    F  Not dead yet
...
Garcia, Jerry                        M  Wed, Aug.09, 1995
George, Boy                          M  Not dead yet
Harrison, George                     M  Not dead yet
...
Kirkwood, Curt                       M  Not dead yet
Lennon, John                         M  Mon, Dec.08, 1980
Lofgren, Nils                        M  Not dead yet
Longmuir, Alan                       M  Not dead yet
Longmuir, Derek                      M  Not dead yet
Manilow, Barry                       M  Not dead yet
McCartney, Paul                      M  Not dead yet
McKeown, Leslie                      M  Not dead yet
Nesmith, Michael                     M  Not dead yet
Orbison, Roy                         M  Thu, Dec.01, 1988
Pavarotti, Luciano                   M  Not dead yet
...
Vaughan, Stevie Ray                  M  Sun, Aug.26, 1990
Walsh, Joe                           M  Not dead yet
Weir, Bob                            M  Not dead yet
Wood, Stuart (Woody)                 M  Not dead yet
```

Using the `risnull()` and `rsetnull()` Functions

As an alternative to using indicator variables, you can use the
risnull() and rsetnull() functions. The risnull() and rset-
null() functions operate directly on the host variable and do not
require a separate host indicator variable.

```
int risnull(int type, char *ptr);
int rsetnull(int type, char *ptr);
```

where *type* is an integer that corresponds to the data type of the variable and *ptr* is a pointer to the variable. The type codes are defined in the `sqltypes.h` header file and are enumerated in Table 15-6. To include `sqltypes.h` in your program, add the following line at the beginning of your program module:

```
exec sql include sqltypes;
```

Table 15-6 Constants for ESQL/C data types defined in
`sqltypes.h.`

ESQL Type	Constant	Integer Value
char	CCHARTYPE	100
short int	CSHORTTYPE	101
int	CINTTYPE	102
long	CLONGTYPE	103
float	CFLOATTYPE	104
double	CDOUBLETYPE	105
decimal	CDECIMALTYPE	107
fixchar	CFIXCHARTYPE	108
string	CSTRINGTYPE	109
date	CDATETYPE	110
decimal	CMONEYTYPE	111
datetype	CDTIMETYPE	112
loc_t	CLOCATORTYPE	113
varchar	CVCHARTYPE	114
interval	CINVTYPE	115

caution

Be sure that you pass the second argument to `risnull()` *or* `rsetnull()` *as a pointer. If the host variable is not already a pointer, you must make it into one by using the C address of operator, (*`&`*). Here is an example:*

```
$ date    bdate;
$ double  num;
$ string  lname[32];

rsetnull(CSTRINGTYPE, lname);
/* lname is already a pointer */
/* Make date and double ptrs; cast to (char *) */
rsetnull(CDATETYPE, (char *) &bdate);
rsetnull(CDOUBLETYPE, (char *) &num);
```

If you don't pass the address of the variables to `rsetnull()` *and* `risnull()`, *you get a core dump.*

It's worth mentioning how `risnull()` and `rsetnull()` work. When Informix selects a value that is null, it sets the variable to an extreme value, such as negative MAX_INT for an integer value, or –Nan (not a number, 0xffffffff on 32-bit computers) for a double. While this is usually not a problem, you need to keep in mind that the value Informix interprets as a null is actually a legitimate value in C. It just may be that you want to put a –MAX_INT value in the database! This is an unfortunate consequence of having a data type try to represent two completely different ideas that overlap.

Listing 15-9 shows how you use the `risnull()` function to test for the presence of nulls.

Listing 15-9 *Handling null values with the* `risnull()` *function.*

```
#include <stdio.h>


exec sql include sqltypes;


exec sql begin declare section;
```

(Continued)

Listing 15-9 *Handling null values with the* `risnull()` *function.*

```
char sel_str[] = "\
select last_name, first_name, sex, death_date \
  from performers \
 where birth_date is not null \
 order by last_name";


exec sql end declare section;


int
main()
{
    exec sql begin declare section;
    string          last_name[16];
    string          first_name[16];
    fixchar         sex;
    date            death_date;
    exec sql end declare section;


    char            date_str[32];
    int             chars_printed;


    exec sql whenever sqlerror stop;
    exec sql whenever not found goto :finished;
```

(Continued)

Listing 15-9 Handling null values with the `risnull()` *function.*

```
exec sql connect to 'music';


exec sql prepare sel_id from :sel_str;

exec sql declare sel_curs cursor for sel_id;


exec sql open sel_curs;

for (;;)

{

        exec sql fetch sel_curs into :last_name,

            :first_name, :sex, :death_date;


        chars_printed = printf("%s, ", last_name);

        printf("%-*s\t%c  ", 32 - chars_printed,

            first_name, sex);

        if (risnull(CDATETYPE, (char *) &death_date))

            printf("Not dead yet");

        else

        {

            rfmtdate(death_date, "ddd, mmm.dd, yyyy",

                date_str);

            printf("%-15.18s", date_str);

        }

        printf("\n");

    }


finished:
```

(Continued)

Listing 15-9 *Handling null values with the* `risnull()` *function.*

```
exec sql close sel_curs;

exec sql free sel_curs;

exec sql free sel_id;


return 0;

}
```

The input is the same as for program `15_8`.

 The `esql -icheck` *option produces code that checks the* `select` *statements for indicator variables if a null is returned from a query. If a null is returned and a host variable does not have an indicator variable, a runtime error is generated.*

ESQL Statement Types

ESQL statements fall into two main categories: those in which the statement is completely specified when the program is compiled, and those that are not specified at compile time. Completely specified ESQL statements are *static*, whereas statements that are not specified at compile time are *dynamic*. All of the previous ESQL example programs have used only static ESQL. For most situations, static ESQL is all you need. However, using dynamic SQL becomes necessary when your application needs to provide the ability to select data from various tables and columns in an ad hoc manner. Trying to enumerate all of the possible select queries would be horribly inefficient, even if possible. Dynamic SQL makes it possible to process any legal SQL statement in your program without having to know the statement in advance.

Static ESQL Statements

An SQL statement is static if the statement type and number of input and output parameters to the statement is known before the application is run.

Executing Nonselect Statements

Nonselect SQL statements are the simplest variety of SQL statements. There are no output parameters, only input. You can use the `prepare` statement to have Informix prepare the statement to do its work. The `prepare` statement parses the SQL string for errors, and translates the SQL statement into an internal representation for subsequent execution. If the `prepare` succeeds, the resulting statement ID is the handle to use for further communication with Informix. When the statement ID is no longer needed, you should free it with an ESQL `free` statement.

caution   *The exec sql `free` statement is in no way related to the standard C function `free()`. Do not make the mistake of trying to free a statement ID with the `free()` function. You'll know it if you do. A core dump is hard to miss.*

tip   *If you are using a function that is called repeatedly to perform a database operation, it may help performance to `prepare` the statement only once and never close it.*

The ESQL `execute immediate` statement does the job of preparing and executing the statement without the need for separate `prepare` and `execute` statements. Use `execute immediate` when you have to `execute` a statement only a few times. If you find that you are using an `execute immediate` inside of a loop or fairly frequently, you should instead consider preparing the statement once and then executing it many times.

Let's look at a simple program that inserts one record into the `genres` table (Listing 5-10). This program is similar to Listing 15-3, except that it uses the `prepare` statement to get a statement ID, and then executes the statement ID.

Listing 15-10 *Using the* prepare *statement.*

```
#include <stdio.h>


int

main()

{

    exec sql begin declare section;

    string          genre[] = "folk";

    string          description[] = "Solo work with a
social conscience";

    char            ins_str[64];

    exec sql end declare section;


    exec sql whenever sqlerror stop;

    exec sql connect to 'music';


    sprintf(ins_str,

            "insert into genres values (\"%s\", \"%s\")",

            genre, description);

    exec sql prepare ins_id from :ins_str;

    exec sql execute ins_id;

    exec sql free ins_id;


    return 0;

}
```

Using Input Parameters

The previous example would be much better if you were not required to build the string before preparing it. It would be better if the insert statement above accepted input parameters. In Listing 15-11, the using clause is added to the execute statement to show this improvement. In addition, performance is improved because the insert statement is prepared only once.

Listing 15-11 Input parameters with the using clause.

```
#include <stdio.h>


int

insert_genre(genre, description)

    $ parameter char *genre;

    $ parameter char *description;

{

    static int init = 0;


    $ whenever sqlerror stop;


    if (!init)

    {

        /* This code will only be executed once. */

        $ prepare inst_stmt from

            'insert into genres values (?, ?)';

        init = 1;
```

(Continued)

Listing 15-11 *Input parameters with the* using *clause.*

```
        }


        $ execute inst_stmt using :genre, :description;


    return SQLCODE;

}


int

main()

{

    $ string genre[] = "folk";

    $ string description[] = "Solo work with a social
conscience";


    $ whenever sqlerror stop;

    $ connect to 'music';


    insert_genre(genre, description);


    return 0;

}
```

Executing `select` Statements

There are two basic types of `select` statements: those that select one row, and those that can possibly select more than one row. The two types of selects have to be handled differently, since you will need a cursor to handle multiple rows. You worked with cursors in Chapter 13.

Executing Singleton `select` Statements   If the SQL statement returns only one row, it is more efficient to use the `exe-cute...into` statement. Listing 15-12 shows an example of a singleton `select`. Save this listing as `15_12.ec`.

Listing 15-12 Executing a singleton `select`.

```
#include <stdio.h>


long

get_num_albums(void)

{

    static int      init = 0;

    $ long          rows;



    $ whenever sqlerror stop;

    if (!init)

    {

        $ prepare num_albums from

            'select count(*) from albums';

        init = 1;
```

(Continued)

Listing 15-12 *Executing a singleton* select.

```
        }

        $ execute num_albums into :rows;


        return rows;

}



int

main()

{

        long            num_albums;


        $ whenever sqlerror stop;


        $ connect to 'music';


        num_albums = get_num_albums();

        printf("There are %ld albums in your collection.\n",

            num_albums);


        return 0;

}
```

Compile and run the listing:

```
$ esql 15_12.ec -o 15_12
$ 15_12
There are 22 albums in your collection.
```

caution *Make sure that the* `select` *is really a singleton* `select` *when using the* `execute...into`. *If the* `select` *returns more than one row, you will get a runtime error. A good way to ensure that the* `select` *is a singleton select is to select only on a primary key or an attribute with a unique constraint. The SQL aggregate functions are also safe since they return only one row.*

Executing `select` Statements That Returns More Than One Row If it is possible that the `select` statement can return more than one row, you must declare a cursor to handle the multiple rows.

You have already seen an example of multiple-statement selects in Listings 15-8 and 15-9, where cursors were used to retrieve multiple rows of data. Let's extend that example to make use of the `open...using` clause to provide input into the `where` clause of the `select`. Save the code in Listing 15-13 as `15_13.ec`.

Listing 15-13 Executing a multiple-row `select`.

```
#include <stdio.h>


exec sql begin declare section;


typedef struct

{

    long int        album_num;

    string          title[31];

    string          artist[21];
```

(Continued)

Listing 15-13 *Executing a multiple-row* select.

```
        short           issue_year;

        string          genre[11];

        short           rating;

        varchar         notes[81];

}

albums;

exec sql end declare section;


int

main()

{

    exec sql begin declare section;

    albums          album;

    string          genre[12];

    exec sql end declare section;

    int             num_recs = 0;


    exec sql whenever sqlerror stop;

    exec sql whenever not found goto :finished;


    exec sql connect to 'music';


    exec sql prepare sel_id from

        'select * from albums where genre = ?';
```

(Continued)

Listing 15-13 *Executing a multiple-row* select.

```
exec sql declare sel_curs cursor for sel_id;


printf("Which genre? ");

scanf("%s", genre);


exec sql open sel_curs using :genre;

for (;;)

{

    exec sql fetch sel_curs into :album;


    printf("%*s %s\n", 12, "Title:", album.title);

    printf("%*s %ld\n", 12, "album_num:",

        album.album_num);

    printf("%*s %s\n", 12, "artist:", album.artist);

    printf("%*s %d\n", 12, "issue_year",

        album.issue_year);

    printf("%*s %s\n", 12, "genre:", album.genre);

    printf("%*s %d\n", 12, "rating:", album.rating);

    printf("%*s %s\n", 12, "notes:", album.notes);

    printf("\n");


    ++num_recs;

}
```

(Continued)

Listing 15-13 *Executing a multiple-row* select.

```
finished:

    printf("There are %d %s records in your

        collection.\n", num_recs, genre);


    exec sql close sel_curs;

    exec sql free sel_curs;

    exec sql free sel_id;


    return 0;

}
```

Compile and run the code.

```
$ esql 15_13.ec -o 15_13
$ 15_13
Which genre? rock
      Title: Abbey Road
  album_num: 3
     artist: Beatles
 issue_year 1969
      genre: rock
     rating: 9
      notes: Paul is not dead.

      Title: Help!
  album_num: 4
     artist: Beatles
 issue_year 1965
      genre: rock
     rating: 8
      notes:
```

```
. . .

       Title: Only a Lad
   album_num: 17
      artist: Oingo Boingo
  issue_year 1981
       genre: rock
      rating: 2
       notes:

       Title: Traveling Wilburys
   album_num: 19
      artist: Traveling Wilburys
  issue_year 1988
       genre: rock
      rating: 5
       notes:
```

There are 9 rock records in your collection.

Dynamic ESQL Statements

In all of the ESQL programs we have written so far, we have always known the number and types of the input and output parameters. However, by using dynamic ESQL, it is possible to determine the number and types of all of the return columns from a `select` statement. This is one of the great strengths of ESQL. The EC `describe` statement processes a prepared SQL statement and populates an EC data structure with this information. There are two different data structures that can be used to hold the output from a `describe`. The first is called an Informix descriptor, and is X/Open-compliant. The other data structure for holding the output of a `describe` is the `sqlda` structure. We will use the `sqlda` method in our program, since it is a little easier to work with than the X/Open descriptor. The X/Open descriptor is accessed by commands such as `exec sql set descriptor`, `exec sql get descriptor`, while the `sqlda` is processed directly through C.

Store the contents of Listing 15-14 in a file named 15_14.ec. This instructive program allows you to type in any select statement for the music database.

Listing 15-14 *Using dynamic ESQL to process arbitrary select statements.*

```
#include <stdio.h>

#include <stdlib.h>


exec sql include sqltypes;

exec sql include decimal

exec sql include sqlda;


void

print_row(int i. struct sqlda *da_ptr)

{

    long            dt;

    struct sqlvar_struct *col;

    int             len;

    int             cnt;

    char            date_format[] = "mm/dd/yy";

    char            *ds;

    int             decpt;

    int             sign;


    printf("Row %-3d, i);
```

(Continued)

Listing 15-14 *Using dynamic ESQL to process arbitrary* `select` *statements.*

```
col = da_ptr->sqlvar;

cnt = 0;

while (cnt < da_ptr->sqld)

{

    switch (col->sqltype)

    {

    case SQLCHAR:

        len - col->sqllen;

        printf("%-*.*s", len, len, col->sqldata);

        break


    case SQLINT:

    case SQLSERIAL:

        printf(" %8d ", *(int *) col->sqldata);

        break;


    case SQLDATE:

        dt = * (long *) col->sqldata;

        rfmtdate(dt, date_format, str);

        printf("%10.10s", str);

        break;


    case SQLMONEY:
```

(Continued)

```
                    *str - '\0\';

                    ds = decfcvt((dec_t *) col->sqldata, 2,

                         &decpt, &sign);

                    sprintf(str, "%-*.*s.%s", decpt, decpt, ds,

                         ds + decpt);

                    printf("7.7s", str);

                    break;


               default:

                    printf("Type %d not handled", col->sqltype);

                    break;



               }



               ++cnt;

               ++col;

          }

     printf("\n");

}


void

allocate_descriptor_memory(struct sqlda *da_ptr)

{
```

(Continued)

```
struct sqlvar_struct *col;

int            cnt;

int            size;


col = da_ptr->sqlvar;

cnt = 0;

while (cnt < da_ptr->sqld)

{

    if (col->sqltype == SQLCHAR)

        col->sqllen++;

    size = rtypmsize(col->sqltype, col->sqllen);

    col->sqldata = (char *) malloc(size);


    ++cnt;

    ++col;

}

}


int

main()

{

    exec sql begin declare section;

    string          stmt[255];
```

(Continued)

```
string          prep_name[] = "dyn_stmt1";

exec sql end declare section;

struct sqlda    *da_ptr;

int             i;


exec sql whenever sqlerror stop;

exec sql connect to 'music';


fprintf(stout,

    "Enter a SQL select statement: ");

fgets(stmt, sizeof(stmt), stdin);


exec sql prepare :prep_name from :stmt;

exec sql describe :prep_name into da_ptr;

exec sql declare sel_curs cursor for :prep_name;

exec sql open sel_curs;


allocate_descriptor_memory(da_ptr);


for (i = 1;; ++i)

{

    exec sql fetch sel_curs using descriptor da_ptr;

    if (SQLCODE ==100)
```

(Continued)

```
          break;


     print_row(i, da_ptr);

  }


  return 0;

}
```

Compile and run the code in `15_14.ec`.

```
$ esql 15_14.ec -o 15_14
$ 15_14
Enter a SQL select statement: select * from genres
    where genre = 'funk';

Row 1  funk    Heavy, thumping beat with plenty of wah
```

Experiment with `15_14.ec` and find out what it can and can't do.

Summary

This was a complex chapter. ESQL/C is a big subject, but you managed to cover the critical topics in significant detail. You now know enough about ESQL/C to program some substantial projects. As you work in ESQL/C it is important to keep in mind that EC can be very unforgiving. It is easy to make seemingly subtle errors in an EC program that cause catastrophic failures. It is the nature of C programs that you have great performance, power, and flexibility, but at the cost of protection from runtime errors such as memory overwrites. Make friends with your debugger.

On our whirlwind tour of ESQL/C, you have progressed from simple programs with no variables or error checking to an example that can execute any `select` statement. You have learned the details of adding exception handling to your programs. You have seen the ins and outs of host variables, and how they allow the C program to communicate with the SQL engine. You have also learned how to do many different types of tasks with ESQL, from executing simple statements such as `insert`, `update`, and `delete`, to handling the more complicated jobs of selecting data with a cursor.

Extra Credit

Q&A

Question	Answer
Does ESQL/C have to be implemented as a preprocessor that produces C code as output? Why or why not?	No, the ESQL/C interface could be written entirely by C function calls. The reason to use the precompilation method is for programming convenience and to allow for conformance to the X/Open standard.
If you attempt to execute a `delete` statement without a `where` clause in DB-Access, it lets you know that you will empty the entire table, and asks you if this is what you really want. Howdoes DB-Access know that the `delete` statement does not contain a `where` clause?	After the statement is described, the descriptor contains a warning variable that indicates whether the statement is a `delete` without a `where` clause.
In program `15_8.ec`, we assumed that if the `death_date` of a performer were null, he/she is not dead yet. Is this a good assumption?	It depends. In the strictest sense, no—a null value is an unknown value. However, you could apply business rules to your database that say that any null value in `death_date` means

the artist is still alive; otherwise, you must have a death date. This is not as good as redefining your schema so that the information is apparent to anyone reading the schema. Business rules that are not defined in the schema are often hard to enforce, and even then can sometimes be circumvented.

The `esql` program provides the `-g` option to add debugging symbols to the final executable. How does this work?

C compilers support the `-g` option, which adds debugging information to the object modules. These object modules are linked into the final executable program. The debugging information tells the debugger specific details about the program that are not strictly necessary to simply run the program.

Exercises

1. Extend program `15_14.ec` to handle more data types in the `print_row()` function. Modify `15_14.ec` so that it can directly handle null return values.

2. Compile an EC program with the `-g` option. Run the program through your favorite debugger. If your debugger is good, you will notice that the current line indicator follows the source from the original EC program and not the generated C file. How is this possible, given that the original EC program file is not really a C program?

3. When using `describe` with dynamic SQL, any `?` characters that indicate future inputs with the `using` clause are not placed in the descriptor. It turns out that you need an input descriptor and an output descriptor for these types of statements. How would you code a method for building an input descriptor?

Exercise Answers

1. There are many possible answers for this exercise.
2. Look at the intermediate .c program file. You will notice the C preprocessor directives `#line` and `#file`. These tell the compiler to override the actual line number of the .c file with the file name and line number provided by the preprocessor directives. Clever.
3. This is not an easy one. You will need to write a parser that can scan the SQL text looking for the ? character. The parser will then have to determine which table and column the ? is meant to reference, and build an `sqlda` structure by hand that has the proper number and types of the input variables. The next step is to populate the input descriptor with the data values that you would normally use in the `using` clause. Instead of `using (:host_variable,...)`, you will be `using descriptor descriptor_name`.

Advanced Topics

This part is the final leg of our Informix world tour, which continues where others might have stopped. Since you signed up for the complete package, you've still got two chapters of adjunct meta-programming topics to cover. In them, you'll learn enough about data migration and administration topics to almost merit the "dweeb" moniker. But we know better. While Isaac prepares mocha lattes for everyone, I'll preview our last two chapters together. For this part's background music, we've got Culture Club's "Colour by Numbers" on the laser disc player.

In Chapter 16, "Data Migration," Kevin Kempter shows you a bag of tricks that can make your development lifecycle easier. This chapter is about more than just moving data from one place to another. It's about backing up your private database; it's about unloading selected data in custom formats, such as for spreadsheets; it's about saving time in the real world. It's good stuff.

Finally Robert Davis returns in Chapter 17 to complete the story he began in the first chapter. With "Database Administration Fundamentals," he opens the Informix kimono to reveal some crucial behind-the-scenes mechanics. By knowing the basics of these administration topics, you'll be more self-sufficient, and be able to write more sturdy and efficient programs.

At the end, I'll return with your cap and gown. You can look forward to the commencement ceremony, with so many freshly scrubbed faces all dolled up in those caps and gowns. The little propellers on top will be Isaac's doing. The music will be the Bay City Rollers' "Once Upon a Star." Fitting, I'd say. Remember, when you hear your name called, file past the champagne fountain and the ice sculpture of a referential constraint—that Isaac is a genius!

If you need to pause just a moment before starting your final journey, you can wait here with me. I'll be turning up the volume on "Soul to Soul," one of Stevie Ray Vaughan's finest. Haven't heard it? Stick around and listen to The Man. SRV. The roadhouse bluesman whose mongrel chocolate brown Strat burned with incendiary, scorched-earth genius. Can't get enough.

Chapter

16

Data Migration

Informix offers several tools to help you migrate data. Data migration can be from an external system into the database, from one database to another, or from a previously unloaded table within the same database. This chapter details the breadth of Informix tools available to help you perform these common and essential tasks.

Introduction

Both developers and DBAs find themselves needing to move, copy, import, back up, and restore data on occasion. In production environments, it is common that data must be extracted from an external system and loaded into an Informix database. Equally often, the reverse is true: an unloaded subset of data must be prepared for delivery to another application. As well, subsets of data are often needed as local restorable archives or to generate working sandboxes for testing new application code. The tools in this chapter make these tasks of migrating data easier.

The following list describes the categories of migration tools available, and the principal advantage of each:

- Binary utilities, for best performance
- Database-level utilities, for easiest use
- Table-level utilities, for most flexibility

The binary tools are the `onunload` and `onload` utilities, which create a binary unload file that contains both data and system catalog information. The database-level tools `dbexport` and `dbimport` easily unload and load entire databases, along with all the DDL needed to recreate them. The `load` and `unload` SQL statements are table-level tools that can quickly unload or load a set of data from a database table. The remaining table-level tool is `dbload`. Its ability to load a variety of data files, based on custom command files you create, makes it a valuable addition to the toolkit. Table 16-1 provides an overview of these tools, designed to make the job of a developer or DBA easier. The remainder of this chapter describes these tools in detail.

Table 16-1 Informix migration tools overview.

	Import Tools	*Export Tool*	*File Type*	*Scope*	*Platform Dependent*
Binary Format	`onload`	`onunload`	binary	database or table	Yes
Database-Level	`dbimport`	`dbexport`	ASCII	database	No
Table-Level	`load, dbload`	`unload`	ASCII	table	No

Binary Format Utilities

Available only with Informix-OnLine, the `onunload` and `onload` utilities allow a single table or an entire database to be migrated in binary format. All relevant contents such as the system catalog structure and any default settings are migrated as well. You can use these utilities in numerous ways, such as reloading original data after you have modified a database with a test program. As with all of the other data export tools described in this chapter, `onunload` does not delete the original object it copies. Consequently, if you use `onload` to refresh a database or table, you first need to drop the object that you are importing.

The `onunload` Utility

The `onunload` utility unloads a backup copy of data to a binary file on disk or to tape. It's easy to use, fast, and makes keeping a spare set of data about for emergencies simple. Its syntax follows:

```
onunload [destination-parameters]
    database-name[:[owner.]table-name]
```

where *destination-parameters*, if not specified, uses the default values from the `onconfig` file for the following settings:

- LTAPEDEV, the tape device name or file name
- LTAPEBLK, the tape block size in kilobytes (ignored for unload to disk)
- LTAPESIZE, the total tape size in kilobytes (ignored for unload to disk)

You may set any of the following values for *destination-parameters* to override the defaults:

```
-t tape-device
```

```
-b blocksize
```

```
-s tapesize
```

where *tape-device* may also be the name of an existing file.

Unloading to Disk

Now let's unload a table. Suppose you want to unload the `albums` table from the `music` database and migrate it to another database. First, you need to own the table or have DBA permissions on the `music` database. This is because the unloaded data contains all of the table's contents, however privileged. Next, you must be able to obtain an exclusive lock on the `albums` table. This means that no one else may be accessing the table at the time of the unload. Let's say you want to place the table in the UNIX file `/tmp/albums.unl`, and the table is owned by `informix`. Make sure that an empty file named `/tmp/albums.unl` exists, then type the following at the command line:

```
$ onunload -t /tmp/albums.unl music:albums
Please mount tape and press return to continue…
$ <Return>
Please label this as tape number 1 in the tape sequence.
```

You have just unloaded the `albums` table in binary format into the UNIX file `/tmp/albums.unl`. This file also contains the system catalog information needed to recreate the table correctly.

Now let's unload the entire `music` database. In this case you need to have DBA permissions on the `music` database, and must be able to obtain an exclusive database lock. Let's say you want to place the database in a file called `/tmp/music.unl`. Make sure an empty file named `/tmp/music.unl` exists and type the following at the command line:

```
$ onunload -t /tmp/albums.unl music
Please mount tape and press return to continue…
$ <Return>
Please label this as tape number 1 in the tape sequence.
```

You have just unloaded the entire `music` database, table definitions, data, and system catalog information into the UNIX file `/tmp/music.unl`. Now you can easily recreate the `albums` table in the `music` database using the `/tmp/albums.unl` file, or recreate the `music` database using the `/tmp/music.unl` file.

Unloading to Tape

The `onunload` utility can also be used to unload to a valid tape device. Table 16-2 shows two common usages.

Table 16-2 `onunload` ***Examples.***

Syntax	Description
`onunload music:albums`	Unload the `albums` table from the `music` database using the default onconfig file parameters for the tape device, block size, and tape size parameters.
`onunload -t /dev/ rmt0 -b 2048 -s 5000000 music`	Unload the `music` database to the tape device `/dev/rmt0` using a block size of 2 kilobytes and a total tape size of 5 gigabytes.

The most common reason to unload data to tape is for long-term off-line storage. Used in that way, `onunload` can be an important adjunct to a robust database archiving strategy.

The `onload` Utility

The `onload` utility is the importing counterpart to `onunload`. It loads data from a binary `onload` file or tape, and creates a database or table.

Restrictions

There are a few constraints to remember when using `onload`. The first is that it can only be used to import data created with the `onunload` utility. Additionally, if the machine from which you exported the data is different from the one to which you are importing it, the source and target database servers must share the following traits:

- Informix version
- Page size
- Byte alignment of the CPUs

Reloading Data

Once an unload file is generated, it can be used repeatedly to copy the same data to any number of databases. Its syntax follows:

```
onload source-parameters [-d dbspace-name]
    database-name[:[owner.]table-name]
```

where *source-parameters* is the same as for `onunload`, and *dbspace-name* is the name of the dbspace into which the table or database is to be placed. If you do not specify *dbspace-name*, the root dbspace is used. You may use a different value for *database-name* than the name of the database that was exported. When you create a database with `onunload`, you own the database, but the original table ownerships are preserved. When you create a table, you own the table unless you specify a new *owner*.

Now let's create a database. Suppose you want to load the `music` database that was just unloaded. For example, say you test a careless co-worker's new program and it corrupts the data in your database. Instead of trying to correct the data, it is much simpler to reload the database. First, use DB-Access to drop the

existing `music` database (for a reminder of how to do this, refer to
Chapter 4, "Creating Databases and Tables"). Now type the following at the command line:

```
$ onload -t /tmp/music.unl music

Please mount tape and press return to continue…

$ <Return>

The load has successfully completed.
```

You have just reloaded the entire `music` database, including
not only the data but also all of the system information such as
indexes, default values, and constraints.

The onunload utility does not preserve a database's logging
mode, but instead creates its databases with no logging. You can
use the `ontape` command, as in the following example, to restore
buffered logging to the `music` database:

```
$ ontape -s -B music
```

Executable by only `informix`, the `ontape` command can be
used to reset the logging mode for any database. In the example
shown, the `-B` option dictates buffered logging. The other options
are:

`-N` (no logging)

`-U` (unbuffered logging)

`-A` (ANSI logging)

Now let's consider the case where you want to load only the
`albums` table. Because onload creates objects with no logging,
and a database cannot contain a mix of logged and unlogged
tables, you must turn database logging off before using `onload` to
import a table. You use the `-N` option of `ontape` to execute this
change.

You need to have resource permissions on the target database
to create a table. This coincides with the intent that those with
resource permissions can extend a database. In this case, imagine
that a co-worker's program corrupted the `albums` table data. First,
use `DB-Access` to drop the `albums` table. Then, type the following at the command line:

```
$ onload -t /tmp/albums.unl music:albums
```

Please mount tape and press return to continue…

```
$ <Return>
```

The load has successfully completed.

In this case, you have created and loaded the albums table, but not all of the adjunct table information such as constraints and ownership privileges. This data is not maintained when you use the onunload and onload combination to migrate a table.

Database-Level Utilities

The dbexport and dbimport utilities allow you to easily migrate an entire database from place to place. Because the data and the schema are unloaded in ASCII format, these migration tools are platform-independent.

The dbexport Utility

The dbexport utility unloads all the data for a database, and creates a file that contains the database schema. These components are later used by dbimport to create a copy of the exported database. The essential syntax for the dbexport command follows:

```
dbexport [destination-parameters] [-ss] [-q]
    database-name
```

where *destination-parameters* describes the disk location or tape format of the exported data. When excluded, the default is to export the data to disk in the current directory. To export to disk, use the following option:

```
-o directory-name
```

where *directory-name* is the pathname to the target directory on disk for both the schema file and the data files. For exporting to tape, use all of the following options, in any order:

-b *blocksize*

-s *tapesize*

-t *tape-device*

The -ss option preserves the server-specific information such as table locations, lock modes, and fragmentation schemes. This makes it easy to migrate the database to an exact duplicate configuration. Finally, the -q (quiet) option suppresses the display of progress to the screen.

Let's unload a database. Say you made some major changes to the music database and want to distribute it to users for their token look. First, choose a directory where the exported files will be placed. For this example, create a directory in /tmp called music. Then type the following at the command line:

```
$ dbexport -o /tmp/music music
```

Look in the /tmp/music directory. You will find a directory named music.exp. In the music.exp directory, you will find a music.sql file (the schema file) and the table unload files. Because these are ASCII files, you can examine or modify them with a text editor, such as vi. Notice also that another file was created in the directory where you launched the export. The dbexport.out file contains error messages as well as the data definition statements that dbexport generated.

The database could instead have been exported to tape with a command like the following:

```
$ dbexport -t /dev/rmt/0 -b 2048 -s 50000000 music
```

Once you have used the straightforward dbexport utility to create the ASCII unload files, you can migrate the database with little effort.

The **dbimport** Utility

The dbimport utility creates a database and loads all the data unloaded via the dbexport utility. Together, these two utilities simplify the migration of databases from machine to machine. The `dbimport` syntax follows:

```
dbimport [source] [create-options] [-q] database-name
```

where *source* is the input file location, and must match the values used during a previous `dbexport`. When excluded, the default is to import the data from the current directory. To import from another directory on disk, use the following option:

```
-i directory-name
```

For importing from tape, use all of the following options, in any order, with values that match the previous `dbexport`:

```
-b blocksize
```

```
-s tapesize
```

```
-t tape-device
```

The optional *create-options* include

```
-d dbspace
```

where *dbspace* is the name of the dbspace in which to create the database (the default is root), and one or none of the following logging mode options:

`-ansi` (ANSI-compliant)

`-l` (unbuffered logging)

`-l buffered` (buffered logging)

If no log mode is specified, the database is created without logging. Refer to Chapter 4 for more details on the log modes of databases. Finally, the `-q` (quiet) option suppresses the display of progress. In any case, those details are captured in a `dbimport.out` file, which is created in the current directory.

Let's use `dbimport` to create and load a database. In this case, imagine that you want to reload the database as it existed when you performed the previous `dbexport`. First, drop the music database using DB-Access. Then type the following at the command line:

```
$ dbimport -i /tmp/music music
```

This is all that is needed to recreate the `music` database and load all of its data.

Table-Level Utilities

The Informix `unload` and `load` SQL statements are two of the most commonly used tools to move data about. Since the `load` and `unload` statements are simply SQL statements, it is easy to unload and load data whenever you need. Furthermore, since the `unload` statement subsumes a `select` statement, it allows you to customize your data exports with great flexibility. However, the `load` statement does not offer similar flexibility for importing data. When you need to import custom data, perhaps because you've received formatted data from an external source, the `dbload` utility is appropriate. Each of these three tools is explored in this section.

The `unload` Statement

The `unload` statement is both powerful and easy to use. It generates a delimited file containing one line for each row returned by a `select` statement that you specify. You might use it to preserve a table's data before some test script is run. Unlike the previous exporting tools, it does not capture the database or table structure. Its syntax follows:

```
unload to outfile select-statement
```

where *outfile* is the path and name of the file to contain the unloaded data, and *select-statement* is any standard `select` statement.

Let's unload some data. Suppose you decide to back up the data in the `album_copies` table prior to executing some dubious program. Execute the following SQL statement:

```
unload to '/tmp/alcopies.unl'

select *

  from album_copies;
22 row(s) unloaded.
```

You have just unloaded the `album_copies` table to the file named `/tmp/alcopies.unl`. With the following command, examine the file to see how Informix uses delimiters to separate the data values:

```
$ cat /tmp/alcopies.unl
3|CD|shelf 5|16.95|

5|CD|shelf 5|13.5|

4|tape|work|9.95|

...

22|CD|shelf 4|17.5|

1|laser|shelf 2||
```

Later, if needed, you can use the `load` statement to insert this data into the `album_copies` table.

Another effective use of the `unload` command is to export a small database into a directory so that a backup copy is always on hand. The shell script in Listing 16-1 does this by using SQL (and some knowledge of Informix's internal `systables` system table) to generate more SQL—a database unloading script.

Save Listing 16-1 as an executable shell script named `dbase_unl`. First, create a directory for the unload, then unload the database, as follows:

```
$ mkdir /tmp/music_unl
$ dbase_unl music /tmp/music_unl
```

Listing 16-1 *Unload a database.*

```ksh
#!/bin/ksh

# dbase_unl: unload all data from a database.

#               dbase_unl [dbname] [target_dir]


# check params

if [ $# -ne 2 ]

then

    echo "\ndbase_unl: unloads all data from a database"

    echo "Syntax: $0 [dbname] [target_dir]"

    exit 1

else

    dbname=$1

    target=$2

fi


dbaccess $dbname -<<EOF

output to $target/unl_tables.sql

without headings

select 'unload to ', trim(tabname) || '.unl',

        'select * ',

            'from ', trim(tabname) || ';'

    from systables

  where tabid > 99;
```

(Continued)

Listing 16-1 *Unload a database.*

```
EOF


# Create a schema.sql file

dbschema -d $dbname -ss $target/schema.sql


cd $target

dbaccess $dbname unl_tables


echo "Done\n"
```

After these commands execute, the `/tmp/music_unl` directory will contain not only the scripts necessary to create and unload the `music` database, but also all of the data from each component table.

One of the nice features of the `unload` statement is that since it's simply an SQL statement, you can use a `where` clause to restrict the `unload` to only the rows you want. For example, you could unload all the unique `formats` from the `album_copies` table along with a count of each. This would give you a single row per unique format. You could further restrict this query to group the rows by the `artist`. The following examples show the versatility of the `unload` statement:

```
-- unload a count of formats from album_copies

unload to '/tmp/sample1.unl'

select format, count(*)

  from album_copies

 group by format;
```

```
-- unload counts of all artists and formats

unload to '/tmp/sample2.unl'

select format, artist, count(*)

  from album_copies, albums

 where album_copies.album_num = albums.album_num

 group by format, artist;
```

The load Statement

The load SQL statement is easy to use, and, as the counterpart to the unload statement, makes that statement more useful. The syntax for the load statement follows:

```
load from infile insert into table-name
```

where *infile* is the path and name of the file containing the unloaded data and *table-name* is the name of the table you wish to load.

Let's load a file that you previously unloaded. Imagine that you accidentally deleted all the rows from the album_copies table. Using DB-Access, simulate this occurrence with the following statement:

```
delete from album_copies;
22 row(s) deleted.
```

Use the following SQL statement to repopulate the table from your backup copy of the data in the album_copies table:

```
load from '/tmp/alcopies.unl'

insert into album_copies;

22 row(s) loaded.
```

You now have the `album_copies` table back to its original
state. The `unload/load` combination can be very helpful; don't
hesitate to unload tables before doing anything that could harm
your data.

Refer now back to Listing 16-1, a script that unloaded an entire
database. Listing 16-2 shows the complement to that script. It uses
the `load` statement to help rebuild a database that was previously
exported with the `dbase_unl` script.

Notice first that this script recreates an entire database, so its
use is restricted to those occasions when the database that is being
reloaded does not already exist, or when you explicitly drop it.
Second, if your database uses referential constraints, you'll need
to load any referenced tables before you load any tables that reference them. Otherwise, attempts to violate referential integrity
could make the load fail.

Listing 16-2 *Load a database.*

```ksh
#!/bin/ksh

# dbase_load: loads all data from a database unload into
a new database

#     dbase_load [dbname] [target_dir]

#



# check params

if [ $# -ne 2 ]

then

    echo "\ndbase_load: loads a new database"

    echo "Syntax: $0 [dbname] [target_dir]"

    exit 1

else

    dbname=$1
```

(Continued)

Listing 16-2 *Load a database.*

```
     target=$2

fi


# Create the new database

dbaccess <<EOF

     create database $dbname;

EOF


# Run the schema.sql file

dbaccess $dbname $target/schema.sql


# For each data file, run the load.

for filename in 'ls $target/*.unl'

do

tab='basename $filename.unl'

dbaccess $dbname <<EOF

     load from $filename insert into $tab;

EOF

done


echo "Done\n"
```

The `dbload` Utility

The Informix `dbload` utility is a versatile data importing tool that can load data from multiple types of input files, such as those created using the `unload` or `dbexport` commands or from external sources. It gains versatility by relying on a custom instruction file that you create, which is specific to the format of the file being loaded. The essential components of the syntax for the `dbload` statement follows:

```
dbload -d database-name -c command-file
    -l error-file [options]
```

where `database-name` is the name of the database to receive the data, `command-file` is the name of the `dbload` command file you've defined, and `error-file` is the name of the file to which diagnostic information is written during the load. If you include at least one of the required parameters, but not all of them, `dbload` prompts you for the missing specifications. The remaining useful `options` are:

```
-n batch-size

-e max-errors

-i rows-to-ignore
```

where `batch-size` is the number of rows inserted before `dbload` commits each batch (the default is 100), `max-errors` is the maximum number of bad rows to allow before aborting (the default is 10), and `rows-to-ignore` is the number of initial data rows to be skipped (the default is 0). By default, shared locks are placed on the tables being loaded. With either of the following options, you can change the locking mode:

`-r` (no" table-level locking)
`-k` (lock the tables in exclusive mode)

To use `dbload` you need to create a `dbload` command file. A command file is the file that tells `dbload` what to load and how to load it. Its contents must conform to the following structure:

```
FILE filename DELIMITER 'character' num-fields;
insert-statement;
```

where `filename` is the name of the data file to load, `character` is the character used as the field delimiter, `num-fields` is the number of fields in the unload file, and `insert-statement` is the insert statement used to load the file.

Listing 16-3 shows what a `dbload` command file might look like for reloading part of the `music` database.

Listing 16-3 A `dbload` *command file.*

```
FILE /tmp/music/music.exp/formats.unl DELIMITER '|' 3;

insert into formats;

FILE /tmp/music/music.exp/performers.unl DELIMITER '|' 5;

insert into performers;

FILE /tmp/music/music.exp/albums.unl DELIMITER '|' 7;

insert into albums;
```

If somehow the data from these three tables got deleted, you could run a command like the following to load the `formats`, `performers`, and `albums` tables:

```
$ dbload -d music -c music.cmd -l music.err -r -n 10 -e 1
```

A command like this would restore values to the `formats`, `performers`, and `albums` tables. One advantage of `dbload` is its ability to import data from any ASCII file. When the data you need to import has been created with another database system, `dbload` is often the best tool to use.

Summary

Informix offers several utilities that allow you to migrate data, whether it's moving data between machines and databases, or simply reloading a previously unloaded table. It is important for you as a developer to know how to use these utilities; they can make your life much easier.

The `onload` and `onunload` utilities can quickly transfer data in binary format. The binary format makes the transfer very fast, and the system catalog information is unloaded for you automatically—so restoring indexes, default values, constraints, and such is easy.

The `dbexport` and `dbimport` utilities make it easy to unload or create an entire database. The `dbexport` utility creates a schema file and creates data files for each table in the database.

The `unload` and `load` SQL statements make it easy to unload the data from a table or to reload that same data. Since the `unload` statement is simply an SQL statement, you can restrict the parameters via a `where` clause. The third table-level migration tool, `dbload`, is extremely versatile. With it, you can load almost any source files by creating a command file that tells `dbload` how to load the data.

These tools all have similarities. Your personal preference and comfort level, as well as your database source and target, will help determine which tool to use.

Extra Credit

Q&A

Question	Answer

How can I force `onload` to place my load (database or table) into a specific dbspace?	You can use the `-d` flag, as in the following example:
	`$ onload -t /tmp/unloadsource.unl`
	`-d mynew_dbspace music`

Question	**Answer**

I have a comma-delimited file that I exported from a spreadsheet. Can I easily load in into a table?	Yes, you can use `dbload`. If the file contained `formats` data, the command file would appear as follows:
	`FILE /tmp/export_file.csv`
	`DELIMITER ',' 2; insert into`
	`formats;`

Exercises

1. Unload a list of all the performers who issued an album between `1980` and `1990`, and a count of the albums on which they performed.

2. Create a `dbexport` file of the `music` database. Drop the database and recreate it using the `dbimport` utility.

3. Delete all rows from the `album_copies` table, then use the `load` statement and the `album_copies` unload file generated by the `dbexport` utility to reload it.

4. Create a `dbload` command file that loads all the unload files that were created with the `dbexport` utility.

5. Create a spreadsheet that matches the `formats` table. Add several of your own formats and export the data to a comma-delimited file. Now create the proper `dbload` command file and load the data into the `formats` table.

Exercise Answers

1. Run the following statement from DB-Access:

```
unload to '/tmp/perf_count.unl'
select album_performers.last_name, album_performers.first_name,
    count(*)
  from album_performers, albums
 where album_performers.album_num = albums.album_num
   and album.issue_year between 1980 and 1990
 group by 1, 2;
```

2. Create the backup with the commands like the following:

```
$ mkdir /tmp/ex2
$ dbexport -o /tmp/ex2 music
```

Use DB-Access to drop the music database. Recreate it with the following dbimport command:

```
$ dbimport -i /tmp/ex2 music
```

3. Use DB-Access to execute the following delete and load commands:

```
delete from album_copies;

load from '/tmp/ex2/music.exp/album_copies.unl'

    insert into album_copies;
```

4. Create a command file with the following contents:

```
FILE /tmp/ex2/music.exp/formats.unl DELIMITER '|' 2; insert into
    formats;
FILE /tmp/ex2/music.exp/genres.unl DELIMITER '|' 2; insert into
    genres;
FILE /tmp/ex2/music.exp/performers.unl DELIMITER '|' 5; insert
    into performers;
FILE /tmp/ex2/music.exp/albums.unl DELIMITER '|' 7; insert into
    albums;
FILE /tmp/ex2/music.exp/album_copies.unl DELIMITER '|' 5; insert
    into album_copies;
FILE /tmp/ex2/music.exp/performers.unl DELIMITER '|' 3; insert
    into performers;
```

5. If your spreadsheet file is called /tmp/spsht.csv, store the following dbload instructions in a file named /tmp/ex5.cmd:

```
FILE /tmp/spsht.csv DELIMITER ',' 2;
    insert into formats;
```

Now execute the following dbload command:

```
$ dbload -d music -c /tmp/ex5.cmd -l music.err -n 10 -e 1
```

Database Administration Fundamentals

This chapter is designed to give the Informix developer a basic "behind the scenes" look at the internals of the INFORMIX-OnLine Dynamic Server Architecture (DSA). An understanding of the material in this chapter can help you write more efficient code, use system resources better, and cooperate more politely in a multi-user environment.

Introduction

This chapter discusses how Informix manages database tasks by using lightweight processes, or *threads*, and shows how you can examine the threads on your system. The chapter also describes how Informix manages its physical processing spaces, both in memory and on disk.

It also explores other administrative fundamentals that can benefit the Informix developer. These include topics relevant to both local and networked database environments. You'll see what factors influence when a table should be fragmented for performance, why your transactions should be as small as possible, and where Informix stores the structure of the databases you create. You need to understand, however, that these are advanced topics, and are best explored when you have a need for the material within.

 Elective Chapter: You can be an effective Informix developer without knowing any of the topics in this chapter. Some of the sections describe intricate topics; others may be inapplicable in your environment. Be your own guide. But if time permits, revisit this chapter to gain an extra facility with Informix databases.

Process Architecture

This section describes the fundamental components of the Informix database server, its *virtual processors (vps)*. Every task that the server executes is performed by a vp, and each vp is specialized. The virtual processor is so named because of its similarity to a CPU. Just as a CPU runs multiple operating system processes for multiple users, a virtual processor runs multiple threads for multiple client applications. A thread is often called a lightweight process because of its similarity to a UNIX process and because it makes fewer demands on the operating system than a UNIX process does. Because a vp can run *multiple concurrent threads*, it is called a *multithreaded process*.

Virtual Processor Classes

Each virtual processor is a member of one particular *virtual processor class*. Each vp class uses threads to perform a specific set of tasks such as disk I/O, writing to the physical log, or handling client/server communication. The number of concurrent active vps in most of the classes is configurable, while the number in others is controlled by OnLine. Table 17-1 shows some of the different vp classes.

Table 17-1 Virtual processor classes.

VP Class	Class Type	Description
CPU	Central Processing Unit	Virtual processor class where most processing occurs. All user threads and some internal threads run in this class.
LIO	Logical I/O	Runs internal threads that write to the logical logs.
PIO	Physical I/O	Runs internal threads that write to the physical log.
AIO	Asynchronous I/O	Performs all disk I/O except writes to logs.
SHM	Shared Memory	Runs internal shared memory communication threads.
SOC	Sockets	Runs TCP/IP Berkeley sockets network communication threads.
TLI	Transport Layer Interface	Runs TLI programming interface—TCP/IP or IPX/SPX—network communication threads.

To list the vps that are running on your system, enter the following variant of the complex `onstat` command:

```
$ onstat -g glo
```

The glo (global) option displays usage statistics for each virtual processor. The list of global vp statistics that you see may include any from Table 17-1, but might also include a few other more obscure classes.

Thread Management

Threads may be shared among vps of the same class, although OnLine tends to keep a thread running on the same virtual processor if possible. Since Informix tries to balance the load between processes, a thread may migrate between many vps during its life. Likewise, a virtual processor—a UNIX process like any other—will typically switch between CPUs as the operating system deems it necessary.

Thus, in the same way that a vp is a UNIX process that the operating system schedules for processing on the CPUs, a thread is a lightweight process that vps schedule for internal processing. Figure 17-1 illustrates the relationship between CPUs, virtual processors and threads.

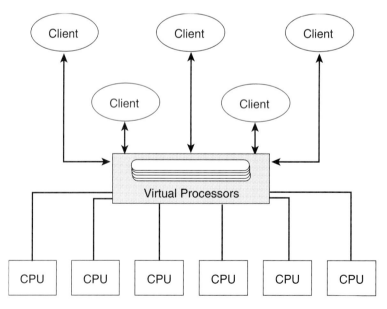

Figure 17–1 *OnLine process architecture.*

There are two different types of OnLine threads: *session threads* and *internal threads*. A session thread—or `sqlexec` thread—is the primary thread that services requests from client applications. Any time a client connects to a database, an `sqlexec` thread is started. Internal threads perform server-specific tasks such as page cleaning, database I/O, and logging I/O.

To see a list of all threads on the server, enter the following command:

```
$ onstat -g ath
```

If you do not see an `sqlexec` thread when you execute the `ath` (all threads) option, connect to the `music` database in another window. When you run the command again, you should now see the `sqlexec` thread that represents the connection you just made.

Shared Memory

The second component of DSA is shared memory. Shared memory is a feature that allows Online processes and threads to share data by storing and accessing the data in pools of memory. As seen in Chapter 1, "The Informix Product Suite," the use of shared memory reduces overall disk I/O and memory usage as well as permits high-speed communication between processes.

When an Informix instance is initialized it acquires at least three shared-memory segments. At least one segment is allocated to each of the *resident, virtual,* and *message* portions. To see the shared-memory segments active for your server, type the following:

```
$ onstat -g seg
```

You can identify the Resident, Virtual, and Message segments by the value in the sixth column. The size of each segment is listed in bytes in the fourth column.

Resident Portion

The resident portion is so named because on operating systems that support shared-memory residency, the Informix instance can be configured to take advantage of this feature. Typically, the UNIX operating system will *swap* the contents of portions of memory to disk as it switches between processes. When a portion of memory is designated as resident, however, it will not be swapped. When frequently accessed data—such as the data in the resident portion—is kept resident, performance is improved because the number of disk I/Os to access this data is reduced.

The most important component of the resident portion is the *buffer pool*, a collection of buffers that cache data pages that have been read from disk. This buffer pool is the structure that allows users to share database data, thereby minimizing disk reads and writes. A common performance-tuning tactic is to increase the number of buffers assigned to the server. The more buffers configured—to a point—the more data pages may be cached in shared memory to reduce disk I/O. Eventually, however, adding additional buffers becomes only a waste of memory resources.

Virtual Portion

The virtual portion of shared memory is made up of a number of fluid shared-memory pools that track similar memory allocations. For example, the virtual portion is where sorting occurs, and where information unique to each user session is stored in its own memory pool. At times of high activity, existing memory pools may be expanded while more pools are created. If there is insufficient memory in the virtual portion to either create a new pool or expand an existing one, OnLine dynamically adds another virtual memory segment.

Carefully monitoring and controlling the number of virtual memory segments is important because system memory is finite. Once the available memory is exhausted, systems will begin using *swap space* or *paging space* that is reserved on disk to accommodate any overflow memory operations. This symptom is known as *thrashing*, and significantly degrades performance. The DBA can place a ceiling on the size of the virtual shared-memory segment. When the server reaches a point where it needs more memory than this cap permits, the server will halt all processing until the situation is remedied.

Message Portion

This third portion of shared memory is initialized only if at least one of the connection types in the `onconfig` file is defined as an IPC shared-memory connection. If so configured, this portion contains the message buffers used by local client applications that communicate via shared memory. Client connections are discussed in "The Connection Process" section later in this chapter.

Disk Management

The third major component of DSA is its disk management, critical in many environments because it is so often the source of performance bottlenecks. All database data and OnLine system information is stored on disks, whose efficient configuration is fundamental to good server performance. Disks are organized into *physical units of storage* and *logical units of storage*. You allocate disk space with physical units of storage, and employ logical units of storage to assign database objects to physical storage units.

Units of Storage

The fundamental atomic unit of I/O in an OnLine system is the *page*, a unit whose size is system-defined. All disk and memory I/O that take place in the OnLine system are performed in page increments. At the highest level of organization is a logical unit of storage called a *dbspace*, a defined collection of pages on disk. Every database and every table within a database must be created in a dbspace. The default dbspace for a database is the root dbspace, whereas the default dbspace for a table is the dbspace in which the database was created. The tables in a database do not need to be created in the same dbspace; in fact, each table in a database could be created in its own dbspace if the resources existed. Each table can exist in only one dbspace unless fragmentation, discussed later in this chapter, is implemented.

Physical Units of Storage

A dbspace is made up of at least one *chunk*, a contiguous physical unit of disk whose maximum size is 2 gigabytes. The size of a dbspace is defined by the number and size of the chunks that compose it.

In Chapter 4, "Creating Databases and Tables," you were introduced to a physical unit of storage called an *extent*, which is made up of contiguous pages on disk. You also learned that the data within a table could reside in one or more extents, the sizes of which are configurable, but which default to eight pages. Although the pages within an extent are contiguous, the extents themselves are not necessarily contiguous. For the most efficient disk access, it is best to keep data pages within a table contiguous, which means limited to one extent. This is generally not a problem when dealing with *static* tables, where the data is not modified, but becomes difficult when dealing with *dynamic* tables, where the number of data pages required continuously grows or shrinks. Performance can degrade when table data is scattered in multiple extents across a disk. This scattering of extents is called *extent interleaving*.

tip   *For best performance, create your tables with a initial extent large enough to contain all of the table's data.*

Figure 17-2 shows the hierarchical relationships between the units of storage discussed so far. It reveals that an extent consists of four or more pages, a chunk consists of one or more extents, and a dbspace consists of one or more chunks.

Logical Units of Storage

Informix uses logical units of storage to organize its physical units of storage into manageable groups.

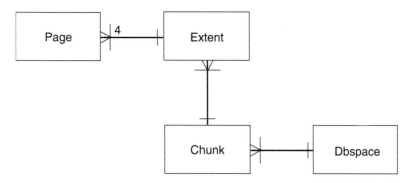

Figure 17–2   Relationships of OnLine units of storage.

Dbspaces   At the highest level of organization is the dbspace, already discussed. A dbspace is the most obvious logical storage unit, and is the granularity you specify when you create a table in a specific storage location.

Tablespaces   A tablespace is the name given to all the disk space allocated to a particular table. It comprises data pages, index pages, and bitmap pages, those pages that track page use within an extent.

The relationship between the various units of storage is less hierarchical now, since tablespaces can be composed of more than one extent and can span multiple chunks. This point makes it clear that a tablespace is a logical rather than physical unit of storage. Figure 17-3 displays the relationships of the various units of storage.

Blobspaces   The remaining unit of logical storage is the *blob-space*, characterized by consisting of chunks that contain only *blobpages*. A blobpage is a specially sized unit of disk space identified to store only blobs, or binary large objects. When a blobspace is created, the OnLine administrator assigns it an appropriate blobpage size at that time. Chapter 4 identified the two blob data types as `byte` and `text`.

Blobspaces are used solely to improve Informix's handling of blob data types. One way this happens is that blob data stored in a blobspace is written directly to disk rather than passing through the buffer pool in resident shared memory. If the buffer pool were used, the volume of data could occupy so many buffer pages that

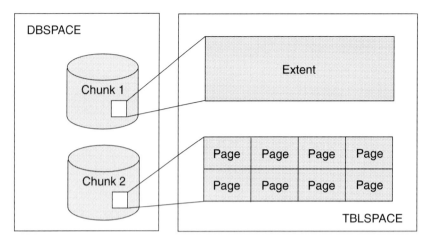

Figure 17–3 *OnLine units of storage.*

all other data and index pages would be forced out. Another difference is that blob data stored in a blobspace never passes through the logical logs. This circumvention of the logs enhances performance for these typically large data types.

  For best performance, store blobs of two or more pages in a blobspace.

Device Management

When you create a chunk in Informix, you must assign it to a UNIX *device* that maps to a physical disk. A UNIX device is a peripheral such as a tape drive, disk drive, or terminal.

Block versus Character Devices

All device files can be classified as either *block* or *character* devices. Block devices transfer data using the system buffers, one block at a time. Using the buffers speeds I/O transfer, but at the cost of having the operating system intervene to perform the buffering. Character device files do not utilize the system buffers, and instead transfer one character at a time.

In most cases, the disk devices can be addressed in either block mode or character mode. Although mountable UNIX file systems use block file access, you should assign your Informix chunks to use only character file access, or *raw I/O*. This is because Informix handles its own data buffering, and can directly transfer data between shared memory and the disk using *direct memory access*, a high-performance type of memory mapping.

Raw Devices versus Cooked Files

When assigning a chunk to a specific disk space, you have the choice of addressing the disk directly, via its character device name, or of using space on a mounted file system. Character devices you access directly are called *raw devices*. Space in a raw device is physically contiguous. Space on a mounted file system, organized into UNIX files, is accessed via block file mode. Such buffered files are called *cooked files*.

Cooked files are not ideal for Informix's use. In a UNIX file, the logically contiguous blocks are not necessarily physically contiguous. Also, although OnLine manages the contents of a cooked file to which a chunk has been assigned, the UNIX operating system manages all cooked file I/O.

You will see better performance and more reliability when you create your OnLine chunks in raw disk space. Data transfer to cooked space is slower: the data is often read twice—once from disk to the kernel buffer pool, and then again from the buffer pool into shared memory. Also, committed data is guaranteed to be stored on disk when using a raw device, but because of the possibility of an initial write to the kernel buffer pool, OnLine cannot make such a guarantee when using a cooked file system. If your system were to crash while committed data was still in the kernel buffer pool, Informix would be unable to recover successfully.

For best performance and reliability, use raw character devices for your OnLine chunks.

Configuration Issues

This section addresses two common Informix configuration obstacles that every developer needs to recognize. Each involves overtaxing a system resource—locks or logical log space—and describes how best to avoid reaching the system limit.

Every Informix instance has a server configuration file, named `onconfig`, that contains all the configuration parameters for the server. This file is located in the `$INFORMIXDIR/etc` directory. Many of the parameters within this file place limits on system resources in order to reduce overall shared-memory usage and to prevent users from monopolizing the engine. Although these resource limits help, they cannot prevent all incidents from occurring. This section describes two scenarios where these limits are approached.

Minimizing Lock Usage

The `LOCKS` configuration parameter in the `onconfig` file sets a limit on the concurrent number of locks that OnLine processes can hold at any given time. Whenever a client connects to a database, or performs any SQL statement, one or more locks are placed at the database, table, page, row, or key (index) level. If the server runs out of locks, all user processes come to a halt until enough used locks are freed. The various types of locks are described in Chapter 7, "Intermediate SQL."

Locks can accumulate rapidly. For example, suppose you have a database where the tables have been created with row-level locking for maximum concurrency. Imagine that you decide to execute an SQL statement to delete all 100,000 rows of data from a particular table. At a minimum, you have accumulated 100,002 of the available locks on the server—a database lock, a table lock, and 100,000 row locks. For each index that exists on that table, you add another 100,000 key locks. If four indexes exist on the table, you now hold 500,002 locks.

From this example, it is easy to see that many hundreds of thousands of locks could be generated if each user on a multi-user system were not lock-conscious. The best solution for problems like this one is to lock a table in exclusive mode before performing a massive insert, update, or delete. If this cannot be done because of concurrency issues, you may have to break your transaction into smaller pieces and perform the operation on smaller sections of data.

 To avoid squandering limited system resources, lock at the highest granularity possible.

Avoiding Long Transactions

A *long transaction* is a transaction that consumes so much logical log space that no other transactions can proceed. The logical logs, used only when a database has transaction logging, are where transactions in progress are stored. Every Informix system has multiple logs, which are used in a cycle. As each log is filled, OnLine begins logging to the next log in sequence. Once all processing and checkpoints have been completed in a logical log, that log may be backed up to some type of media so it is free to be reused when its turn comes around again.

As long as a transaction continues processing without being committed, the logs that it spans cannot be backed up. When a long transaction occurs, no more processing can be done because there is no more logical log space for writing. None of the logs can be backed up because there is no room to either commit or roll back the transaction. The only way to recover from this disaster is to perform a complete restore from a server archive.

It is important you realize that you do not necessarily have to be processing to cause a long transaction. All users share the same logical logs. If you begin a transaction and leave it open for a length of time, other users can fill the logs while your process is otherwise idle. Because logs must be backed up in order, and the log you started the transaction in cannot be freed, none of the other logs can be freed either.

The `onconfig` file provides a safety net for long transactions in the form of two configuration parameters: LTXHWM (*Long Transaction High Water Mark*) and LTXEHWM (*Long Transaction Exclusive High Water Mark*). Both of these parameters represent a percentage of the total logical log space available. When a transaction spans the percentage of the logs indicated by LTXHWM, it stops and begins to roll back everything it did up to that point. As a transaction rolls back, it continues to write to the logical logs along with other processes. As the rollback is occurring, if the amount of used log space reaches the LTXEHWM—a higher percentage—all other user processes are suspended until the offending transaction completes its rollback.

Even though these parameters are very effective at preventing long transactions, if your administrator has these set too high when you run a large transaction, the rollback could potentially cause a long transaction to occur. Even if LTXHWM and LTXEHWM are set appropriately to prevent a transaction from spanning all the logs, the rollback alone can be troublesome. It is especially annoying to other developers when their processing is suspended while waiting for your rollback to complete. The way to avoid this situation is to minimize the number of operations within one transaction and to keep your transaction time to a minimum.

 To avoid filling the transaction logs, keep your transactions as small and brief as possible.

Networked Databases

Informix supports remote connectivity, with which you can run client/server applications or work in distributed database environments. This section is devoted to covering the processes that OnLine uses to make client connections to local and remote databases.

The Connection Process

Before a client application can be of any use, it must first be able to connect to a database server. It can do this via either a local or remote connection. Informix determines what connection method to use based on the value of the INFORMIXSERVER environment variable. OnLine searches through the $INFORMIXDIR/etc/sql-hosts file, looking for this servername in the first column.

Look in your system's `sqlhosts` file and follow along with the connection process. Your file might look a little like the following sample `sqlhosts` lines:

```
server1_shm     onipcshm      moosehead      whatever
server1_soc     onsoctcp      moosehead      server1soc
server2_soc     onsoctcp      becks          server2soc
server3_soc     onsoctcp      pauligirl      server3soc
```

For these examples, consider that the local machine is called `moosehead` and that there are two other machines on the network, named `becks` and `pauligirl`.

The `sqlhosts` file

Table 17-2 describes the contents of the `sqlhosts` file.

Table 17-2 The `sqlhosts` file contents.

Column	Contains	Description
1	Dbservername	Represents a valid DBSERVERNAME or DBSERVERALIAS entry from the `onconfig` file.
2	Nettype	Specifies the type of connection to be made to a server.
3	Hostname	The host name of the machine on which the server resides.
4	Servicename	A unique key name within `sqlhosts` used to identify the port number and protocol in the `/etc/services` file. An internal place holder is used for shared-memory and stream pipe connections.

Once OnLine finds the `dbservername` that is currently defined, it determines which connection method to use by the value in the

Nettype field. Table 17-3 shows the meaning of the various Nettype values.

Table 17-3 The Nettype values.

Value	Connection	Description
onipcshm	Local	A shared-memory connection using the *Inter-Process Communication* (*IPC*) interface.
onipcstr	Local	A stream pipe connection using IPC.
onsoctcp	Remote	A socket connection using *Transmission Control Protocol/Internet Protocol* (*TCP/IP*).
ontlitcp	Remote	A *Transaction Layer Interface* (*TLI*) connection using TCP/IP.
ontlispx	Remote	A TLI connection using Internetwork Packet Exchange/Sequenced Packet Exchange (IPX/SPX) protocol.

Only remote connections use the Servicename value in the /etc/services file. This unique Servicename indicates which port number to connect across and which protocol to use for the remote connection. Local Nettype connections ignore the value in the Servicename column.

 The TCP/IP (onsoctcp and ontlitcp) connection Nettypes may also be used to make local connections. When this type of connection is made, the entry in the /etc/services file is used to designate a port number. Informix then uses this port number to perform a local loopback connection.

 For best performance when accessing a local database server, use a shared-memory connection.

The `/etc/services` File

The `/etc/services` file is where Servicename values are mapped to port numbers. The following lines might appear in the `/etc/services` file of the `moosehead` database server.

```
server1soc      4001/tcp
server2soc      4002/tcp
server3soc      4003/tcp
```

The first field lists the entries from the Servicename fields in `sqlhosts`. The second field lists the respective port numbers—you may use any valid available port number—and protocols to use when making a connection to the remote server. Note that an entry is still required for `server1soc` even though it is a local connection on `moosehead`. When OnLine makes the local connection to `server1` using this TCP/IP port number, Informix uses local loopback.

Trusted Computers

Informix requires the ability to connect to remote database servers without supplying a password. To resolve this problem, a list of all the trusted machines must be supplied to OnLine within one of two files. The `/etc/hosts.equiv` file lists system-wide trusted computers, while individual `$HOME/.rhosts` files list specific trusted computers for specific users. In many production environments, the use of personal `.rhosts` files is forbidden as a security risk. When trying to make a remote server connection to a machine that is not listed as a trusted computer, you will get an error stating that the client host or user is not trusted by the server.

Synonyms

Synonyms, introduced in Chapter 8, "Advanced SQL Queries," allow you to create permanent table aliases. A common use for synonyms is to create a local reference to a remote table. You create a synonym with the following SQL syntax:

```
create synonym synonym-name for
[database-name[@database-server-name]:]
    [table-owner.]table-name
```

where *database-server-name* must exist in the first column of your `sqlhosts` file. When you create a synonym, you specify the remote database—possibly on a remote server—in the creation statement. When you perform operations on this local synonym, you are actually working with data in its associated remote database table. A synonym retains the permissions of its associated table.

Fragmentation

Fragmentation is an OnLine feature that allows you to control where fractions of a table's data are stored. Introduced in Chapter 4, fragmenting a table splits it into sections and stores each section in a different dbspace. Both tables and indexes can be fragmented. When a table is very large, fragmenting it can increase performance, concurrency, and data availability.

The way in which a table is spread across a set of dbspaces and the distribution of data and index keys across this spread is called a *fragmentation strategy*. The actual distribution of data and index keys within the fragmentation strategy is called a *distribution scheme*. When an end user accesses a fragmented table, the fact that it is fragmented will be transparent. No modifications need to be made to perform SQL operations on fragmented tables. The following sections discuss when fragmentation should be considered.

Improving Concurrency

Concurrency is a concern in environments where a large number of users are accessing the same table's data at the same time. Fragmentation can improve concurrency by placing each table fragment on a separate I/O device, thereby reducing user contention for rows in the same table.

Improving Single-User Response Time

Single-user response time is often a concern in decision-support environments where single queries perform sequential scans of large amounts of table data. In such an environment, the fragmentation strategy objective is to distribute data in a balanced fashion across multiple fragments on separate I/O devices. The primary advantage of fragmenting data in this way is to permit parallel data scans.

Improving Data Availability

When implemented properly, a fragmentation strategy can ensure that some data within a table is still accessible when one of its table fragments becomes unavailable, due perhaps to a disk failure.

Improving Archive/Restore Granularity

Informix's backup utilities (ON-Bar and ON-Archive) can both perform archives and restores at the dbspace level. This allows you to be very selective when defining a unit of archive and recovery. In theory, you could define a very small number of rows and index keys per fragment and then have the option to archive and restore only this fragment. In implementing this type of fragmentation strategy you should keep your fragment sizes small, grouping related rows within each fragment.

Distribution Schemes

OnLine supports round-robin and expression-based distribution schemes. The round-robin method is simplest, whereas the expression-based method offers the most flexibility. With the round-robin scheme, OnLine distributes data as evenly as possible across the fragments you specify. Its primary purpose is to balance I/O across multiple disks and to allow parallel data scans.

With an expression-based distribution scheme, you define specific rules in the table creation statement that mandate how fractions of the table's data are stored. By using relational operators, you dictate that rows that meet certain criteria should be stored in the dbspaces you specify. The syntax for creating a table that implements expression-based fragmentation follows:

```
create table table-name (
    column-and-constraint-definitions

  ) fragment by expression

    fragmentation-expression in dbspace-name,

    fragmentation-expression in dbspace-name

 [, fragmentation-expression in dbspace-name …]

   [remainder                  in dbspace-name];
```

where *table-name* is the table to be fragmented, *column-and-constraint-definitions* define the table structure, *fragmentation-expression* is a rule you specify, and *dbspace-name* is the name of the dbspace where rows matching the expression are stored. Database rows that match no *fragmentation-expression* are stored in the remainder *dbspace-name*.

In practice, you'll need to work with your system's DBA to identify the dbspaces available for fragmenting a table, and to craft the appropriate expressions that will define your expression-based distribution schemes.

The System Catalog

The system catalog tables are generated automatically whenever a database is created. There is one set of 29 system catalog tables for each database on a server. These tables always exist in the dbspace where the database was created. A system catalog tracks primarily the following objects within its database:

- Tables
- Indexes
- Views
- Triggers
- Stored procedures
- User privileges
- Constraints

Each time an SQL statement is run, the server accesses one or more of the system catalog tables to perform tasks like determining user privileges, enforcing constraints, and verifying column data types. Table 17-4 shows the most important tables in the system catalog.

Table 17-4 Important system catalog tables.

Table Name	Function
systables	Describes each table, view, and synonym in a database.
syscolumns	Contains information about each table and view column in a database.
sysindexes	Contains information about each index in a database.
systabauth	Describes the privileges that are granted to users in each table.
sysviews	Describes each view defined in the database.
sysusers	Contains database-level privileges for a database.
sysconstraints	Contains information about every constraint in a database. This includes primary key, foreign key, check, and unique constraints.
sysreferences	Describes all the referential constraints placed on columns.
sysprocedures	Contains the characteristics of each stored procedure.
sysprocbody	Contains the compiled version of each stored procedure along with the stored procedure text.
systriggers	Contains information about each trigger in a database.

(Continued)

Table 17-4 Important system catalog tables.

Table Name	Function
systrigbody	Contains trigger text and code for each trigger.
sysfragments	Contains fragmentation information for tables and indexes. There is one row for each table or index fragment.
sysroleauth	Describes all roles granted to users.

On occasion, you may find value in selecting data directly from the system catalog tables to verify a certain component of your database structure. At the least, you should recognize the existence of these tables to help understand and demystify how Informix records its database schemas.

Summary

In this chapter you learned about some of the more important internal components of INFORMIX-OnLine Dynamic Server as well as some fundamentals of server administration. The three primary components of OnLine are virtual processors, shared memory, and disk management.

A virtual processor is a UNIX process that manages multiple concurrent threads. Shared memory is divided into three separate portions. The resident portion contains primarily the buffer pool, the place where data that has been read from disk is cached for efficiency. The virtual portion is composed of a number of different pools that track similar memory allocations. The disk component of OnLine comprises physical and logical units of storage. A page is the smallest physical unit of storage that OnLine uses, and is the building block from which extents are built. OnLine uses the sqlhosts and /etc/services files to define local and remote database connectivity. The value of your INFORMIXSERVER environment variable ultimately determines the method OnLine uses to establish a database connection.

Fragmentation is a method used to distribute database data and indexes across multiple dbspaces. For very large tables, performance, concurrency, and reliability can be improved by implementing a round-robin or expression-based distribution scheme.

Finally, the system catalog tables were described as tracking resources within a database. System catalog tables store data about all aspects of a database's structure, its tables, indexes, views, triggers, stored procedures, privileges, and constraints.

Extra Credit

Q&A

Question	**Answer**
Can I dynamically add a buffer to the resident portion of shared memory?	No, structures in the resident portion of shared memory cannot dynamically change in size.
I want to delete all the rows from a large table, but I don't want to monopolize all of the available locks. Is there a way to achieve this without dropping and rebuilding the table?	Yes, you can lock the table in exclusive mode inside your transaction and then perform the delete. Sometimes, however, dropping the table is so much faster that you may want to consider that option.
I want to see good performance when I make local connections to my database, but I don't want to risk shared-memory corruption. Can I do this without using my remote connection method?	Yes, have your OnLine Administrator configure a stream pipe connection method.

Exercises

1. Using the UNIX command ipcs, identify your server's shared-memory segments.
2. All UNIX devices are listed in the /dev directory. Block special devices are identified with a b in the first column of a listing

with the `-l` option. Likewise, character special devices have a c in the first column. The devices allocated to OnLine are owned by the Informix ID. List the Informix-owned contents of that directory, and notice how the character and block devices compare.

3. Study your `sqlhosts` and `/etc/services` files so that you understand how each dbservername value identifies a specific network or local connection.

Exercise Answers

1. The following is one possible `ipcs` command:

```
$ ipcs -mb | grep informix
```

2. A command like the following should reveal these devices:

```
$ ls -l /dev | grep informix
```

3. Your mileage may vary.

The Sample Database

This appendix contains all of the instructions you need to create the sample `music` database. This database is used to help illustrate many of the exercises in this book, so you should make every effort to build it before working through the chapters.

Configuring Your Environment

Before you can create and load the database, you need to be connected to an Informix database server. Chapter 3, "DB-Access," described the fundamentals of configuring your environment for this purpose.

If your environment is not set up to access your database server after login, you will need to set some environmental variables from the command line. If you are using the Bourne shell or K shell, enter the following commands:

```
$ export INFORMIXDIR=Informix-directory
$ export PATH=$INFORMIXDIR/bin:$PATH
$ export TERMCAP=$INFORMIXDIR/etc/termcap
$ export DBDATE=MDY4/
$ export INFORMIXSERVER=dbserver-name
```

where *Informix-directory* is the fully qualified path to the directory where Informix was installed, and *dbserver-name* refers to the Informix configuration parameter DBSERVER or DBSERVERALIAS. If you are unsure about what either of these values should be set to, ask your local database administrator or system administrator.

If you are using the C shell, type the following instead:

```
$ setenv INFORMIXDIR Informix-directory
$ setenv PATH $INFORMIXDIR/bin:$PATH
$ setenv TERMCAP $INFORMIXDIR/etc/termcap
$ setenv DBDATE MDY4/
$ setenv INFORMIXSERVER dbserver-name
```

At this point, you should have access to your Informix database server. If you type the following command, you should see the DB-Access main menu:

```
$ dbaccess
```

If you still need help configuring your database environment, you can find some pointers in Chapter 3, "DB-Access."

Building Your Database

Building your copy of the `music` database is a three-step process, summarized below. Each step is described in detail in the following sections.

1. Download the creation files. These include `makedb.sql` and `maketbls.sql`, also included in this appendix. Instructions follow for extracting these files from the Internet. Should you extract them, you will also get three utility scripts (`loaddata.sql`, `deldata.sql`, and `droptbls.sql`) and six data files (`formats.unl`, `genres.unl`, `perfs.unl`, `albums.unl`, `alcopies.unl`, and `alperfs.unl`).
2. Run the creation scripts. The script `makedb.sql` builds the `music` database, and the `maketbls.sql` script builds each table within the database.
3. Load the sample data. The script `loaddata.sql` populates each table in the `music` database with the data from its respective data file.

Download the Creation Files

The easiest way to build your copy of the `music` database is to download the files from the Internet. Point your browser to the following URL:

`ftp://ftp.prenhall.com/pub/ptr/informix_sco.w-052/miller`

Click on `Informix Basics` to download a file named `basics.zip`. Use the `pkzip` utility to extract the component files from this compressed `basics.zip` file. The following files are included in the `basics.zip` archive:

- `albums.unl`
- `alcopies.unl`
- `alperfs.unl`
- `deldata.sql`
- `droptbls.sql`
- `formats.unl`
- `genres.unl`
- `loaddata.sql`
- `makedb.sql`
- `maketbls.sql`
- `perfs.unl`

Extract these files to your local directory.

Run the Creation Scripts

If you need help with the general concepts described in these steps, refer to Chapter 4, "Creating Databases and Tables." Enter the following command to create the `music` database:

```
$ dbaccess - makedb

Database created.

Database closed.
```

Now enter the following command to build the tables in the `music` database:

```
$ dbaccess music maketbls

Database selected.

Table created.

Table created.

Table created.

Table created.

Table created.

Table created.

Database closed.
```

Load the Sample Data

The last step in building your database is to load each table with the sample data. Of course, you can skip this step and enter your own data. Should you elect to do so, you can find some guidance in Chapter 5, "Basic SQL," and Chapter 6, "ISQL Forms and Reports." Each describes the fundamentals of data entry.

Before loading the data, be sure that your environmental variable DBDATE is set to MDY4/ as described in the "Configuring Your Environment" section. Enter the following command to load the music database with the sample data:

```
$ dbaccess music loaddata

Database selected.

20 row(s) loaded.

7 row(s) loaded.

73 row(s) loaded.

22 row(s) loaded.

22 row(s) loaded.

94 row(s) loaded.

Database closed.
```

If you need help understanding the tools used to load data, refer to Chapter 16, "Data Migration."

Reload the Sample Data

You may find over time, after having modified the sample data, that you would like to reload the pristine data. Two SQL utility scripts are included to help you perform this operation.

The deldata.sql script deletes all data from the music tables. After running it, you can then execute the loaddata.sql script again, as shown in the previous section.

Finally, should you care to rebuild the tables themselves rather than merely the data in them, you can execute the drop-tbls.sql script. Following that, you can run the maketbls.sql script, followed by the loaddata.sql script, to repopulate the tables.

The Sample Files

This section shows the contents of the various files used to create and load the sample `music` database.

The Creation Scripts

The scripts in Listings A-1 and A-2 are used to create the `music` database and the tables within it.

Listing A-1 *The makedb.sql script.*

```
create database music with buffered log;
```

Listing A-2 *The maketbls.sql script.*

```
create table formats (

    format          char(6) not null primary key

                    constraint pk_formats,

    default_value money,

    description     char(40)

);


create table genres (

    genre           char(10) not null primary key

                    constraint pk_genres,

    description     char(60)

);
```

(Continued)

```
create table performers (

     last_name     char(15) not null,

     first_name    char(15) not null,

     sex           char(1)  not null

                            check (sex in ('F', 'M'))

                            constraint ck_performer_sex,

     birth_date    date,

     death_date    date,

     primary key (last_name, first_name)

                            constraint pk_performers

);


create table albums (

     album_num     serial   not null primary key

                            constraint pk_albums,

     title         char(30),

     artist        char(20),

     issue_year    smallint,

     genre         char(10) references genres

                            constraint albums_fk_genres,

     rating        smallint check (rating between 0 and 10)

                            constraint ck_album_rating,

     notes         varchar(80),

     unique (title, artist) constraint ak_albums
```

(Continued)

```
);


create table album_copies (
      album_num        integer  not null references albums
                                constraint ac_fk_albums,
      format           char(6)  default 'CD' not null
                                references formats
                                constraint ac_fk_formats,
      location         char(15) default 'shelf 1'
      amount_paid      money,
      primary key (album_num, format) constraint pk_album_copies
);


create table album_performers (
      last_name        char(15) not null,
      first_name       char(15) not null,
      album_num        integer  not null references albums
                                constraint ap_fk_albums,
      foreign key (last_name, first_name) references performers
                                constraint ap_fk_performers,
      primary key (last_name, first_name, album_num)
                                constraint pk_album_perfs
);
```

The Load Script

The script in Listing A-3 loads each table in the `music` database with its sample data.

Listing A-3 *The loaddata.sql script.*

```
load from formats.unl   insert into formats;

load from genres.unl    insert into genres;

load from perfs.unl     insert into performers;

load from albums.unl    insert into albums;

load from alcopies.unl insert into album_copies;

load from alperfs.unl   insert into album_performers;


update statistics;
```

The Reload Scripts

The scripts in Listings A-4 and A-5 allow you to reload the `music` database with its sample data.

Listing A-4 *The deldata.sql script.*

```
delete from album_performers;

delete from album_copies;

delete from albums;

delete from performers;

delete from genres;

delete from formats;
```

```
drop table album_performers;

drop table album_copies;

drop table albums;

drop table performers;

drop table genres;

drop table formats;
```

The Sample Data

This section shows the sample data used in the examples throughout this book.

The formats Data

```
format    default_value description


8track           $8.00 when only the best will do

CD              $15.99 compact disc

tape             $9.99 cassette tape

LP              $12.00 vinyl record, complete with scratches

DAT             $18.50 digital audio tape

video           $24.99 VHS format videocassette

laser           $32.50 laser disc
```

The genres Data

genre	description
blues	Chicago, Texas, and Memphis heartache
calypso	Steel drums and coconut drinks with little umbrellas
classical	Rock me, Amadeus
country	Songs about trains, dogs, and trucks
disco	Do the hustle in your platform shoes
gospel	Inspirational voices from the choir
hip hop	Rap, and urban rhythmic screeds
jazz	From beatnik to new acoustic
metal	Loud and rebellious screeching guitars
polka	Beer barrel Bohemian sounds in 2/4 time
pop	Easy, catchy, even bubble gum tunes
punk	Edgy, cacophonous anger, with instruments
reggae	The sun-splashed Jamaican beat of Bob Marley
rock	Tunes your kids (or your parents) hate
rockabilly	High energy nascent country rock
salsa	Songs with irresistible Latin spice
ska	Reggae plus six cups of coffee
soul	Earthy rhythm and blues
world beat	Rhythms from the many corners of the globe
zydeco	Blackened Cajun beat, with pepper sauce

The performers Data

Last Name	First Name	Sex	Born On	Died On
Avila	John	M	01/14/1957	
Bartek	Steve	M	01/30/1952	
Bostrom	Derrick	M		
Briley	Alexander	M		
Caffey	Charlotte	F		
Capello	Tim	M		
Carlisle	Belinda	F	08/16/1958	
Carreras	Jose	M		
Craig	Michael	M		
Cummings	Burton	M	12/31/1947	
Dolenz	Mickey	M	03/08/1945	
Domingo	Placido	M	01/21/1941	
Dylan	Bob	M	05/24/1941	
Edmunds	Dave	M	04/15/1944	
Elfman	Danny	M	05/29/1953	
Faulkner	Eric	M	10/21/1955	
Fitzgerald	Warren	M	09/15/1968	
Garcia	Jerry	M	08/01/1942	08/09/1995
George	Boy	M	06/23/1962	
Harrison	George	M	02/25/1943	
Hart	Mickey	M	09/11/1943	
Hay	Roy	M		
Hernandez	Vatos	M	09/05/1951	
Hughes	Glenn	M		
Jacks	Terry	M		
Jackson	Jackie	M	05/04/1951	
Jackson	Jermaine	M	12/11/1954	
Jackson	Marlon	M	03/12/1957	

Jackson	Michael	M	08/29/1958	
Jackson	Tito	M	10/15/1953	
Jones	Davy	M	12/30/1945	
Jones	Randy	M		
Kirkwood	Cris	M	01/10/1959	
Kirkwood	Curt	M	10/22/1960	
Layton	Chris	M		
Lennon	John	M	10/09/1940	12/08/1980
Lofgren	Nils	M	06/21/1951	
Longmuir	Alan	M	06/20/1951	
Longmuir	Derek	M	03/19/1952	
Lynne	Jeff	M		
Manilow	Barry	M	06/17/1946	
McCartney	Paul	M	06/18/1942	
McKeown	Leslie	M	11/12/1955	
Morvan	Fabrice	M		
Moss	John	M		
Nesmith	Michael	M	12/30/1942	
Orbison	Roy	M	04/23/1936	12/01/1988
Pavarotti	Luciano	M	10/12/1935	
Petty	Tom	M	12/31/1953	
Phipps	Sam	M	10/01/1953	
Pilatus	Rob	M		04/03/1998
Preston	Billy	M	09/09/1946	
Rose	Felipe	M		
Rundgren	Todd	M	06/22/1948	
Scaggs	Boz	M	06/08/1944	
Schmit	Timothy B.	M		
Schneiderman	Leon	M	01/25/1954	
Schock	Gina	F		
Shannon	Tommy	M		
Starkey	Zak	M		

Starr	Ringo	M	07/07/1940	
Sublett	Joe	M		
Tork	Peter	M	02/13/1942	
Turner	Dale	M	07/02/1941	
Valentine	Kathy	F		
Vaughan	Stevie Ray	M	10/03/1954	08/26/1990
Walsh	Joe	M	12/31/1947	
Weir	Bob	M	10/06/1947	
Wiedlin	Jane	F		
Williams	Nathan	M		
Willis	Victor	M		
Wood	Stuart (Woody)	M	02/25/1957	
Wynans	Reese	M		

The albums Data

```
album_num    1
title        Absolute Rollers - The Best of
artist       Bay City Rollers
issue_year   1995
genre        pop
rating       4
notes        First time All of Me Loves All of You appeared on
    a CD.


album_num    2
title        Once Upon A Star
artist       Bay City Rollers
issue_year   1975
genre        pop
rating       0
notes
```

```
album_num    3

title        Abbey Road

artist       Beatles

issue_year   1969

genre        rock

rating       9

notes        Paul is not dead.


album_num    4

title        Help!

artist       Beatles

issue_year   1965

genre        rock

rating       8

notes


album_num    5

title        Revolver

artist       Beatles

issue_year   1966

genre        rock

rating       8

notes        Includes George's hit, Taxman.


album_num    6

title        Please Please Me

artist       Beatles

issue_year   1963

genre        rock

rating       10

notes
```

```
album_num    7

title        Live from Montreux: Vol. 2

artist       Ringo's AllStar Band

issue_year   1994

genre        rock

rating       5

notes        Richard Starkey on the road again.


album_num    8

title        Colour by Numbers

artist       Culture Club

issue_year   1983

genre        pop

rating       1

notes


album_num    9

title        Kissing to be Clever

artist       Culture Club

issue_year   1982

genre        pop

rating       2

notes


album_num    10

title        Soul to Soul

artist       Double Trouble

issue_year   1985

genre        blues

rating       9

notes
```

```
album_num    11

title        Dylan and the Dead

artist       Dylan and the Dead

issue_year   1989

genre        rock

rating       0

notes        Quite possibly the worst album by either
             Bob Dylan or the Grateful Dead.


album_num    12

title        Beauty and the Beat

artist       Go-Gos

issue_year   1981

genre        pop

rating       6

notes


album_num    13

title        Jackson 5 Christmas Album

artist       Jackson 5

issue_year   1970

genre        soul

rating       3

notes        Michael at his holiday best.


album_num    14

title        Huevos

artist       Meat Puppets

issue_year   1987

genre        rock

rating       1

notes
```

```
album_num      15

title          Girl You Know its True

artist         Milli Vanilli

issue_year     1989

genre          pop

rating         4

notes          They were lip-synching on the album, too.


album_num      16

title          Barrel Full of Monkees

artist         Monkees

issue_year     1971

genre          pop

rating         7

notes


album_num      17

title          Only a Lad

artist         Oingo Boingo

issue_year     1981

genre          rock

rating         2

notes


album_num      18

title          In Concert

artist         Three Tenors

issue_year     1990

genre          classical

rating         8

notes
```

```
album_num    19

title        Traveling Wilburys

artist       Traveling Wilburys

issue_year   1988

genre        rock

rating       5

notes


album_num    20

title        Cruisin

artist       Village People

issue_year   1978

genre        disco

rating       6

notes        Introduced Y.M.C.A, a gift to the world.


album_num    21

title        Sounds of the Okefenokee Swamp

artist       Ambient Sounds

issue_year   1995

genre

rating       4

notes        Loony!


album_num    22

title        Zydeco Live!

artist       Zydeco Cha Chas

issue_year   1994

genre        zydeco

rating       7

notes        Nathan cooks up some Cajun spice.
```

The album_copies Data

album_num	format	location	amount_paid
1	laser	shelf 2	
2	8track	car	$6.95
3	CD	shelf 5	$16.95
4	CD	shelf 5	$0.00
4	tape	work	$9.95
5	CD	shelf 5	$13.50
6	CD	car	$14.95
7	CD	shelf 5	$14.95
8	laser	in player	$29.99
9	CD	shelf 5	
10	CD	shelf 1	
10	tape	pocket	$8.99
11	tape	work	
12	CD		$9.50
13	LP	closet	$13.00
14	video	shelf 2	$17.50
15	CD	work	$2.95
16	8track	car	$8.00
18	video	shelf 2	$21.50
20	LP	closet	$12.00
21	tape	shelf 1	$9.99
22	CD	shelf 4	$17.50

The album_performers Data

last_name	first_name	album_num
Faulkner	Eric	1
Longmuir	Alan	1
Longmuir	Derek	1

McKeown	Leslie	1
Wood	Stuart (Woody)	1
Faulkner	Eric	2
Longmuir	Alan	2
Longmuir	Derek	2
McKeown	Leslie	2
Wood	Stuart (Woody)	2
Harrison	George	3
Lennon	John	3
McCartney	Paul	3
Preston	Billy	3
Starr	Ringo	3
Harrison	George	4
Lennon	John	4
McCartney	Paul	4
Starr	Ringo	4
Harrison	George	5
Lennon	John	5
McCartney	Paul	5
Starr	Ringo	5
Harrison	George	6
Lennon	John	6
McCartney	Paul	6
Starr	Ringo	6
Capello	Tim	7
Cummings	Burton	7
Edmunds	Dave	7
Lofgren	Nils	7
Rundgren	Todd	7
Schmit	Timothy B.	7
Starkey	Zak	7
Starr	Ringo	7

Walsh	Joe	7
Craig	Michael	8
George	Boy	8
Hay	Roy	8
Moss	John	8
Craig	Michael	9
George	Boy	9
Hay	Roy	9
Moss	John	9
Layton	Chris	10
Shannon	Tommy	10
Sublett	Joe	10
Vaughan	Stevie Ray	10
Wynans	Reese	10
Dylan	Bob	11
Garcia	Jerry	11
Hart	Mickey	11
Weir	Bob	11
Caffey	Charlotte	12
Carlisle	Belinda	12
Schock	Gina	12
Valentine	Kathy	12
Wiedlin	Jane	12
Jackson	Jackie	13
Jackson	Jermaine	13
Jackson	Marlon	13
Jackson	Michael	13
Jackson	Tito	13
Bostrom	Derrick	14
Kirkwood	Cris	14
Kirkwood	Curt	14
Morvan	Fabrice	15

Pilatus	Rob	15
Dolenz	Mickey	16
Jones	Davy	16
Nesmith	Michael	16
Tork	Peter	16
Avila	John	17
Bartek	Steve	17
Elfman	Danny	17
Fitzgerald	Warren	17
Hernandez	Vatos	17
Phipps	Sam	17
Schneiderman	Leon	17
Turner	Dale	17
Carreras	Jose	18
Domingo	Placido	18
Pavarotti	Luciano	18
Dylan	Bob	19
Harrison	George	19
Lynne	Jeff	19
Orbison	Roy	19
Petty	Tom	19
Briley	Alexander	20
Hughes	Glenn	20
Jones	Randy	20
Rose	Felipe	20
Willis	Victor	20
Williams	Nathan	22

Administrative Tools

This appendix is for the Informix tinkerer, the person who wants to peer under the hood of a database server as it operates. In most development environments, only database and system administrators use these tools. Nonetheless, even the casual developer can benefit from knowing the full range of tools that are available. The two types of tools included here are monitoring tools, those used to examine the structure and performance of a database environment, and administrative tools, those used to configure and manage the database environment.

Monitoring Tools

This section examines the `onstat`, `oncheck`, `onperf`, and *DB/ Cockpit* database monitoring utilities. All of these come bundled with the UNIX-ported 7.xx OnLine engines. These tools have value not only for the Informix DBA, but also for the developer who has an interest in monitoring and optimizing system performance.

onstat

The information retrieved using the `onstat` command line utility is a snapshot of shared memory structures at the instant the command executes. Since the contents of shared memory change as the `onstat` output is displayed, the statistics of the output are only accurate at that particular instant in time. The `onstat` does not place any locks on shared memory, so it can be run safely at any time without hindering the performance of other user processes. Of all the monitoring and administrative tools available, `onstat` is probably the most often used. Its commands can be run interactively or incorporated into UNIX shell scripts to provide a very powerful DBA monitoring arsenal.

The `onstat` utility must be run directly on the database server, not via a remote database connection, because the contents of shared memory are only available on a local machine. Any user with database connectivity can run the `onstat` commands.

Since there are over 70 options that can be passed to `onstat`, you will not be seeing a fully printed option list here. However, assuming you are logged in and pointing to your database server, you can find out all the `onstat` options from the command line. At the UNIX command line, type in the following:

```
$ onstat --
```

There is no space between the dashes. You might want to pipe the command to `more` or `pg` since there is more than one screen of output. As you can see, this generates a list of all the available `onstat` options. You'll notice that about a third of the way down the list is a line reading:

```
MT COMMANDS:
```

All the options beneath this line became available when the DSA architecture was introduced. These three-letter MT commands require that the `-g` subcommand precede them.

Although there are over 70 `onstat` options available, a DBA
will typically use less than half of these options, and fewer than
that on a regular basis. Informix developers used many of the `-g`
options as the INFORMIX-Online Dynamic Server was being
designed to help them in their development process. These options
were left available in the event a DBA ever had the need to use
them, but also for use by Informix on-site support personnel to aid
in diagnosing performance problems. The goal of this section is
not to give you an understanding of all the `onstat` options, but
rather an appreciation for the different ways in which the `onstat`
utility may be used.

Begin by examining statistics for all user and server threads.
Enter the following command:

$ **onstat -g ses**

You will see output similar to the following:

```
INFORMIX-OnLine Version 7.12.UC1    -- On-Line -- Up 00:24:09 -- 24864
    Kbytes

session                                         #RSAM    total      used
id         user      tty     pid    hostname threads  memory    memory
12         informix -       0      -        0        8192      7124
11         davisr    0       16596  loanc10 1        180224    36188
7          informix -       0      -        0        8192      5268
6          informix -       0      -        0        8192      7124
4          informix -       0      -        0        16384     7956
3          informix -       0      -        0        16384     8296
2          informix -       0      -        0        8192      5268
1          informix -       0      -        0        8192      5268
```

To see specific statistics for a particular session, type in the following, where the *session-id* is a number in the first column
from the last command:

$ **onstat -g ses** *session-id*

You can gather multiple statistics in the same command by
combining two or more option flags. Try this by executing the following command:

```
$ onstat -dp
```

where the -d option displays statistics for *dbspaces* and *chunks*, and the -p option displays the server profile.

As described in Chapter 17, "Database Administration Fundamentals," a *chunk* is a unit of contiguous disk space assigned to the OnLine system and managed by the Informix engine. A *dbspace* is a chunk or collection of chunks. A database must be created in one particular dbspace, while the tables in that database may reside in many dbspaces. Additional chunks can be added to a dbspace to increase its size.

The -r option repeats an onstat command every *n* seconds. If no number is given, the default is five seconds. To display currently active threads at three-second intervals, type in the following:

```
$ onstat -g act -r 3
```

The onstat utility also provides an interactive mode. You enter an interactive session by typing the following:

```
$ onstat -i
onstat>
```

This interactive mode allows you to enter any onstat option without requiring the onstat - format. To see all active threads again, type in the following:

```
onstat>act
```

Now try to combine multiple onstat options in interactive mode with the following command:

```
onstat>dp
```

You'll notice that you got a listing of options similar to when you ran onstat -- earlier. This is because the interactive mode does not allow multiple statistics to be generated in the same command; nor does it recognize the -r option. In fact, any time you supply an option that onstat does not recognize, whether you are in interactive or standard mode, you will get the full listing of options. To exit interactive mode, enter q for quit.

oncheck

The `oncheck` utility is both an administrative tool and a monitoring tool. It not only supplies configuration and disk usage information, but can also repair certain corrupted indexes.

The `oncheck` utility can perform the following functions:

- Display information about disk structures, such as tables, indexes, and chunks
- Check disk structures for inconsistencies
- Repair indexes found to contain inconsistencies

The only disk structures that can be repaired are indexes. To generate the list of oncheck options, enter the following at the UNIX command line:

```
$ oncheck
```

You will notice that two sections of options correspond to the check (`-c`) and print (`-p`) primary functions. The repair function can be performed by any of the check or print options involving indexes.

All of the `oncheck` options except those that display database data can be run by anyone. Because the following options display potentially sensitive database data, they can be run only by one of the two super-user IDs, `informix` and `root`: `-pk`, `-pK`, `-pl`, `-pL`, `-pd`, `-pD`, `-pp`, and `-pP`.

Another function that can be performed only by one of the super-user logins is index repair. If an `oncheck -ci` command, which checks the consistency of table indexes, finds an inconsistent index during its execution, it will prompt you to specify whether or not you want to repair the index. If you supply the `-y` option, which answers `yes` to any questions, the index will be repaired automatically. Conversely, the `-n` option instructs `oncheck` to not repair the index.

Try the following to check the integrity of the indexes for the `albums` table in the `music` database:

```
$ oncheck -ci music:albums
```

The following output shows that there are four indexes on the
albums table, and that none are corrupted.

```
Validating indexes for music:informix.albums...

                        Index   104_11

                        Index   104_12

                        Index   104_13

                        Index   104_14
```

If you created the music database under your own login, you
should see your login ID in place of informix. This signifies that
you are the owner of the table.

The following command shows a section of the -pk output for
the music:albums table. Remember, this command performs the
same checks as the -ci option, but can only be run by informix
or root because it displays data.

```
$ oncheck -pk music:albums

Index   104_13 on TBLspace music:informix.albums

Level 0 Node 3 Prev 0 Next 0

Key:        "<00>            " :

Key:        "blues       " :

Key:        "classical " :

Key:        "disco       " :

Key:        "pop         " :

Key:        "rock        " :

Key:        "soul        " :
```

The partial output displayed shows information pertaining
only to one of the indexes. Since no inconsistency errors were generated, oncheck did not find any corruption within that index.

If you enter the following command without specifying a table,
oncheck verifies the integrity of every index in the database,
including those for the system catalogs:

```
$ oncheck -ci music
```

onperf

The `onperf` utility is a graphical interface used to monitor performance of the INFORMIX-OnLine Dynamic Server. It can monitor most of the same types of statistics or *metrics* that the `onstat` utility can, but in a graphical format. One advantage of `onperf` is that it provides a scrollable line graph tool you can use to monitor a metric or a set of metrics over time. Another advantage over `onstat` is the capability to save a timeline graph of this type to disk so that events can be played back at a later date exactly as they occurred. Figure B-1 depicts a timeline metric of system CPU usage and user CPU usage.

Whereas `onstat` can be run on the database server only, `onperf` can be run on any client that has access to the database.

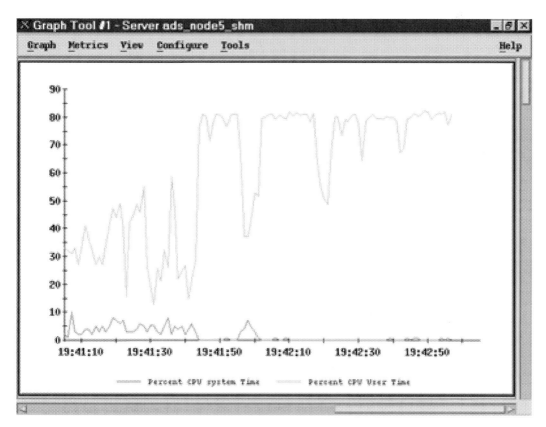

Figure B–1 *Onperf timeline graph displaying system and CPU usage.*

Whether you run `onperf` on a client or the server, the machine on which `onperf` is running must support the X display server and the mwm window manager. Besides these machine capabilities, you need only set two more environmental variables to run `onperf`. The first is your `DISPLAY` variable. Set it as follows, depending on your UNIX shell:

```
$ export DISPLAY=display-name:0.0
$ setenv DISPLAY display-name:0.0
```

where *display-name* is either the IP address or name of the computer or X terminal where the `onperf` windows will be displayed. Since `onperf` uses Motif windows, the `LD_LIBRARY_PATH` environmental variable will also need to be set to the directory path of the Motif libraries on the display machine. Once your environment is set properly, enter the following command:

```
$ onperf
```

The `onperf` utility provides four Motif windows, called *tools*, each of which displays different types of metrics. The tools are:

- Graph tool: the primary tool that `onperf` uses to monitor general performance activity. The timeline graph shown in Figure B-1 is one of the metric displays available. Multiple metrics can be gathered at the same time.
- Data-collection tool: allows you to choose which metrics to store in a data collector buffer and then save the buffer contents to a file. This file can be opened at a later time to play back the metrics that were gathered.
- Query-tree tool: displays the progress of a database query.
- Activity tools: a set of tools designed to display specific OnLine activities such as disk usage, physical processor usage, and user session activities.

DB/Cockpit

DB/Cockpit is a GUI tool that provides a superset of the `onstat` utility within a point-and-click environment. The DB/Cockpit architecture is composed of two components, `onprobe` and `oncockpit`.

The `onprobe` program is a data collector that is run on the database server. It gathers data from both the *System Monitoring Interface (SMI)* database and shared memory. It uses this data to trigger alarms and to evaluate the severity of any conditions that initiated these alarms. It can function without `oncockpit`, acting as a watchdog over systems that do not have an OnLine administrator, activating alarms when necessary and recording user-defined events. These alarms can be any task that the UNIX system can initiate, such as sending e-mail or pager messages to key personnel, or displaying messages on an X terminal.

The `oncockpit` program sends requests for database activity and configuration information, and displays the data returned. It can also display alarms sent to it by `onprobe`. It can be run from any remote client with access to the server running `onprobe`.

note *Before the `oncockpit` process can be started, `onprobe` must be running on the database server.*

Figure B-2 depicts the DB/Cockpit main window.

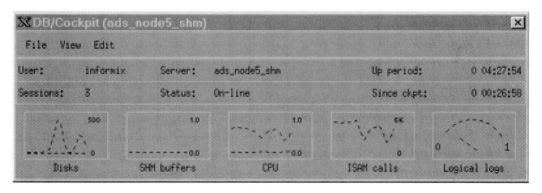

Figure B–2 *DB/Cockpit main window.*

DB/Cockpit comes with three tools:

- Alarm setter: a tool that can be customized to warn against specific behavior and events.
- Viewer: an information collector and data evaluator. It displays sets of point-in-time statistics, each in a separate view window.

- Severity analyst: a color-coded data analyzer that alerts to out-of-range behavior. The four severity levels are normal, warning, error, and fatal. These severity alerts are based on ranges defined by the user. When you set normal ranges for certain parameters of interest, DB/Cockpit passes their data through an evaluator that uses color codes to indicate which parameters stray out of range.

A separate service entry needs to be defined in the `/etc/services` file prior to starting `onprobe` or `oncockpit`. If you are using TCP/IP, a typical entry in the services file might look like

```
cockpit          2000/tcp
```

You will need to check with your DBA or SA to add a new service entry. It may be that there is already a service defined for DB/Cockpit on your system. Once you have either created or determined your DB/Cockpit service name, you start `onprobe` on the local server with the following command:

```
$ onprobe -service service-name
```

where `service-name` is the name of your DB/Cockpit services entry. Once `onprobe` is running on the server, you start `oncockpit` with the following command:

```
$ oncockpit [-host host-name] -service service-name
```

where `host-name` is the name of the host you are running your DB/Cockpit windows on, and `service-name` is the name of your DB/Cockpit service entry. If you omit the `-host` option, the `host-name` defaults to the local host.

Administrative Tools

The following sections cover five administrative tools: `dbschema`, `onspaces`, `onparams`, `onmode`, and `onmonitor`. Each of these utilities comes bundled with the UNIX versions of the Informix engine.

dbschema

The dbschema utility displays the exact SQL statements needed to rebuild a database or any objects within it, such as its tables or indexes. The SQL statements required to create a database or database object are collectively called a *schema*. Any user can generate a schema with the dbschema utility.

The dbschema utility may be used for a variety of reasons. Many DBAs like to use it as a substitute for traversing the DB-Access menus to gather information about a particular object. It is also used to recreate the structure of entire databases or to reproduce database objects in other databases. It may also be used to rebuild objects in the same database from which the schema was extracted. For example, if a table's data becomes corrupted, a DBA may need to drop and recreate the table, and then reload it with uncorrupted data. To obtain the exact SQL needed to recreate the table, dbschema could be used to obtain only the schema associated with that particular table. This schema would include any other objects associated with it, such as indexes, primary and foreign keys, and constraints.

To display the dbschema options available, enter the following:

```
$ dbschema
```

To view the server-specific version of the schema for the performers table in the music database, enter:

```
$ dbschema -ss -t performers -d music
```

onspaces

The onspaces utility is used to modify *blobspaces* and dbspaces. A blobspace is a logical storage unit that stores nothing but byte or text data. Only users informix and root can execute onspaces.

Using onspaces, you can perform the following tasks:

- Create and drop blobspaces
- Create and drop dbspaces
- Create and drop chunks
- Start and end dbspace mirroring

- Change chunk status, marking a chunk in a mirrored pair as On-line or Down
- Set the DATASKIP parameter

The onspaces options are as follows:

```
onspaces  { -a spacename -p pathname -o offset -s size [-m path offset]
        |

        -c {-d DBspace [-t] | -b BLOBspace -g pagesize}
                -p pathname -o offset -s size [-m path offset] |

        -d spacename [-p pathname -o offset] [-y] |

        -f[y] off [DBspace-list] | on [DBspace-list] |

        -m spacename {-p pathname -o offset -m path offset [-y] |
                -f filename} |
        -r spacename [-y] |

        -s spacename -p pathname -o offset {-O | -D} [-y] }

    -a - Add a chunk to a DBspace or BLOBspace
    -c - Create a DBspace or BLOBspace
    -d - Drop a DBspace, BLOBspace or chunk
    -f - Change dataskip default for specified DBspaces
    -m - Add mirroring to an existing DBspace or BLOBspace
    -r - Turn mirroring off for a DBspace or BLOBspace
    -s - Change the status of a chunk
```

It is good administrative practice to use onspaces commands to create the database environment. A script containing such commands serves as a type of archive file for future reference. It is not uncommon that dbspace devices mysteriously disappear, or that a DBA needs to create similar database environments on other platforms. Scripts such as these prove invaluable in such situations.

note *The onspaces utility is used primarily to create dbspaces and chunks, both during the initial creation of an Informix instance and as future disk space is required. The other options are used less often.*

onparams

The `onparams` utility is used to modify *logical log* and *physical log* configuration parameters. Only users `informix` or `root` can run it. Its list of options is shown here:

```
onparams  { -a -d DBspace [-s size]           |
            -d -l logid [-y]                   |
            -p -s size [-d DBspace] [-y] }


    -a  - Add a logical log

    -d  - Drop a logical log

    -p  - Change physical log size and location

    -y  - Automatically responds "yes" to all prompts
```

Logical logs are used to record changes to a database since the last database archive. The following types of records are stored in the logical logs:

- DDL statements
- DML statements
- Changes to the server configuration
- Changes to the logging status of a database
- *Checkpoints*, operations used to synchronize the pages on disk with the pages in shared memory

The logical logs are used during a database restore to bring a database up to its most current and consistent level.

The physical log is used to store unmodified copies of pages called *before-images*. Before a page is modified in shared memory and stored on disk, a before-image of the page is written to the physical log. All dbspace page modifications are physically logged. The primary reason for physically logging these before-images is to ensure that, in the case of a server failure, all data can be brought to physical consistency, to the point of the most recently committed transaction.

Both the physical log and logical logs must be originally created in the initial dbspace called the root dbspace, but may be moved to other dbspaces after initialization. The sizes of each are configurable. After a logical log is created, its size cannot be changed; however, new logs can be created using new sizes. The physical log can be resized at any time, although the Informix engine must be brought Off-Line to make the change.

onmode

The onmode utility is used by informix or root to perform server-mode and shared-memory changes. Its options follow:

```
onmode -abcDdFklMmnpQRrSsuyZz
    -a <kbytes>     Increase shared memory segment size.
    -b <version>    Revert OnLine disk structures.
    -c    Do checkpoint
    -D    <max PDQ priority allowed>
    -d    {standard|{primary|secondary <servername>}} set DR server type
    -F    Free unused memory segments
    -k    Shutdown completely
    -l    Force to next logical log
    -M    <decision support memory in kbytes>
    -m    Go to multi-user on-line
    -n    Set shared memory buffer cache to non-resident
    -O    Override dbspace down blocking a checkpoint
    -p <+-#> <class>   Start up or remove virtual processors of
          class cpu, aio, lio, pio, shm, soc, or tli.
    -Q    <max # decision support queries>
    -R    Rebuild the /INFORMIXDIR/etc/.infos.DBSERVERNAME file
    -r    Set shared memory buffer cache to resident
    -S    <max # decision support scans>
    -s    Shutdown to single user
    -u    Shutdown and kill all attached sessions
    -y    Do not require confirmation
    -Z <address> heuristically complete specified transaction
    -z <sid>    Kill specified session id
```

There are three primary modes of operation for the OnLine engine: *On-Line, Quiescent,* and *Off-Line.* On-Line mode is the multi-user, operational mode required to connect to the database server, and to perform any database activity. Quiescent mode is the administrative mode where only users informix or root are capable of performing server administration activities. In this mode, no other users are permitted to connect to the database server. Most administrative functions, such as creating or dropping dbspaces, can be performed while in On-Line mode, although Quiescent mode provides a more stable environment to perform these functions. Other functions, such as adding a logical log, require that the engine be in Quiescent mode. Off-Line mode is the mode in which the OnLine server is not running at all. In this mode, the server has not been initialized, and therefore, no Informix shared-memory segments have been created. The onmode options -k, -m, -s, and -u, are used to place the server into a specific mode.

Other onmode commands that are used frequently within most environments include:

- onmode -a   Increase shared-memory segment size
- onmode -c   Force a checkpoint
- onmode -l   Move to the next logical log
- onmode -F   Free unused shared-memory segments
- onmode -z   Kill a specified session ID

ON-Monitor

ON-Monitor is a menu-based administrative tool that performs most of the functions of onparams, onspaces, and onmode, as well as a few of the functions of the onstat utility. Its menus and screens behave the same as the ones in DB-Access or ISQL.

Although any user may run On-Monitor, only the users informix or root can view the six restricted options, shown below. Just as a normal user is restricted from running the options in onspaces, onmode, and onparams, On-Monitor restricts the same types of operations by restricting menu access. Use the following operating system command to invoke ON-Monitor:

$ **onmonitor**

The following nonrestricted STATUS menu options display information of the type listed to all users:

- Profile   (onstat -p)
- Userthreads   (onstat -g ses)
- Spaces   (onstat -d)
- Databases   (dbaccess database name -dib)

- Logs   (onstat -l)
- Archive
- data-Replication
- Output
- Configuration (onstat -c)

The commands in parentheses are the onstat or dbaccess counterparts to the menu option. Try maneuvering through the STATUS menu options to compare the On-Monitor output to the equivalent command-line output.

Users informix and root gain access to the following six additional main menu items:

- Parameters   (configuration file, onparams)
- Dbspaces   (onspaces)
- Mode   (onmode)
- Force-Ckpt   (onmode)
- Archive   (configuration file)
- Logical-Logs   (ontape, configuration file)

Each of these ON-Monitor options leads to a submenu that lists another set of options. The parenthetical items in the list show that either a utility or a change to the server configuration file is duplicated by this menu option. For example, the Dbspaces menu lets a DBA perform the same tasks as the onspaces utility does, such as creating a dbspace or a adding a chunk to an existing dbspace. The Parameters menu provides options that permit changes to the server configuration, as well as options that perform the same functions as the onparams utility. The ontape utility performs database archives and logical log backups, and changes the logging status of a database.

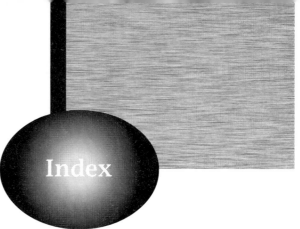

Index

A

abs function, 123
.ace extension, 176
action-clause clause, 263
Active set, 157-58
Add command, Create Table
    submenu, 88
Add operation, PERFORM menu,
    156
Administrative tools, 628-34
    dbschema, 105-6, 629
    monitoring tools, 619-28
        DB/Cockpit, 619, 626-28
        oncheck, 619, 623-24
        onperf, 619, 625-26
        onstat, 619, 620-22
    onmode, 632-33
    ON-Monitor, 633-34
    onparams, 631-32
    onspaces, 629-30
Advanced SQL queries, 211-37
    joining, 212-22
        Cartesian products,
            216-18
        composite joins, 214-15
        defined, 212
        equijoins, 212-14
        multitable joins, 215-16
        outer joins, 221-22
        restrictive joins, 220-21
        self-joins, 218-20
    subqueries, 229-33
        in delete statements, 233
        in select statements,
            229-31

        in update statements,
            232-33
    synonyms, 228-29, 587-88
    views, 222-28
        create view statement,
            222
        defined, 222-23
        hidden comparison
            condition, 223-25
        hiding a complex join,
            226-27
        presenting an aggregate
            as a column, 227-28
        restricting the select list,
            225-26
after group of control block,
    formatting, 463, 464-65
Aggregate expressions, using in
    select statement,
    124-26
Aggregate functions:
    group by clause with,
        187-90
    group by clause without,
        187
Alarm Setter tool, DB/Cockpit,
    627
album_copies data, sample
    database, 614
album_performers data,
    sample database,
    614-17
albums.4gl program, 365-77,
    424-28
    error checking, 426-28

albums data, sample database,
    608-14
Algorithms, defined, 290
Alias, 128, 219
    for tables, 118
all operator, 230
Altering tables, 103-4
Alternate keys, 27
alter table statement, 103-4
and operator, select
    statement, 134, 136
any operator, 230
Application programming
    interface (API), 5
.arc extension, 176
Archive/restore granularity, 589
arg_val(int), 330
arg_val() method, 344
Arithmetic expressions, using in
    select statement,
    126-27
Arrays, declaring, 302
arr_count(), 330
arr_curr(char), 330
artist_value.4gl report,
    465-69, 479-80
Assignment, 313
attribute clause, 347
Attributes, 4, 20, 343
    defining, 26-27
Attribute specifiers, 348
attributes section, form
    specification file, 164
Auditions:
    Dwarf, 422
    Spice Girl, 402

Audit trail, creating, 264-68
autonext attribute, ISQL
    forms, 165
autonext specifier, 364
avg function, 124

B

Back-end software, 5-6
Bad thing, *See* Cartesian
    product
Base tables, 222
Bay City Rollers Fan Club,
    214-15
before group of
    variable-name
    control block, 463, 464
Before-images, 631
between clause, select
    statement, 131-32
Binary data types, 87-88
Binary format utilities, 548-54
    onload utility, 548, 552-54
    onunload utility, 548,
    549-51
Binding statements, 363
black attribute, 348
blink attribute, 347, 348
blobpages, 579
Blobs, 87
blobspaces, 579-80
Block vs. character devices,
    580-81
blue attribute, 348
bold attribute, 348
bottom margin element, ISQL
    report output section,
    173
Boyce-Codd normal form, 39
Branching, 308-11
Buffer pool, 576
Built-in functions, 329-30
byte data type, 82, 87-88, 502

C

c4gl compiler, 293-95
Candidate keys, 27

Cardinality, 29
Cartesian product, 216-18
    use of term, 217
case statement, 308-11
cc compiler, 294
c file extension, 294, 295
Character data types, 82-83
char data type, 81, 82, 500
Checkpoints, 631
ChooseAlbum() function,
    325-26
Choose command, DB-Access,
    48
Choose option,
    Query-language
    menu, 61
ChooseRptDest() function,
    477-79, 481
Chronological data types, 84-87
    date data type, 85
    date/time data types, 85-87
Clauses, combining in a single
    line, 118
clear statement, 377
clear window statement, 388,
    397
Client/server computing, 5-6
clipped formatting qualifier,
    174
close statement, cursors,
    418-19
close window statement, 388,
    398
Column expressions, using in
    select statement, 122
Column gutter, arranging
    statement around, 117
Column-level constraint
    definitions, tables,
    94-102
Column-level permissions, 201
Columns, 4-5, 20
    presenting aggregates as,
    227-28
Columns option, Table Info
    submenu, 49, 52-53
Command files, 59
Command line arguments,
    reading, 379

Command scripts, 59
comment method, 344
comments attribute, ISQL
    forms, 165
comments =
    'message-string',
    364
Committed Read isolation level,
    207-8
Comparison conditions, 129-30
Compiler directives,
    Informix-4GL, 308-9
Complex join, hiding, 226-27
Composite joins, 214-15
Concurrency, 588
Conditionals, 246
Configuration issues, 582-84
    lock usage, minimizing,
    582-83
    long transactions, avoiding,
    583-84
Connection command,
    DB-Access, 48
Constants, using in select
    statement, 120-21
Constraint command,
    Create Table
    submenu, 89
Constraint naming
    recommendations,
    tables, 100-101
Constraints, 20, 35-36
Constraints option, Table
    Info submenu, 50,
    54-57
construct statement, 357,
    434-37
continue statement, and
    exiting a loop in SQL,
    248
Control block formatting,
    463-65
    after group of control
    block, 464-65
    before group of control
    block, 464
    first page header
    control block, 464

define statements, 300-301, 308

define *variable-name* like statements, 301

delete statements, 142-44
subqueries in, 233

Dependency, 29

Derived value, maintaining, 268-72

Detail operation, PERFORM menu, 156

/dev/null, 66

Development tools:
Informix-4GL, 14-15
Informix-ESQL, 15
Informix-NewEra, 16-17
stored procedures, 15-16

Device management, 580-81
block vs. character devices, 580-81
raw devices vs. cooked files, 581

dim attribute, 348

Dirty Read isolation level, 207-8

Discard-new-database command, Create Database submenu, 77

Disk management, 577-81
device management, 580-81
units of storage, 576-80

display array statement, 401-3, 409
by example, 404-7
details of, 407-8
keys for navigating, 408
syntax for, 407-8

Display attributes, defining, 347-48

Display labels:
defined, 127
using for selected values, 127

display method, 344

DisplayNotes() function, 322-23

display statement, 350-51, 357

Distribution schemes, 589-90

Domains, 21, 34, 80

Double dash (--), 133

Double quotes, 118

downshift, 364

downshift attribute, ISQL forms, 165

downshift(char), 330

Drop command:
Create Table submenu, 88
DB-Access, 48
Query-language menu, 62-63

drop table statement, 102

Dumb terminal, 6

Dweeb, 65

Dynamic ESQL statements, 534-40

Dynamic Scalable Architecture (DSA), 8-9

Dynamic SQL statements, 307, 429-37
assembling, 435
construct statement, 434-37
execute statement, 432-34
placeholders, 429-32
prepare statement, 430-32
query-by-example, 434-37

E

ec file extension, 294

.ec source file, 293

Embedded Structured Query Language, *See* ESQL/C

EnterNewNotes() function, 322, 327-28

Entities, 4, 21
defining, 23-25
entity types, 25
traits of, 24

Entity integrity, 32-34

Entity-relationship diagram (ERD), 22

Environmental variables, reading, 379-80

Equijoins, 212-14
defined, 213

error method, 344

error statement, 349-50

ESQL/C, 485-534
dynamic ESQL statements, 534-40
error checking, 490-95
error status codes, 490-91
get diagnostics statement, 491-92
whenever statement, 492-95
host variables, 496-502
arrays of, 502-6
arrays of structures of, 510-13
character data types, 499-501
as C structures, 506-8
data types, 498-99
ESQL/C special types, 501-2
as function parameters, 513-14
indicator variables, 514-18
null variables in, 514-23
risnull() function, 518-23
rsetnull() function, 518-23
how it works, 487
program variables, 496-502
purpose in using, 486-87
sample program, 488-89
static ESQL statements, 524-34
input parameters, 526-27
nonselect SQL statements, 524-25
select statements, 528-34

esql compiler, 293, 294

/etc/services file, 587

Evaluating your collection, 258-61

Exceptions, 255-57
on exception statement, 255-56
raise exception statement, 256-57

Executables, 293

Moore, Mary Tyler, 438
Multimodule programs,
    compilation of, 296-97
Multiple-row `select`, 530-34
Multitable joins, 215-16
Multi-user SQL, 198-207
    isolation levels, 206-7
    locking, 203-6
        database-level, 204
        page-level, 205
        row-level, 205
        table-level, 204-5
        wait mode, 206
    permissions, 198-203
        column-level, 201
        database-level, 199-200
        roles, 202-3
        stored procedures, 201-2
        table-level, 200-201
Musical Therapy ring menu,
    352-55

N

Naming conventions, 36
Naming functions, 322
Native Language Support
    (NLS), 83
`nchar` data type, 81, 83
Networked databases, 584-88
    connection process, 584-85
    `/etc/services` file, 587
    `sqlhosts` file, 585-86
    synonyms, 587-88
    trusted computers, 587
`New` command, DB-Access, 47
`New` option:
    `Query-language` menu,
        57-58
    `Report` submenu, 167
`Next` operation, PERFORM
    menu, 156, 158
Nodes, 9
`noentry` specifier, 364
`normal` attribute, 348
Normalization, 37-39
    first normal form, 38
    higher forms, 39

second normal form, 38
third normal form, 39
`NOTFOUND` global variable, 304
`not` operator, `select`
    statement, 134-35
Null, 21
Null comparisons, `select`
    statement, 132-33
`NULL` global variable, 304
`num_args()`, 330
Numerical data types, 83-84
    real number data types, 84
    whole number data types,
        83-84
Numeric expressions,
    formatting, 472-74
`nvarchar`, 81, 83

O

`o` file extension, 294
`oncheck`, 619, 623-24
`oncockpit` program,
    DB/Cockpit, 627
One-to-many relationships, 29
One-to-one relationships, 29
`on every row` control block,
    463
`on exception` statement,
    255-56
`on last row` control block,
    463
Online help screens, creating,
    398-400
Online transaction-processing
    (OLTP), 8
`onload` utility, 548, 552-54
`onmode`, 632-33
    commands, 633
    modes of operation, 632
ON-Monitor, 633-34
`onparams`, 631-32
`onperf`, 619, 625-26
`onprobe` program, *DB/Cockpit*,
    627
`onspaces`, 629-30
`onstat`, 619, 620-22
`onunload` utility, 548, 549-51

`open` statement, and cursors,
    418
`open window` statement, 388,
    396-97
Operating system commands,
    running, 380-81
Operators, 4GL expressions,
    314-15
`options` statement, 345-46,
    377-78
`order by` clause, `select`
    statement, 139-41
`or` operator, `select`
    statement, 135
Outer joins, 221-22
`Output` command, DB-Access,
    48
`Output` operation, PERFORM
    menu, 156
`Output` option,
    `Query-language`
    menu, 62

P

Page, 577
`page header` control block,
    463
`page length` element, ISQL
    report output section,
    173
Page-level locking, 205
`page trailer` control block,
    463
Paging space, 576
Passing arguments, 251-55
    to functions, 322-24
Pattern matching expressions,
    `select` statement,
    136-39
pcode, 293
pcode interpreter (fglgo), 293
`performers` data, sample
    database, 606-8
`performers` table:
    customized form
        specification for, 163-64
    customized report
        specification for, 170-71

default form specification
for, 157-62
default report:
executing, 168-69
generating, 168
default report specification for,
170
Permissions:
multi-user SQL, 198-203
column-level, 201
database-level, 199-200
roles, 202-3
stored procedures, 201-2
table-level, 200-201
Physical modeling, 21
Physical units of storage, 577,
578
Pina colada recipe, 41
Placeholders, 429-32
Pointy-headed geek, 21
megadweeb as, 65
pow function, 123
prepare statement, 430-32,
524-25
Previous operation, PERFORM
menu, 156, 158
Primary keys, 21, 27, 33
updating--not!, 37, 147
printf(), 500
print statement, 174, 471-72
Process architecture, 572-75
thread management, 574-75
virtual processor classes,
572-74
Program blocks, 307-8
Program flow control, 308-13
branching, 308-11
looping, 311-13
Program variables:
arrays, declaring, 302
data type, declaring,
300-303
defining, 299-305
ESQL/C, 496-502
global scope, 300
like notation, 301
local scope, 299
modular scope, 300
naming, 303

dos/don'ts for, 303-4
records, declaring, 301-2
scope of, declaring, 299-300
Project scope, defining, 22-23
prompt method, 344
prompt statement, 351-52
Pseudo-code (p-code), 14

Q

QBE operators, ISQL forms,
159-60
Query-by-example (QBE), 153,
285-86, 358, 434-37
Query-language command,
DB-Access, 47
Query-language menu, 57-63
Choose option, 61
Drop option, 62-63
Modify option, 61
New option, 57-58
Output option, 62
Run option, 58-59
Save option, 59-60
Query operation, PERFORM
menu, 156
Query output, redirecting,
141-42
Query plan, 197
QUIT_FLAG global variable, 304

R

raise exception statement,
256-57
and exiting a loop in SQL,
248
Rapid Development System
(RDS), 298
Raw devices vs. cooked files, 581
Real number data types, 84
Records, declaring, 301-2
red attribute, 348
Referential constraint
definitions, tables,
98-100
Referential integrity (RI), 28-29,
36-37

Relational database, 4-5, 21
Relational operators, 130-31
Remove operation, PERFORM
menu, 156
Repeatable Read isolation
level, 207-8
Report destination, changing
dynamically, 476-81
Report driver, 456, 457
Report execution, 314
Report execution statements,
470-11
Report formatter, 456, 457-63
format section, 460-63
order by section, 460
output section, 458-60
report declaration section,
458
report to element, ISQL
report output section,
173
required attribute, ISQL
forms, 165
required specifier, 364
reserve attribute, 348
Reserved screen lines, 344-45
Resident memory, 576
Restrictive joins, 220-21
Returning values from a
function, 325-29
return statement, and exiting
a loop in SQL, 248
reverse attribute, ISQL forms,
165
reverse specifier, 364
revoke SQL operator, 198-203
rfmtdate() function, 498
Ring menus, 352-57
Musical Therapy ring menu,
352-55
risnull() function, 518-23
Roadhouse bluesman, See
Vaughan, Stevie Ray
round function, 123
Row-level locking, 205
Rows, 4-5, 21
rsetnull() function, 518-23
Run command, DB-Access, 47
run method, 344

W

weekday function, 124
whenever compiler directive,
      309
whenever statement, 492-95
where clause, select
      statements, 129-30
while loop, 311-13
white attribute, 348
Whole number data types,
      83-84
Williams, Nathan, 73
wordwrap specifier, 365
Writing functions, 320-24

X

XPS, *See* INFORMIX-OnLine XPS
      (Extended Parallel
      Server)

Y

year function, 124
yellow attribute, 348

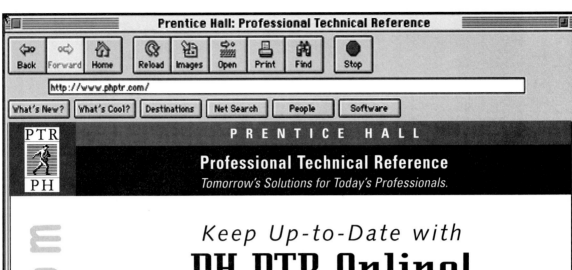

PRENTICE HALL

Professional Technical Reference
Tomorrow's Solutions for Today's Professionals.

Keep Up-to-Date with
PH PTR Online!

We strive to stay on the cutting-edge of what's happening in professional computer science and engineering. Here's a bit of what you'll find when you stop by **www.phptr.com**:

Special interest areas offering our latest books, book series, software, features of the month, related links and other useful information to help you get the job done.

Deals, deals, deals! Come to our promotions section for the latest bargains offered to you exclusively from our retailers.

Need to find a bookstore? Chances are, there's a bookseller near you that carries a broad selection of PTR titles. Locate a Magnet bookstore near you at www.phptr.com.

What's New at PH PTR? We don't just publish books for the professional community, we're a part of it. Check out our convention schedule, join an author chat, get the latest reviews and press releases on topics of interest to you.

Subscribe Today! **Join PH PTR's monthly email newsletter!**

Want to be kept up-to-date on your area of interest? Choose a targeted category on our website, and we'll keep you informed of the latest PH PTR products, author events, reviews and conferences in your interest area.

Visit our mailroom to subscribe today! **http://www.phptr.com/mail_lists**

CBT SOFTWARE LICENSE AGREEMENT

IF YOU DO NOT AGREE WITH THESE TERMS AND CONDITIONS,
DO NOT INSTALL THE SOFTWARE.

This is a legal agreement you and CBT System Ltd. ("Licensor"). The licensor ("Licensor") from whom you have licensed the CBT Group PLC courseware (the "Software"). By installing, copying or otherwise using the Software, you agree to be bound by the terms of this Agreement License Agreement (the "License"). If you do not agree to the terms of this License, the Licensor is unwilling to license the Software to you. In such event, you may not use or copy the Software, and you should promptly contact the Licensor for instructions on the return of the unused Software.

1. **Use.** Licensor grants to you a non-exclusive, nontransferable license to use Licensor's software product (the "Software") the Software and accompanying documentation in accordance with the terms and conditions of this license agreement ("License") License and as specified in your agreement with Licensor (the "Governing Agreement"). In the event of any conflict between this License and the Governing Agreement, the Governing Agreement shall control.

You may:

a. (if specified as a "personal use" version) install the Software on a single stand-alone computer or a single network node from which node the Software cannot be accessed by another computer, provided that such Software shall be used by only one individual; or

b. (if specified as a "workstation" version) install the Software on a single stand-alone computer or a single network node from which node the Software cannot be accessed by another computer, provided that such Software shall be used by only one individual; or

c. (if specified as a "LAN" version) install the Software on a local area network server that provides access to multiple computers, up to the maximum number of computers or users specified in your Governing Agreement, provided that such Software shall be used only by employees of your organization; or

d. (if specified as an "enterprise" version) install the Software or copies of the Software on multiple local or wide area network servers, intranet servers, stand-alone computers and network nodes (and to make copies of the Software for such purpose) at one or more sites, which servers provide access to a multiple number of users, up to the maximum number of users specified in your Governing Agreement, provided that such Software shall be used only by employees of your organization.

This License is not a sale. Title and copyrights to the Software, accompanying documentation and any copy made by you remain with Licensor or its suppliers or licensors.

2. **Intellectual Property**. The Software is owned by Licensor or its licensors and is protected by United States and other jurisdictions' copyright laws and international treaty provisions. Therefore, you may not use, copy, or distribute the Software without the express written authorization of CBT Group PLC. This License authorizes you to use the Software for the internal training needs of your employees only, and to make one copy of the Software solely for backup or archival purposes. You may not print copies of any user documentation provided in "online" or electronic form. Licensor retains all rights not expressly granted.

3. **Restrictions**. You may not transfer, rent, lease, loan or time-share the Software or accompanying documentation. You may not reverse engineer, decompile, or disassemble the Software, except to the extent the foregoing restriction is expressly prohibited by applicable law. You may not modify, or create derivative works based upon the Software in whole or in part.

1. **Confidentiality**. The Software contains confidential trade secret information belonging to Licensor, and you may use the software only pursuant to the terms of your Governing Agreement, if any, and the license set forth herein. In addition, you may not disclose the Software to any third party.

2. **Limited Liability**. IN NO EVENT WILL THE Licensor's LIABILITY UNDER, ARISING OUT OF OR RELATING TO THIS AGREEMENT EXCEED THE AMOUNT PAID TO LICENSOR FOR THE SOFTWARE. LICENSOR SHALL NOT BE LIABLE FOR ANY SPECIAL, INCIDENTAL, INDIRECT OR CONSEQUENTIAL DAMAGES, HOWEVER CAUSED AND ON ANY THEORY OF LIABILITY., REGARDLESS OR WHETHER LICENSOR HAS BEEN ADVISED OF THE POSSIBILITY OF SUCH DAMAGES. WITHOUT LIMITING THE FOREGOING, LICENSOR WILL NOT BE LIABLE FOR LOST PROFITS, LOSS OF DATA, OR COSTS OF COVER.

3. **Limited Warranty**. LICENSOR WARRANTS THAT SOFTWARE WILL BE FREE FROM DEFECTS IN MATERIALS AND WORKMANSHIP UNDER NORMAL USE FOR A PERIOD OF THIRTY (30) DAYS FROM THE DATE OF RECEIPT. THIS LIMITED WARRANTY IS VOID IF FAILURE OF THE SOFTWARE HAS RESULTED FROM ABUSE OR MISAPPLICATION. ANY REPLACEMENT SOFTWARE WILL BE WARRANTED FOR A PERIOD OF THIRTY (30) DAYS FROM THE DATE OF RECEIPT OF SUCH REPLACEMENT SOFTWARE. THE SOFTWARE AND DOCUMENTATION ARE PROVIDED "AS IS". LICENSOR HEREBY DISCLAIMS ALL OTHER WARRANTIES, EXPRESS, IMPLIED, OR STATUTORY, INCLUDING WITHOUT LIMITATION, THE IMPLIED WARRANTIES OF MERCHANTABILITY AND FITNESS FOR A PARTICULAR PURPOSE.

4. **Exceptions**. SOME STATES DO NOT ALLOW THE LIMITATION OF INCIDENTAL DAMAGES OR LIMITATIONS ON HOW LONG AN IMPLIED WARRANTY LASTS, SO THE ABOVE LIMITATIONS OR EXCLUSIONS MAY NOT APPLY TO YOU. This agreement gives you specific legal rights, and you may also have other rights which vary from state to state.

5. **U.S. Government-Restricted Rights**. The Software and accompanying documentation are deemed to be "commercial computer Software" and "commercial computer Software documentation," respectively, pursuant to FAR Section 227.7202 and FAR Section 12.212, as applicable. Any use, modification, reproduction release, performance, display or disclosure of the Software and accompanying documentation by the U.S. Government shall be governed solely by the terms of this Agreement and shall be prohibited except to the extent expressly permitted by the terms of this Agreement.

6. **Export Restrictions**. You may not download, export, or re-export the Software (a) into, or to a national or resident of, Cuba, Iraq, Libya, Yugoslavia, North Korea, Iran, Syria or any other country to which the United States has embargoed goods, or (b) to anyone on the United States Treasury Department's list of Specially Designated Nations or the U.S. Commerce Department's Table of Deny Orders. By installing or using the Software, you are representing and warranting that you are not located in, under the control of, or a national resident of any such country or on any such list.

7. **General**. This License is governed by the laws of the United States and the State of California, without reference to conflict of laws principles. The parties agree that the United Nations Convention on Contracts for the International Sale of Goods shall not apply to this License. If any provision of this Agreement is held invalid, the remainder of this License shall continue in full force and effect.

8. **More Information**. Should you have any questions concerning this Agreement, or if you desire to contact Licensor for any reason, please contact: CBT Systems USA Ltd., 1005 Hamilton Court, Menlo Park, California 94025, Attn: Chief Legal Officer.

IF YOU DO NOT AGREE WITH THE ABOVE TERMS AND CONDITIONS, SO NOT INSTALL THE SOFTWARE AND RETURN IT TO THE LICENSOR.

LICENSE AGREEMENT AND LIMITED WARRANTY

READ THE FOLLOWING TERMS AND CONDITIONS CAREFULLY BEFORE OPENING THIS SOFTWARE MEDIA PACKAGE. THIS LEGAL DOCUMENT IS AN AGREEMENT BETWEEN YOU AND PRENTICE-HALL, INC. (THE "COMPANY"). BY OPENING THIS SEALED SOFTWARE MEDIA PACKAGE, YOU ARE AGREEING TO BE BOUND BY THESE TERMS AND CONDITIONS. IF YOU DO NOT AGREE WITH THESE TERMS AND CONDITIONS, DO NOT OPEN THE SOFTWARE MEDIA PACKAGE. PROMPTLY RETURN THE UNOPENED PACKAGE AND ALL ACCOMPANYING ITEMS TO THE PLACE YOU OBTAINED THEM FOR A FULL REFUND OF ANY SUMS YOU HAVE PAID.

1. **GRANT OF LICENSE:** In consideration of your payment of the license fee, which is part of the price you paid for this product, and your agreement to abide by the terms and conditions of this Agreement, the Company grants to you a nonexclusive right to use and display the copy of the enclosed software program (hereinafter the "SOFTWARE") on a single computer (i.e., with a single CPU) at a single location so long as you comply with the terms of this Agreement. The Company reserves all rights not expressly granted to you under this Agreement.

2. **OWNERSHIP OF SOFTWARE:** You own only the magnetic or physical media (the enclosed CD-ROM) on which the SOFTWARE is recorded or fixed, but the Company retains all the rights, title, and ownership to the SOFTWARE recorded on the original CD-ROM copy(ies) and all subsequent copies of the SOFTWARE, regardless of the form or media on which the original or other copies may exist. This license is not a sale of the original SOFTWARE or any copy to you.

3. **COPY RESTRICTIONS:** This SOFTWARE and the accompanying printed materials and user manual (the "Documentation") are the subject of copyright. You may not copy the Documentation or the SOFTWARE, except that you may make a single copy of the SOFTWARE for backup or archival purposes only. You may be held legally responsible for any copying or copyright infringement which is caused or encouraged by your failure to abide by the terms of this restriction.

4. **USE RESTRICTIONS:** You may not network the SOFTWARE or otherwise use it on more than one computer or computer terminal at the same time. You may physically transfer the SOFTWARE from one computer to another provided that the SOFTWARE is used on only one computer at a time. You may not distribute copies of the SOFTWARE or Documentation to others. You may not reverse engineer, disassemble, decompile, modify, adapt, translate, or create derivative works based on the SOFTWARE or the Documentation without the prior written consent of the Company.

5. **TRANSFER RESTRICTIONS:** The enclosed SOFTWARE is licensed only to you and may not be transferred to any one else without the prior written consent of the Company. Any unauthorized transfer of the SOFTWARE shall result in the immediate termination of this Agreement.

6. **TERMINATION:** This license is effective until terminated. This license will terminate automatically without notice from the Company and become null and void if you fail to comply with any provisions or limitations of this license. Upon termination, you shall destroy the Documentation and all copies of the SOFTWARE. All provisions of this Agreement as to warranties, limitation of liability, remedies or damages, and our ownership rights shall survive termination.

7. **MISCELLANEOUS:** This Agreement shall be construed in accordance with the laws of the United States of America and the State of New York and shall benefit the Company, its affiliates, and assignees.

8. **LIMITED WARRANTY AND DISCLAIMER OF WARRANTY:** The Company warrants that the SOFTWARE, when properly used in accordance with the Documentation, will operate in substantial conformity with the description of the SOFTWARE set forth in the Documentation. The Company does not warrant that the SOFTWARE will meet your requirements or that the operation of the SOFTWARE will be uninterrupted or error-free. The Company warrants that the

media on which the SOFTWARE is delivered shall be free from defects in materials and workmanship under normal use for a period of thirty (30) days from the date of your purchase. Your only remedy and the Company's only obligation under these limited warranties is, at the Company's option, return of the warranted item for a refund of any amounts paid by you or replacement of the item. Any replacement of SOFTWARE or media under the warranties shall not extend the original warranty period. The limited warranty set forth above shall not apply to any SOFTWARE which the Company determines in good faith has been subject to misuse, neglect, improper installation, repair, alteration, or damage by you. EXCEPT FOR THE EXPRESSED WARRANTIES SET FORTH ABOVE, THE COMPANY DISCLAIMS ALL WARRANTIES, EXPRESS OR IMPLIED, INCLUDING WITHOUT LIMITATION, THE IMPLIED WARRANTIES OF MERCHANTABILITY AND FITNESS FOR A PARTICULAR PURPOSE. EXCEPT FOR THE EXPRESS WARRANTY SET FORTH ABOVE, THE COMPANY DOES NOT WARRANT, GUARANTEE, OR MAKE ANY REPRESENTATION REGARDING THE USE OR THE RESULTS OF THE USE OF THE SOFTWARE IN TERMS OF ITS CORRECTNESS, ACCURACY, RELIABILITY, CURRENTNESS, OR OTHERWISE.

IN NO EVENT, SHALL THE COMPANY OR ITS EMPLOYEES, AGENTS, SUPPLIERS, OR CONTRACTORS BE LIABLE FOR ANY INCIDENTAL, INDIRECT, SPECIAL, OR CONSEQUENTIAL DAMAGES ARISING OUT OF OR IN CONNECTION WITH THE LICENSE GRANTED UNDER THIS AGREEMENT, OR FOR LOSS OF USE, LOSS OF DATA, LOSS OF INCOME OR PROFIT, OR OTHER LOSSES, SUSTAINED AS A RESULT OF INJURY TO ANY PERSON, OR LOSS OF OR DAMAGE TO PROPERTY, OR CLAIMS OF THIRD PARTIES, EVEN IF THE COMPANY OR AN AUTHORIZED REPRESENTATIVE OF THE COMPANY HAS BEEN ADVISED OF THE POSSIBILITY OF SUCH DAMAGES. IN NO EVENT SHALL LIABILITY OF THE COMPANY FOR DAMAGES WITH RESPECT TO THE SOFTWARE EXCEED THE AMOUNTS ACTUALLY PAID BY YOU, IF ANY, FOR THE SOFTWARE.

SOME JURISDICTIONS DO NOT ALLOW THE LIMITATION OF IMPLIED WARRANTIES OR LIABILITY FOR INCIDENTAL, INDIRECT, SPECIAL, OR CONSEQUENTIAL DAMAGES, SO THE ABOVE LIMITATIONS MAY NOT ALWAYS APPLY. THE WARRANTIES IN THIS AGREEMENT GIVE YOU SPECIFIC LEGAL RIGHTS AND YOU MAY ALSO HAVE OTHER RIGHTS WHICH VARY IN ACCORDANCE WITH LOCAL LAW.

ACKNOWLEDGMENT

YOU ACKNOWLEDGE THAT YOU HAVE READ THIS AGREEMENT, UNDERSTAND IT, AND AGREE TO BE BOUND BY ITS TERMS AND CONDITIONS. YOU ALSO AGREE THAT THIS AGREEMENT IS THE COMPLETE AND EXCLUSIVE STATEMENT OF THE AGREEMENT BETWEEN YOU AND THE COMPANY AND SUPERSEDES ALL PROPOSALS OR PRIOR AGREEMENTS, ORAL, OR WRITTEN, AND ANY OTHER COMMUNICATIONS BETWEEN YOU AND THE COMPANY OR ANY REPRESENTATIVE OF THE COMPANY RELATING TO THE SUBJECT MATTER OF THIS AGREEMENT.

Should you have any questions concerning this Agreement or if you wish to contact the Company for any reason, please contact in writing at the address below.

Robin Short
Prentice Hall PTR
One Lake Street
Upper Saddle River, New Jersey 07458

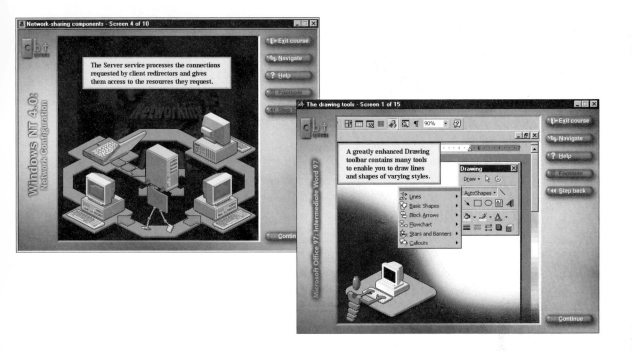

Other curricula available from CBT Systems:

- Cisco
- Informix
- Java
- Marimba
- Microsoft
- Netscape
- Novell

- Oracle
- SAP
- Sybase
- C/C++
- Centura
- Information Technology/
  Core Concepts

- Internet and Intranet
  Skills
- Internetworking
- UNIX

REAL Books by REAL Authors for REAL Professionals

FROM PRENTICE HALL PTR

NEW!
INFORMIX-OnLine Dynamic Server Handbook

Carlton Doe

Hands-on information that will help INFORMIX-OnLine Dynamic Server administrators get their job done as effectively as possible. This book transforms the dry technical details of Informix documentation into practical, hands-on techniques and ideas for effective administration. It serves the needs of both DBAs and administrators responsible for multiple database environments. This book covers the entire process of starting up and running an INFORMIX-OnLine Dynamic Server database environment, including preparing for initialization; initializing an OnLine Dynamic Server instance; building a database environment; archiving and restoring; monitoring and optimization. It reviews issues related to high availability and distributed transaction environments. There is cogent, careful coverage of how to recover from a crash. The accompanying CD-ROM's extensive library of scripts can save you hundreds of hours by automating many essential administration tasks.

1997, 496pp., paper, 0-13-605296-7

A Book/CD-ROM Package

Informix Performance Tuning, Second Edition

Elizabeth Suto

Maximize the performance of your INFORMIX-OnLine System. This insider's guide to Informix performance has been completely updated to reflect all recent releases of INFORMIX-OnLine, INFORMIX-OnLine Dynamic Server and INFORMIX XMP. No matter which release you're running, this book will walk you through all the performance-related issues you need to understand, including: query optimization, database design, disk layout, memory utilization, and processor usage.

1997, 192 pp., cloth, 0-13-239237-2

NEW!
JDBC Developer's Resource

Art Taylor

JDBC allows developers to create Java applications which fully leverage their existing corporate database resources. This book is the first comprehensive tutorial and reference for learning and using JDBC. The author begins by introducing the JDBC standard and its relationship to ODBC; then shows how JDBC can be used to enable a wide variety of applications. It shows how JDBC provides for enhanced security, through techniques such as trusted applets. There is detailed coverage of Java database access application design, including both two-tiered and three-tiered applications. Techniques for using JDBC are also covered. An extensive tutorial section walks developers through every step of developing three sample applications, demonstrating most of the techniques developers will need, including how to implement multithreading support, register drivers, and execute SQL statements. The book also contains listings of every JDBC class method, with usage examples and tips. All code appears on the accompanying CD-ROM — along with the exciting new Mojo rapid application development environment for Java, and JDBC/ODBC drivers from Visigenic — everything a developer needs to build database-enabled Java applications.

1997, 752pp., paper, 0-13-842352-0

A Book/CD-ROM Package

Informix Stored Procedure Programming

Michael L. Gonzales

Informix stored procedures, which can be used to dramatically improve the performance of SQL code, tighten security, reduce maintenance of permissions, and maximize data integrity, are often difficult to understand. This book offers numerous examples and illustrations that show how stored procedures can be used to optimize code while improving security and data integrity. Also included is a comprehensive SPL syntax reference, as well as more than 20 stored procedures that can be used or adapted as needed.

1996, 200 pp., paper, 0-13-206723-4

ABOUT THE CD

The enclosed CD-ROM contains the following computer-based training (CBT) course module from CBT Systems:

INFORMIX OnLine Dynamic Server.

The CD can be used on Windows 3.x and Windows 95.

Technical Support

If you have a problem with the CBT software, please contact CBT Technical Support. In the US call 1 (800) 938-3247. If you are outside the US call 3531-283-0380.

Prentice Hall does not offer technical support for this software. However, if there is a problem with the media, you may obtain a replacement copy by e-mailing us with your problem at: disc_exchange@prenhall.com